The Language of the Heart

The Language

of the Heart

A Cultural History of the Recovery Movement
from Alcoholics Anonymous to Oprah Winfrey

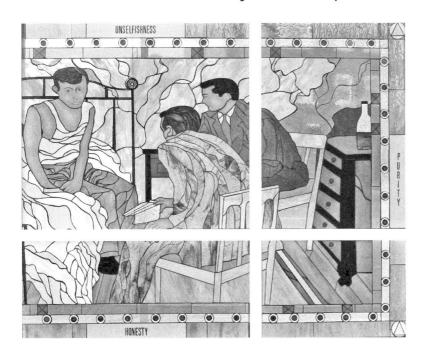

TRYSH TRAVIS

THE UNIVERSITY OF NORTH CAROLINA PRESS
CHAPEL HILL

© 2009
THE UNIVERSITY
OF NORTH CAROLINA
PRESS
All rights reserved
Designed by
Kimberly Bryant
Set in Arnhem and
The Sans by Keystone
Typesetting
Manufactured in
the United States of
America

Library of Congress Cataloging-in-Publication Data
Travis, Trysh.

 The language of the heart : a cultural history of the
recovery movement from Alcoholics Anonymous to Oprah
Winfrey / Trysh Travis.

  p. cm.

 Includes bibliographical references and index.

 ISBN 978-0-8078-3319-3 (cloth: alk. paper)

 1. Alcoholics Anonymous—History. 2. Recovery movement—
History. I. Title.

 HV5278.T79 2009

 362.292'86—dc22

 2009018549

The excerpts from Alcoholics Anonymous literature are
reprinted with permission of Alcoholics Anonymous World
Services, Inc. ("AAWS"). Permission to reprint these excerpts
does not mean that AAWS has reviewed or approved the
contents of this publication, or that AAWS necessarily agrees
with the views expressed herein. AA is a program of recovery
from alcoholism *only*—use of these excerpts in connection
with programs and activities which are patterned after AA,
but which address other problems, or in any other non-AA
context, does not imply otherwise. Additionally, this
publication is not affiliated with the AA Grapevine
publication *The Language of the Heart: Bill W.'s* Grapevine
Writings.

Portions of this work appeared earlier, in somewhat
different form, as "'Handles to Hang on to Our Sobriety':
Commonplace Books and Surrendered Masculinity in
Alcoholics Anonymous," *Men and Masculinities* (DOI:
10.1177/1097184X08318182): 1–26; and " 'It Will Change the
World If Everybody Reads This Book': New Thought Religion
in Oprah's Book Club," *American Quarterly* 59, no. 3 (Fall
2007): 1017–41. They are used by permission.

13 12 11 10 09   5 4 3 2 1

For my mother,
who taught me the language of both heart and head

It is not a thing of a day; it is not confined to a few;

it is not local. It is true that many failures are recorded,

but that only adds to the argument. There must be many

and striking successes to counterbalance the failures,

otherwise the failures would have ended the delusion.

—H. H. Goddard, "The Effects of Mind on Body as Evidenced by Faith Cures," American Journal of Psychology, 1899

CONTENTS

Gratitude xi   Abbreviations xvii

INTRODUCTION: The Sex Addict, the Dry Drunk, and the
Ubiquitous Recovery Movement *1*

PART ONE: ADDICTION AND RECOVERY

1: The Metaphor of Disease *21*

2: The Antidote of Surrender *61*

PART TWO: ALCOHOLICS ANONYMOUS AND PRINT CULTURE

3: Reading the Language of the Heart *107*

4: The "Feminization" of AA Culture *143*

PART THREE: POLITICS AND SPIRIT

5: The Varieties of Feminist Recovery Experience *187*

6: Oprah Winfrey and the Disease of Difference *229*

AFTERWORD: Recovery as a "Populist" Culture *265*

Appendix A: Alcoholics Anonymous Membership *273*

Appendix B: Reprintings and Distribution of *Alcoholics
Anonymous 275*

Notes 279   Bibliography 319   Index 347

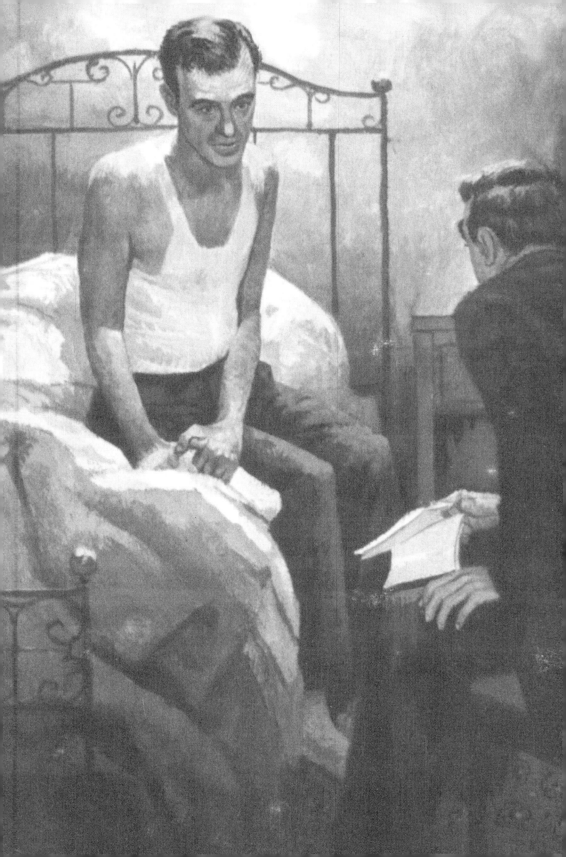

FIGURES

1.1 Locally produced pamphlet literature helped to spread the idea of alcoholism as disease *51*

2.1 The "man on the bed" as he appeared in the *Saturday Evening Post*, 1941 *89*

2.2 Robert M.'s interpretation of the man on the bed for the AA *Grapevine*, 1955 *90*

2.3 Stained glass interpretation of the man on the bed from the Akron AA Archives, 2001 *91*

3.1 Regionally produced flyer encouraging active Big Book reading *108*

3.2 Big Book page with highlighting and marginalia *109*

3.3 Hand-tooled leather Big Book cover showing "Stepping Stones" *110*

3.4 "Lady's" Big Book cover in needlepoint, ribbon, and fabric *111*

4.1 Tom P. Jr.'s "COWD AA" *177*

4.2 Mose Y.'s *Grateful Thoughts* *178*

5.1 Lesbian sobriety inscribed at the center of feminist space *188*

5.2 Cartoon suggesting that alcohol is a tool of patriarchal oppression *208*

GRATITUDE

For me, writing is not unlike an addiction. It occupies enormous amounts of time, much of which is spent chasing a high that comes infrequently and rarely satisfies. The visceral thrill of crafting a particularly deft sentence, or the rush that comes as the swarming ideas begin to align themselves into a clear and discernible logic—these pleasures pass swiftly, and I sink back into the decidedly drab routine of moving words around on paper, hoping to hit the sweet spot again soon, and nearly paralyzed with fear that I never will. Although my obsession is licensed, even demanded by my employer (the large university where I work), there remains something unseemly about it. Few of my colleagues share my compulsions; they just write their books and articles and it's no big deal—why can't I treat my writing like that? Instead I scheme to make time for it, sneaking away from students and colleagues, family and friends. Rather than vacation, I go on long writing binges. I spend a great deal of time alone.

It is perhaps because my writing life is so solitary that I feel such gratitude to the friends and colleagues who have helped and supported me as I have worked on this book. Although I began this project after leaving graduate school, its roots are in New Haven, the place I first encountered 12-Step culture up close. Susan G., Scott H., Candy R., Beth R., Susan S., Mark, Dan, and the rest of the crowd at the (now long-defunct) Café Diesel all participated in this book, though they probably didn't realize it at the time. More conscious contributors have been my graduate school writing group, Julia Ehrhardt, Juliette Guilbert, and Cristina Ruotolo. Though we live far apart and are absorbed in radically different lives than the one we shared in school, they remain among my best readers, carving out time to think through this project with me. In Julia's case, this meant commenting on every chapter and offering editorial suggestions frequently as hilarious as they were insightful. Less formally but no less usefully, I have benefited from the editorial acumen of Susanna Ashton, Tim Aubry, Jonathan Auerbach, Rita Barnard, Anne Brannen, Laura Callanan, Jerry Christensen, Richard Fox, Brian Herrera, Gordon Hutner, Lisa Jerry, Julie Kim, Fred Pfeil, Leah Rosenberg,

Joan Shelly Rubin, John Henry Schlegel, Jodi Schorb, Erin Smith, and Ed White at various stages in the composition process. Sian Hunter at UNC Press has been a steadfast supporter, never fazed by setbacks and delays; in the production process, Paul Betz and Eric Schramm helped me fix my profligate loose ends.

In addition to these readers, I owe a special debt to John W. Crowley, Joan Hedrick, Joli Jensen, and Lori Rotskoff. To put it in 12-Step terms, they shared their "experience, strength, and hope" regarding this project at a variety of critical junctures; their enthusiasm supported me when my own confidence waned. Likewise, Janice Peck deserves a special and outsized thanks. When I was beginning my research on Oprah Winfrey, she not only shared her precious archive with a total stranger, but also engaged me and my work with incredible warmth and humor. Our readings of recovery culture are ultimately quite different, but there are few critics with whom I so respectfully disagree.

This project was not my dissertation; it began when I left graduate school and took up a more grown-up life as a faculty member. My interest in the popular literature of recovery began in earnest when, as a new member of the Southern Methodist University English department, I was invited to give a lunchtime talk on popular fiction in the Godbey Lecture Series. The "Godbey Ladies," as they are often called, propelled my first formal and in-depth exploration of recovery during our discussion of Rebecca Wells's best-selling novel *The Divine Secrets of the Ya-Ya Sisterhood*. My unexampled department chair, Dennis Foster, was the first to suggest that there might be a book-length project in this recovery stuff; he was seconded by Nina Schwartz and Beth Newman, whose own predilections for psychoanalytic criticism did not bar them from seeing the potential value in a quite different explanatory and discursive mode. Since that first public lecture, I have had the great good fortune to be invited to present my recovery-related research to a variety of audiences —at book history and print culture colloquia at Drew, Rutgers, and Harvard Universities, as well as the American Antiquarian Society, and to student and faculty groups at Duquesne University, the Honors College of the University of Oklahoma, and the University of Texas at Dallas. The response in these academic settings has varied, ranging from enthusiastic approbation (indeed, relief that someone was writing seriously about recovery) to hostile dismissals of the project's intellectual foundations. Both of these, as well as the frank curiosity and genial bafflement that were more common responses, provided fuel for my inquiries.

Nothing, however, has been as helpful to me—either as inspiration or as practical assistance—as the insights of the AA historians that I have met over the last ten years. Some of these names may be well known within the world of alcoholism and addiction studies. Ernest Kurtz, who wrote the first serious history of Alcoholics Anonymous; William L. White, whose overview of alcoholism and addiction treatment in many ways suggested the framework for this book; and Glenn Chesnut, who has done more careful, thoughtful, and balanced intellectual and social history of midcentury AA than anyone I know—all three have given unstintingly of their time and energy as I have toiled away on this book. Their scholarly examples and their unfailing kindness have truly made my work possible.

Similarly, Matt Dingle of the East Ridge Community, Gail LaC. of the Akron Archives, and Art Sheehan have all helped me with documents, facts, and artifacts, responding to questions new to me but whose answers they learned long ago. While these are the names on this volume's proverbial speed dial, there are others whose help has been crucial along the way: Jim A. and Geoff C. of the Chicago Area Archives; Don B. in Illinois; Charlie Bishop; Pam C. in Oklahoma; Tony C.; Tom D. and Bruce S. in Akron; Jared Lobdell; Mitchell K.; Pete K. in Tennessee; Phil McG., David N., and Janeen T. in Northern California; Tim Ryan in Cleveland; David W. in Daytona Beach; the late Bill Pittman; and the late and truly great Searcy W. in my hometown of Dallas. Not necessarily in AA, but very much of the 12-Step world are the Hazelden veterans who graciously consented to share their stories with or otherwise assist me: Allan Borne, Mark Crea, Jim Erickson, Karen Casey Elliott, Tom Grady, Bill Hammond, Elisabeth L., Damian McElrath, Rebecca Post, Ruby Rott, Jerry Spicer, David Spohn, Harry Swift, and Barbara Weiner. Their patience and generosity made what began as a minor structural element in this story into a major piece of the larger narrative.

The generosity and enthusiasm of these collaborators is matched only by that of the professional staff at the AA General Services Office in New York. Archivist Judit Santon paved the way for me to obtain access to the archives there; Amy Filiatreau and Michelle Mirza picked up where she left off, assisting me in locating, checking, and rechecking the information on AA's print culture that forms the backbone of much of my narrative. In addition to the archives staff, Valerie O. and the late Vinnie M. offered insights and history during my research trips, and Tom J. and Darlene S. provided valuable logistical assistance.

Work on the non-12-Step portions of this project has posed its own special set of challenges. For help in disentangling some of the complexities of Women for Sobriety, I am most grateful to Lee Kaskutas and to Mary, the current WFS outreach coordinator. Tim Wilson and Christina Moretta at the San Francisco Public Library and, through them, Gen Guracar, Marian Michener, and Carol Seajay made Jean Swallow and the broader lesbian feminist recovery culture into tangible things I could write about rather than just abstractions. For sharing their research and evolving ideas about esoteric religion and New Thought, I thank Marie Griffith, Lyn Harbaugh, Tace Hedrick, and Beryl Satter. And for pushing me to make more of Oprah's Book Club than I had originally thought possible, I am forever indebted to James English, Melani McAlister, and Kathryn Lofton.

This project has been a long time in the making, and I have received generous support for it from a variety of sources. Southern Methodist University's Graduate Research Fund provided money for a complete set of Oprah Book Club transcripts and an initial visit to the Alcoholics Anonymous Archives in New York. A John Nicholas Brown fellowship in American Civilization, a travel to collections grant from the Chester H. Kirk Collection on Alcoholism and Alcoholics Anonymous, and a Sam Taylor Grant for Methodist College Faculty from Texas combined to support sustained work in the Kirk Collection at Brown University's John Hay Library, where I was ably assisted in excavating an unprocessed collection by librarian Tovah Reis. The Bibliographical Society of America's William Reese Fellowship and a Humanities Scholarship Enhancement Fund Grant from the University of Florida underwrote additional travel to the AA Archives; and Deborah Cantrell provided me a comfortable office at the University of Colorado's Wolf College of Law for a beautiful summer's worth of writing. Finally, and possibly most important, a National Endowment for the Humanities fellowship allowed me to take the time necessary to broaden the scope of the project and sharpen its writing. Some version of this book would no doubt have been completed even without the generosity of these funders, but I could never have pulled off such a rich and strange project without the time that their money bought me.

While this project began in the English department at Southern Methodist University, it has come to conclusion in the Women's Studies program at the University of Florida. Kendal Broad and Florence Babb have patiently answered my questions about social movements and feminist methodology; Anita Anantharam has shared my enthusiasms for feminist print culture. Particularly heartfelt thanks, however, are in order for the students who have helped me: Leila Adams and HavreDe Hill, who read and commented on several chapters in draft form; Mallory Szymanski and Desi Krell, who ably assisted me in teaching; and Amy Long, who provided research and proofreading assistance that unfailingly lived up to her motto of "always correct, and always on deadline."

With unabashed sentimentality in the best sense of that word, I turn to the friends and family members who may not have played instrumental roles in seeing this book to completion, but without whom it would never have existed. To Jean-Christophe Agnew, Laura Cook, Jim and Kate Corona, Ann Fabian, Bret Gilbert, Jack Gendelman, Tova Herman, Leah Hochman, Alejandra Irigoin and Regina Grafe, Jamie Gassman, Steve Rice and Jacqui Lunchik, Kio Stark, Chris Sterba, Elizabeth Teare and Salim Yaqub, Carla Tischler, Amy Travis, Jennifer Travis Lange, Thom Travis, Daniel Webster, Mark Weiner and Stephanie Kuduk, and Elizabeth and Frankie Young: I thank you—for your patience, for your humor and intelligence, and for your ability to drag me out of this project and into the revivifying light of your friendship from time to time. I offer the same debt of gratitude to my mother, Julie Travis, and her partner, John Raht. Mom, your confidence in me has never wavered; you have unfailingly modeled intellectual curiosity, patience, thoroughness, and the importance of a job well done. Had I not learned these traits so thoroughly by your example, at the end of the day no amount of brain power or education would have mattered much. I learned most everything that really matters from you.

Finally, to Mark Fenster, my true love and great friend, who enriches my heart and challenges my mind every day, I say thanks. No one has paid more of a price for my writing addiction than you, and I cannot imagine anyone else bearing it as gracefully. Your far-reaching intellect, your great generosity of spirit, and your persistent sense of the absurd make every day better. You are truly the best thing that has ever happened to me.

I have tried to list here all the good angels who helped move this book to completion, but there have been many, and it is quite likely that a few have escaped me. I offer apologies in advance to anyone I have unintentionally slighted. I note as well that while the good works of many parties contribute to what is best about this book, any mistakes in it—

and I am sure there are many—are my own. My hope is that both the volume's insights and its errors of fact or of interpretation will form the basis for future discussion about the nature, history, and meaning of 12-Step recovery and its inheritors. I welcome such discussion, conducted in the language of the heart or in whatever other tongue best suits the subject.

ABBREVIATIONS

BB   *Alcoholics Anonymous: The Story of How Many Thousands of Men and Women Have Recovered from Alcoholism* [The Big Book]. New York: AA World Services, 2001.

COA   *Alcoholics Anonymous Comes of Age: A Brief History of AA.* New York: AA World Services, 1957.

Dr. Bob   *Dr. Bob and the Good Oldtimers: A Biography, with Recollections of Early AA in the Midwest.* New York: AA World Services, 1980.

LOH   *The Language of the Heart: Bill W.'s* Grapevine *Writings.* New York: AA Grapevine, 1988.

PIO   *Pass It On: The Story of Bill Wilson and How the AA Message Reached the World.* New York: AA World Services, 1984.

SD   *Slaying the Dragon: The History of Addiction Treatment and Recovery in America.* Bloomington, Ill.: Chestnut Health Systems/Lighthouse Institute, 1998.

12/12   *Twelve Steps and Twelve Traditions.* New York: AA World Services, 1952.

The Sex Addict, the Dry Drunk, and the Ubiquitous Recovery Movement

Though he may be remembered more vividly for some of his other accomplishments, Bill Clinton will also go down in history as America's first recovery president. During his 1992 presidential bid, Clinton spoke candidly about his step-father's alcoholism and his step-brother's cocaine problems, and the media was quick to pick up on the role addiction had played in the life of the candidate whose campaign biography called him "the Man from Hope." "There are many possible ways to respond to an alcoholic parent," opined *New York Magazine*. "Bill Clinton's was to become the perfect child." The would-be president's childhood exposure to alcoholism became the preferred explanation for what could only be described as a lifetime of manic overachievement. "I understand addictive behavior," Clinton said the week of his inauguration. "You know, a compulsive politician is probably not far from that."[1]

Clinton's intimate understanding of addiction took on new significance in the wake of the Monica Lewinsky scandal. Former president Gerald Ford was only the most prominent of the commentators who argued that "Clinton has a sexual addiction," and suggested that he seek professional treatment for his apparently uncontrollable womanizing.[2] "A lot of men have gone through the treatment with a lot of success," explained Ford's wife Betty (herself a recovering alcoholic), "but he won't do it, because he's in denial." The self-awareness about the dynamics of addiction that had seemed so refreshing during Clinton's campaign now became a bitter irony: clearly, knowing how addiction worked had done nothing to elevate him above its insidious grasp. Ultimately, the Fords and many other observers concluded that the sexual addiction of the man from Hope "damaged his presidency beyond repair."[3]

Americans weary of what critics had taken to calling "the recovery presidency" breathed easier once George W. Bush took over the White House in 2001.[4] Bush admitted to having been a heavy drinker for much of his youth, but quit cold turkey the year he turned forty, the beneficiary, allegedly, of an old-fashioned gospel temperance appeal delivered to him by family friend Billy Graham.[5] His ability to stop drinking without recourse to a 12-Step program, he claimed, demonstrated that he was no alcoholic. "I've had friends who were, you know, very addicted [and needed] AA," Bush told the *Washington Post*. "I don't think that was my case."[6] As his presidency wore on, however, voices in the blogosphere begged to differ. Bush might not be drinking, but in his prosecution of the War on Terror he displayed all the characteristics of a "dry drunk," a term used in Alcoholics Anonymous to describe someone who no longer drinks alcohol, but who still manifests the "attitudes and pathologies of their drinking years," including impatience and incoherence, obsessive behavior, self-aggrandizement, and black and white thinking.[7] Bush's "obsession that he alone is right in his view of the world is driven by the complex ingredients of egomania and inferiority . . . found in the medical diagnostic description of the illness of alcoholism," one recovering alcoholic observed.[8] The president's "my way or the highway" version of diplomacy, his single-minded pursuit of the terrorists, his glassy-eyed swagger and apparent eagerness for violence —all these suggested to a growing number of observers that here, once again, was a president "in denial."[9] For disenchanted citizens under both administrations, the discourse of addiction and recovery became a prism that focused disparate and seemingly incomprehensible acts into coherent (if deplorable) approaches to governance.

Critics on both the left and right talked about the Clinton and Bush regimes in terms of addiction and recovery, and recovery-inflected readings of the two presidencies appeared in the most respectable media outlets as well as those on the far fringes of polite society. The popularity of such readings—their appeal across the lines of class, culture, and party affiliation—suggests the degree to which the matrix of ideas, practices, and institutions known as "the recovery movement" has unobtrusively woven itself into the fabric of our late twentieth- and early twenty-first-century lives. As they parsed these wildly dissimilar presidents according to the logic of addiction and recovery, none of the commentators who wrote about Bush and Clinton's distinctive histories of addiction felt it necessary to define what it means to be addicted to sex or alcohol, to interrogate addiction's causes, or to question the distinctions between addiction and moral turpitude. Quite the opposite: whether sympathetic or caustic, their accounts assumed that readers accepted the idea of addiction as a mental, physical, and even spiritual disease that, in its many guises, compels individual behavior, distorts the fabric of social relationships, and is largely beyond the addict's control.

Complementing this depiction of addiction was the image of "recovery," which, while deployed with equal certainty, was far more vaguely and gesturally defined: Clinton could have sought "treatment" to end his sex addiction; Bush should be "sober" rather than merely "dry." But what kind of treatment is this? And what, beyond the forswearing of alcohol, constitutes "sobriety"? Recovery emerged implicitly from stories of Clinton's and Bush's foibles as a negative state, as freedom from the destructive compulsion to dally with interns or make unilateral declarations of war. Beyond this somewhat obvious baseline, however, its substance remained fairly nebulous. The authors of these accounts assumed that their audiences, taking a cue from Supreme Court Justice Potter Stewart's famous description of pornography, knew recovery when they saw it—or, more precisely, saw the lack of it. By the dawning of the Clinton-Bush era, the state of being in recovery, like the logic of addiction, had become a matter of common sense, a concept so familiar that it seemed to evade—or perhaps not even to require—definition.

This book seeks to challenge this common sense. By looking at the evolving canon of literature about recovery by recovering people, it aims to historicize and explicate the frequently deployed but somewhat sloppily defined category of "recovery," and to examine its connections to broader historical and cultural currents in the contemporary United States. Such definitional work is necessary, I believe. Future chief executives may yet evade inscription into the discourse of recovery, but the power of the addiction/recovery dyad to frame and interpret reality has already been well established. Since recovery is here to stay, we would do well to develop an adequate sense of what the term means. It is only with such a definition in hand that we can hope to determine whether it bodes well or ill for us—as individuals and as a nation—that Americans gesture to recovery to explain public, political behaviors and trends as well as personal states of being.

WHAT IS RECOVERY?

The number of people who identify themselves as "in recovery," in one way or another, is staggering. Alcoholics Anonymous, which originated the 12 Steps and is still the best-known recovery organization, reported a membership in 2006 of just under 2 million, with over 100,000 meetings around the world.[10] The total number of AAs, however, may be much larger. The rule of thumb for estimating membership at AA's General Service Office (the organization's headquarters and global information clearinghouse) is to assume that only about one-third of the groups that meet and call themselves "Alcoholics Anonymous" actually bother to register their existence.[11] Thus the known membership may be only the tip of the AA iceberg.

Membership in other 12-Step groups pales by comparison to that of AA but is nevertheless significant. The estimated membership of Narcotics Anonymous is 645,000; of AA's allied organization, Al-Anon (for family and friends of alcoholics), 340,000. Overeaters Anonymous, which along with Al-Anon is one of the oldest 12-Step groups dedicated to "process" rather than "substance" addictions, estimates its membership at between 50,000 and 65,000.[12] Co-Dependents Anonymous, which became somewhat notorious for its explosive growth soon after it appeared in the late 1980s, now counts only around 11,000 members.[13]

Separate from AA and its offshoots (though there are many points of overlap in their philosophies and, sometimes, in personnel, as chapter 1 makes clear) is America's professional addiction treatment industry encompassing the public, private, and military facilities that offer in- and out-patient services to men, women, and juveniles. In 2005, the last year for which data is available, these facilities treated nearly 1.1 million patients.[14] While precise data on the industry's finances is difficult to obtain, healthcare economist Christopher Roebuck has estimated that the weekly cost of treatment per patient runs between $91 (for outpatient methadone maintenance) and $700 (for extended stay residential treatment).[15] The treatment industry is thus a substantial economic sector, with vested political interests and considerable lobbying power.

Beyond these organized institutions lies the larger and more fluid territory of recovery-infused popular culture. In that space, thousands of recovering people and professional therapists hawk their personal recovery philosophies in the form of textbooks, memoirs, and novels as well as through live, televised, and web-streamed public appearances. Audiences for these products conservatively number in the millions and, increasingly, span the globe. In the chapters that follow, I refer frequently to recovery as a "subculture," but I do so advisedly. That term accurately captures the sense of distance from the mainstream shared by many recovering people (in different ways and to different degrees), but it does occasionally seem silly to apply it to a group whose members number in the millions.

If few people in the United States today grasp the size of recovery culture, even more fail to understand its substance. Most people, for example, have heard of Alcoholics Anonymous—certainly many seem to have an opinion about it. But those opinions are not necessarily well informed. As I have worked on this book, any number of educated people have expressed curiosity about AA, which they have variously believed to be a feminist therapy group ("Everyone *I* know in it is a woman"), a religious organization ("Well, they always meet in churches, don't they?"), or some kind of cultish pyramid scheme ("Somebody's got to be making money off of it!"). Such perceptions of AA are common, and result at least in part from the organization's decentralized and somewhat anarchic structure, a defining characteristic that has carried over into the broader recovery movement.

The AA Preamble, an introduction to AA frequently read aloud at the start of a meeting, concisely explains that organization's aims, interests, and limitations:

> *Alcoholics Anonymous* is a fellowship of men and women who share their experience, strength and hope with each other that they may solve their common problem and help others to recover from alcoholism. The only requirement for membership is a desire to stop drinking. There are no dues or fees for A.A. membership; we are self-supporting through our own contributions. A.A. is not allied with any sect, denomination, politics, organization or institution; does not wish to engage in any controversy, neither endorses nor opposes any causes. Our primary purpose is to stay sober and help other alcoholics to achieve sobriety.[16]

Thus the qualities that make AA what it is are precisely the things that create enormous confusion about what it is: there are no rules about who can join or what constitutes an AA group, and while the General Service Office in New York conducts the organization's business and coordinates the flow of information around the world, it has very little power over its constituents.[17] AA and other organizations like it are structured rhizomatically, growing laterally, with new groups proliferating at will; a common saying holds that "all that is required to start a new AA meeting is a resentment and a coffeepot." As a result, meetings around the world reflect not only their historical moment and their national, regional, and even neighborhood cultures, but also individual and communal personalities. The internal dynamics shaping AA as a whole, as well as those informing individual meetings, or in regional or national collectives, vary widely, shift over time, and cannot be easily pigeonholed; what is true for AA holds for most other 12-Step groups as well.

As if size, diversity, and resistance to generalization were not enough to create confusion, 12-Step or "Anonymous" organizations are hardly the be-all and end-all of recovery. The habitual and unthinking assumption that 12-Step groups equal "the recovery movement" is one critical commonplace that this book aims to disrupt. In fact, the movement (if it can even be called a movement) consists of a wide range of organizations and individuals with distinctive and, in some cases, irreconcilable points of view.[18] Central to it are AA and the groups modeled on it, which are best understood as nonprofit mutual-help organizations that advocate a spiritual approach to understanding and ending addiction. These types of groups, which number in the hundreds, use versions of AA's 12 Steps, along with its 12 Traditions for self-governance, to address all manner of addictions, whether to substances (as in Alcoholics Anonymous, Narcotics Anonymous, et al.) or to processes (as in Al-Anon, Debtors Anonymous, Co-Dependents Anonymous).[19] What I refer to in this book as "12-Step culture" is marked by an emphasis on spirituality and on the mutuality and non-commercialism inscribed in AA's 2nd and 8th Traditions, which note that "our leaders are but trusted servants; they do not govern" and that "Alcoholics Anonymous should remain forever non-professional" (12/12, 10–11).

Operating alongside of and often as a complement to this expansive 12-Step culture is a vast network of professional therapeutic entities (such as counselors, clinics, and treatment centers) concerned with addiction and recovery. Unlike the 12-Step organizations and their devotees, however, they are not necessarily or are only secondarily invested in addiction and recovery's spiritual dimensions. Typically employing an eclectic range of diagnostic tools, what I call "therapeutic recovery culture" unfolds through private clinical practice, the public health system and its allies in the educational and criminal justice sectors, the looser channels of popular culture, or, as we shall see in later chapters, some combination thereof.

Finally, there are the agents of what I term "post-12 Step recovery."

The work of these healing practitioners and cultural producers is informed by 12-Step and/or therapeutic discourses, but they use them critically and/or draw their definitions of addiction and recovery in part from other sources, including feminism, postcolonial theory and ideals of ethnic nationalism, and esoteric spirituality. Sometimes grassroots and activist in their orientation, other times operating on a mass commercial scale, post-12 Step theorists and activists typically disseminate their ideas through networks that have few or no formal ties to traditional 12-Step groups or to the health services sector.

It is these quite different entities, taken together, that constitute the cultural formation known as "recovery." The energies that animate it spring from religious history, from the republican tradition of mutual aid, from progressive notions of identity and community, and from secular and commercial discourses of self-improvement. They are routed through and around grassroots networks, state bureaucracies, professional organizations, and ideological conceptualizations of the self. Recovery's indebtedness to these diverse and sometimes competing traditions helps to explain its persistence (it is both deeply and widely rooted) as well as the tendency toward lax definitions (it is not easily categorized). In addition, the fact that recovery partakes of so many varied traditions of thought and practice suggests that its adherents understand it and, more important, use it in different ways. An adequate definition must take this complexity into account. It is as an inheritor and an extension of these other institutions and traditions that recovery has come to do meaningful cultural work in people's lives.

BLINDNESS AND INSIGHTS

Recovery's unrecognized or unacknowledged diversity, then, combined with sheer numbers and a lack of standardization, have historically worked together to make it little known and poorly understood. Even many people who are themselves recovering in 12-Step or therapeutic groups often have only a fuzzy grasp of the world of recovery outside their immediate experience. For every person I have met outside the recovery movement who had serious misconceptions about AA, for example, I have also encountered a person in AA who was surprised to learn of that organization's long and sometimes vexed relationships with, among other things, Christian evangelicalism, the professional therapy and addiction treatment community, New Thought religion, and the feminist movement. At one level, this book is for such people; it can be read simply as an attempt to bring these relationships—in all their category-confounding complexity—into the public eye.

At another level, however, this book addresses a blind spot that seems particularly to affect academic researchers. Many recovering people have good reasons for not inquiring into the intellectual genealogies of their programs. For good or ill, their interests in recovery philosophy are primarily practical. Later chapters discuss the fact that they may even be urged by those around them not to take an overly analytical or intellectual view of their program lest they derail their quests for sobriety. The same is not true, however, for academics, whose lack of knowledge of and incuriosity about recovery is often so complete as to seem decidedly willful. While the well-educated humanist or qualitative social scientist is expected to have at least a passing familiarity with the standard premises of psychoanalysis, the recovery movement's most basic history and its structuring ideas are, for all intents and purposes, a terra incognita to most such scholars. Therefore, a second aim of this book is to establish recovery—its history, its organizing principles, and its culture, among other things—as a legitimate subject for sustained scholarly analysis.

There are exceptions to this rule of academic neglect, of course. Existing scholarly research on recovery falls into two general categories, and though neither type of work has sought to answer the cultural questions that I find most compelling, I have drawn heavily on both while writing this book. First and not surprisingly, an abundant body of research has explored the medical/psychological and public health dimensions of 12-Step approaches to alcoholism and other addictions. Since it began to be generated during the late 1940s, the vast bulk of this scholarship has centered on questions of efficacy: does 12-Step recovery, with its focus on abstinence and spirituality, successfully break addictive habits? This practical question would seem well suited to empirical social scientific inquiry, but the "Anonymous" nature of 12-Step culture means that collecting meaningful data on the topic is and always has been difficult. Moreover, much research on this question is fiercely partisan, undertaken by scholars whose stakes in particular treatment protocols (and the private and governmental funds that legitimate them) often seem to predetermine their research outcomes. As a result, the question of whether, how, and to what degree 12-Step approaches to addiction are effective remains largely unresolved.[20]

Does recovery work? Pushing past this utilitarian question, some scholars of culture and society began during the late 1970s to inquire more broadly into a different question: What does recovery mean? Their research has generally developed along two lines. The first seeks to understand the recovery movement as a part of the modern "medicalization of deviance" and thus a form of social control, while the second looks at the ways that participation in recovery culture confers a sense of identity and community on participants.[21] Both lines of inquiry typically observe specific groups to discern how members respond to and/or resist the larger world that surrounds them; they often look at the ways that narrative form and the practice of storytelling within the group affect identity formation and group dynamics.[22] This common methodology, along with a shared investment in social theorist Michel Foucault's ideas about the relationships between the individual and social institutions, means that questions about recovery culture as a form of social control and as a source of identity frequently circle around to meet: people in recovery gain a sense of identity and community by investing in a set of ideas that, in some ways, delimits their freedoms. Robyn Warhol and Helena Michie exemplify this logic in their analysis of how experience-sharing within 12-Step meetings affects members: "The more one hears and internalizes the structure of the master narrative in the infinite iterations that get played out in every speaker meeting, the more one will be able to reconceive one's own story to fit that narrative."[23] Seen from this angle, recovery culture becomes important chiefly because it presents an opportunity for self-formation within a fragmented postmodern world devoid of culture-wide systems of meaning.[24]

To varying degrees, the existing scholarship on the recovery movement gestures to the historical contexts in which its various iterations appear: AA originated in the Great Depression, Co-Dependents Anonymous is part and parcel of the post-1960s "culture of narcissism," and so on. But professional scholars' historical investigations have been noticeably sketchy, especially when compared with the rich 12-Step history compiled both in the official publications of 12-Step organizations themselves and in the writings of AA historians. Addressing the development of AA at the local and the national levels, authors like Mel B., Dick B., Charles Bishop, Audrey Borden, David Brown and Sally Brown, Glenn Chesnut, Mary Darrah, Richard Dubiel, Ernest Kurtz, Katherine Ketcham, Mitchell Klein, Jared Lobdell, Nancy Olson, Bill Pittman, Arthur Sheehan, and innumerable local AA archivists have disinterred key details of AA's past and carefully recorded the evolution of the fellowship over time.[25] Only a handful of academic researchers—Matthew J. Raphael, Ron Roizen, Robin Room, Lori Rotskoff, and William L. White chief among them—have shared AA historians' interest in giving sustained attention to the evolution of AA or its offshoots or sought fully to historicize the origins and development of the broader recovery culture to which they gave rise.[26]

Such historicizing is the goal of this book. I use the term "historicize" rather than the simpler "history" because my aim is not simply to recount the order and details of events that occurred at distinct moments in time, but to embed those events within the larger cultural contexts and flows of power that shaped them. These include the power of the state, the marketplace, and social institutions; the diffuse ideologies of gender, race, and sexuality; and the more direct power of charismatic individuals. Placing the *specific* institutional and intellectual evolution of 12-Step culture and its inheritors within the *general* frame of these larger issues works, I think, to reveal the nuances of both the specific and the general histories at stake and to shed light on the relationships between them. Such a "historicizing" of the recovery movement is important because, like a war or a public protest, like "the Communist Party" or "Abstract Expressionism," recovery is a multifaceted, dynamic, and evolving cultural formation—a set of beliefs and practices that arises from specific historical and material circumstances because it is able effectively to make sense of those circumstances for the people affected by them.

Since AA's founding in 1935, recovery culture has been shaped by both individual personalities and impersonal material constraints; its appeals are firmly grounded in the intellectual, political, and psychic realities of its time. Readers of this book may seek to champion, reform, or resist the recovery movement, or they may simply want to understand it better. Whatever their aims, it is my contention that both recovery's internal complexities and its relationships to forces and events seemingly external to its workings deserve to be better known.

BOUNDING AND GROUNDING RECOVERY CULTURE

Part of the reason there has been so little wide-ranging historical work on recovery culture is that it both borrows from and evades traditional categories of humanistic and social science inquiry. The drive to curtail drinking and drug use is a reformist project, but the 12-Step organizations at the center of the recovery movement focus almost exclusively on enabling and sustaining personal change, and therefore fit only uneasily into the progressive, community-minded tradition of social reform. At the same time, 12-Step culture's non-creedal spiritualism, which has been taken up by its therapeutic and post-12-Step offspring, means recovery aligns somewhat awkwardly with the history of religious life as traditionally defined. And while many latecomers to recovery culture fit clearly within the evolution of modern therapeutic ideas and practices, a significant number of recovering people and institutions refute the therapeutic label and insist that recovery is in essence a spiritual, not a psychological project. Thus recovery is simultaneously a reform effort, a spiritual practice, and a therapeutic exercise—except when it is not those things. Without question, a part of what makes recovery difficult to grasp is its polyglot and sometimes internally contradictory discourse, the evolution of which I trace in the chapters that follow. But in addition, the interpretive frameworks offered by traditional academic fields of inquiry seem inevitably to blur some aspects of recovery even as they bring others into focus.

This substantive slipperiness is compounded by the evanescence of recovery culture. The organizational features mentioned above, such as anonymity, organizations' refusal to maintain records of membership or efficacy, overall lack of rules, wide variations in practice across time and from place to place—all these make it nearly impossible to isolate even Alcoholics Anonymous, the biggest and best-known 12-Step organization, as an object of study. Identifying the most rudimentary boundaries of recovery culture—determining when it began, deciding what texts and practices are included within it, evaluating what kind of cultural formations it can be most usefully compared to, and so on—is a daunting project.

In an attempt at such bounding, this book focuses on recovery's manifestations in print culture. At first blush, this choice may seem bizarre. Familiar images of Alcoholics Anonymous, for instance, depict it as a fundamentally oral and participatory culture, one with little interest in reading or contemplation. Yet printed matter features prominently in most AA meetings, present in proud displays of books and pamphlets, framed versions of inspirational slogans in fancy calligraphy, and banners emblazoned with the 12 Steps and 12 Traditions. Print's importance to AA is reiterated by displays of reading within meetings—whether of the aforementioned Preamble, the Steps and Traditions, a passage from *Alcoholics Anonymous* (the AA "Big Book"), or the page for the day from a reader like *Daily Reflections*—and, in many groups, by focused, collaborative discussion of sanctioned texts. While AA, as the oldest and largest 12-Step organization, has the most robust print culture, most other well-established 12-Step fellowships publish and distribute at least some of their own literature.[27]

Beyond 12-Step organizations, print's importance to recovery culture has registered in a somewhat different way, namely in a proliferation of titles so intense that it has drawn critical attention. The principal spark to a flurry of academic criticism of recovery in the late 1980s and early 1990s was a trend that *Publishers Weekly* called "the rage for recovery"— a seemingly endless stream of best sellers (and would-be best sellers) touting an equally abundant array of 12-Step and therapeutic principles, and appealing almost exclusively to women.[28] Written primarily by professional therapists (some of whom were themselves recovering people) and published by addiction treatment centers or specialty publishers, the first recovery best sellers were sold via direct mail. As the "rage" wore on, however, recovery became a mainstream commodity, sold both in chain bookstores and in specialized "sobriety boutiques," and promoted through a seamless apparatus that placed authors at the center of recovery lifestyle magazines and newspapers, mainstream television talk shows, and an ongoing calendar of conferences and retreats. This promiscuous print culture, which treated reading as a key pathway to psychic healing and growth, became the focal point for much of the criticism of the recovery movement, as if recovery's simultaneous adoption by women and incarnation in popular literary forms had rendered its propositions suspect.[29] These examples—one of pride in print, and one of anxiety about print—suggest that while 12-Step group culture may center on face-to-face communication and participation, print is clearly and has long been an important part of the larger cultural formation of the recovery movement.

While this project began as an attempt to answer the fairly narrow question of how reading came to play such a central role in Alcoholics Anonymous (a question taken up in chapter 3), I discovered that a focus on recovery's print culture had a practical side effect: it fixed an otherwise amorphous mass of individual actors, groups, and ideas into a fairly stable (if still expansive) object of analysis. By tracking the development of the canon of 12-Step culture, I could map not merely the growth of Alcoholics Anonymous, but also the evolution of distinct strands of thought within and beyond it, and the attitudes and beliefs that had led to splinter groups, spin-offs, and commercial adaptations. Tracking the flow of print through the complex history of the recovery movement as a whole emphasizes both the similarities and the differences among the movement's constituent parts, and clarifies both what has remained consistent and what has varied over time. In short, print allowed me to track what Michel Foucault has called the "swarming" of a discourse, in this case recovery's movement from its original institutional location in the 12-Step group out into the broader culture, where diverse and seemingly unrelated institutions have refined its forms and, in doing so, increased its visibility, legitimacy, and power.[30]

A focus on print materials has value beyond mere expediency, however. In addition to simply demonstrating the speed, direction, and nature of recovery's movement into the mainstream, a look at printed texts also reveals the ways the marketplace has helped to shape recovery's evolution. While the spoken word and personal communication formed the heart of early Alcoholics Anonymous, that organization's development was, if not conditioned upon, at least closely connected to distinctive modes of textual production, distribution, and sales. AA developed its own writing, editing, and publishing enterprise in part so that it could maintain a distance from the larger world of for-profit commercial publishing. This anti-market attitude was challenged during the 1970s and 1980s when distinct—and distinctly profitable—publishing and reading communities began to develop within the professional treatment industry. The therapeutic best sellers coming out of presses like Hazelden and HCI attracted the attention of trade publishers who had previously turned up their noses at the idea of books by, for, and about addicted people. Once the polite literary world realized the commercial viability of recovery discourse, new avenues for exploring its nuances opened up: niche and mass markets for all manner of expository writing on addiction and recovery appeared during the 1980s and 1990s, followed by a widespread and seemingly insatiable craving for memoirs and, ultimately, best-selling fiction. Throughout this evolution, authors working in different genres, for different audiences, and with different relationships to the centers of mainstream cultural and economic power revised AA's original insights into a variety of literary commodities. Just like changing clinical knowledge about addiction, the opportunities and pressures afforded by the literary marketplace played a role in shaping the complex cultural formation that is recovery.

With this fact in mind, the chapters that follow trace the development of the "communications circuits" of the recovery movement: the interconnected loops of authors, publishers, distributors, promoters, retailers, readers, and critics who collaboratively give writing about addiction and recovery its enduring public life.[31] Book historian Robert Darnton developed the model of the communications circuit from a study of the book trade in Enlightenment-era France, the period when books were first becoming a mass medium, aiming to demonstrate the way that the ideas and influence that shaped literary and intellectual culture flowed laterally and reciprocally among a wide range of interested parties, rather than simply trickling down from the top. This distinctive circuit of cultural production, Darnton argued (sonatas and paintings, for example, were not made in this way), made books uniquely suited to be the conveyors of the democratic ideals that characterized the Enlightenment. Despite the passage of time and the increased complexity of the publishing business, Darnton's concept of the communications circuit remains a remarkably useful one, well suited to explicating the development of recovery print culture. Its image of reciprocal exchange and influence neatly captures the evolution of ideas within the recovering community. Also, and perhaps most important, it offers the opportunity to illustrate the dialogical process by which what began as a marginal or subcultural worldview and its material culture came to intersect with and to effect the larger mainstream.

Observing this give-and-take at work is important if we want to see the finer grains of difference within the recovery subculture. As the popular rage for recovery died down, some 12-Step authors and readers who had crossed over into "official" print culture stayed on there, while others returned to smaller, less visible enclaves. From among the latter emerged some vocal critics of commercial literary norms and of the recovery ideals promoted in mainstream print forms; their robust discourse is discussed in some detail in chapter 4. It is tempting to see this evolving relationship between amateur and professional print producers as a simple narrative of authenticity and co-optation: a couple of mom-and-pop AAs peddled workbooks out of the trunk of their car until a big New York publisher bought them out and made a killing selling slicked-up, expensive versions of what they had previously made with hands and heart. While versions of that dynamic may be accurate, over the long term what emerges is a more complex picture of resilient authors and publishers operating outside the commercial literary world. Recovery's communications circuits create a flow of ideas and texts into, out of, and around a cultural mainstream that does not dominate or exhaust the category of recovery culture. Revealing the diversity of recovery authors' relationships to the dominant print culture dismantles the shibboleth of a homogeneous "recovery culture" whose meaning and purpose can be easily characterized and conveniently dismissed.

Print culture, then, has been both a channel through which recovery ideas have been expressed and a material and social force that has helped give those ideas their form. What I refer to in this book as "recovery philosophy" or "recovery ideology" has been shaped by distinct ideas about authorship, writing, distribution, and reading, and by access to specific technologies that help bring those ideas to fruition. With the goal of illuminating those ideas, this book has a three-part structure. The first section, "Addiction and Recovery," traces the appearance and maturation of the institutions that formed the material base out of which recovery print culture precipitated: the professional addiction treatment industry and Alcoholics Anonymous. Separately and together over the course of several decades, these two entities generated the theories of addiction and recovery that would feed into the narratives of the sex addict and the dry drunk at the turn of the century. To disseminate that knowledge to their various constituencies (which sometimes overlapped with and at other times were kept apart from one another), they developed a distinctive rhetoric—what AA cofounder Bill Wilson would call "the language of the heart"—and a communications infrastructure that distanced them, albeit in quite different ways, from the literary mainstream (LOH).

Part 2, "Alcoholics Anonymous and Print Culture," builds on this broad foundation to depict the little known but large and complex world of 12-Step print matter. It traces the midcentury creation and formation of the AA canon in the AA General Service Office in New York, and the simultaneous rise of amateur AA authorship in the Midwest. While different from one another, both of these literatures emerged from the experiences of the middle-class, middle-aged, heterosexual white men who founded AA and saw alcohol addiction as a spiritual sickness. Not surprisingly, their hegemony was challenged during the 1970s and 1980s by the coming into visibility and voice of alcoholics (and other kinds of addicts) from different walks of life. The treatment center literature that addressed these emergent audiences seemed to touch a cultural chord, and it captured the attention of trade publishers seeking new markets and revenue streams in a constricting economy. It also sparked a "back-to-basics" backlash by amateur authors within AA, who deplored what they saw as the encroachment of therapeutic and multicultural insights onto what they believed to be a universal spiritual language.

If the book's first two sections focus on the masculinist culture of AA, the final part, "Politics and Spirit," treats the world of post-12-Step recovery and its varied print forms, which speak almost exclusively to women. Free from Tradition 10's mandate to "ha[ve] no opinion on outside issues" (12/12, 12), post-12-Step authors and audiences brought a range of feminist insights and political consciousness to their under-standings of addiction as a spiritual sickness; that range of ideas was paralleled by the multiple print networks through which they circulated their ideas. The spectrum of attitudes that post-12-Step recovery writers display toward the individual and the community make it difficult to identify the political implications of women's investments in recovery spiritualism, and that difficulty is compounded by the sometimes frank commercialism of their texts and the marketing strategies that bring them to the public eye. But, like the 12-Step and therapeutic forms that preceded it, post-12-Step recovery points its adherents toward a larger social and political world beyond the self, and offers them a spiritual language with which to address that world.

The book's three sections can be read as explorations of different strains of Bill Wilson's "language of the heart," dialects that formed in response to specific local circumstances. Part of what interests me in this project are the relationships among those dialects and their speak-ers. But I am at least as intrigued by the difference between recovery's language of the heart, in all its various patois, and the common speech of intellectuals and progressive critics. A short afterword, "Recovery as a 'Populist' Culture," speculates about the origins and the implications of the gap between these two discursive regimes.

WHAT THIS BOOK IS NOT

While this book ranges quite broadly, there remain any number of topics that it does not touch upon, along with scores of narrative threads and methodological niceties that it has not made its own. Such may be the fate of any lengthy piece of writing. However, one particular thing that this book is not merits mention here, before the chapters begin to unfold, since awareness of it may condition the way that readers approach the text.

This book makes no claims about the effectiveness or lack thereof of 12-Step recovery or professional addiction treatment. It does not attempt to debunk or to celebrate recovery, although it does draw on and try to understand many works that do both those things. While I make generalizations about recovery discourse throughout this book—about its origins, its intersections with other cultural forms, its connections to various structures of power—given the nature of this project it seems foolish to generalize a position that is "for" or "against" recovery as such. As I have tried to explain in this introduction, the term denotes a variety of ways of thinking, a spectrum of acts of faith; these varied positions are put into practice differently by people around the globe. Some people improve their lives by being in recovery, becoming more thoughtful, more self-possessed, and better able to gain critical traction on the world around them. Others do not, and in fact go on to weave recovery's principles into their own justifications for self-delusion and the domination of others. Like any other belief system, from "Compassionate Conservatism" to Marxist-Leninism, recovery can be used well or badly by the individuals who take it up as their own. Readers who come to this book looking for blanket condemnation or praise will be disappointed.

My sense, however, is that such readers are rare, outnumbered by curious and critical minds interested in complicating, rather than simply confirming, their existing ideas about this multifaceted topic. The history of recovery ideas and practices that follows is written with such an audience in mind.

PART ONE **Addiction and Recovery**

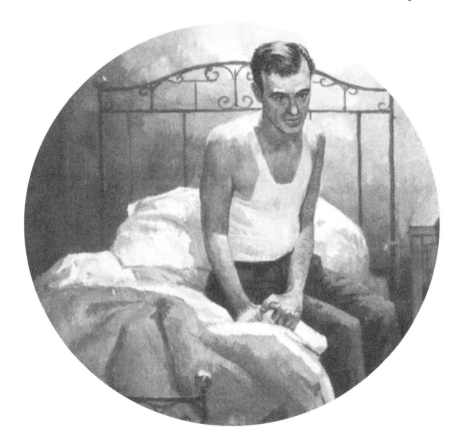

CHAPTER ONE

The Metaphor of Disease

When she was diagnosed with cancer in 1977, cultural critic Susan Sontag did what comes naturally to intellectuals faced with complicated and unnerving circumstances: she turned to writing. *Illness as Metaphor* was her attempt to better understand her experiences as a patient by exploring the extra-clinical discourses about cancer and tuberculosis that had helped to make those diseases cognizable to generations of sufferers and caregivers alike.[1] In a host of literary works, as well as in the language of fashion, military strategy, and urban planning, Sontag discerned a set of connotations and assumptions about the "nature" of TB and cancer that acknowledged their corporeal manifestations, but ultimately had little to do with them. Thanks largely to the nineteenth-century Romantics and their followers, tuberculosis had become in the popular mind a "disease of liquids . . . and of air" that affected the "upper, spiritualized body" (13, 17). It "was thought to come from too much passion, afflicting the restless and the sensual"; its victims were "sensitive, passive people who are not quite life-loving enough to survive" (21, 25). Cancer, on the other hand, was a disease of the "opaque body," caused by "insufficient passion [and] afflicting those who are sexually repressed, inhibited, unspontaneous, incapable of expressing anger" (12, 21). While TB had been a disease of the Bohemian city, cancer was a disease of "middle-class life" amid suburban sprawl (15), of all that was "most ferociously energetic" in modernity, as well as what was most corrupt and polluted (68–71).

Sontag argued that the connotations of both diseases—their literary as opposed to their material existence—had real consequences. Woven inextricably into the rhetorical and conceptual fabric of culture, they conditioned diagnosis and treatment, symptom progression and mortality rates. Her aim in explicating this intangible dimension of disease, she stated flatly, was "liberation"; she believed "the most truthful way of regarding illness—and the healthiest way of being ill—is one most purified of, most resistant to, metaphoric thinking" (4, 3). But the terms of her own project suggested how difficult such purification and resistance might be. Scores of examples demonstrated that the labor of constructing disease through language went on in every precinct of culture, and the omnipresence of disease imagery was only compounded by its evocativeness and imprecision. The fundamentally nonrational appeal of the *image* of disease, Sontag was forced to concede, endowed it with great power, since few people are willing "to apply that quixotic, highly polemical strategy, 'against interpretation,' to the real world" (102). The sick and the healthy alike, as well as the institutions that sought to bridge the gaps between them, at some level preferred to derive their understanding of disease from what Sontag called the "lurid metaphors" with which "the kingdom of the ill . . . has been landscaped" (4).

Sontag's attention to the nature and purpose of metaphor was absent from a flurry of popular books that appeared in the late 1980s and early 1990s to deride what psychologist Stanton Peele called "the diseasing of America." Peele's book of that name (1989), along with his 1991 *The Truth about Addiction and Recovery*, joined works like Herbert Fingarette's *Heavy Drinking: The Myth of Alcoholism as a Disease* (1988), Charles Sykes's *A Nation of Victims*, Wendy Kaminer's *I'm Dysfunctional, You're Dysfunctional*, and Jack Trimpey's *The Small Book: A Revolutionary Alternative for Overcoming Alcohol and Drug Dependence* (all 1992) to attack the disease concept of addiction. Developed over the course of half a century, this theory holds that addiction "is a primary, chronic, neurobiologic disease, with genetic, psychosocial, and environmental factors influencing its development and manifestations. It is characterized by behaviors that include one or more of the following: impaired control over drug use, compulsive use, continued use despite harm, and craving."[2] The recommended course of treatment typically includes detoxification, followed by total abstinence and an admission of powerlessness over the addictive substance, which is usually concretized by ongoing commitment to a 12-Step program. The disease critics assailed both grassroots groups like Alcoholics Anonymous and the interlocking arms of the medical and social service organizations that formed the professional addiction treatment industry, and derided the idea of addiction as a disease—like the discourses of cancer and TB that Sontag had traced—for being simultaneously ubiquitous and vague. "Few people," Herbert Fingarette noted, can articulate all the presuppositions of the disease concept, "and many people either do not believe every detail of the doctrine or hold some beliefs inconsistent with it." Nevertheless, "versions of the classic disease concept remain a dominant theme in the public's thinking."[3]

Like Sontag, the disease critics were concerned about what they perceived to be a set of "fantasies," "fictions," "mystifications," and "myths" that they believed exercised a negative effect in the world.[4] Some of them were medical professionals disturbed by what they perceived to be shoddy science; others were cultural critics worried about the ways in which the concept of addiction as a disease deflected attention from larger social questions. Some wrote from a socially conservative perspective, enraged by the ways that the involuntary nature of "disease" seemed to moot questions of personal responsibility, while others came out of a left-wing tradition, arguing that medicalizing addiction conveniently overlooked deeper and more intractable questions of political economy and social inequality. All agreed, however, with Peele's central contention: "The disease version of addiction does *at least* as much harm as good . . . excusing crime, compelling people to undergo treatment, and wildly mixing up moral responsibility and disease diagnoses."[5]

The disease critics' combined works mounted a persuasive critique of the concept's hegemony, but were less clear on explaining precisely *how* it had achieved its ascendancy. Populist authors like Peele invoked the specter of a conspiracy within the professional treatment community, which they believed had barred alternative conceptualizations of addiction from entering into the public discourse and tapping available funding streams. Mandarins like Kaminer and Sykes tended to fault the feckless public. But while most noted that media representations of addiction had played a role in popularizing the disease concept, none drew on Sontag's earlier insight and sought to investigate the essentially literary and discursive nature of the disease metaphor they so reviled. The disease critics' inattention to the cognitive, emotional, and practical work that the metaphor did for the individuals and the culture that embraced it severely undermined their ability to change the terms on which addiction is known and discussed. Two decades after their critical manifestoes, a perpetual fountain of memoirs and tabloid news stories, along with reality TV shows like *Celebrity Rehab* and *Intervention*, suggest that a broad cross-section of Americans continues to believe that addiction is a disease for which treatment and recovery are the only appropriate responses.[6]

The bulk of this book traces the cultural life of the disease metaphor of addiction's counterpart—the similarly ill-defined and omnipresent concept of "recovery." In preparation, this chapter examines the metaphorical dimensions of the disease concept that the critics of the 1980s and 1990s glossed over. My purpose here is not necessarily to debunk the disease concept; following Sontag, I take as my subject "not physical illness itself but the uses of illness as a figure or a metaphor" (3). With this in mind, this chapter examines why, how, and to what degree the founders and early members of Alcoholics Anonymous, physicians and psychiatrists, clergy, educators, employees of the criminal justice system, public relations experts, lobbyists, and policy makers came to endorse the particular understanding of the excessive consumption of alcohol that had come to be dominant by the end of the twentieth century.[7] The persistent appeal of the disease metaphor cannot be understood apart from their various investments in it—investments that sometimes aligned and sometimes clashed, but that cumulatively bestowed upon the disease concept an apparently unshakeable degree of cultural legitimacy. That legitimacy was achieved by the individuals and organizations whose stories unfold in the pages that follow; together they succeeded in "landscaping" the twentieth-century United States with the metaphor of addiction as disease.[8]

FROM VICE TO NEUROSIS

Historians of alcoholism and addiction generally agree that the disease concept arose as a backlash against, or at least an exhaustion with, "the passionate, moralistic, and legislative social controversies of the hundred-year temperance-prohibition-repeal eras."[9] Prior to the twentieth century, American attitudes toward drink and drunkards were complicated, and a variety of ideas about how to deal with them competed for hegemony. The physician Benjamin Rush, generally recognized as the first American authority on drunkenness, argued in the late eighteenth century that people who have become addicted to spirits "should abstain from them *suddenly* and *entirely*. 'Taste not, handle not, touch not' should be inscribed upon every vessel in the house of a man who wishes to be cured of habits of intemperance."[10] However, by "spirits," Rush meant only distilled liquors; like many early temperance advocates, he believed that cider, beer, and wine posed no threat. Advocates of "cold water temperance," on the other hand, promoted total abstinence from all forms of alcohol and gleefully looked forward to the day when "all who are intemperate will . . . be dead [and] the earth will be eased of an amazing evil."[11] Also committed to total abstinence, but taking a somewhat different view of the habitual drunkard, were the physicians, neurologists, and proto-psychologists who would come to be called, by the late nineteenth century, "inebriety physicians." These reformers—like J. Edward Turner, founder of the New York State Inebriate Asylum (1864), and his protégé Thomas Crothers, founder of the American Association for the Cure of Inebriates (1870)—believed that "inebriety was a disease and must be treated in hospitals the same as other diseases."[12] These contradictory ideas, rooted in competing scientific frameworks, cultural norms, and moral schemas, jostled together in the popular imagination for much of the nineteenth century.

This heterodoxy declined, however, toward the end of the century, as the push for national Prohibition became what Joseph Gusfield has described as a "symbolic crusade." Outraged by the nature and the rapid pace of change in Gilded Age America—the influx of immigrants, the increased political power of women, and the rise of consumerism, all of which were linked to and manifested themselves in changes in drinking habits—white, native-born Protestants from the Midwest and South embraced antiliquor legislation as a chance "to assert the public dominance of old middle-class values." Positions on all sides of the drink question hardened. "Dry" advocates asserted the "abstemious, ascetic qualities of American Protestantism" while "wets" championed a pluralist, cosmopolitan worldview in which "tolerance, good interpersonal relationships, and the ability to relax oneself and others are greatly prized."[13]

The product of these starkly diverging worldviews was an incendiary language of vice, sin, and racial hysteria. To the Board of Temperance, Prohibition, and Public Morals of the Methodist Church, the liquor traffic was "the crime of crimes, the devil's headquarters on earth, a ponderous second edition of hell, revised, enlarged, and illuminated." The largest organization advocating national prohibition, the Anti-Saloon League, rallied its troops in its 1911 *Yearbook* by reminding them that they were involved in a " 'war—continued, relentless war.' "[14] Even previously even-handed inebriety physicians joined in, moved by the belief that alcohol was a "racial poison," capable of diluting the genetic stock of the ruling classes and thus undermining Western civilization.[15] They ceased to advocate for compassionate rehabilitation of chronic inebriates, and began to argue instead for their quarantine in public workhouses and mandatory sterilization. The eugenicist belief that certain populations were predisposed to alcohol abuse and related vices made sterilization seem more than justified as a public health measure: "It might be curative; it surely would be preventive, and better, by far . . . than hav[ing them] beget a brood tainted with this curse of the world."[16]

Anti-prohibition forces were equally vehement in their castigation of dry reformers, and they countered their adversaries' moral outrage primarily with libertarian arguments. The Brewers' and Distillers' Association, one of the most powerful anti-prohibition lobbies, formed a National Protective Association that was quickly renamed the Personal Liberty League, and its members routinely took dry advocates to task for their "sumptuary and tyrannical" laws, antibusiness practices, and attempts to meddle in private life. Much wet propaganda focused on the economic disruption that would ensue with national prohibition. Its rootedness in facts and figures meant that while, in general, "in volume the wet propaganda probably equaled that of the drys . . . in quality it was inferior." However, the wets occasionally trafficked in more colorful invective. "A typical outburst," according to historian Herbert Asbury, was the magazine *Barrels and Bottles'* denunciation of the Anti-Saloon League as "the most arrogant organization of canting hypocrites and jesuitical grafters the world has ever known."[17]

It was these fevered sentiments that led to the passage of the Volstead Act, banning the manufacture, sale, or transportation of intoxicating liquors in 1919, and they were not cooled when repeal came in 1933. The triumph of wet culture, or what sociologist Mariana Valverde has called "enlightened hedonism"—the urbane, secular, and pluralist culture of consumerist America—relegated dry forces to the position of a discarded remnant.[18] From that position, they continued to rail against what they saw as government's willingness to soften its stance on moral legislation, and to agitate stridently at the state and local levels for liquor control measures. As Gusfield notes, their declining political potency hardened into a sense of disenfranchisement and betrayal (which in some cases later fed into midcentury anticommunism) and lent their language a hysterical tone.[19] Neither excessive drinking nor its personal and social costs vanished overnight with repeal, but by the 1930s, people who wanted to talk seriously about those things had begun to search for a new language with which to do so.[20]

For a little while, at least, it seemed that the new jargon of psychoanalysis would fit the bill. Even before repeal, psychoanalysis had begun to establish itself as the ideal modern discourse through which to rethink excessive drinking; the proto-psychologists known as "alienists" had played an important role in the development of the American Association for the Cure of Inebriates.[21] Lay therapist (and reformed drunkard) Courtney Baylor began to advance the idea of compulsive drinking as a form of neurosis as early as 1912. Working with New Thought minister Dr. Elwood Worcester in Boston's Emmanuel Movement, he sought to cure the mental "tenseness" that drove people to drink through a variety of techniques pioneered by both analysts and mental healers: hypnosis, affirmation, guided relaxation, and so on.[22] Baylor's protégé Richard Peabody (another reformed inebriate) continued this approach in New York City, arguing that "the behavior of the alcoholic is [best] explained as an abnormal search for ego maximation or self-preservation," and could thus be successfully treated by "hypnoidal suggestion."[23]

Worcester and Peabody's spiritualist diagnostics would inspire later thinkers, but they were pushed to the margins of the debate over drinking in the rush to embrace the structures of Freudian symptomatology during the 1920s. Although many well-educated practitioners might have read the German language text when it appeared in 1908, the 1926 translation of Karl Abraham's "Psychological Relations between Sexuality and Alcoholism" was the first in the United States to advance the theory that would become analytic gospel, namely that "dipsomaniacs" suffered from unresolved oral fixations, and that liquor was their unhealthy substitute for mature heterosexual relationships.[24] Karl Menninger, whose eponymous clinic in Topeka, Kansas, was one of a handful of new treatment facilities for alcohol addicts to open during the 1910s and 1920s, similarly described excessive drinking as "a typical infantile revenge reaction. In the first place, it is performed with the mouth; in the second place, it places a fictitiously high value upon the magical virtues of the substance desired; more important still, its practical aggressive virtues are indirect."[25] Assimilated handily to Freud's general theory of symptom formation, obsessive drinking was easily read as a working-out of infantile neurosis.

In alcoholism as in other matters, psychoanalytic diagnosticians eschewed ideas of inherited degeneracy: "Alcoholism cannot possibly be an hereditary trait," Menninger asserted (177). What Freud called the family romance took on the causal role that inbreeding had once played. Just as in centuries past, the default alcoholic in the early twentieth century was male, and psychoanalysis was quick to lay his constellation of pathologies (like so many others) at the feet of bad mothering. Either a too-distant or a too-smothering mother led her son to incorrect object choice, and compulsive drinking was but one of the symptoms of this maladaptation. "Drunkards suffer from serious paraphilias," asserted Freud's colleague William Stekel. "Nearly all of them are latent homosexuals; they are incestuously fixed . . . they are unable to obtain their sexual objective or have lost it" because of a failed cathexis on the mother early in life.[26] The bottle could serve as a substitute for the breast, and alcohol's disinhibiting qualities allowed for a regression to childhood. "All the component instincts of the polymorph-perverse child, described by Freud, break loose," observed Simon Weijl.

> The anal-erotic tendencies and sadistic drives emerge out of the sublimatory and cultivated reactions. . . . Men together in a saloon need only a little alcohol to become very familiar and aggressive . . . The fraternal feelings increase until the drunkards leave the bar arm in arm. The stage of direct genital homosexual acts is omitted, due to the remaining resistance, and the anal-sadistic stage is reached. Violence and fights are a direct manifestation, just as are throwing one's money about and paying another man's debts in the bar.[27]

To address this tortured constellation of drives, the analyst aimed "to replace the patient's own 'bad' mother with a new and better one who could succeed where the first one had failed in furthering personality development."[28] Analysis—and the transference relationship with the analyst himself—would end what Menninger called the alcoholic's "essential passivity and the wish to win love from people by excessive friendliness and essential subservience rather than by masculine achievement" (176). Once this reordering of the libido was complete, the desire for bad objects—including drink—would simply drop away. In the meantime, there was little that could—or should—be done about excessive drinking, and few analysts even prescribed abstinence as part of their treatment regimes (SD 98).

Psychoanalysis's conceptual schema for understanding the world became ingrained in the thinking of many mainstream middle-class Americans by the middle of the twentieth century. In the post-Repeal period, its tidy explanation for obsessive drinking seemed a perfect replacement for the super-heated language of wets and drys: its focus on desire within the family unit was a sophisticated acknowledgment of human complexity, yet it came with a sheen of scientific rigor. But while Freud's many followers adopted his explanatory paradigms with glee, psychoanalytic understandings of compulsive drinking never fully captured the public imagination. Unlike other forms of "deviant" behavior—homosexuality, for example, or female "frigidity"—excessive drinking seemed not to lend itself to the Freudian cure. The lessons of psychoanalysis caused some highly educated urbanites to change the way they viewed the causes and the treatment of drunkenness in the first part of the twentieth century, but they did not become the default explanation for the problem among medical professionals or within popular culture.

One reason for this may have been the difficulty of instantiating psychoanalytic treatment regimes for alcoholics. "Psychological 'surgery,' i.e., psychoanalysis[,] *theoretically* . . . is the treatment of choice" for alcohol addiction, Menninger argued. But he confessed that "*practically*, there are many serious difficulties in the way." The talking cure required a long, intense, routinized, and expensive commitment that few alcohol addicts were willing to make. "Furthermore," Menninger admitted, "most persons addicted to alcohol are too 'far gone' . . . to be treated by psychoanalysis under the ordinary circumstances" (183; original emphasis). This considerable practical problem was magnified by a related strategic issue. Even as interest in Freud and his disciples flourished in the 1920s and afterward, psychoanalytic practitioners remained on the margins of a skeptical American medical establishment, one that had already defined alcoholics as a distinctly unappealing and largely hopeless group. Drunks were aggressive, noncompliant patients with a reputation (well deserved in many cases) for abusive behavior and nonpayment of bills; more often than not, when they did seek admission to legitimate hospitals, physicians remanded them instead to a holding cell in the local prison. Analysts seeking professional legitimacy and financial stability had little to gain by hitching their wagons to the decidedly inglorious alcoholic star.[29] It would fall to people outside the medical profession proper to craft a new and fully modern language with which to talk about excessive drinking in the post-Repeal United States.

FROM SPIRITUAL SICKNESS TO "ALLERGY PLUS OBSESSION"

Alcoholics Anonymous began in 1935. Its founders were William ("Bill") Wilson, an unemployed New York stock analyst, and Robert ("Dr. Bob") Smith, a proctologist from Akron, Ohio. They met when Wilson, recently and tentatively sober after his fourth time in detox, found himself craving a drink while in Akron pursuing a business prospect. Fearing that he would succumb to his worst impulses unless he spoke with someone who could understand his feelings, he pulled a clergyman's name at random from the phonebook, called him up, and asked to be introduced to another drunkard. The ideas that Wilson and Smith exchanged when they met—ideas about the nature of their craving for alcohol and possible ways for overcoming it—not only sustained Wilson in his abstinence that night, but also prompted Dr. Bob, a few weeks later, to take his last drink. Inspired, Wilson decided to stay for the summer in Akron, and the two men began to seek out other habitual drunkards with whom to share their ideas. By the time Wilson returned to New York in the fall, four men—all long-term, hard-case inebriates— had achieved sobriety, and he and Smith were convinced they had found a workable solution for men like themselves who had previously been written off as hopeless.

Prior to their meeting, Wilson and Smith had both been involved in the evangelical Oxford Group, a nondenominational Christian fellowship founded by Frank Buchman and devoted to "world-changing through life-changing."[30] Raised a Lutheran Pietist, Buchman trained at the Philadelphia Seminary at Mt. Airy; after his ordination, he worked for the YMCA, directed a settlement house in inner-city Philadelphia, and taught at the liberal Hartford Seminary. But at a Keswick Convention in England in 1908, he had a life-changing experience when he heard a Pentecostal preacher speak on "Higher Life" or "Holiness" teachings, which held that, through the intercession of the Holy Spirit, some humans may reach a sinless state of "sanctification" on earth.[31] He felt himself called to missionary work and, after several trips to China and Britain, renounced the Lutheran church in order to travel the world in pursuit of "a Christian revolution" whose "aim is a new social order."[32] Originally called "Buchmanites," the sect changed its name to the Oxford Group after successful proselytizing at that university in the mid-1920s.[33]

Although it had its share of detractors and was never quite a mass movement in the United States, the Group was still a strong presence from the early 1920s until around the start of the Second World War. Its most reliable historian describes it as "the most vital religious movement of [its] day," with a peak membership of about 50,000.[34] Like many evangelicals before him, Buchman preached a version of "First

Century Christianity"—a creed-less, church-less pietistic faith premised on love and revealed truth and organized according to six principles:

1. Men are sinners.
2. Men can be changed.
3. Confession is prerequisite to change.
4. The changed soul has direct access to God.
5. The Age of Miracles has returned (through changed lives, miraculous coincidences, etc.).
6. Those who have been changed must change others.[35]

Unlike the better-known Evangelicals and Social Gospel reformers of the period, both of whom sought to do Christ's work among the poor and disadvantaged, Buchman focused his missionary work on the wealthy and powerful. His critique of "the worldliness of the average Christian" was manifested in, among other things, an "implicit disapproval of tobacco, alcohol, and other indulgences."[36] Oxford Group principles characterized the attraction to these vices as a symptom of a larger "spiritual sickness." Surrender to God and a reorientation of life around what Buchman called "The Four Absolutes"—honesty, purity, unselfishness, and love—was the required "surgical spiritual operation" necessary to restore the body and soul to health. A significant beneficial side effect of Buchman's "soul surgery" was that it eliminated the desire to drink.[37]

Bill Wilson and Bob Smith both had achieved sobriety (Smith only intermittently) through their participation in the Group, and Wilson routinely claimed that "early AA got its ideas . . . straight from the Oxford Groups . . . and from nowhere else" (COA, 39). Together with other reformed drinkers, Wilson and Smith adapted Buchman's six principles into what they called "the word-of-mouth program," an explicitly religious approach to drink cessation:

1. We admitted we were licked, that we were powerless over alcohol.
2. We made a moral inventory of our defects or sins.
3. We confessed or shared our shortcomings with another person in confidence.
4. We made restitution to all those we had harmed by our drinking.

5. We tried to help other alcoholics, with no thought of reward in money or prestige.

6. We prayed to whatever God we thought there was for power to practice these precepts. (COA, 160)

This approach enjoyed some success, particularly in Akron, but for a variety of reasons (discussed further in chapters 2 and 3) the group that called themselves "the alcoholic squad" broke with Buchman's followers in the late 1930s, preferring to champion a "spiritual" rather than a "religious" antidote to excessive drinking. Wilson revised the six-point word-of-mouth program into AA's 12 Steps, making them "more explicit" so that there was not "a single loophole through which the rationalizing alcoholic could wiggle out" (COA, 161). The basic lineaments of the precursor text, however, remain clearly discernible in Wilson's list:

1. We admitted we were powerless over alcohol—that our lives had become unmanageable.

2. Came to believe that a Power greater than ourselves could restore us to sanity.

3. Made a decision to turn our will and our lives over to the care of God *as we understood Him*.

4. Made a searching and fearless moral inventory of ourselves.

5. Admitted to God, to ourselves and to another human being the exact nature of our wrongs.

6. Were entirely ready to have God remove all these defects of character.

7. Humbly asked Him to remove our shortcomings.

8. Made a list of all persons we had harmed, and became willing to make amends to them all.

9. Made direct amends to such people wherever possible, except when to do so would injure them or others.

10. Continued to take personal inventory and when we were wrong promptly admitted it.

11. Sought through prayer and meditation to improve our conscious contact with God *as we understood Him*, praying only for knowledge of His will for us and the power to carry that out.

12. Having had a spiritual awakening as the result of these steps, we tried to carry this message to alcoholics and to practice these principles in all our affairs.[38]

The 12 Steps recapitulate the insights and the emphasis of the Oxford Group's diagnosis of a "spiritual sickness" that can only be cured by surrender to God, and amplify the Group's pragmatic anti-doctrinalism by making explicit that this is a God "*as we understood him.*" This non-specific pietism became one of the defining features of AA's conceptualization of chronic drunkenness, a condition that, increasingly, was coming to be called "alcoholism."

The second of AA's defining features was the concept of alcoholism as a disease. Although Smith was the doctor, it was Wilson who installed the idea of alcoholism as a disease at the center of AA philosophy. Wilson's drinking binges began with the First World War, and by the early 1930s his family was interring him periodically at New York City's Towns Hospital for Drug and Alcoholic Addictions. A quasi-medical facility founded in 1901, Towns was well known for its attention to the somatic dimensions of addiction, which it addressed with a variety of "purge and puke" therapies (*PIO*, 101).[39] During his stays at Towns in 1933 and 1934, Wilson met neurologist Dr. William Duncan Silkworth, who offered him what was at the time a somewhat unorthodox theory to explain his drinking problem. Silkworth championed the idea of alcoholism as a "manifestation of allergy," one that, if untreated, progressed into a full-blown disease with a "definite symptomatology and a fixed diagnosis indicative of a constant and specific pathology." Diseased drinkers were constitutionally different, Silkworth believed, from common drunkards, who might actually drink more heavily than their allergic peers. What distinguished the diseased drinker's appetite was not necessarily its size but its overweening intensity. Fully cognizant of alcohol's adverse effects on the body, the alcoholic drank anyway, but "whereas he formerly drank for pleasure," Silkworth argued, "he now has to drink from necessity in order to keep going."[40]

Like the nineteenth-century inebriety physicians in whose footsteps he followed, Silkworth was vague about why some individuals suffered this allergy and others did not, what triggered or soothed it, and about the mechanisms through which it asserted itself as a craving. His focus was on the need to "recognize the condition as a species of anaphylaxis occurring in persons constitutionally susceptible to sensitization by alcohol" and, following that, to work at "revitalizing and normalizing [the] cells" and getting them "to produce[e] their own defensive mechanism." But if causation remained murky to him, he was certain about several things: those who were affected by alcoholism had little control over it; the course of the disease was inevitably progressive and usually fatal; and total abstinence was the only remedy. Tolerance, dependence, and mania increased hand in hand and "in order to meet these changes and increasing symptoms, [the alcoholic] is compelled to increase the amount he consumes, and a prolonged spree replaces a short intoxication," despite conscious knowledge of the dire consequences.[41] In a radical departure from the prevailing wisdom, Silkworth suggested to Wilson that "alcoholism could no more be 'defeated' by willpower than could tuberculosis" and that as a result, it should be understood "not as a moral defect, but as a legitimate illness" (PIO, 102).

Wilson would ultimately credit his final turn away from liquor to an ecstatic moment of religious conversion, but Silkworth's theory of alcoholism as "*the obsession of the mind* that compels us to drink *and the allergy of the body* that condemns us to go mad or die" made a strong impression on him (COA, 13; original emphasis). Smith, too, embraced the idea upon learning of it. As the two men began to refine their understanding of Buchman's "spiritual sickness," Silkworth's "obsession plus allergy" (COA, 69) became one of their most important talking points. Silkworth's theorizing never received much validation in the medical community, but lack of scientific bona fides did not inhibit its strategic value—which is what AA's cofounders truly prized.[42] AA historian Ernest Kurtz notes that while Wilson was preparing the manuscript of *Alcoholics Anonymous* (the "Big Book"), he queried Smith about the wisdom of employing "disease" or similar terms. "Bob's reply, scribbled in a large hand on a small sheet of his letterhead, read, 'Have to use disease—sick—only way to get across *hopelessness*,' the final word doubly underlined and written in even larger letters."[43] This rhetorical functionality, ultimately, is what sold the cofounders on disease.

Accordingly, the Big Book began with an essay by Silkworth entitled "The Doctor's Opinion," which laid out his belief that "the action of alcohol on these chronic alcoholics is a manifestation of an allergy. . . . These allergic types can never safely use alcohol in any form at all; and once having formed the habit and found they cannot break it. . . . The only relief we have to suggest is entire abstinence" (BB, xxviii, xxx).[44] Although it explicitly compares the alcoholic to a cancer patient, the text makes no attempt to explain the somatic dimensions of the disease in any detail, or to defend the concept. "The doctor's theory that we have an allergy interests us," the narrative notes, but immediately goes on to acknowledge that "as laymen, our opinion as to its soundness may, of course, mean little." The question of "soundness" was deemed somewhat beside the point. What is important is that the allergy theory serves a useful purpose: "As ex–problem drinkers, we can say that [t]his explanation makes good sense," the text continues. "It explains many things for which we cannot otherwise account" (BB, 18, xxvi). To Wilson, Smith, and their early followers, nothing more than the explanatory power of common sense was required. As Kurtz deftly explains, the early members of Alcoholics Anonymous routinely spoke "of their alcoholism as disease," simply because "the vocabulary of 'disease' was . . . handy."[45]

The importance of this "handiness" to the success of Alcoholics Anonymous cannot be overestimated. The professional and dispassionate language of medicine appealed to the educated but not necessarily cosmopolitan men who were AA's earliest affiliates.[46] It distanced their organization not only from the moral pronouncements of the drys, but also from the psychoanalytic bizarreries of "infantile neurosis" and "latent homosexuality" that had begun to circulate through some realms of American popular culture. Furthermore, as William L. White observes, the comparison of alcoholism to diseases like tuberculosis, heart disease, diabetes, and cancer (all of which were referenced in various AA materials published during the 1940s) simply felt right—and for many reasons. In each of those cases, the progress of the disease could be easily observed although its origin remained obscure; the prospect of arresting though not fully curing alcoholism via self-scrutiny and lifestyle change fit with contemporary understandings of those more clearly somatic illnesses as well. For individual alcoholics, White argues, figuring their alcoholism as a disease served as a way "to understand their vulnerability to addiction and their need for complete abstinence." That practical need met, AA members deemed coherent and empirically demonstrable understandings of onset, pathology, and resistance to be mere quibbles. AA's understanding of alcoholism as a disease "drew, not on empirical science, but on an experiential truth confirmed in the lives of AA members." The validity of this "felt truth" was demonstrated to early AAs by the fact that once they named and approached their drinking as a disease, they began to recover as never before (SD, 198, 151).

By embracing the language of "allergy," "illness," or "malady," then, AA's cofounders and early members laid the groundwork necessary to establish the idea of alcoholism as a disease in the popular mind. But

AA was not the sole—and possibly not even the most important—agent in the creation of the "diseasing" that late twentieth-century critics decried. Rather, as Robin Room has argued, AA's "success was a precondition" for the later and larger work of a professional "Alcoholism Movement" that overlapped with and worked alongside of but was not coterminous with AA itself.[47] The midcentury activists sometimes called "alcohologists" also warmed to disease terminology because of its redoubtable "handiness." But both the ways in which they laid claim to disease and the results of their doing so proved quite distinct from their nonprofessional counterparts in AA.

"ALCOHOLISM IS A DISEASE"

Membership in Alcoholics Anonymous increased steadily during the early 1940s, skyrocketed after the Second World War, and exceeded 100,000 by 1950 (appendix A). Despite this growing visibility, at midcentury a hodgepodge of ideas about the causes and effects of alcoholism competed for legitimacy among reformers, policy makers, and the members of the helping professions who concerned themselves with drink-related issues. Both the allergy-plus-obsession model of AA and the symptomatic-of-infantile-neurosis theory of psychoanalysis contributed to a diagnostic cacophony that also included ideas drawn from gospel temperance and nineteenth-century inebriety medicine as well as from good old-fashioned quackery. As a term of art to indicate the habit of "repetitively drinking quantities of alcohol, usually enough to cause intoxication," the scientistic "alcoholism" jockeyed for position not only with "drunkenness" but also with the more archaic "inebriety" and "dipsomania."[48] Not until well into the 1950s did Americans begin to develop a common vocabulary for talking about drink and excessive drinking. When that language did emerge, it was the product of a loose coalition of laboratory scientists, public health officials, educators, clergy, criminal justice workers, and recovering alcoholics working in concert—the forces that sociologists and historians of addiction have dubbed the Alcoholism Movement.

The moniker is in some ways deceptive; William L. White notes that the work of the various players can be called "a movement only in retrospect" (SD, 180), and the chief chronicler of their efforts, historian Bruce Holley Johnson, admits that what "might appear to have been a well-orchestrated campaign . . . [was] rarely coordinated in any significant sense."[49] Participants shared an interest in legitimating the academic study of alcohol and alcohol-related social problems and providing humane rehabilitation to alcoholics, but they varied enormously on the question of what kinds of study mattered most. Even as a shared discourse of alcoholism-as-disease was emerging, there was no across-the-board consensus as to whether—or how—such an assertion might be true.

Despite this "theoretical anarchy,"[50] the Alcoholism Movement was very successful in its attempts "to produce legitimacy, credibility, [and] publicity for the idea that the habitual drunkard is the victim of a disease" and deserving of help rather than scorn.[51] Johnson notes that the first edition of Collier's *Encyclopedia*, published in 1950, defined alcoholism as "a morbid state resulting from ingestion of alcohol or alcoholic compounds" that primarily affected "delinquents, degenerates, criminals, tramps and chronic moral offenders." By the time Collier's second edition appeared in 1961, that definition had transmogrified into "an illness, and one so widespread that it constitutes a public health problem [and] affects some of our most promising people; individuals who have demonstrated abilities, who have raised families successfully, or who have occupied respectable positions in society and business."[52] Members of AA, clearly, were not the only ones who found the disease concept "handy," and the ranks of those who profited—literally and figuratively—from seeing the overconsumption of alcohol in this light would continue to swell as the decades passed. As these stakeholders in the hard and social sciences tried to determine how best to frame the discussion of alcohol, the disease metaphor began to supplant competing explanations of excessive drinking in both popular and scholarly discourse.

A host of forces was responsible for this phenomenon, but two institutions deserve special mention as nodal points for the elaboration and dissemination of the disease concept. The Yale Center of Alcohol Studies and the National Council for Education on Alcoholism were perhaps the most influential representatives of the research and the public relations dimensions of the Alcoholism Movement. Although their relationships with each other—and, it should be noted, with Alcoholics Anonymous—were not entirely harmonious, both contributed significantly to the disease concept's ascendancy at midcentury.

The Yale Center began in the 1930s as a research project surveying alcohol intake and metabolic rates in the university's Applied Physiology Laboratory; it became a separate entity under the direction of physician Howard Haggard and biostatistician E. M. Jellinek in 1943. The Yale Center, Mariana Valverde has argued, was the first attempt by research professionals to repopulate the "intellectual vacuum that [had] appeared after the somaticist degeneration paradigm" of the late nineteenth century was discredited.[53] Its agenda was ultimately sociological rather than medical: research focused on "alcohol studies," which ranged from the psychological and cultural factors contributing to individual overconsumption to questions of highway safety, workplace absenteeism, and similar socioeconomic issues (*SD*, 187).

Because of the interdisciplinary, collaborative, and evolving nature of the Yale Center, it would be incorrect to impute to it a singular perspective on the causes and nature of alcoholism. Some Yale personnel expressed "discomfort with the term 'alcoholism' [and] attack[ed] elements of th[e] emerging disease concept" (*SD*, 197). Despite this internal dissent, E. M. Jellinek's writings—along with his connections to the National Council on Alcoholism, discussed below—meant that the Center became closely identified with the disease concept during the 1940s. Jellinek had originally worked for the Research Council on Problems of Alcohol (RCPA), a free-standing research entity founded in 1937 to study a broad range of alcohol-related social issues in the wake of repeal. Under financial duress, however, the RCPA refocused its research agenda two years later to center specifically on problem drinking. This shift in emphasis opened the way for funding from the liquor industry, which was eager to establish a clear distinction between pathological and "normal" drinking, and to publicize the fact that the former affected a mere handful of the population. Jellinek's job, first at the RCPA and then at Yale (which also received liquor industry monies), was to compile a mammoth review of the existing scientific literature on alcohol problems, and to outline a plan for future research based on that review. The resulting Classified Abstract Archive of the Alcoholism Literature framed the discourse of alcohol research through the 1970s, and the will to see alcoholism as a disease arose from within it.

The first director of the Yale Center, Howard Haggard, had founded the *Quarterly Journal of Alcohol Studies* in 1940 to bring the RCPA's work to the public, and Jellinek became the *Journal*'s managing editor when he came to Yale in 1941. The following year, he published the results of his four-year literature review there, in an article that announced that "the central problem[s] of alcohol" are "the origins and development of addiction" and the "prevention and cure of abnormal alcoholic habits."[54] He followed up on his own mandate to investigate these questions with the landmark 1946 article "Phases in the Drinking History of Alcoholics," which established an enduring image of alcoholic symptomatology among clinicians and lay readers alike. "Phases" argued that alcoholics devolved over time from convivial social tipplers into heavy drinkers who persisted in their alcohol consumption despite rising personal and social costs. From there they declined more precipitously, first into psychological and then to true physical dependence. Once they reached this final "chronic" phase, Jellinek argued, the "entire *rationalization system fails* and the addict admits defeat. He now becomes spontaneously accessible to treatment."[55] This picture of alcoholism as progressive, characterized by increased tolerance, craving, loss of control, and, finally, a bottoming out that made treatment possible became the industry standard by midcentury.

Jellinek's conclusions were based on deeply problematic data, and he acknowledged as much in "Phases." His map of the varying types and levels of alcohol addiction was derived from ninety-eight responses to a questionnaire that had been made up by AA members, published in the AA newsletter the *Grapevine* in 1945 and returned by anyone who cared to do so—hardly a "scientific" study. But since other research by the RCPA and the Yale Center had already established alcohol addiction's "origins and development . . . prevention and cure" as the most pressing research questions of the day, Jellinek concluded that the "methodological deficiencies and numerical limitations" of the survey data could be brushed aside.[56] Despite the fact that these were the self-reported experiences of a self-selected fraction of the alcoholic population, who were responding to a questionnaire prepared by nonprofessionals seeking validation for their own self-diagnoses, he argued that "the material [was] so suggestive of future possibilities" that it was "practically imperative to submit the data to students of alcoholism" and to elaborate future research agendas and policy statements out of it.[57]

Jellinek revised his definitions and diagnostics somewhat over time—he administered a more detailed questionnaire to 2,000 alcoholics for a 1952 follow-up article—and was always careful to note (perhaps in deference to liquor industry philanthropists) that the percentage of drinkers who fit the profile of "chronic alcohol addicts" was very small.[58] But the original characterization of alcoholism derived from the *Grapevine* questionnaires quickly became ingrained in both popular culture and clinical practice. As Robin Room has pointed out, studies of alcoholic behavior to this day frequently rely on "a drinking history—often a 'modified Jellinek form' "—as their primary mode of data collection. Equally if not more important, the simple "Phases of Alcoholism" chart that illustrated Jellinek's 1952 article became "probably the most widely diffused artifact of the Alcoholism Movement," reproduced in all manner of educational and public relations literature.[59] His disclaimers and caveats notwithstanding, Jellinek's tools invited problem drinkers and those who sought to diagnose or help them to inscribe themselves into the narrative elaborated by the handful of AA members who had returned the *Grapevine* survey.

Jellinek left Yale in 1948 to advocate on a wider stage for the idea that "alcohol problems, regardless of their etiology, were medical problems." Prior to his departure from New Haven, however, he established the Yale Center as the American hub for "research, knowledge dissemination, professional education and public awareness" of alcohol problems.[60] It carried out this mission through two principal avenues. The first of these was the Yale Plan Clinics, outpatient alcoholism treatment services located in New Haven and Hartford and, by 1957, copied in over thirty other states. The main role of the clinics was to test "the possibilities of large-scale rehabilitation" of alcoholics who could not afford in-patient treatment by offering low-cost diagnostic tests and "habit guidance." Initially, that guidance "follow[ed] in general the principles of psychotherapy," suggesting to patients not that they suffered from a disease, but that they used "alcohol as a remedy for a real problem the nature of which [they] must learn to understand." But clinical practice soon drifted toward an embrace of key aspects of the disease model: diagnoses relied heavily on patients' drinking histories and on categorization according to Jellinek's phases. In addition, all patients were "informed on the activities of Alcoholics Anonymous and . . . encouraged to join that organization."[61] Thus while they served as rehabilitative and educational venues, the clinics also performed an important public relations function, helping "to spread the idea that alcoholism was a disease until that concept was fully accepted" (*SD*, 184).

The other Yale-based nodal point through which disease-concept ideology was disseminated was the Summer School of Alcohol Studies, founded to redress the fact that "the prevention of inebriety through civic activities is seriously hampered by the lack of a sufficiently large number of persons who have a broad and scientific understanding of the problems of alcohol and who could qualify as leaders in their communities." Beginning in 1943, clergy, attorneys, teachers, temperance workers, hospital administrators, and employees in the criminal justice system attended the Summer School to learn about current theories of alcoholism and research on alcohol problems; physicians and psychologists enrolled beginning in 1948. Scholarships were available, and close to 1,200 students had attended the Summer School by 1950. They took state-of-the-art knowledge about alcohol problems and treatment—including the disease concept—back to forty-seven different states, where they typically created new institutions or lobbied existing ones to create ways of addressing problem drinking that reflected new research paradigms. As state and local commissions on alcoholism and public health were established during the 1950s, they began to subsidize employees' attendance at the Summer School. In addition, the school opened a special "Industrial Institute" in 1953, with the goal of educating business professionals who sought to improve employee productivity through early intervention and counseling. Working through a variety of institutions in their home states, this loose confederation of alcoholism advocates helped to advance the "scientific" understanding of alcohol and alcohol problems developed in the Yale Center.[62]

In addition to the clinics and the Summer School, from 1944 to 1950 Yale was the institutional home of another organization—perhaps the most important one—that worked to popularize the disease concept. This was the National Council for Education on Alcohol (NCEA), a public relations/public education venture begun by Marty Mann, the first women to achieve lasting sobriety in Alcoholics Anonymous. After getting sober in 1939, Mann drew on the examples of the National Tuberculosis Association and of mental health advocate Dorothea Dix to begin a national campaign to destigmatize alcoholism and prompt communities to create humane and widely available rehabilitative treatment options for alcoholics.[63] She attended the Yale Summer School in 1944, and Jellinek offered to provide a home for her burgeoning endeavor at Yale.

A professional publicist (before devoting herself full-time to alcoholism education, she had worked for Macy's and the American Society of Composers, Authors, and Publishers, and helped to organize, edit, and write the AA Grapevine), Mann envisioned the NCEA as an educational organization devoted to disseminating a three-point message to all Americans:

1. Alcoholism is a disease and the alcoholic is a sick person.
2. The alcoholic can be helped and is worth helping.
3. This is a public health problem and therefore a public responsibility.[64]

For much of the 1940s and 1950s, Mann traveled the country, sharing this insight at medical conferences and rotary clubs, clerical retreats and women's benevolent organizations. By all accounts a gifted strategist as well as a mesmerizing public speaker and witty conversationalist, the "lady ex-lush," as she was sometimes called, proved an extremely compelling spokesperson and, ultimately, a lobbyist.[65] Her indefatigable personal testimony, recapitulated and extended in the NCEA's pamphlet literature and her popular *Primer on Alcoholism* (1950), played a central role in introducing the American public to the disease concept of alcoholism.

Mann's success in swaying public opinion was in part due to the fact that her crusading spirit meant she had few qualms about overstating her case. In an article announcing the founding of the NCEA in the *Quarterly Journal of Studies on Alcohol*, she proclaimed that the fact "that alcoholism is a disease, rather than a moral shortcoming, has been known to scientists for a considerable time, but unfortunately this knowledge has never become public property." Her aim was to make what she called the "unguarded secret" of the disease into public knowledge.[66] This zeal—which was shared by other key early members of the NCEA whose lives had been touched by alcoholism—made Mann remarkably effective at public relations and lobbying.

It also led to complications in her relationships with both the Yale Center and Alcoholics Anonymous. Given their own investments in the "handy" nature of the disease concept, many members of Alcoholics Anonymous—including Bill Wilson, who was her sponsor—agreed with Mann's perspectives, but the organization cooled to the NCEA after Mann sent out a fundraising letter implying that AA endorsed and helped to fund its work. Arguing that her campaign violated the principle of anonymity at the core of its program, Wilson prevailed upon Mann to remove references to AA from NCEA literature, and to refrain from referring to herself as a member of the group in her presentations.[67] At the same time, Yale researchers found themselves increasingly uneasy with Mann's lack of interest in the scientific validity (or lack thereof) of her claims. After Jellinek left the Yale Center in 1947, his replacement, sociologist Selden Bacon, made no attempt to hide his distaste for what he called the "propagandistic . . . crusade" of Mann's "alcoholism cult."[68] The NCEA and the Yale Center parted ways in 1950, just as Mann published her *Primer on Alcoholism*, a popular volume of disease-concept ideas. Featured in the *Book of the Month Club News*, the *Primer* instantly spread the word of the "baffling disease of alcoholism" to the club's nearly 1 million members.[69]

Growing public support for Mann's ideas meant that despite falling afoul of the nascent scientific community (and thus losing its primary funding stream), the NCEA continued to score public relations victories for the disease concept during the early 1950s. In 1951 the World Health Organization's Expert Committee on Alcohol and Alcoholism (chaired, perhaps not surprisingly, by E. M. Jellinek) declared alcoholism a disease. Five years later, the American Medical Association somewhat more equivocally acknowledged that alcoholism should not prohibit admission to hospital, and that the alcoholic should be treated as a sick person; 1954 saw the founding of the New York Medical Society on Alcoholism—later the American Society of Addiction Medicine (*SD*, 188). Mann was made a fellow of the American Public Health Association in 1952, and in 1954 was named one of the ten greatest living Americans by journalist Edward R. Murrow.[70] By 1954, over fifty local branches of the NCEA had been created across the country, and their volunteer outreach efforts were successfully eroding the stigma that had attached to chronic drunkenness since the nineteenth century. By the early 1960s, survey data suggested that around 65 percent of Americans had come to believe that "alcoholism is an illness," up from about one-fifth of the population in the mid-1940s.[71]

The only thing inhibiting the NCEA's efforts at this point was lack of funding. To raise money for treatment programs, Mann mounted an ambitious campaign to furnish New York City bars with coin boxes emblazoned with the message, "You can drink. Help an alcoholic who can't. Alcoholism is a disease." Nevertheless, by the mid-1950s the NCEA was teetering on the brink of collapse. Mann, however, remained undaunted. A member of the New Thought Church of Religious Science, and thus a strong believer in visualization, self-affirmation, and intentional prayer, she held fast to the belief that "there is a rich drunk out there somewhere who will get sober and help us out." Her prediction proved right in 1954 when R. Brinkley Smithers, heir to the IBM fortune and a recovering alcoholic, joined the NCEA board and became its principal benefactor. Smithers, who had supposedly "dried out" fifty times before achieving lasting sobriety in AA, brought with him the commitment, the drive, and, most important, the funds necessary to take disease concept advocacy to the next level.[72]

THE ALCOHOL AND DRUG INDUSTRIAL COMPLEX

Smithers's entry into the Alcoholism Movement accelerated the process of "diseasing" that Peele, Fingarette, and others would come to lambaste in the early 1990s. Over the course of his life, Smithers donated more than $25 million of his personal fortune to alcoholism-related causes, and funneled another $12 million in the same direction through the Christopher D. Smithers Foundation (named after his father, a founder of IBM) (*SD*, 193). His philanthropic commitment helped the NCEA attract both additional high-level donors and the attention of government policy makers. Its financial footing secured in 1954 by a gift from Smithers of $10,000, the NCEA changed its name to the National Council on Alcoholism (NCA) and shifted its focus from grassroots education and outreach to institution-building and lobbying. Over the course of several decades, the NCA and its offshoot organizations succeeded in aligning and making interfaces among a host of social sectors—the business community, healthcare providers, and the social services and criminal justice systems among them.

In a 1946 speech that was heavily publicized within the business community, Jellinek had noted that 29.7 million work days were lost each year to alcoholism (*SD*, 189). Smithers's business background meant that workplace alcoholism was a particular passion, and beginning in the late 1950s he and Marty Mann elaborated Jellinek's observations into a campaign aimed at getting business and industry leaders to "Save the man, save the investment!" The result was a steady growth in alcohol education, intervention, and treatment programs based in the workplace. It culminated in the establishment, in 1959, of what NCA members believed to be their "most successful" program, the Office for Industrial Services.[73] Another sub-organization, the National Committee for the Homeless and Institutional Alcoholic, developed the NCA's ties to the world of hospitals, asylums, and prisons, as well as to the growing network of state and federally financed social workers. By the early 1960s, forty state alcohol education programs—mostly quite modest—that disseminated information through these professional networks as well as directly to the community had come into existence. Their goal, adopted from the NCA, was the same no matter their audience: reduce the stigma of alcoholism and encourage humane treatment. As a result, although most hard-case drunkards continued to wind up in psychiatric hospitals through the middle decades of the twentieth century, continued prodding by disease concept advocates meant that some public general hospitals began to develop specific alcoholism or detox wards during the 1950s and 1960s. In addition, "by the end of the 1950s, there were some 200 small private alcoholism treatment programs in the United States . . . many [of them] birthed within the previous fifteen years" by long-term alcoholics who had finally found sobriety in AA (*SD*, 216–17).

Using a mixture of community-based and professional organizations, Mann and Smithers's NCA created a discursive and institutional infrastructure that connected a range of constituencies concerned about alcoholism. That infrastructure's strength, and with it the hegemony of the disease concept, increased exponentially after Lyndon Johnson assumed the presidency. Johnson, whose father (and perhaps one or both of his siblings) was an alcoholic, had himself joined the NCEA in 1948.[74] Personal conviction, along with the increasing visibility of young alcohol abusers across the country, may explain Johnson's 1966 declaration to Congress that "the alcoholic suffers from a disease which will yield eventually to scientific research and adequate treatment" and his willingness to back that contention with federal funds. Between 1963 and 1974, William L. White notes, the federal government enacted thirteen separate pieces of legislation addressing the needs of alcohol and drug addicts, and created a specific alcohol division within the National Institute of Mental Health (NIMH) (*SD*, 263–65).

The first of these was the 1963 Community Mental Health Centers Act, which mandated that facilities receiving government funding provide some kind of alcoholism treatment.[75] A number of additional measures followed, leading up to what White calls "the single piece of legislation that birthed today's system of addiction treatment," the Comprehensive Alcohol Abuse and Alcoholism Prevention, Treatment, and Rehabilitation Act, commonly known as the Hughes Act after its sponsor, Iowa senator (and recovering alcoholic) Harold Hughes. Marty Mann and Bill Wilson, as well as actress Mercedes McCambridge (a recovering alcoholic), were among those who testified at the public—and highly publicized—hearing of the Senate Subcommittee on Alcoholism and Narcotics in 1969, arguing for a policy-level embrace of the disease concept and for federal funds to expand access to treatment. The hearing resulted in the passage of the Hughes Act and the founding in 1970 of the National Institute on Alcohol Abuse and Alcoholism (NIAAA), a division of NIMH intended to unify the patchwork of state and local organizations that had grown up in the previous decades (*SD*, 265–66).

Taxpayer dollars, not surprisingly, were the thread intended to bind those patches. The NIAAA was an important advance over earlier governmental fact-finding and advisory commissions because it was authorized "to confer *formula grants* (i.e. based on a population formula) to the states in order to establish programs for treatment and prevention; *project grants* to public and private non-profit agencies to conduct demonstration projects, and provide education and training and services for the treatment of alcoholism; and *contracts* with public and private agencies for the above services."[76]

The surge of federal money into both public and private alcoholism programs during the 1960s and 1970s created what Harold Hughes would later call an "alcohol and drug industrial complex" of unprecedented scope and reach.[77] By 1978, some 250,000 alcoholics were being treated in federally supported facilities. These included both in-patient units—most of which resembled the private facilities founded by AA members during the 1940s and 1950s—and out-patient clinics—many modeled on the Yale Plan Clinics. Total national expenditure on alcoholism treatment in 1960, White has calculated, was around $6 million. By 1980, it was estimated at $795 million (*SD*, 266).[78]

Treatment protocols varied from facility to facility, and it would be wrong to say that all treatment providers hawked an identical version of the disease concept to their clients. While the diagnosis and treatment of late-stage alcohol addiction dominated alcohol programs, some clinicians and educators focused on early intervention, harm reduction, and abuse prevention strategies as well.[79] In addition, the monolithic picture of "the alcoholic" was beginning to disintegrate under closer epidemiological scrutiny and cultural pressure. Beginning in 1978, the NIAAA had called on Congress to fund treatment tailored to the needs of what it called "special populations," groups organized according to age, gender, race, and sexuality, and during the early 1980s "set-aside" allocations for treatment of those populations proliferated.[80] Some of these identity-based programs incorporated cultural and political consciousness-raising into the treatment milieu. A few women's treatment programs, for example, took on a feminist slant (discussed in more detail in chapter 5), while others in African American and American Indian communities linked alcoholism and addiction to systemic racism and internal colonization, using arguments like the Black Panther Party's succinct "Capitalism Plus Dope Equals Genocide." But such politicized approaches to addiction, not surprisingly, were exceptional.[81]

William L. White notes that "addiction services had existed in America before the 1970s, but there had never been a national *system* of addiction treatment" (*SD*, 267; original emphasis). By the early 1980s, however, a system was definitely in place. It was not without glitches and there were a few heretics within it, but for the most part it was unified, cohering around Jellinek's *Grapevine*-derived image of alcoholism as progressive and potentially fatal, characterized by loss of control, blackouts, denial, and "bottoming-out," and subject to arrest only by total abstinence. Despite growing skepticism within the scientific community about the validity of the disease model and the efficacy of the treatment protocols that grew out of it, the Alcoholism Movement's understanding of addiction remained encoded in the default structures of diagnosis and treatment—even as "alcoholism" morphed into the larger category of "chemical dependency" or "substance abuse."[82]

The final consecration of the disease concept's legitimacy occurred in the late 1970s when alcoholism began to be widely recognized as what White calls "an insurable illness" (*SD*, 269). Reversing the nineteenth-century practice of denying both health and life insurance to known alcoholics, a handful of private companies had begun in the late 1960s to cover the costs for hospital-based alcoholism treatment then, tentatively, to pay for residential care in non-hospital treatment facilities. This trend accelerated precipitously when the NIAAA began to promote the idea "that health insurance for alcoholism was the best way to assure a stable funding base for alcoholism treatment" and made securing that insurance one of its primary goals.[83] The push to cover residential alcoholism treatment grew out of the "save the investment, save the man" arguments Mann and Smithers had begun to make in the 1950s, but extrapolated them to a larger arena. Underwriting the costs of treatment, the NCA, the NIAAA, and various other stakeholders argued, would not only save employers money in terms of "worker productivity, on-the-job safety, absenteeism, and even corporate security," but would also cut down on healthcare costs currently borne by the American public at large, since "alcoholics use health care services at a rate that is 100% higher than their age and gender cohorts."[84] Convinced by this argument, by the early 1980s thirty-three states "had passed legislation requiring group health insurance providers to offer optional coverage for alcohol treatment," and 32 percent of all funding for alcohol treatment came from third-party insurance.[85] As the recession deepened toward the end of the decade, imperiling the flow of federal grant and contract money, cash from third-party insurers became increasingly important "as a means of transcending local funding inadequacies" that threatened many community-based programs.[86]

The increased flow of insurance money toward alcoholism treatment occurred just as demographic shifts and improving medical technology were leaving general hospitals with fewer patients. The downside of this underutilization became glaringly apparent after a major overhaul of Medicare in 1983 discouraged prolonged hospital stays. Under the new payment schema, institutions no longer received inclusive "reasonable cost"–based reimbursements, but "diagnosis-related grouping" payments, which offered a fixed dollar amount per patient, based on the diagnosis. Fledgling addiction treatment units, however, were able to wring an exemption from the new Medicare protocols for three years and continued to be reimbursed under the old and more generous reasonable-cost standard.[87] A dearth of medical patients combined with lower rates of reimbursement per patient meant that converting underutilized facilities into specialized alcoholism treatment wards became an attractive option for many hospitals—and for a growing number of for-profit companies specializing in addiction treatment. An NIAAA study in 1986 found that the number of privately funded treatment facilities increased by almost 50 percent between 1979 and 1982, with much of that growth "accounted for by a steady growth in the number of units owned by profit-making organizations."[88]

This entrepreneurial spirit was complemented during the 1980s by the continuing expansion of the overlaps between the treatment community and the criminal justice system. "Perhaps no other social agency is so well situated to provide a steady flow of clients [into treatment] as the criminal courts," Constance Weisner and Robin Room have argued. Their research demonstrates that, in California at least, "the trickle of cases from the courts to alcoholism treatment . . . increased to a flood" during the early 1980s, with clients referred "not only for public drunkenness and drunk driving, but also for wife battery, child abuse, robbery, forgery, and assault." Citizen groups like Mothers Against Drunk Driving lobbied for changes in sentencing guidelines that would make treatment mandatory upon conviction, resulting in a steady flow of "diseased" offenders into both in- and out-patient rehab during the 1980s. At the same time, the push for "drug-free" workplaces initiated under President Ronald Reagan's "War on Drugs" moved more people into treatment, including casual users who were targeted for "early intervention" by Employee Assistance Programs eager to improve workplace productivity.[89]

Together, these factors meant that addiction treatment "grew from a handful of programs in the 1950s, to 2400 programs in 1977, to 6800 in 1987, to 9057 in 1991" (*SD*, 276). Across the board, the model for diagnosis and treatment in these programs "emphasized therapy based on the disease concept, education about the medical effects of alcoholism, and attendance at AA meetings."[90] By the end of the 1980s, the disease of alcoholism had been more than destigmatized, it had been routinized and made—in some quarters at least—hugely profitable.

The role of Alcoholics Anonymous in this classic transformation of "vice" into "disease" is complex and, on the surface, somewhat contradictory. Officially, AA holds itself apart from the professional treatment world. In part as a response to the growing power and visibility of the Alcoholism Movement, in the mid-1950s AA developed a code of self-governance in the form of the 12 Traditions (discussed more fully in the next chapter), which specifically distance AA proper from "outside . . . enterprise[s]" (Tradition 6) and discourage opining on "outside issues" (Tradition 10) like alcohol control legislation, the veracity of the disease concept, whether treatment should be mandatory, and so on. The gap between AA, the treatment community, and the increasingly intertwined criminal justice and public health systems was further ratified by Traditions stipulating that AA be "fully self-supporting" and "forever non-professional," with a "public relations policy based on attraction rather than promotion" that observes "personal anonymity at the level of press, radio, and films" (Traditions 8 and 11).

Even the schematic history I have presented here, however, should make clear that despite these provisos AA was intimately involved in the legitimation and spread of the disease concept and in the development of the education/treatment/policy network that elaborated and institutionalized it. AA grew willy-nilly in the two decades before the Traditions were codified and adopted by the organization; during that time a range of attitudes and practices that ratified the disease concept was firmly enshrined within local and regional cultures. Once the Traditions were put in place, individuals and groups interpreted them in wildly varying ways. And, most important, the Traditions placed no restriction on how individual members of AA might proselytize, educate, or lobby on behalf of the disease model of alcoholism; they merely stipulated that they do so as individuals, rather than as spokespersons for the larger organization. The result was a significant if not systematic overlap between AA and the alcoholism treatment industry.[91]

Just as Jellinek drew his ideas about the nature and progress of the disease from AA experience, many local AA groups cribbed the work of Alcoholism Movement experts for their own publications. Pamphlets like "Thirteen Steps to Alcoholism" (Birmingham, ca. mid-1950s) and "Alcoholics Anonymous: The Program for Recovery from Alcoholism" (Des Moines, ca. late-1950s) included questions on drinking habits that they proudly announced had been developed by Jellinek.[92] Similarly, "Alcoholics Anonymous: An Interpretation of Our Twelve Steps" (Washington, D.C., 1944), "Birds of a Feather" (St. Louis, ca. 1950), and countless other local publications featured a thirty-five-item questionnaire attributed to Dr. Robert Seliger of Johns Hopkins University Hospital.[93] Many pamphlets using the Seliger questions preserved a nominal distinction between AA and the Alcoholism Movement by acknowledging that "the Test Questions are not AA Questions," but not every local AA publisher bothered to observe such fine distinctions. The first page of the pamphlet "Who, Me?" (Fig. 1.1) makes it clear that many AAs, whether persuaded by the merits or simply by the "handiness" of the disease concept, were happy to see themselves as part of the larger Alcoholism Movement.[94]

Similarly, the attitude Bill Wilson characterized as "Let's Be Friendly with Our Friends" helped to shape the theory and practice of alcoholism treatment outside AA proper.[95] Without claiming to speak on behalf of the organization, individual AAs gave presentations on the 12-Step approach to alcoholism at the Yale Summer School, and worked alongside the professionals at the Yale Plan Clinics. In communities across the country, members of AA worked with local NCEA (and later NCA) chapters to reform hospital admissions policies—often putting up the funds for detox and/or keeping watch over alcoholic patients to allay hospital administrators' fears that they were too troublesome to merit beds. Some recovered alcoholics, like Marty Mann, Brinkley Smithers, and Harold Hughes, saw their public relations and lobbying efforts as responses to the 12th Step's injunction to "carry this message to alcoholics and practice these principles in all our affairs"; others took it

HEART DISEASE . . .
TUBERCULOSIS . . .

ALCOHOLISM . . .

DIPHTHERIA . . .
PNEUMONIA . . .
SYPHILIS . . .

You're Wrong Mister . . .

It Does
Belong
On This List!

There is no medical cure for Alcoholism. Its victims are usually forced to wage a losing battle, not only against the ravages of the disease, but also against the ignorance of a society which refuses to regard the Alcoholic as a diseased person. This ailment has stalemated all resources of the highly organized research institutions of the medical and scientific professions and Church efforts.

Many Alcoholics continue to suffer when they either fail or **REFUSE** to recognize their illness because of the stigma that has been attached to its name through centuries of neglect to treat alcoholism as a disease.

Figure 1.1. Pamphlet emphasizing disease concept, Salt Lake City AA Group #1, ca. early 1950s. Courtesy of Chester H. Kirk Collection on Alcoholism and Alcoholics Anonymous, John Hay Library, Brown University.

upon themselves to carry the message to hospitals and prisons and, later, treatment centers. And of course AA enabled the criminal justice system's growing investment in 12-Step ideology during the 1970s and 1980s by absorbing into its meetings (though not without friction) the thousands of criminal offenders mandated to attend them.

As the subsequent chapters demonstrate, this interpenetration of the civic, commercial, professionally managed institutions developed by alcoholism activists and AA's rhizomatic and voluntarist spirit—what William L. White has termed its "spiritually driven anarchy" (*SD*, 153)—was a source of considerable tension. Alcoholics Anonymous, as an organization and as a host of individuals, did contribute to the "diseasing of America." But it was not the driving force, and perhaps not even the most important force, behind that development. Although the disease critics discussed at this chapter's outset do not make note of it, many AAs, as we shall see, deplored "the diseasing" themselves. Much of their ire focused on the professionalization of recovery within the treatment industry and what they believed to be the concomitant dilution of AA's spiritual orientation. This anger and dismay became especially pronounced during the last phase of the disease concept's mutation during the 1980s and 1990s, as a new category of "process addictions" broadened the disease model's scope to include virtually everyone in the United States.

FROM SUBSTANCE TO PROCESS ADDICTION

As it became a fixture within American life during the middle of the twentieth century, AA spawned a host of imitators focused on substances other than alcohol. The earliest of these was Narcotics Anonymous—founded in 1947 or 1953, according to different accounts. A steady succession of additional substance-addiction groups followed, typically founded by members of AA who wanted to apply 12-Step principles to other habits but felt constrained from doing so within their groups because Tradition 5 stipulates that the "primary purpose" of AA is recovery from alcoholism, not from anything else. Groups like Overeaters Anonymous (1960), Potsmokers Anonymous (1968), Pills Anonymous (1975), and Nicotine and Cocaine Anonymous (both 1982) adopted the 12 Steps and Traditions nearly verbatim and with the permission of the AA General Service Office. Equally important, they retained AA's decentralized organizational structure, tradition of financial self-support, and emphasis on spirituality and mutual aid.[96]

More important than the growth of these additional substance-focused 12-Step groups to the "diseasing" dynamic, however, was the rise of organized groups that sought to apply the 12 Steps to the obsessive behaviors or habits of mind that some clinicians call "process addictions."[97] The first such organization was Al-Anon, founded by Bill Wilson's wife, Lois, in 1951. Alateen, for children of alcoholics ages twelve to twenty, and Gamblers Anonymous followed, both in 1957. Debtors Anonymous appeared in 1968, and Emotions Anonymous, for "recovery from emotional difficulties," in 1971. The first of many groups devoted specifically to sexual issues, The Augustine Fellowship, was founded in 1977.[98] Like the substance addiction offshoots described above, these groups were founded by members of AA who, having coped with their alcohol addictions, wished to use the Steps to address their other problems. The number and type of these process addiction groups increased via a similar refining process: members of one group would decide that the specific nature of their addictions would be best addressed in a group that was unified by and focused on shared experience, and so would split off to form such a group. Thus in the 1980s, Robin Room has argued, "it became common and praiseworthy to shift from one 12-Step group to another in a sequential process of facing up to different issues in one's life."[99] That trend only accelerated in the 1990s thanks to the Internet, which effectively canceled out barriers of time and space and made it possible for far-flung individuals to find and relate to one another. Twelve-Step groups devoted to a host of increasingly rarefied problems—workaholism, Hepatitis C, a propensity for clutter, to name just a few—found comfortable constituencies in cyberspace.[100]

Within the mutating and expanding universe of 12-Step possibilities, Al-Anon and the groups that spun off from it to treat relationships soured by the presence of alcohol or drug addiction bear special mention; their history is the longest and has left the deepest imprint on the broader popular culture. Reflecting the default assumptions about gender common to their class and culture, early AAs assumed that alcoholism was a man's disease.[101] AA meetings, as a result, were almost exclusively male, and Al-Anon began quite consciously as a kind of ladies' auxiliary to AA. Although wives often attended AA meetings with their husbands in the earliest days of the fellowship, as the custom of alcoholics-only meetings developed in the 1940s, wives (and some mothers and daughters) found themselves with time on their hands while their menfolk talked and prayed in the next room. "At first we either played bridge or gossiped," Lois Wilson recalls, "but soon we began to discuss our own problems and what we could do about them."[102] Following her example and that of Bob Smith's wife, Anne, the "co-alcoholics," as they were sometimes called, turned to the spiritual path of the 12 Steps to address their problems. They sought a Higher Power's guidance in dealing with their own "addictions," namely the undesirable behaviors and habits of mind that they had adopted to compensate for their loved ones' drinking.

The patterns of thought and action from which they prayed to be released typically included nagging, blaming, and quarrelling; taking on financial and decision-making responsibility within the family; and coddling or covering up the misbehavior of drunk or absent breadwinners. As the husband reformed, so must the wife. His project focused on relinquishing alcohol, hers on giving up a more diffuse poison: the myriad tiny thought processes and behaviors that had allowed her to cope with him when he was drunk. Both the substance and the "process" abuser were bound together—and aided in their ongoing journeys —by the acknowledgment that a spiritual sickness formed the root of their troubles, and by the belief that a spiritual antidote would best address it.

That AA and Al-Anon relied on (and contributed to) a host of historically specific gendered stereotypes to conceptualize their ideas of diagnosis and treatment is patently obvious, and I discuss the more far-reaching implications of this gendered understanding of addiction and recovery in the chapters that follow. At this juncture it is sufficient to note that, as Lori Rotskoff has persuasively argued, the two groups worked together in many ways to reinforce the conservative gender norms of the Cold War era, creating not only "sober husbands" but also the "supportive wives" necessary to complete and nurture them.[103] As Janice Haaken has noted, however, Al-Anon's official literature moved beyond this rigidly heteronormative stance over the decades, influenced by the growing visibility of female alcoholics—and of male Al-Anons— as well as by "an emerging feminist critique" of traditional caregiver roles.[104] This loosening of gender roles and assumptions in Al-Anon helped to influence its steady growth during the 1960s and 1970s. Despite this nuancing of some key assumptions, however, Al-Anon retains the same philosophical core as AA: it declares a focus on alcohol as such, emphasizes spiritual rather than traditional psychological diagnostics, exalts voluntary association over professional hierarchy and commercial exchange, and sees as its most important therapeutic tools submission to a Higher Power and service to the group.

Al-Anon's closely defined mandate prompted the appearance in the 1980s of two groups with a more heterodox approach to process addictions. Founded in 1978 and 1989, Adult Children of Alcoholics and Co-dependents Anonymous mushroomed quickly; by 1990 there were 1,500 ACOA meetings in the United States and another 200 abroad. CODA, in the space of one year, grew to 2,100 meetings.[105] While both groups invoked the 12 Steps and the idea of recovery associated with them, they also departed significantly from the pragmatic and spiritual approach to recovery developed within Alcoholics Anonymous. In doing so, they drew the concepts of disease and recovery out of a well-established but still marginal subculture and into the floodlit mainstream of popular discourses of the self. Mobilizing a set of ideas from the family systems therapy and humanist psychology that had become popular in the 1970s, codependence put 12-Step culture on the front pages of national news magazines and made it a staple of television talk shows.

Unlike the 12-Step groups that preceded them, ACOA and CODA were fundamentally therapeutic rather than spiritual in orientation. ACOA's official history notes that the organization, which was founded by several Alateens and an adult member of AA who had grown up in an alcoholic home, split off from its two more traditional feeder groups precisely because members wished to focus "on recovering from the effects of being raised in a dysfunctional family rather than [on] being powerless over alcohol."[106] CODA, "a fellowship of men and women whose common problem is an inability to maintain functional relationships," similarly focused on "the dilemmas of the conflicts in our relationships and our childhoods . . . born out of our sometimes moderately, sometimes extremely dysfunctional family systems."[107] Both groups shared Al-Anon's insight into the ways that the presence of alcoholism (or any other addiction or obsessive behavior) within the family unit disrupts emotional development, conditioning affected individuals into a host of suboptimal behaviors and thought processes that may persist into adulthood. In keeping with the professional turn away from the category of "alcoholism" and toward "chemical dependence," they called these process addictions "codependence."

ACOA and CODA addressed codependence and framed a solution to it via the work of midcentury therapists like Virginia Satir, Carl Rogers, and Abraham Maslow, whose work centered on the stress that the family and related institutions places on the self that longs to be free and self-determined. When combined with traditional 12-Step spirituality, this humanist self-actualization project resulted in a hybrid psychospiritual discourse whose nonspecificity attracted thousands of adherents. The groups' adoption of the moniker "Anonymous" and the use of the 12 Steps and Traditions prompted most observers to assume that ACOA and CODA were simple extensions of AA. But as John Steadman Rice and Leslie Irvine have observed, while groups like ACOA and CODA utilize many of the rituals and the language of 12-Step culture, they in fact represent "a radical reversal in the traditional 12-Step view of the relationship between self and society [and] cannot be interpreted as the logical continuation of the legacy of AA."[108] Because they seek to explicate the damage wrought in the family of origin, these therapeutic 12-Step organizations diametrically oppose AA's focus on personal responsibility in the present.

Despite this foundational difference from their forebears, process addiction or codependence advocates have demonstrated a similarly pragmatic (and even less circumspect) investment in the disease metaphor. Thinking in terms of disease may have come easy because some of the earliest framers of codependence were professional therapists working in the addiction treatment world, an impressive number of whom identified as recovering addicts themselves. Individuals who identify as ACOAS and CODAS use disease vernacular in the same loose and opportunistic way that early AAs did. But professional codependence advocates early on recognized the instrumental value of disease status. Two of the earliest books on the topic frame codependence as a disease in their introductory chapters, linking and analogizing it to addiction but also insisting on its specificity. "We are accustomed to thinking of [chemical dependence] as having three facets—physical, emotional/psychological, and spiritual," explains Timmen Cermak in *Diagnosing and Treating Co-Dependence*. "But chemical dependence is also a *family* disease in the most profound sense of the word. Sooner or later, everyone around the sick person 'catches' it in one form or another." Similarly, Anne Wilson Schaef's *Co-Dependence: Misunderstood-Mistreated* notes approvingly that "we are beginning to recognize that co-dependence is a disease in its own right [with] an *onset* (a point at which the person's life is just not working . . .), a *definable course* (the person continues to deteriorate . . .) and, untreated . . . a *predictable outcome* (death)."[109]

Codependence advocates operated from the same rationale that had powered the Alcoholism Movement before them: recognizing codependence as a disease would reduce stigma and help to make effective and humane treatment available. It is difficult to overlook, however, the decidedly material dimension of their interest in "diseasing." It cannot be denied that Bill Wilson, E. M. Jellinek, Marty Mann, and others ultimately made comfortable livings as advocates for their versions of the disease concept of alcoholism. Adult Children of Alcoholics and Codependents Anonymous retain Tradition 8's commitment to "remain forever non-professional," but the professional therapists who advanced the cause of codependence through their books, workshops, and television appearances became celebrities and, in many cases, millionaires.

The treatment industry as a whole, not just the fortunate few who became its spokespersons, had a similarly significant financial stake in codependence being recognized as a disease. The push to categorize and treat codependence as a stand-alone disease entity occurred simultaneously with the enormous growth of the addiction treatment industry in the 1980s. "Family treatment" became a customary part of the treatment regimen at many facilities during this period, and champions of codependence lobbied to make it, like alcoholism before it, an "insurable illness." "If the client's home environment impedes therapy," Cermak argued, "residential treatment should be strongly considered. . . . The concept of detoxification applies not only to the need for chemical dependents to withdraw from the effects of the chemicals they have ingested. . . . Co-dependents [need] to 'detox' from the insanity of a chemically dependent family system in order to fully break their denial."[110]

Arguments like Cermak's met with limited success: lobbying to provide insurance coverage for process addictions began just as insurers began to cut back on coverage for substance addictions. But while therapists who wished to enshrine codependence as the latest iteration of the disease concept of addiction lost a key battle with insurers, they nevertheless may have won the war. As public and private third-party reimbursements for in-patient addiction treatment declined in the shift to managed care during the late 1980s, out-of-pocket payments to participate in family treatment programs became increasingly common. Diseased codependents willing to pay for their own treatment assumed a privileged position within the economic structure of the treatment industry at the same time that they became the most prominent facet of the disease concept within the popular culture of the late twentieth century.[111]

THE POLITICAL ECONOMY OF RECOVERY CULTURE

In *Illness as Metaphor*, Susan Sontag incisively looked beyond medical discourse to understand how ideas about disease actually worked in and on the psyches of both the ill and those who cared for them. Her exploration of the literary dimensions of disease—those elements that, while constructed merely through language and image nevertheless shape how we understand, what we believe, and how, as a result, we act and feel—revealed that what we often assume to be a straightforward (if complicated) physical condition is in fact also a multifaceted and diffuse cultural construction. But Sontag was, in many ways, an old-fashioned close reader of literature. In *Illness as Metaphor*, the texts through which she derives the metaphorical lives of TB and cancer are remarkably context-free: they appear out of nowhere, articulated in nonspecific material forms. Thus while the essay brilliantly answers the question the addiction-as-disease critics evaded—"How did disease become so culturally resonant?"—it does so in a deceptively simple way: "Metaphor made it so." In her move to assert the centrality of the literary, Sontag ignored the social networks, institutions, and practices that allow the literary to take on cultural life.

More so than cancer or tuberculosis, the disease concept of addiction is a literary construction. The brief history above should make clear that while it drew on and mobilized empirical "science," it was produced through language, in distinct historical circumstances, by interested (though not completely unified) parties who had access to powerful technologies of cultural production and distribution as well as to the legitimating powers of the state. Rooted in this political economy, various individuals and groups articulated and promoted a coherent (though, again, not completely unified) philosophy of disease and recovery, sometimes in original ways, sometimes by reference to a host of preexisting cultural assumptions, stereotypes, and historical and aesthetic traditions. The result, by the end of the century, was the development of what Robin Room has called a "generalized 12-Step consciousness"—an epistemological and moral framework constructed primarily through language, but made meaningful through lived experience—that understood the totality of the world and the self as manifestations of or resistances to addictive "disease," broadly defined.[112]

As that consciousness developed, it produced new institutions, and as we shall see in subsequent chapters, a host of cultural products and practices: not only texts, but also publishing strategies and reading protocols. Like Susan Sontag, I am interested in the ways in which a metaphorical construction comes to have the power to organize reality for the people who are exposed to it. Unlike Sontag, however, I believe that understanding the material conditions and the communications structures through which a metaphor—or any other discursive formulation—moves is a crucial factor in explaining its power. The physical forms that encode and embody literary meanings not only influence the ways and the extent to which such meanings can circulate, but also tacitly instruct audiences on how, and how seriously, to engage with them.

What I have called the recovery communications circuit had its origins in the broader political economy of recovery culture, the institutions that, in the collaborative process described here, promulgated the disease concept of addiction. The chapters in parts 2 and 3 explore the material, formal, and imaginative dimensions of the printed matter that issued from that circuit. Those varied print forms—among them pamphlets, flyers, newsletters, hand-made and mass-marketed books and workbooks—sprang from a common impulse: the desire to promulgate some version of the ideas espoused by the men who founded and developed the 12-Step program of Alcoholics Anonymous. AA's answer to the disease concept of addiction, which I call the "antidote of surrender," is the subject of the next chapter.

CHAPTER TWO

The Antidote of Surrender

A s the disease concept of addiction percolated within American popular culture, a complimentary discourse developed alongside it that characterized 12-Step groups as strange religious sects. In a 1963 *Harper's* magazine article, psychologist Arthur Cain described AA as "one of America's most fanatical religious cults," whose controlling and anti-rational devotees believed the 12 Steps to be the result of "divine revelation."[1] This perception was fed during the 1970s and 1980s by the scandals surrounding 12-Step-derived treatment communities like Synanon, The Seed, and Straight, Inc., which kept members virtual prisoners.[2] By the 1990s, Jack Trimpey, founder of the anti-12-Step sobriety organization Rational Recovery, could comfortably rage that "*Of course AA is a cult!* AA is not only a religious cult, it is a radical cult, an evil cult, a widespread cult, and a dangerous cult." The organization works, he argued, as "the embodiment of the Beast," with the single aim of hectoring members into "withdrawal from normal social activities where alcohol may be present. Fear of travel or moving to a new home. . . . Profound self-doubt. . . . Uncertainty and indecision in simple matters. . . . Increasing depression. . . . [All prompt] suicidal thoughts that invariably lead to drinking or using."[3]

Various authors picked up on Trimpey's theme, first in books with titles like *Alcoholics Anonymous: Cult or Cure?* and *Resisting 12-Step Coercion* and then on Internet sites like "AADeprogramming" and "The Orange Papers." All voiced a version of the same message: in Trimpey's words, "Self-destruction is a direct result of 12-step programming."[4]

With their code words and rituals, their canonical literature and hallowed spaces, 12-Step programs can certainly seem cult-like. In the case of AA, the nature of sobriety itself is partly to blame: as Mariana Valverde has noted, since the normalization of social drinking in the wake of Prohibition, abstaining from drink has, paradoxically, become a kind of deviance in most American communities. While the social stigma that attends upon that deviance may vary, performing abstinence in public places nevertheless signals an allegiance to a restricted lifestyle, one that seems out of step with the mainstream values of a consumer society oriented to the cultivation of pleasing personalities and the celebration of leisure.[5]

The pronounced clannishness sometimes found within AA groups may complement the essential weirdness of refusing alcohol. Trimpey's claim that AA prohibits its affiliates from associating with people outside the group is wrong, but the often-invoked slogan "stick with the winners"—an injunction to fraternize with people who enjoy strong sobriety—does have a decidedly prescriptive ring to it. In his aptly titled study *Becoming Alcoholic*, David Rudy describes AA as a "greedy organization" that is "not content with claiming a segment of the energy of individuals but demand[s] their total allegiance." Although he does not use Trimpey's term "programming," Rudy nevertheless confirms that AA invites its members to take on a new identity; to "becom[e] alcoholic" means to remake the self in the light of both shared past experience and highly ritualized, routinized behavior in the present.[6]

What is most responsible, however, for making 12-Step groups seem like communities in the eyes of their adherents and cults in the eyes of their detractors is a core set of ideas, elaborated in early AA and carried reverentially forward into the present, that link addiction to spiritual malaise. Influenced by both the evangelical Oxford Group and by popular spiritualism and New Thought religions, early AAs created a sense of self and of community loosely premised on what Max Weber has called a "religious rejection of the world," a contrarian form of self-definition found among many followers of dissenting religions as well within less reputable "cults." Weber saw such rejections as attempts to repudiate the logic of modernity, with its progressive dehumanization and rationalization—its "disenchantment"—of all interpersonal and spiritual relations.[7]

Although AA's cofounders emphasized the practical dimensions of their enterprise, and consciously used "spiritual" rather than "religious" language, they were motivated by a critique of modernity similar to that described by Weber, and defined their newly sober selves against the logics of possessive individualism and market rationality that were the birthright of white men of their class and generation. Those logics, they argued in the Big Book, mandated a life of "self-propulsion" and "self-will run riot" (60, 62), psychic and behavioral traits that fed into and were complemented by compulsive drinking. In place of that toxic norm, AA posited a spiritually grounded ideal of the self and the world—

and of the self *in* the world—intended to counter what Bill Wilson called the cultural norms of "domination or dependence" that drove men to drink (*12/12*, 117). As they admitted their powerlessness over both alcohol and the world associated with it, AAs cultivated a surrendered sense of self rooted in personal humility and love and, along with that individual identity, a community founded on what Weber calls a "religious ethic of brotherliness [and] reciprocity."[8] They argued that only when they abandoned the competitive values of the American mainstream and adopted in their place the surrendered life of the AA fellowship would compulsive drinkers be able to arrest the degenerative disease of alcoholism.

Then as now, AA's members live and work in the regular world, can enter and exit the group as they please, and are actually limited in the financial contributions they can make to it; such freedom and distance directly oppose the organizational norms of true cults.[9] But AA *can* seem a world unto itself, and its critics are not wrong to see a certain cultishness in both the nature and intensity of its "religious rejection" of the world. This chapter examines the canonical texts of early AA to better understand what it rejected—specifically, the broad identity of possessive individualism as it was exemplified in turn of the century norms of white, middle-class, heterosexual masculinity. It also explores the larger ramifications and the limitations of that rejection. Reading the 12 Steps and 12 Traditions, the writings of cofounder Bill Wilson, and a cluster of long-lived midcentury midwestern sobriety aids, I look at early AA's critique of the gendered behavioral norms embedded in mainstream consumer culture. Out of that critique came lessons in how to replace the alcoholic self with one that was truly sober (as opposed to merely "dry"), a condition that entailed being surrendered to a Higher Power as well as grounded in the personal qualities of humility, gratitude, and love. Living what was called the "AA Way of Life" entailed renouncing the default practice of competition with others and adopting instead a hermeneutical stance I call "alcoholic equalitarianism," a compassionate worldview that emphasized the essential similarity and imperfection of all humans.[10]

The sober and surrendered life, with its incantatory Steps and Traditions, its regime of meetings and its ongoing contemplation of a Higher Power, may look cultish to some outside observers. For the businessmen, artisans, and entrepreneurs of early AA, however, an embrace of 12-Step surrender and community life was anything but restrictive. On the contrary, for them (as for many 12-Step affiliates today), the life of the Steps and Traditions offered a newfound freedom, an unprecedented opportunity to become spiritually and emotionally alive and nothing less than fully human.

DIAGNOSING THE STRANGE ILLNESS

Scholarly analyses of AA that seek to situate the organization and its ideas in historical context typically treat the Roaring Twenties and the subsequent stock market crash of 1929 as key backdrops. Born, in many cases, in the last decade of the nineteenth century, the early members of AA belonged to what Robin Room calls "the wet generations," the "middle-class youth in America [who were] coming of age during and after the First World War." Less adamant in their rejection of Victorian life than the vanguardist Lost Generation, members of this group nevertheless felt "their lives pulled out of accustomed orbits by the First World War, and [used] national Prohibition [as] an archetypal symbol of the values and lifestyles they were rejecting." The Crash held special significance for them because when the "affluence of the Twenties was succeeded suddenly by the privations of the Depression . . . their sustained heavy drinking bec[ame] problematic for them."[11] Lori Rotskoff leverages this historical argument to understand the gendered dimensions of AA, noting that both surgeon Bob Smith and stock market analyst Bill Wilson, "as members of the professional-managerial class . . . enjoyed perquisites of manly authority in the 1920s, only to lose those privileges in the 1930s, when the Depression, combined with their drinking, exacted a more formidable toll." Taking this interpretation one step further, John Rumbarger argues that it was not compulsive drinking and public brawling that caused Bill Wilson to be laid off in the early 1930s, as "Bill's Story" in the Big Book claims, but "the circumstances of the Depression," specifically Wilson's failure "to persuade people to speculate in the stock market at a time when there was every reason not to do so." His subsequent "descent into 'alcoholic hell'" reflected less the power of alcoholism than the power of self-loathing in the face of . . . failure in the marketplace."[12]

While this analytical lens brings one facet of 12-Step experience into sharp relief, it obscures another. Scholars habituated to the secular and materialist frameworks privileged by the modern academy read both drinking and creating AA as compensatory activities, ways to numb the sense of ideological betrayal and existential drift that ensued when the white men of the expanding and upwardly mobile middle class crashed on the rocks of economic reality during the 1930s. Thus in Rumbarger's account, AA spirituality becomes a simple version of false consciousness: Wilson's "call for submission to a Higher Power is finally a call to surrender to the powers that be." Rotskoff makes a similar though more nuanced claim, arguing that AA's concept of alcoholism as the result of spiritual dysfunction " 'contribute[s] ideologically' to normative constructions of race, class, and gender identity" and as such extends and helps to naturalize the hegemony of white male privilege.[13]

While such readings are not without merit, they miss both the tools for cultural critique that AA offered to its adherents and the opportunity to consider the ways in which involvement in a spiritual community (even a community of resolutely bourgeois white men) might constitute a criticism of or challenge to existing structures of socioeconomic order. Without denying that 12-Step discourse, particularly as it gained in legitimacy during the late twentieth century, has an ideological effect, it is important to note as well that both the metaphor of disease and what I am calling the antidote of surrender posed their own critiques of the dominant culture within which they appeared. Although AA self-consciously ruled questions of political-economic power out of its purview (for reasons discussed later in this chapter), a significant portion of early AA literature devotes itself to denigrating the beliefs and practices dedicated to mass-producing the productive capitalist citizen known as the "self-made man."

The ideal of the self-made man has had an important place in U.S. culture since the early Republican period, when earlier models of white masculinity (the genteel patriarch, the heroic artisan) began to be crowded out of the collective imagination by the shift toward industrial capitalism. It was at this time, Michael Kimmel has argued, that American men "began to link their sense of themselves as men to their position in the volatile marketplace." They were "born anxious and insecure, uncoupled from the more stable anchors of land ownership or workplace autonomy. Now manhood had to be proved."[14] By the end of the nineteenth century, the degree of uncertainty and anxiety in men's lives had increased perceptibly, thanks to continually evolving economic and geopolitical conditions as well as to the increasing visibility and power of white women and men of color (native born and immigrant); all these factors further destabilized middle-class white men's cultural centrality. To compensate, the cluster of beliefs commonly known as Victorian success ideology—a "tendency to equate moral and material progress" and an unshakeable belief that at "the center of that morality was the autonomous individual, whose only moral master was himself"—took on ever-increasing importance within mainstream American culture.[15]

As white middle-class men's real power of self-determination declined, popular discourse that trumpeted that power and aimed to bolster it increased proportionally. Body-building, competitive sports, and nature adventures kept the physical body strong and toned; fraternal organizations and the rhetoric and rituals of "muscular Christianity" elevated and purified the spirit; institutionalized racism, sexism, and anti-immigrant activism, along with imperialist rhetoric, trumpeted the white male mind as the repository of "civilization," and venerated an analogous ideal white male self that was "the master of my fate . . . the captain of my soul."[16] This discourse without question afforded middle-class white men unwarranted amounts of privilege. But it also imposed a set of severe moral, characterological, and economic constraints upon them: "Ambition was not an opportunity but an obligation," and one that weighed increasingly heavily on masculine shoulders as the twentieth century opened.[17] It was on this way of being in the world that early AA trained its sights.

Bill Wilson's various biographers have made clear the degree to which, despite coming of age in the twentieth century, he was a product of Victorian success ideology; its tenets dominated his rural Vermont hometown long after the official end of the Victorian period. Wilson's father, a mining manager, abandoned the family when young Billy was ten years old. Shortly afterward, his mother obtained a divorce and moved to Boston, leaving her son to be raised by her elderly parents. Wilson's grandfather, Gardner Fayette Griffith—a teetotaling Civil War veteran who had grown rich on timber and water interests—became Wilson's role model. Pushed to succeed by family and community expectations, Wilson spent much of his young life believing that "I had to be first in everything because in my perverse heart I felt myself the least of God's creatures" (COA, 53). This motivation worked. In high school, Wilson was a star athlete, orchestra leader, and president of his class. But he was also neurasthenic and depressive; after his first year at Vermont's Norwich University, mysterious heart palpitations, stomach upset, and generalized malaise laid him low for a year. Once he did return to school, in 1916, his National Guard unit was called up. Determined to make a heroic name for himself in the war, Wilson went through officer training in Plattsburgh, New York. After marrying Lois Burnham in January 1918 he shipped out, but his regiment was quarantined in England due to the influenza pandemic and he never saw active combat. When he returned to the United States, Wilson drifted from job to job in New York, typically in positions created for him by Lois's well-connected family. His drinking, which had begun during officer training, escalated throughout the 1920s, even as he found himself becoming rich off stock market speculation.[18] As Matthew J. Raphael notes, for Wilson, drinking was not a way of flouting Victorian propriety as it was for so many of the writers and artists of his generation; quite the contrary. It was first a way for the ambitious but unworldly country boy to fit in among genteel urbanites, and then, as Wilson explains, a means to perform his self-importance: "I was drinking to dream greater dreams of power, dreams of domination. Money to me was a symbol of security. It was the symbol of prestige and power," and alcohol was its natural accompaniment.[19]

Although he was an ardent Republican and anti–New Dealer, Wilson came to believe that it was precisely the culturally mandated and uncritical belief in the market values of individual competence, efficacy, and power that underpinned the disease of alcoholism.[20] Unchecked, the characteristically American faith in "unreasonable individualism" (*LOH*, 40) became an out-of-control egomania with deadly potential. As described in the previous chapter, Dr. William Silkworth's "allergy plus obsession" formula was the primary means for explaining AA to new prospects in the organization's earliest days. But what Silkworth called "the hard medical facts" existed primarily as a starting point, a way into understanding what Wilson ultimately called a "strange illness of body, mind, and spirit."[21] Because the spiritual dimensions of that illness were rooted in key elements of modern, middle-class, white male identity, alcoholism could only be remedied by rejecting that identity. The necessity of that rejection was made plain by the Big Book's radical assertion that "the first requirement" for sobriety was recognizing that "any life run on self-will can hardly be a success" (60).

This explanation of alcoholism's cause made AA's remedy oddly counterintuitive. Drawing on his own experiences, Wilson suggested that the alcoholic began simply as a man of his time and place—a habitué of the parties and watering holes that formed the glittering showplaces of modern consumer culture, and a believer in his own capacity to monitor and control his alcohol use. At the moment that alcohol began to exact a social or physical toll, normal people would easily discern that it was time to change their ways and would simply cut back on drinking. But the alcoholic's overinvestment in social norms kept him from making that logical decision. Instead, a fixation on fitting in, on appearing *au courant* and in the swim, pushed him to continue drinking. "No person likes to think he is bodily and mentally different from his fellows," the Big Book noted. As a result, "the great obsession of every abnormal drinker" was the proper exercise of willpower, which would allow him to "control and enjoy his drinking" (30). Driven to participate in what his peer culture deemed "normal," and armed with belief in his own capacity for self-control, the alcoholic would head out to a social occasion, clasping the "threadbare idea that this time we shall handle ourselves like other people" (24). But the physical craving for more liquor—and the allergic reaction to it—would quickly kick in, and a pleasant evening out would become a bender. Illness and shame inevitably followed the drinking spree, triggering a new will to reform and prove oneself "normal," then periods of white-knuckle abstinence, and finally the return of delusional self-confidence. This inevitably prompted another fall off the wagon and a cycle down into "pitiful and incomprehensible demoralization" (30).

Explanations of chronic drunkenness from eighteenth-century physician Benjamin Rush through the Dry crusaders of the twentieth century had argued that a shortage of manly self-mastery was the cause of problem drinking. As Elaine Frantz Parsons bluntly puts it, the drunkard "was not a true man because he was unable to exert his will over his own body and interests."[22] By envisioning drinking behavior as the result of a gendered ideology that believed "the autonomous self [was] only in need of even heavier doses of self-control," Wilson inverted that commonplace: the root of the alcoholic's problem was not a lack of willpower, but a surfeit of it.[23]

Thus while ultimately personal in nature, the strange illness was nevertheless inextricably enmeshed in and facilitated by the gendered norms of early twentieth-century American culture. The alcoholic was not the only one cut off from resources that would allow him to admit the limitations of self-will. His loved ones and expert authorities, drawing from the same limited cultural reservoir that he did, continually urged him toward the futile grail of self-mastery, never realizing that it was loyalty to that sense of self that precipitated the intractable cycle of drunkenness. An extended metaphor in the Big Book illustrates the pervasiveness of this belief:

Most people try to live by self-propulsion. Each person is like an actor who wants to run the whole show; is forever trying to arrange the lights, the ballet, the scenery and the rest of the players in his own way. If his arrangements would only stay put, if only people would do as he wished, the show would be great. . . . What usually happens? The show doesn't come off very well. He begins to think life doesn't treat him right. He decides to exert himself even more. . . . Still the play does not suit him. Admitting he may be somewhat at fault, he is sure that other people are more to blame. He becomes angry, indignant, self-pitying. What is his basic trouble? . . . Is he not a victim of the delusion that he can wrest satisfaction and happiness out of this world if only he manages well? (60–61)

Were it not for the culture-wide "delusion that . . . happiness" can be achieved through "manag[ing] well," the alcoholic might have psychic resources sufficient to deal with his physical allergy. But the "absurd and incomprehensible" (37) middle-class masculine norms of autonomy and self-definition made creative and flexible responses highly unlikely. Given these circumstances, the Big Book argued that only by rejecting the usual ways of defining the self and adopting wholly new ones could alcoholics halt their drinking.

The Big Book framed this choice starkly. To achieve sobriety required that "first of all, we had to quit playing God" (62). The 12 Steps offered the means to do so, with the first three—"admitted that we were powerless over alcohol," "came to believe that a Power greater than ourselves could restore us to sanity," and "turned our lives and our will over to the care of God"—breaking the process of surrender into constituent parts. They prompted alcoholics to recognize the falsity of the autonomy and self-control promised—indeed, mandated—by modern market culture, and to embrace instead the ideal of self promised by and premised on an older, more deferential cosmology. Working the Steps would replace what AA historian Ernest Kurtz calls a "distorted dependency" on the self—a faith symbolized and reinforced by dependence on alcohol—with a generative faith in a Higher Power, a divine force that Kurtz describes as the "proper object" of dependence.[24] Once they exchanged the "life of self-propulsion" for the life of powerlessness, the masters of their fates and captains of their souls would find an antidote to the "strange illness" that preyed upon them.

Twenty years before Bill Wilson and Bob Smith named the life of self-propulsion as the root cause of alcoholism, sociologist Max Weber had made his own observations of Victorian success ideology. What interested him were the spiritual antidotes crafted by men who longed to be free of "the cold skeleton hands of rational orders [and] the banality of everyday routine" that increasingly defined the life of the professional middle class.[25] He argued that these salvific spiritual practices, which he called "religious rejections of the world," typically take two forms. The first is the ascetic—a set of active practices that seek to "tame what is creatural and wicked" in the world and "in the actor's own nature," and replace it with values and practices that will draw him closer to God. The second form of rejection is the mystical—a passive and "contemplative *possession* of the holy" in which "the creature must be silent so that God can speak" (325–26; original emphasis). Both rejections share a desire to reenchant the world: to achieve a social and cosmic order of the type presumed to precede the modern era, one characterized by interpersonal connectedness and infused with divine mystery and thus uniquely able to counter the "functionality, rationality, and generality" of the present day (347). This common antimodern root means that while they differ in emphasis and style, ascetic and mystical practices often blur into one another, especially among believers that do not "flee from the world, but . . . remain in [its] orders" (326).

Alcoholics Anonymous was founded by such believers, and, while it is a spiritual rather than a religious organization, it is premised on a "rejection of the world" similar to those observed by Weber. AA's versions of asceticism and mysticism derive from the two theological traditions that informed it at its founding, the active and evangelical Protestantism of Frank Buchman's Oxford Group and the passive, idealist, harmonial optimism of New Thought religions.[26] These faith traditions may seem so different as to be irreconcilable, but within AA they evolved into an odd but complimentary relationship. By vigorously embracing the ascetic "surrendered life," AAs became able to pursue a deliberately diffuse, non-creedal, and sometimes mystical spirituality.

The Oxford Group was itself a strange conglomeration of the ascetic and the mystical, and I discuss the Group's ritualistic reading and meditative practice of "listening for guidance" in the next chapter. Its ascetic dimension is more readily observed and contributed more directly to

the shaping of AA's core philosophy and practice. Following his ordination in the Lutheran church, Buchman ran a settlement house and
mission in inner-city Philadelphia, served as the secretary of the YMCA
at Penn State University, performed missionary work in India, England,
and China as well as on college campuses throughout the northeastern
United States, and taught at the Hartford Seminary. In each instance,
conflicts with institutional authorities prompted his departure. In 1921
this history of friction culminated in his decision to quit the church
proper and create his own organization, which he vowed would be a
"voice of protest against the organised, committeeised and lifeless
Christian work" of doctrinal and institution-based religion.[27]

Buchman believed in personal, practical, one-to-one evangelizing,
but he differed from many of his contemporaries in that he focused not
on mass revivals, but on converting what he called "key men" in the
community—members of the comfortable middle and upper middle
classes "whose transformation would most quickly affect society at
large."[28] In addition, he seems to have been largely unconcerned with
the main issues roiling conservative churchmen during the time: the
apostasy of evolution and other scientific challenges to biblical literal-
ism. Instead, his primary focus was on what he called "soul sickness," a
condition defined by a Group member who wrote under the pseudonym
"The Layman with a Notebook" as "morbidity of outlook and the feeling
that the physical is predominant in life."[29]

Like many of the evangelical "religions of the heart" that have come
into being since the Protestant Reformation, Buchman laid this "morbidity" at the feet of an impersonal and secular consumer society. He saw
the contemporary glorification of the physical and the material as a kind
of debased Mammonism: what he called "materialism" encompassed
sexual acting out, profligacy, vanity, envy, gluttony, and of course excessive drinking. These physical indulgences were exacerbated and compli-
mented by distinctly modern forms of intellectual self-aggrandizement,
which denied the nature of the "disease . . . and disorder of the soul" (20).
Grabbing on to the "fashionable cult" of "pathological psychology,"
"modern . . . 'highbrows' " sought to evade their soul sickness by treating
human failings as "repressed desires; inhibitions; fixations; morbid introspection; suppression of natural instincts and other words ending in
'ism,' 'phobia,' 'mania'—anything but what they are—just plain Sin" (19–
20). Such prevarications, obviously, only compounded the problems
they claimed to describe. The Oxford Group offered its adherents a more

salutary framework for understanding modern unhappiness: the simple realization that "sin is the disease, Christ is the cure, the result is a miracle."[30]

The dimension of Oxford Group asceticism most obviously germane to AA is the rejection of intoxicating liquor, but the Group was primarily concerned with spiritual and psychic abstinence, with abandoning worldly notions of happiness and success in favor of "relinquishing our lives to God" (51). A life thus relinquished was prosecuted according to what Buchman identified as "the Four Absolutes": Honesty, Purity, Unselfishness, and Love. Fealty to these simple principles, the Group believed, would distance believers from the tainted world, where "everything is judged by its financial value [and] souls are for sale cheap" (89). Like other "First Century" or "primitive" Christian groups, the Oxford Group held that once the community of believers grew large enough, it would redeem the world beyond it, delivering humanity writ large to what Buchman (apparently without a trace of irony) called "the dictatorship of the living spirit of God."[31]

The Layman with a Notebook proclaimed unequivocally that "Frank Buchman is not an ascetic" (14), and the Oxford Group made no attempt to cloister its members or to dress them in sackcloth and ashes.[32] But even the brief sketch above should make clear that the Group tended toward what Weber had called the "religion of virtuosos."[33] Buchman and his followers constituted their identities through a series of rejections—of the rationalized, depersonalized modernity embodied in the organized church; of the "mental snobs" and "commercialize[d] indecencies" of consumer culture (91); and of all those "who arrogate to themselves the external purity of a lovely flower" but who "behind the velvet delicacy of its petals [have] heart[s] rotten and worm-eaten" (87). The trappings of modern life were simply not consistent with the life of faith. To "live in Christ to the best of our spiritual ability," the Layman with a Notebook observed, it was first necessary to "die to the world in which are the very roots of our being" (45). Preaching against all that was worldly, Buchman's followers sought to erect in its place an uncorrupted community of believers bound to one another and to God by a direct and personal faith. Along with the more narrow practice of abstaining from alcohol, AA's cofounders retained this broad conceptual asceticism after they split off from the Oxford Group in 1939.

Such a giving over of oneself to a higher power came hard to the average alcoholic, Bill Wilson acknowledged, because a life steeped in the secular self-congratulation of Victorian success ideology militated strongly against it. "Bill's Story" in the Big Book recounts Wilson's own urbane indifference to religion: "To Christ I conceded the certainty of a great man . . . his moral teaching—most excellent. For myself, I had adopted those parts which seemed convenient and not too difficult . . . [but] judging from what I had seen in Europe [during the First World War] and since, the power of God in human affairs was negligible, the Brotherhood of Man a grim jest" (11). For Wilson, as for the Layman with a Notebook, however, the intellectual sophistication that allows the modern cynic to believe he sees through the panaceas of traditional religion is just another version of the life of self-propulsion. Freedom from alcoholic craving only becomes possible when the alcoholic finally rejects his know-it-all attitude and embraces instead the reality of his finitude, abjection, and dependence on God.

In Wilson's case, that reality manifested itself during his penultimate stay at Towns Hospital. "I, who had thought so well of myself and my abilities, of my capacity to surmount obstacles, was cornered at last. Now I was to plunge into the dark, joining that endless procession of sots who had gone on before. . . . No words can tell of the loneliness and despair I found in that bitter morass of self-pity. Quicksand stretched around me in all directions. I had met my match. I had been overwhelmed. Alcohol was my master" (8).

The experience of what AAs would later call "hitting bottom" is the analogue to traditional Protestantism's "deep and despairing experience of 'conviction under The Law,'" the moment in which, stripped once and for all of his worldly accomplishments and plunged into total despair, the sinner truly realizes the infinitude and surpassing love God has for His creatures.[34] Though lacking theological specifics, Wilson's experience retains that classical structure:

> I still gagged badly on the notion of a Power greater than myself, but finally, just for the moment, the last vestige of my proud obstinacy was crushed. All at once I found myself crying out, "If there is a God, let Him show himself! I am ready to do anything, anything!"
>
> Suddenly the room lit up with a great white light. I found myself caught up in an ecstasy which there are no words to describe. . . . All about me and through me there was a wonderful feeling of Presence. . . . And I thought, "No matter how wrong things seem to be, they are still all right. Things are all right with God and His world." (COA, 63)

The language of this realization is significant, for as he narrates his experience of surrender, Wilson moves out of a secular modern frame of reference. In the Big Book passage acknowledging that "alcohol was my master," Wilson had figured the destruction of his bodily and psychic autonomy—the typical hallmarks of successful Western masculinity—in the direst terms. Once an individuated and self-contained achiever, he had fallen, via drinking, into an undifferentiated selfhood. From a distinct individual he had declined into merely one in an "endless procession of sots," and would soon, he imagined, lose even the vestiges of humanity, as the oozing "morass" and "quicksand" around him overran the boundaries of his once triumphant male body.[35]

Seen from the other side of the "great white light," however, depersonalization and the dissolve of bodily boundaries is liberating—a cause for celebration. Once freed from his normative and limited worldview, Wilson becomes able to sense a "wonderful . . . Presence" moving "about me and through me." A new and miraculous feeling of unboundedness replaces the terrifying isolation that is the marker of modern personhood and social organization. Having finally surrendered his futile modern selfhood and "die[d] to the world," Wilson achieves the sense of ecstatic interpenetration that has been familiar to religious seekers from antiquity forward.[36] "A peace and serenity [like] I had never known . . . as though the great clean wind of a mountaintop blew through and through" (14) is asceticism's reward, and the surrendered self—in AA as in other religious rejections of the world—submits gratefully to the loss of the worldly identity that had once seemed so precious.

THE EXPANSIVE SPIRIT

Although the alcoholic's surrender structurally resembles that which is made in traditional Protestantism, it is not made to a traditional Protestant God but rather to "whatever or whoever can stop his drinking."[37] This deliberately nonspecific spirituality is technically another inheritance from the Oxford Group. Bill Wilson was drawn into the Group by his friend Ebby T., a former drinking buddy who shared his dislike of gospel temperance but had learned in the Group to "pray to whatever God I thought there was . . . and if I did not believe there was any God, then [to] try the experiment of praying to whatever God there *might* be." It was this expansive sense of the divine, Ebby told Wilson, that had made his spiritual change possible (COA, 59; original emphasis). The Group's commitment to ecumenism may have been somewhat strategic; for all Buchman's antidoctrinal contrarianism, his writings and speeches remain steeped in the language not only of sin and redemption, but also of Christ and the cross. But the investment in "whatever God there *might* be" became in AA a core philosophy. This broad conceptualization of the spiritual marked the point where the ascetic dimension of AA ended and its mysticism began.

Part of AA's spiritual rather than religious orientation was itself strategic.[38] After their own transformative experiences, Wilson (and, somewhat more reluctantly, Smith) came to believe that any explicit religiosity, much less the stringent "absolutes" of Frank Buchman, would drive away as many drunkards as it attracted. In addition, it might deter participation by Catholics, who were forbidden by canon law from joining religious organizations outside the church.[39] But an equally important factor in AA's embrace of the spiritual was Wilson and Smith's own eclectic religious beliefs. Both cofounders had been raised in liberal New England Protestant churches and, as AA historian Glenn Chesnut has noted, it is that theology, even more than Buchman's supercharged revisions of it, that probably had the most enduring effects on them.[40] But AA's conceptualization of the divine was influenced as well by the fact that the cofounders were avid spiritualists—what religious studies scholars call "seekers" or "restless souls," with "a tendency to identify 'true' spirituality with mysticism or occultism: the knowledge of ultimate reality experienced as something outside common expressive forms."[41] Like many nineteenth-century Anglo-American religious iconoclasts, they participated regularly in séances and used ouija boards to communicate with spirits. Wilson may have taken the lead in this regard, devoting a special room in his house to weekly "spook sessions," but as AA's official history points out, both cofounders "work[ed] away at spiritualism; it was not just a hobby" (*PIO*, 280).

In addition to popular mystical pursuits, Wilson and Smith were also familiar with a variety of esoteric religious traditions. Lois Wilson hailed from a family of followers of the Swedish mystic Emmanuel Swedenborg (1688–1771), whose New Church and its teachings are generally seen as the main theological precursors to the New Thought sects that developed in the United States and Britain in the nineteenth century. Her grandfather was a minister in the Swedenborgian Church of Lancaster, Pennsylvania, and her father, Nathan Clark Burnham, was a homeopathic physician whose training at the Hahnemann School of medicine in Philadelphia would have included discussion of the doctrines of spiritual healing.[42] In the years just prior to AA's founding, while Wilson was drunk and unemployed, he and Lois lived with Burnham, and as he absorbed mystical ideas of mind and spirit around the family dinner table, Wilson also investigated them through reading. Lois Wilson's memoir notes that during this period he explored the mental healing practices of Christian Science, "read[ing] and re-read[ing]" Mary Baker Eddy's *Science and Health with Key to the Scriptures* in the hope of overcoming his drinking.[43] Though he practiced a fairly straightforward version of Congregationalism, Bob Smith, too, "believed vigorously and aggressively" (*PIO*, 280) in precognition, second sight, and communication with the spirit world. He attended the New Thought retreats known as Camps Farthest Out and followed the teachings of the Unity Church as well as various Theosophical leaders.[44]

Not only the pietist Protestantism of the Oxford Group, then, but also the expansive mysticism that philosopher William James, in his influential *Varieties of Religious Experience* (1902), had called "the religion of healthy-mindedness" informed AA's ideas of spirituality.[45] James's explication of New Thought sheds useful light on the principles of this diffuse and eclectic tradition and its place in 12-Step philosophy. *Varieties* posits that the religion of healthy-mindedness is best understood not as a doctrine but as an idealist tendency, a habit of "conceiving good as the essential and universal aspect of being [and] deliberately exclud[ing] evil from [one's] field of vision" (86). Such an outlook was a matter of temperament for some people (St. Francis of Assisi and Walt Whitman were James's examples) and of theology in some denominations, like Lutheranism and Methodism. James argued that during the nineteenth century, however, organized Western religions of all stripes had begun to drift toward such optimistic outlooks, moving away from the "morbidness with which the old hell-fire theology" had been associated (89). This "New Thought," which James also referred to as the "Mind-cure" movement, spoke directly "to persons for whom the conception of salvation has lost its ancient theological meaning, but who labor nevertheless with the same eternal human difficulty. *Things are wrong with them*; and 'what shall I do to be clear, right, sound, whole, and well?' is the form of their question." To that enduring human inquiry, New Thought gave a decisive and optimistic answer: "You *are* well, sound, and clear already, if you did but know it" (103; original emphasis). The goal of its various sects and schools was to make such knowing possible—to instruct adherents in how to slough off the false perceptions that blocked their access to an essentially beneficent reality.

Recognizing the self's baseline harmony with the universe entails a religious rejection of sorts: to the New Thought idealist, it is the world's false definitions of health, wealth, and happiness that weigh down and sicken the soul. Devotional practice—affirmations, prayers, meditations —works to loosen the hold of those false definitions on the spirit and thus restore its "natural" health and prosperity. But because the idealist bent also holds that evil has no essential reality, evil does not need to be actively renounced; surrender therefore takes a mystical rather than an ascetic form. Echoing Weber's description of the mystical as "a state of 'possession,' not action,"[46] James characterized New Thought's highest aim as an undoing of the modern norms of vigilance and aggression, the cultivation of "passivity, not activity; relaxation, not intentness." By "giv[ing] up the feeling of responsibility, let[ting] go your hold, re-sign[ing] the care of your destiny to higher powers, be[ing] genuinely indifferent as to what becomes of it all," the believer gives the "little private convulsive self a rest, and find[s] that a greater Self is there" (104–5). Seen in this light, surrender of the self is less the relinquishment of sin than of what James identified as "fear" and "the misery habit," both of which are brought on by misplaced belief in the power of material forces to shape human reality (93, 95).

Like traditional creedal religions, New Thought recognizes that relinquishing such beliefs is seldom easy. To achieve surrender, James explained, "a native hardness must break down and liquefy" (105). But once that dissolution occurs, the rewards are profound indeed. Weber had described the culmination of the mystic's quest somewhat abstractly, as the spirit "flowing out into an objectless acosmism of love."[47] James's explanation of New Thought was considerably more pragmatic: "The powers of the universe will directly respond to your individual appeals and needs" (112).

Significantly, AA's interest in New Thought did not extend to its "power of mind" dimension. Such a cultivation of personal mental power was another form of the life of self-propulsion and, as Bill Wilson had discovered during his fruitless perusal of *Science and Health*, no prophylactic against alcoholism. What interested the cofounders, AA historian Mel B. has noted, was New Thought's capacious image of a beneficent natural order and its many practical devotional techniques.

They used the latter to keep themselves aligned with the former and to cultivate an ongoing "conscious contact with God" (Step 11).[48]

AA historians have long acknowledged the influence of *Varieties* on AA's cofounders: in *Alcoholics Anonymous Comes of Age*, Wilson acknowledges that "it was Ebby, I think, who brought me a copy of . . . *Varieties of Religious Experience*. It was rather difficult reading for me, but I devoured it cover to cover" (64). The book was also a "favorite" of Dr. Bob's, and appears on the "List of Books that Early AAs Read" compiled by secretary Nell Wing (*Dr. Bob*, 306). James's comparative religions perspective and his extensive treatment of the conversion experience, Matthew J. Raphael has argued, combined to provide Bill Wilson with "the conceptual framework by which to comprehend what had happened to him" and, by extension, to conjecture about what had happened or could happen to other men like himself. Though he "seldom, if ever, revisited the book that once had touched him so profoundly," he nevertheless " 'frequently and avidly' recommend[ed it] 'to correspondents telling of difficulty with the AA program.' "[49]

Another virtue of *Varieties* may have been its treatment of New Thought alongside the great religions of the world. Like James's Harvard pedigree, this conferred a degree of legitimacy on a set of heterodox spiritual and mystical practices that AA's cofounders knew from personal experience and the popular culture around them. By claiming that faith is simply "the belief that there is an unseen order, and that our supreme good lies in harmoniously adjusting ourselves thereunto," James disaggregated spirituality from specific theologies—both high- and lowbrow—and thus made it available for use by anti-authoritarian alcoholics.[50] As with the concept and language of "disease," this pragmatic value rather than the theological or theoretical nuances of "spirituality" was what AA valued most.

The ascetic traditions of Western religion are more highly codified, better known, and, ultimately, more easily translated into narrative form to American audiences than the more diffuse and individualistic mystical rejections of the world. It is perhaps for this reason that the printed literature of midcentury AA, as we shall see, emphasized the pietist inheritance of the Oxford Group. But New Thought mysticism—especially the idea of an accessible, personal, and nonjudgmental Higher Power—was an equally important taproot within the fellowship, informing both the theory and the practice of AA spirituality. A notable early example of AA's enmeshment with New Thought was the Ministry of

High Watch, a Kent, Connecticut, retreat founded on the teachings of Christian Science minister Emma Curtis Hopkins. Originally a sanitarium and generic drying-out facility, during the 1940s High Watch became one of the first treatment communities to address alcoholism solely through spiritual means.[51] The mystical strain of 12-Step philosophy became more pronounced when demographic and cultural changes during the 1960s and 1970s stimulated its roots, prompting them to branch out and to blossom. In that period, which I discuss in later chapters, the tensions between the ascetic and the mystical routes to surrender and the question of which offered the best path to sobriety took on new urgency for many AA members.

For Bill Wilson, Bob Smith, and their contemporaries, however, any tensions that might have existed between the two very different spiritual traditions that undergirded AA were defused by the fact that each worldview celebrated an all-powerful divine force that actively worked in the lives of the faithful, supporting them in their repudiation of the mainstream values of competition and aggression. In doing so, they offered a clear path not only to a sober but also to a vastly rich life. The pragmatic focus of AA meant (and for many, still means) that members spent their time not on adjudicating a balance of power between pietist humility and idealist self-expansion, but on carrying to new prospects the joyous message of sober and spiritual life. They were aided in that process by literature that invited readers accustomed to the life of self-will run riot to see instead the complex virtues of powerlessness, and that taught by inspiring example how to live as surrendered men.

OPENING THE DOOR OF THE HEART

Since the seventeenth century, more women than men have been active in religious life in the United States. The same set of values and beliefs that installed the ideal of the self-made man at the center of bourgeois culture made it hard for that man—for any man—to embrace the psychodynamics of religious transport, especially the "submission, yielding, giving oneself over to the will of another, and . . . visible emotionalism" that characterize surrender to God. The result has been what religious historians refer to as a "feminization of piety"—an indelible marking of spiritual life as the precinct of women.[52]

Although their de facto sexism meant that their fellowship was dominated by men, early AAs nevertheless faced their own version of this problem. A group that sought to distance itself from the toxic life of self-propulsion would need to build into its vision of the surrendered self a recognizable and solid masculine identity. If it could not, members insecure about their manliness might be swept back out into the gender-normal mainstream and return to drinking. Their relative cultural blindness where questions of gender and power were concerned means that early AAs did not address this issue directly, but it was nevertheless a subject of concern for them. The issue was taken up most distinctively by amateur authors who had sobered up in midwestern cities where the ascetic inheritance of the Oxford Group was the strongest. In pamphlet and book publications that quickly became canonical, they addressed the question of how to balance the competing claims of spiritual and masculine life.[53] As they explored the nature and purpose of sober living, they extended the critique of normative male identity that the Big Book had begun and sketched its alternative: a manly identity grounded in the loving brotherhood of AA believers and, as a result, somewhat distanced from what Weber calls "natural relations and . . . the matrimonial community."[54]

This project unfolds most clearly in a group of midwestern pamphlets that treat the move from what the authors call "sobriety, period" —defined as "no drinks [and thus] no hangovers, no jams, no troubles" —to the true "AA sobriety" of the surrendered and spiritual life.[55] At the outset of these stories, "sobriety, period" satisfies the narrators because it allows them to continue to indulge in the boisterous pleasures of modern masculinity. Hanging on to a few of these pleasures is particularly important to men who feel keenly that they have already been deprived of the masculine prerogative of drink. Rationalizing his continuing leisure-time pursuits, "The Devil and AA's" narrator makes the potential emasculation that comes with sobriety clear: "What am I, a man or a mouse? . . . Now that I've quit drinking, can't I have a little fun? Can't I toss away a sawbuck or two on the horses? Isn't it all right for me to sit up all night playing poker? After all, the guys I'm playing with are AAs." Similarly, even after he swears off drink, the narrator of "AA Is a Tender Trap" retains a keen sense of what constitutes "life's necessities" for a real man: "a big front; a glamorous social life; plenty of spending money borrowed, begged, or stolen; attractive women friends and a moral standard that guaranteed a man's freedom."[56]

The pamphlet narrators learn, however, that "sobriety, period" turns out to be an "inferior, substitute brand of AA."[57] Those who would find true release from the life of self-propulsion must go further in renouncing its soul-deadening values. Failure to do so will lead inevitably back to drinking. "The AA who does just enough in AA to maintain his sobriety" faces a grim prospect, warns the author of "The Long Haul." "When growth ceases, death begins. A plant that is rooted in stony ground, that has little water, that has little sunshine, manages to stay alive, but it's a puny thing." The pamphlet narrators hit a new kind of bottom when they realize that "sobriety, period" has left them vulnerable to a despair familiar from drinking days—"the kind that forced me, sooner or later, to look at myself through sober eyes, and in revulsion and disgust to hustle back to the bottle."[58] Each Chicago pamphlet describes the narrator's arrival at a spiritual crossroads, where he realizes that, just as he relinquished alcohol, so must he now give up the habits that, while allowing him to retain his nominal masculinity, have kept him spiritually "puny."

Most obvious among those habits are the pursuit of sensual vices rooted in ego gratification: "padding the old swindle sheet, or making a play for that red-headed dice girl, or socking the rent money on some horse's nose."[59] But these spectacular foibles are the least dangerous forms of self-sabotage. More pernicious are the "modern highbrow" vices that the Layman with a Notebook had identified, specifically the spiritual dishonesty of intellection and rationalization. Demonstrating the continuing influence of Oxford Group–style asceticism, the pamphlet authors excoriate such self-aggrandizing and self-delusional modes of thinking.

In doing so, they built on a tradition that originated in the best-known and most respected midwestern sobriety aid, *The Little Red Book*. The text originated in Minneapolis in 1942, when Barry C. and Ed W. of the Nicollett Group began to teach a series of required classes for AA newcomers and their families, modeled on the strict practices observed by Dr. Bob's home group in Akron.[60] The two men worked from a set of handwritten notes, which over time were transcribed, edited, and mimeographed by friends and admirers; circulated hand to hand, versions of their teaching document spread across the United States and Canada under the title "An Interpretation of the Twelve Steps." In 1946 the authors founded Coll-Web Publishing and, after a final editing of their materials by Dr. Bob himself, began producing a hardbound version of their study guide.[61]

The Little Red Book efficiently explicates the three-part disease in its first two chapters, but its focus is the surrendered life, which it defines in stark opposition to alcoholism's "false pride" (37), "self-exaltation" (39), and "self-centeredness" (27 and passim). These mental habits, the authors contend, are exacerbated by the modern tendency toward intellectualizing. While it acknowledges that reading and studying AA literature and the Bible can aid in the larger project of self-surrender, *The Little Red Book* is careful to remind its readers that the "constructive reconditioning" (38) necessary to achieve sobriety occurs at God's pleasure, not through heightened self-knowledge or understanding of alcoholism as such. Readers are cautioned not to "waste time in useless discussion of the . . . word sanity in Step Two" (28). Although it only makes sense to "use intelligence to avoid further alcohol addiction" (61), any attempts to problematize, complicate, or read against the grain are discouraged. Such critical engagement, *The Little Red Book* argues, is merely evidence of persistent self-will, a "mental binge" that will soon escalate into a "spiritual blackout" and then a "physical drunk" (34). Instead of flaunting their ability to quibble over meanings and ramifications, readers are urged simply to "accept the Twelve Steps in their entirety," since "it might very well be suicide to disagree with any part of [them]" (28). In place of the ego-gratifying habits of analysis and rationalization, *The Little Red Book* counsels quiet acceptance, the willingness to "take on an understanding of God's will and make ourselves a channel for its expression" (39).

The pamphlet authors elaborated on this argument. The narrator of "AA Is a Tender Trap" explains that the belief in "cynicism as the mark of smart sophistication" could no longer be tolerated by a man seeking lasting and meaningful sobriety. The cosmopolitan narrator of "Out of the Fog" goes so far as to explain that he has renounced his allegiance to H. L. Mencken, despite a previous fondness for that author's flippant definition of "conscience [as] an inner voice that warns us somebody is looking." The move from puny to robust spirituality, he admits, has compelled him to acknowledge instead that "conscience, in almost anybody's language, is a synonym for God."[62]

Intellection, sophistication, and irony, like the more recognizably masculine "vices" of drinking, gambling, promiscuity, and the pursuit of glamour, were thus cast by midwestern authors as soul-killing habits. Renouncing both forms of mainstream pleasures was necessary for the man who wanted to move from the shaky ground of "sobriety, period" to "AA sobriety" or what *The Little Red Book* called the "AA Way of Life." When he was at last purged of these vestiges of soul-sickness, a man could begin "to pray in words *and* to pray in deeds" and to reestablish his identity on a new foundation, the cornerstones of which the pamphlet authors enumerated as "LOVE," "grace," "peace of spirit," and "gentleness."[63]

Midwestern literature extolled these qualities—not typically seen as "manly"—as the centerpiece of the sober masculinity AA offered its members. While we cannot know the ways in which or the extent to which this schema of virtues played out in the lives of real people, their discursive presence is nevertheless important. The rigorous vision of the midwestern authors would become the centerpiece of a distinct strain of AA that I call "traditionalist." Reflective of the relatively homogenous (middle-class, white, male, and Protestant) AA cultures of Akron and Cleveland, highly attuned to the influence of the Oxford Group, and consequently emphasizing an ascetic rather than a mystical spiritualism, traditionalist AA inflected the development of a regionally specific (though not monolithic) 12-Step culture at midcentury. Equally if not more important, it also informed a contrarian counter-culture that developed as AA evolved and diversified in later years, a process I take up in chapters 3 and 4.

The significance of traditionalist ideas within the history of AA is complemented by the important ways that they complicate assumptions about the gendered work that the fellowship performed for its members. Lori Rotskoff has argued that AA rehabilitated alcoholic men into their socially sanctioned role as "sober husbands"—wage earners whose performance in the labor market supported the families in which they functioned as good-natured patriarchs.[64] Anecdotal evidence suggests that this frequently happened, but the midwestern authors expend scant energy on sobriety's implications for family or work life. Proving Barbara Ehrenreich's contention that psychic "maturity" was the code word for masculine success at midcentury, the narrator of "The Long Haul" does explain that "what we have to do in AA [is] Grow UP."[65] But he is alone in his invocation of maturity as such. Neither *The Little Red Book* nor the Chicago and Akron pamphlets devote more than a few sentences to men's roles as workers, fathers, or husbands.[66] Like Weber's ascetics and mystics, the authors devalued "the relationships of the [kin-group] and of matrimony" in favor of a "new community" organized around "religious ethic of brotherliness."[67] Success as a sober man was not measured by family or workplace accomplishment, but in terms of the duration and quality of sobriety and dedication to the AA community.

Thus the narrator of "AA, God's Instrument" acknowledges that sobriety's role in "the recovery of jobs, in the restoration of happy family life, in the rediscovery of self-respect," is significant. But those accomplishments pale beside the realization and acceptance of what he calls "common helplessness" and the "union of mutual liabilities" that AA offers its members.[68] Like Bill Wilson in his postconversion moment, sober AAs came to define themselves not as singular and self-contained individuals within the modern realms of home and office, but through their interdependencies with other AAs—interdependencies that reflected their primal unity with the divine. Weber's "brothers in salvation" became the chief reference point for AAs' new identities because "the group itself has been the graceful means for many to catch a fleeting but convincing glimpse of the Infinite."[69] "We keep AA always as our first love," the narrator of "The Long Haul" reminded his audience, because only other members of the same community would support men who sought to develop and sustain the decidedly unmanly "willing" and "compliant heart[s]" upon which sobriety depended—hearts disallowed them by the relentless competition of the world around them. Only when encouraged and inspired by other surrendered men could they set aside the life of aggression and intellect and find a true home in the world. Significantly, that home was *not* a domicile shared with wife and children, but an interior space of spiritual communion: "a blessed home in myself where I can go in and shut the door and kneel to my Father in secret and be at peace."[70]

That such a "home in myself" would be "secret" suggests the midwestern authors' awareness that the identities they exhorted their readers to embrace were unusual, even slightly deviant versions of masculinity. Claiming and living such a gender role did not come easily for early AAs, who, as salesmen and entrepreneurs in the George Babbitt mold, had long valued rationality and rationalization, masculine competition, and the clearly bounded bodies, hearts, and minds that they implied. Their new understanding of the nature of spiritual sickness, however, had revealed to them the limitations of this worldview and, along with it, of the gender roles that had shaped their lives. Though they spoke of gender only obliquely, the men who founded AA nevertheless sought to fashion new masculine identities for themselves by embracing—and encouraging others to embrace—the logic of spiritual surrender and, with it, the dissolve of the self into the love of the community. Such surrender was of necessity conscious and active: as the narrator of "Willingness" reminded his audience, "the latch to [the] heart is on the inside, and God himself won't enter until you open the door."[71] To live as a surrendered and sober man was to open that door and leave it open, to undo the cultural mandates that had formerly kept men closed off and suspicious, driven away from one another as surely as they had been driven toward alcohol and other markers of masculine "success."

ALCOHOLIC EQUALITARIANISM

What the *Little Red Book* called the "AA Way of Life" and other midwestern authors simply termed "AA sobriety" was not merely abstinence, or even abstinence plus professions of religious faith. It indicated instead the replacement of the normative autonomous masculine self with a "self-in-relation," a self defined and made meaningful not by its difference and distance from others, but by its connection to them.[72] Anthropologist Gregory Bateson has described this phenomenon as a shift in the mind of the individual AA from a Western ethos of "symmetry," in which the self is perceived as a monad that either resists or capitulates to forces outside of it, to one of "complementarity," a holistic worldview premised on empathetic exchange, within which the self is recognized as simply one part of a larger system.[73] Instead of deriving from personal success, well-being is contingent on the condition of the whole alcoholic community.

This rejection of commonplace conceptions of success grounded in masculinist ideals of autonomy, accumulation, and power over others distances AA from the tradition of American self-improvement schemes that originate in Benjamin Franklin's "Project for Moral Perfection."[74] Although the Steps do promise an improved life thanks to an end to drunkenness, they also aim to dismantle the self-propelled and upwardly mobile Franklinesque self. Steps 1 through 3, with their admission of powerlessness, inaugurate that dismantling. The remaining Steps instruct the alcoholic in how to reorient his life so it centers on the others who have been excluded, exploited, and hurt by the "symmetrical" energies of drunken life.

Significantly, Steps 4 through 12 do not outline a master plan for the conscious development of habits or personality traits necessary for success in the public sphere, like those offered by Franklin or his inheritors, Smith and Wilson's contemporaries Dale Carnegie and Napoleon

Hill.[75] Instead, they inculcate passivity: the alcoholic self rejects the modern project of self-fashioning. It cannot be remade except by God, who is asked "to remove our shortcomings" (Step 7) and grant "knowledge of His will for us and the power to carry it out" (Step 12). The exception to this, and the central area in which the alcoholic must take action and responsibility, is in his stunted relationships. Recognizing the ways in which the workings of self-will run riot have warped interpersonal connections, then seeking to straighten and heal those connections, is the substance of Steps 4, 5, 8, 9, and 10.

Step 4 begins this process with an enumeration and explanation of fears and of resentment-inspiring people and circumstances. In the Big Book examples, "Mr. Brown" is resented because he "told my wife of my mistress" and "may get my job at the office"; the resentment affects "sex relations" and "self-esteem." But while the resentment list details the actions of others, its purpose is not to identify *their* faults. The text explicitly reminds readers that "the inventory was ours, not the other man's" (67). Like the fear that "touches about every aspect of our lives," the sources of resentment are catalogued in order to reveal the degree to which "the world and its people really dominat[e] us" (66). This catalog exposes once again the fiction of self-mastery, this time at the psychic rather than simply the physical level, prompting the alcoholic to acknowledge that "these resentments must be mastered, but how?" (66).

The answer to this—and the centerpiece of AA's vision of personal redemption—is the ideology I have chosen to call "alcoholic equalitarianism," an analogue (and in many ways an offshoot) of the Christian equalitarianism that characterized the evangelical Protestant sects that appeared in Europe and the United States during the late eighteenth and nineteenth centuries. Informed by the philosophy of moral sentiments and reacting against both Catholic and Calvinist theologies, Christian equalitarianism's founding premise was the availability of salvation to all who would seek it, irrespective of rank or station. This was a theological innovation of revolutionary proportions, and one that profoundly influenced not only religious history but also a wide range of modern movements for democratic social reform.[76] For my purposes here, however, what is most relevant is the way Christian equalitarianism presumed and helped to validate a new epistemological stance, the way it reformulated ideas about what is real and how we know it to be real. Unlike their more doctrinaire predecessors, who treated outward appearance as an index of sanctification, evangelicals preached the importance of seeing past worldly physical and social difference to the essential reality of beings, to their nature as seen by God. As an analogue to the five physical senses, every individual possessed an innate moral sense that allowed for such true seeing. Because that moral faculty was a gift from God, Christian equalitarianism argued that it was the duty of all who possessed it to use it to see *through* the false distinctions imposed on God's creatures by a corrupt society and *into* the true nature of their souls. This seeing through difference and to similarity was accomplished by the act of imagination that today we typically call "identification." By seeing themselves in those who were superficially "other" to them, evangelicals offered an "experimental extension of humanity" to people like the enslaved, the poor, and the mad, whom law and custom treated as less than human.[77] Alcoholic equalitarianism relied on similar assumptions.

This brief sketch does not do justice to the complexities of evangelical thought, but it should begin to suggest the premises of Christian equalitarianism upon which AA would build. One purpose of the 4th Step inventory was to reveal the degree to which self-will run riot affected the nominally sober as well as the alcoholic, and to invite the recovering self to center relationships on that commonality, rather than on superficial differences and tensions. The resentments list prompted the alcoholic to review the actions of those who had come to be perceived as "others" because they impeded the progress of his ascendant and triumphal self. When the 4th Step "grudge list" (65) was reviewed through the lens of alcoholic equalitarianism, the essential sameness of self and other was revealed: "The people who wronged us were perhaps spiritually sick. Though we did not like their symptoms and the way these disturbed us, they, like ourselves, were sick too." Rather than being stigmatized for their difference, the "nut[s]" and "nag[s]" who had seemed so "unreasonable—unjust—overbearing" must be embraced (65–67)—both for their kinship to "us" and for "our" essential sameness in God's eyes. The epistemological and moral gesture of the phrase "they, like ourselves" recast the resentment makers as "sick" and "like ourselves," which made it possible to "show them the same tolerance, pity, and patience that we would cheerfully grant a sick friend" (67). Thus the 4th Step was a first attempt at folding others into the self, dissolving soul-killing rancor and enmity, and creating "complementarity" where once "symmetry" had ruled.

The magnanimous project of opening the door of the heart to all who suffered from self-will run riot was carried further by the recognition of personal wrongdoing and the making of amends in Steps 9, 10, and 11. True "AA Sobriety" was contingent on the self-humbling that came with a meaningful apology for past wrongs—"a remorseful mumbling that we are sorry won't fill the bill at all," the Big Book noted (83). Admitting wrongdoing and making amends were important not merely as acts of reparation but also as concrete demonstrations of the Big Book precept that "the spiritual life is not a theory. *We have to live it*" (83; original emphasis). Only by consciously recognizing the humanity of people who had previously been wronged would the alcoholic further the project of his own rehumanization. By acknowledging wrongdoing, both in the past and in the moment (Step 10), the sober AA demonstrated his commitment to complementarity and his willingness to subordinate his own will and desires to the other members of the human community.

The most complete demonstration of alcoholic equalitarianism appears in the 12th Step—"Having had a spiritual awakening as the result of these steps, we tried to carry this message to alcoholics and to practice these principles in all our affairs"—which makes plain the evangelical dimension of AA's spiritual program. Carrying the message takes many different forms, including sponsorship (the individual mentoring of another member); speaking at meetings; taking on clerical, administrative, and service work within AA's service structure; and performing "unspectacular but important tasks [like] arranging for the coffee and cake after the meetings" (*12/12*, 110). As in monastic communities, such tasks serve both a functional and a contemplative purpose, reminding the recovering alcoholic both of where he has been and how far he has traveled and of the ongoing nature of the journey.

The most iconic form of carrying the message is the "12th-Step call," the personal visit to the drinking or drying-out alcoholic, during which AAs share their own stories and "lay out the kit of spiritual tools" that have helped them to achieve sobriety (BB, 95). In its treatment of how to talk with the not-yet-sober alcoholic, the Big Book stresses the role that alcoholic equalitarianism plays in that delicate communication: "Tell him enough about *your* drinking habits, symptoms, and experiences to encourage him to speak of *himself*. . . . Describe *yourself* as an alcoholic. . . . If he is alcoholic, he will understand you at once. He will match your mental inconsistencies with some of his own" (91–92; emphasis added). Rather than proselytizing ("Never talk down to an alcoholic from any moral or spiritual hilltop" [95]), the AA who carries the message must

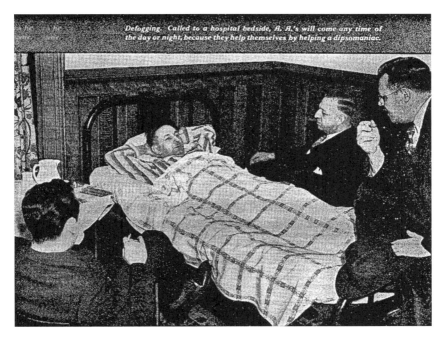

Defogging. Called to a hospital bedside, A. A.'s will come any time of the day or night, because they help themselves by helping a dipsomaniac.

Figure 2.1. The original "man on the bed," as photographed by Art Miller for the Saturday Evening Post, *1 March 1941. Courtesy of Stephen Mette.*

engage in an interpersonal give-and-take, modeling the simultaneous extension and acceptance of empathy that characterize—and enrich—the self-in-relation.

The significance of the 12th Step call, and of the boundary-trans-gressing and democratic dimensions of alcoholic equalitarianism more generally, is demonstrated by the image of "the man on the bed"—the sick or detoxing drunkard being visited by sober AAS. The term origi-nated in the Big Book's description of Bill Wilson and Dr. Bob's first successful outreach to another alcoholic (BB, 157–58).[78] What had been a casual descriptor began to become iconographic in the first national news story about AA, which appeared in the *Saturday Evening Post* in March 1941, and opened with a graphic image: "Three men sat around the bed of an alcoholic patient in the psychopathic ward of Philadelphia General Hospital one afternoon a few weeks ago. The man in the bed, who was a complete stranger to them . . . was a mechanic. His visitors had been educated at Princeton, Yale and Pennsylvania . . . [but] less than a year before, one had been in shackles in the same ward."[79]

A photograph of the visit to the man on the bed (Fig. 2.1) accom-

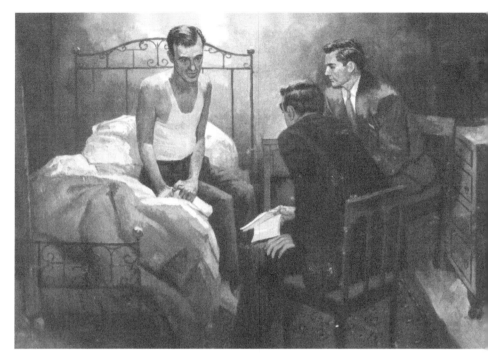

Figure 2.2. "Came to Believe." Illustration by Robert M. for the AA *Grapevine, 1955.*

panied the *Post* article, and the image has since been reinterpreted by
AA artists in a variety of materials (Figs. 2.2 and 2.3). One of the few
figurative representations of AA in action, images of the man on the bed
always stress the putative difference in status between the sober and the
drinking alcoholics, using a variety of visual details (e.g., they are erect
while he is prone; they are respectably dressed while he is not) to convey
this fact. In all its iterations, however, the image of the man on the bed
also undermines that accentuated difference by including composi-
tional elements—the halo-like light around the sick man, the circular
arrangement of bodies—that equalize and unite the various figures,
indicating the universality of the alcoholic condition.

A circle of chairs and a coffee urn in a smoky church basement may
signal AA to the uninitiated, but it is the image of the man on the bed
that captures most accurately AA's commitment to working across social differences in the spirit of alcoholic equalitarianism. As the pamphlet "Do You Think You're Different?" puts it, "Alcoholism . . . is no
respecter of age, sex, creed, race, wealth, occupation, or education . . .

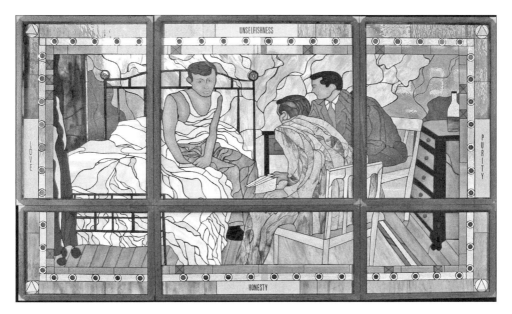

Figure 2.3. Anonymous Artists, "The Man on the Bed." Stained glass embellished with fifty-six sobriety medallions, 2001. Courtesy of Akron Archives of Alcoholics Anonymous.

anyone can be an alcoholic."[80] All AAs have been the man on the bed, and can easily fall back into that position if they begin to believe once more that they are different from or better than he is. Newcomers, who are often encouraged to go on 12th Step calls to remind themselves of what their lives have recently been like, are instructed in this creed via the slogan "Don't Compare—Identify." The crucial act of identification, of seeing themselves in the man on the bed, instantiates the exchange of the normative, "symmetrical" mode of cognition for the radically empathetic and equalitarian one premised on "complementarity."

Like its Christian forebear, alcoholic equalitarianism is at heart a humanist utopian vision that privileges personal rather than societal change. Its focus on the individual, however, does not mean that AA is or has been oblivious to the existence of larger structures and systems of power. If the 12 Steps focus on disrupting Victorian success ideology's hold over individuals within the AA fellowship, the 12 Traditions aim to perform a similar function for the community as a whole. A set of guidelines for self-governance, they are less well known than the Steps that preceded them, but in many ways more important. By suggesting the ways that AA as a whole should conduct and define itself relative to the larger world of possessive individualism, they extend the critique of the self-made man to indict more explicitly the market economy that gives rise to him.

INSTITUTIONALIZING A GIFT ECONOMY

AA's relationship to the modern market economy within and against which it defines itself has been most fully explored by Lewis Hyde, who argues that AA is best understood as a "gift economy," a community self-consciously organized around modes of exchange that evade the logic and norms of market capitalism. The currency of this gift economy is the message of self-surrender and alcoholic equalitarianism, which Hyde describes as an example of a "transformative teaching"—"the lessons in living that alter, or even save, our lives."[81] Only if they are given freely as gifts, however, can AA's teachings become "transformative"; that quality inheres in the fact that they are premised on values fundamentally opposed to those encoded in the formalized, rationalized, and dispassionate exchanges of market society. The foundational opposition between the logic of AA's gift economy and that of the mainstream is encapsulated in the AA slogan explaining the role 12th Step work plays in sobriety maintenance: "You have to give it away in order to keep it." The ability to give the gift is the marker of true sobriety: awareness of and respect for the gift is one of the hallmarks of alcoholic equalitarianism. The sober AA is only sober because another alcoholic gave him the gift at an earlier time. Thus Hyde characterizes 12th Step work as a kind of modern potlatch: "passing the gift along is the act of gratitude that finishes the labor" of the original giver.[82]

Preserving itself as a gift economy has not been an effortless endeavor for AA. The gravitational pull of mainstream Western capitalism, with its quite different logics of giving and getting, is a force that not only individuals but also the fellowship as a whole has had consciously to reckon with. The signal part of that reckoning was undertaken when Bill Wilson crafted the 12 Traditions in the period following the Second World War, a time of growth and change so intense that he would later call it "a truly frightening experience" (COA, 193).[83] Structured as a complement to the 12 Steps, the Traditions outlined an organizational culture that aimed to support and maintain the humbled, relational self created by working the Steps. While intended in part to guide interactions within and between AA groups, their more important function was to delimit the AA community's relationship with the larger world, where self-propulsion remained the norm and the sirens of "money, property, and prestige" (Tradition 6) threatened to undermine sobriety.

In its early years, AA expanded slowly, publicized by word of mouth along the routes of the many traveling salesmen who encountered it in Akron and New York.[84] After some friends of friends interested John D. Rockefeller in the fledgling group, an advisory board called the Alcoholic Foundation, comprising some affiliates and some non-alcoholic trustees, was established in New York in 1938. A small grant from Rockefeller paid $30 weekly stipends to Wilson and Smith and covered the cost of an office where Wilson and secretary Ruth Hock answered mail.[85] By 1940, AA claimed 2,000 affiliates. Membership increased during the war to reach 15,000 by 1945. As military personnel returned home and resumed domestic life, interest in AA exploded, and by 1951 there were 120,000 members meeting in 4,000 groups (see appendix A). Growing pains were endemic and perhaps inevitable.

For several reasons, the cofounders had been reluctant to codify a set of rules or by-laws by which the organization should be governed during AA's earliest years. Smith and other midwestern affiliates remained heavily invested in the idea of a leaderless, unstructured fellowship, modeled on "the man from Galilee" and using "nothing but word of mouth to carry the spirit from person to person, group to group." Wilson's early reluctance to set rules of AA conduct was more practical: he believed that their overweening commitments to the life of self-propulsion made alcoholics inherently anti-authoritarian, "the most rugged of individualists, true anarchists at heart." As such, they would either refuse to join a group with rules or would join with the express purpose of changing them or breaking them (*LOH*, 11–12, 7). By the late 1940s, however, the chaos brought on by rapid growth had prompted both cofounders to reconsider their anti-institutionalist sentiments.

The small New York headquarters was overwhelmed by letters that revealed a fellowship imperiled by "questions of membership, money, personal relations, public relations, management of groups [and] clubs" (*12/12*, 18). Despite the Steps' injunctions to sobriety, humility, and responsibility, AAs stole money intended to pay the rent on meeting space, quarreled over who got to be in charge of meetings, embarked on clandestine love affairs, blabbed about their identities to the press, and, not uncommonly, went off on drinking sprees. While they had neither the desire nor the ability to codify individuals' behavior, both Wilson and Smith agreed that such antics threatened not only individual sobriety but also the integrity and viability of the fellowship as a whole.

Around this time, a *Grapevine* article entitled "History Offers Good Lesson for AA" brought the example of the Washingtonian Temperance Society to AA's attention. Founded in Baltimore in 1840, the Washingtonians had enjoyed enormous success up and down the Eastern seaboard during their ten-year history; one estimate suggests that 600,000 people signed the pledge under their auspices and 150,000 remained abstinent.[86] Unlike most antebellum temperance groups, which lobbied for alcohol control and abstinence among the middle classes, the Washingtonians functioned as a mutual aid society, offering practical and emotional support to all comers, including confirmed drunkards desiring to reform. "With the solicitude of friends and brothers," they reached "hundreds of men that would not come out to . . . churches [or] temperance meetings." Their meetings centered on "experience sharing," unscripted speeches in which the reformed and the desiring-to-reform spoke "from the heart to the heart," telling their drinking stories to audiences who listened with "tearful attention."[87] Not surprisingly, midcentury AAs recognized a version of themselves in both the precepts and the practice of the Washingtonians.

"History Offers Good Lesson for AAs" appeared in the *Grapevine* in July 1945; the following month, a second essay on the Society's rise and fall sounded a somber note, observing that it is "hard for us to believe that a hundred years ago the newspapers of this country were carrying enthusiastic accounts about a hundred thousand alcoholics who were helping each other stay sober [while] today the influence of this good work has so completely disappeared that few of us had ever heard of it" (*LOH*, 4–5). The causes of the Washingtonian's downfall sounded all too familiar. Members had quarreled over whether to endorse moderate drinking (specifically the drinking of fermented, rather than distilled spirits) as an alternative to abstinence, and the Society's explosive popularity and high visibility quickly drew members into political debates about Sabbath observance, Prohibition, and abolition. Some Washingtonian leaders, overwhelmed by their own fame, went off on binges, absconded with funds, and allied themselves (or refused to ally themselves) with controversial political and religious figures. In short, the *Grapevine* suggested, AA's antebellum forebears had been preyed on by familiar demons—what Wilson called "overweening pride, consuming ambition, exhibitionism, intolerant smugness, money or power madness." The Washingtonians became a cautionary tale, and the *Grapevine* opined, "Let us never say, 'It can't happen here' " (*LOH*, 4).

Ruminating on the Washingtonian example, Bill Wilson embarked on a vigorous campaign to promote a set of organizational principles that would keep AA from succumbing to a similar fate. From the bully pulpit of the *Grapevine*, he argued for a set of guidelines that would create a communal culture conducive to ongoing personal humility and capable of containing the effects of individual egos if (or when) they ran amok. The result was the 12 Traditions:

1. Our common welfare should come first; personal recovery depends on AA unity.

2. For our group purpose there is one ultimate authority—a loving God as He may express Himself in our group conscience. Our leaders are but trusted servants; they do not govern.

3. The only requirement for AA membership is a desire to stop drinking.

4. Each group should be autonomous except in matters affecting other groups or AA as a whole.

5. Each group has but one primary purpose—to carry its message to the alcoholic who still suffers.

6. An AA group ought never endorse, finance, or lend the AA name to any related facility or outside enterprise, lest problems of money, property, and prestige divert us from our primary purpose.

7. Every AA group ought to be fully self-supporting, declining outside contributions.

8. Alcoholics Anonymous should remain forever nonprofessional, but our service centers may employ special workers.

9. AA as such ought never be organized; but we may create service boards or committees directly responsible to those they serve.

10. Alcoholics Anonymous has no opinion on outside issues; hence the AA name ought never be drawn into controversy.

11. Our public relations policy is based on attraction rather than promotion; we need always maintain personal anonymity at the level of press, radio, and films.

12. Anonymity is the spiritual foundation of all our Traditions, ever reminding us to place principles before personalities.[88]

The Traditions offered guidance for the performance of routine transactions within the organization, but their largest if unstated goal was to ensure that AA would remain a gift economy structured according to the logic of "transformative teachings," rather than to the impersonal norms of commodity exchange.

Tradition 1 asserts the preeminence of the self-in-relation by linking individual or "personal" fate to the "common welfare." Anticipating some of his critics' likely responses to this communitarian sentiment, Wilson argued that no organization "more jealously guards the individual's right to think, talk, and act as he wishes" than AA. But this liberal and permissive stance was balanced by the individual's knowledge "that he is but a small part of a great whole [and that] the clamor of desires and ambitions within him must be silenced whenever these could damage the group" (12/12, 129–30). Maintaining a sense of self premised on affiliation and complementarity rather than competition and dominance was the first priority of the individual and the collective.

Traditions 2 and 3 treat the means by which such a community enacts the democratic principles of alcoholic equalitarianism. They articulate AA's distance from the fraternal temperance organizations of the late nineteenth and early twentieth centuries, with their rigorous qualifications for and rituals of membership, and their hierarchical, arcane leadership structures.[89] The AA community, by contrast, is open to all comers and premised on consensual rather than majoritarian decision making. To emphasize that fact, the 2nd Tradition asserts the primacy of the "group conscience"—the belief that the divine is manifested within the group itself and that decision making should seek out that divine presence rather than simply allowing the majority to rule. Like Tradition 3's drastically simple qualification for membership, it aims to subordinate individual claims to virtue to a greater, shared good, and to disable potentially ego-inflaming ideologies of exclusion and hierarchy.

While the Traditions guiding AA's self-regulation are important, more striking are those that seek to define the group against—and to define its relationship to—the larger world of individual egos, professional ambition, and the modern marketplace. Wilson observed correctly that if the organization was going to continue successfully to expand within and beyond the United States, it simply could not remain a completely horizontal, all-volunteer institution. Such an idea, he argued, was "only a dream about simplicity . . . not simplicity in fact" (COA, 140). Some division of labor would be necessary in order to attain coherence and consistency: to publish a standard literature and reliable meeting information, to distribute that literature and respond to requests for information, to maintain and pay for office space, and so on. All these tasks, he argued, were made more simple, not more complicated, by a modicum of professionalism. The trick was to achieve this degree of routinization without succumbing to the fate of the Washingtonians—to allow AA to be *in* the world, but not *of* it. These issues were addressed explicitly in Traditions 8 and 9, which allow for some division and specialization of labor through the structure of "service boards" and "special workers," and for the creation of a democratic structure through which recurring questions of money, property, and power might be answered. The letters to the New York office made plain that in the absence of such an infrastructure, chaotic communications garbled the AA message, strained ties with otherwise sympathetic partner institutions, and created exploitative rather than supportive relationships within meetings and communities.

Wilson strongly believed, however, that the drive for clarity and consistency within the organization must be limited, lest AA become simply another arena in which affiliates sought to practice the dominating behaviors characteristic of the normative world. Thus Tradition 9 paradoxically asserts that "AA as such ought never be organized." While the flow of information and the mundane transactions within the organization might be standardized and centralized, there should never be a similar routinization of 12-Step work. Just as Wilson had trumpeted AA's commitment to "jealously guard[ing] the individual's right[s]," Traditions 4 and 5 establish the rights of constituent groups to their individual inflections and idiosyncrasies and ensure that individual, local, and regional differences will not be hostage to a top-down pursuit of philosophical uniformity. So long as each group observes what Tradition 5 calls the "primary purpose" of "carry[ing the] message to the alcoholic who still suffers," it may do so in whatever fashion is deemed appropriate by the personalities and priorities of individual members in concert with local social mores.[90] Although Tradition 4's stipulation that "each group should be autonomous except in matters affecting other groups or AA as a whole" seems to limit the exercise of individual and group peccadilloes, it deliberately leaves those "matters" undefined.

Traditions 6, 7, 10, and 11 clarify those matters somewhat by delimiting the relationships the AA community has to the larger world around it. Crafted in response to the developing Alcoholism Movement described in chapter 1, these Traditions aimed to differentiate AA from professional treatment providers and policy makers. Wilson encouraged individual AAs to carry the message in organizations dedicated to alcoholism rehabilitation or policy, and to share their first-hand experience with institutions eager to learn about it. "Like our good friends the physicians," he argued, AAs are "honor-bound to share what we know with all" (LOH, 44). But sharing should not be confused with commodifying, and he reminded those who spread the word of AA that they should do so as "individuals only." "This means that they will respect the principle of anonymity in the press; that if they do appear before the general public they will not describe themselves as AAs; that they will refrain from emphasizing their AA status in appeals for money or publicity" (LOH, 45).

The effect was to establish an unambiguously anti-politics and anti-market foundation to 12-Step culture, an outlook on the world that is codified most explicitly in Tradition 10. In order to prevent a potentially ego-inflating traffic in sobriety expertise (both within AA and between AA and the outside world), Tradition 10 stipulates that the organization has "no opinion on outside issues," including issues of electoral and cultural politics. Similarly, while the organization might rely on donations to stay afloat, it should shun cash transactions. As Wilson put it elsewhere, "For face-to-face treatment of a drunk, no money, ever" (COA, 116). While legions of critics have reviled AA for its refusal to enter into political— and politicized—debates (including but not limited to struggles over the disease concept, alcohol control legislation, and the efficacy of mandated treatment), Wilson was convinced that only with these boundaries firmly established and universally observed would sobriety remain a gift. Without them, it became simply another alienated commodity.

In addition to articulating these creedal values, Traditions 6, 7, 10, and 11 fed into Tradition 12's reassertion of the primacy of the surrendered self. The final Tradition's claim that "anonymity is the spiritual foundation of all our Traditions" returned attention to the role of personal humility and identification in "the AA Way of Life." Wilson's personal experiences, the letters he read, and his observations of missteps like those taken by Marty Mann and the National Council for Education on Alcohol (described in chapter 1) combined to convince him that the self-in-relation and the gift economy within which it thrived were fragile institutions, continually vulnerable to capture by the powerful toxic discourses that swirled through and shaped the larger culture of the marketplace. Without conscious, ongoing, personal, and organizational commitment, AA would quickly devolve, as the Washingtonians had, into just another social club or fraternal organization—a self-help rather than a mutual-help organization that hawked a canned set of ideas about drinking and abstinence in the crowded modern marketplace, rather than offering the unique and transformative gift of sobriety.

As Wilson worked out the Traditions and promoted them through writings in the AA *Grapevine* and speaking engagements around the country during the late 1940s and early 1950s, he relied heavily on stories of his own foibles to illustrate the necessity of adopting guidelines for collective behavior. His narratives typically focused on his attempts at various points in AA history to make unilateral decisions, set policy, and engage in boisterous self-promotion. Like the midwestern literature that juxtaposed "sobriety, period" to "AA sobriety," these anecdotes aimed to illustrate that "the desires for power, for domination, for glory, and for money" continued long after the desire for alcohol waned, and "could threaten us in ways that alcohol and sex could not" (COA, 98). Failure to pursue "the AA way of life" at the level of the collective would have grave consequences in the long run. Because the self-in-relation was such a fragile construction, Wilson argued in *12 Steps and 12 Traditions*, "the unity of Alcoholics Anonymous is the most cherished quality our Society has. Our lives, the lives of all to come, depend squarely upon it. We stay whole or AA dies. Without unity, the heart of AA would cease to beat; our world arteries would no longer carry the life-giving grace of God; His gift to us would be spent aimlessly. Back again in their caves, alcoholics would reproach us and say, 'What a great thing AA might have been!' " (129).

Ideally, a perpetually renewing awareness of the richness of the surrendered and equalitarian life, along with knowledge of and the desire to do God's will, would influence AA individual and group behavior. When that failed, Wilson noted, the specter of "John Barleycorn," who "ever threatens each AA citizen with torture or extinction," acted as a fine disciplinarian (LOH, 34). Memories of alcohol's effects on their own lives and evidence of it at work in the lives of others reminded AAs that "for us, it is do or die": "The death sentence hangs over the AA member, his group, and AA as a whole. . . . So there is authority enough, love enough, and punishment enough, all without human beings clutching at the handles of power" (COA, 106, 105).

This sense of the ominous power of alcohol hovering over the individual and the group meant that, as Wilson explained, "at first, I obeyed because I had to." Fear of once more becoming the man on the bed acted as a strong check on newcomers' impulses. But as sobriety progressed, fear was replaced by love: "After a while I began to obey because I saw that the Traditions were wise and right. . . . Today I hope I have come to a time in my AA life when I can obey because I really want to obey, because I really want the Traditions for myself as well as for AA as a whole" (COA, 136; original emphasis).

Such a recalibration of desire, away from self-will and toward the collective good, was the result of a changed epistemology, the movement from seeing "myself" as an isolated individual to seeing—and feeling—that self as intimately and irrevocably bound up with "AA as a whole." The generous and equalitarian impulses of that self resulted in the paradoxical assertion that "I really *want* to obey." Living according to the Traditions signaled the successful transition from "sobriety, period" to the "AA Way of Life," from symmetry to complementarity, and from a spiritually puny life to one lived robustly and fully in the grace of God and of the fellowship. For the self-made men who were the earliest members of AA, as for many members today, this transformation into true selves-in-relation was a change that can only be described as radical, one that marked the beginning of a whole new existence.

THE SENTIMENTAL SUBCULTURE

To date, the most sustained exploration of white American men and their restlessness within the confines of Victorian success ideology remains T. J. Jackson Lears's *No Place of Grace*. Although as elite WASP intellectuals their social positions differed somewhat from those of early AAs, Lears's subjects also sought spiritual release from lives of dis-ease. Hoping for gravity in a "weightless" world, they "craved both the authentic experience outside the bounds of Victorian respectability and the intense spiritual ecstasy of communion with God."[91] Their quests, however, were largely futile. While they "long[ed] to experience faith at firsthand," their education and sophistication precluded it. Imprisoned within their own self-consciousness, Lears argued, they could "enter the pre-modern spiritual world only in books, or as spectators at 'picturesque' shrines. They might remain only tourists of the supernatural" (174).

Although he acknowledged that the late nineteenth century also saw the rise of "mystics and mind-curists" (175) with significant followings,

Lears depicted the paralysis of his white male subjects—their positions poised "at the doors of mystical perception, unable to enter" (285)—as inevitable. But early AAs, born in the late nineteenth century and thus perhaps the last generation of Americans fully inscribed within the culture he describes, articulated a similar critique and achieved a quite different response; they succeeded in creating a spiritual sense of self and of community that, when lived fully, successfully contravened the era's imperatives to what Lears called "the internalized ethic of self-control" (13) and Bill Wilson described as "self-will run riot." Unlike the "tourists of the supernatural," AAs did not merely yearn for but actually achieved a working philosophy—and a viable community—of the self-in-relation, a modern self capable, through spiritual surrender, of what Lears described as the utopian capacity to "submerge individual identity in union with the cosmos" (175).

Their ability to do so resulted from their "religious rejections of the world," their embrace of ascetic and mystical spiritual practices through which they consciously marked their distance from the rapacious market culture of possessive individualism, particularly its gendered embodiment in the ideology of the self-made man. Unlike many of the more conventional sects Max Weber describes, AAs did not withdraw physically from their disenchanted world. Indeed, a return to functionality within it—to bodily control, family life, gainful employment—was one of the benefits of sobriety. But as individuals and as a community they criticized the individualism, aggression, and cynicism that were the conventional markers of masculinity, naming them as both symptoms and causes of the soul sickness that lay back of alcoholism.

AA's critique of possessive individualism does not aspire to structural or materialist analysis. Instead, like the evangelical Protestant and New Thought religions that inform it, 12-Step philosophy posits a humanist critique of the alienating structures of modern market capitalism, arguing for the transformative potential of the recognition of an essential human sameness. This universalism means that investment in social categories and markers of identity like class, race, gender, profession, and religious affiliation become, in Bill Wilson's term, mere "phantoms of self-importance." Insistence on their reality, in turn, is the misguided engine that drives addiction by contributing to "big-shotism and phony thinking . . . self-justification, self-pity, and anger . . . the crazy contest for personal prestige and big bank balances" (*LOH*, 210). The principles of alcoholic equalitarianism offer the ability to see through those differences, despite (or perhaps because of) the fact that the rest of the world deems them real. As "Do You Think You're Different?" explains, the sober self recognizes such spurious identities as "prop[s] I can live without now."[92] The use of given names only within meetings puts this theory into practice. At AA's inception, especially, anonymity served a practical purpose, allowing alcoholics to seek help without opening themselves up to stigmatization. But at a deeper level the sloughing off of the surnames that tie individuals into worldly systems of privilege and prestige also signals an ongoing commitment to a value system divorced from those systems and attuned to a higher reality.

Given this epistemological tendency, observers seeking to understand the deep structures of AA's worldview might do well to compare it to the sentimental culture of the nineteenth century. Both cultural formations respond to the depersonalization and competition of market capitalism with understandings of the self and the world drawn from (but not reducible to) the anti-hierarchical, universalizing credos of evangelical Protestantism, most notably the will to see beyond what are deemed to be superficial social designations and into a deeper and truer human essence. Both share an anti-rational, anti-intellectual bent. Because they see in analysis and argument a rhetorical analogue to the competition and deceit of the marketplace, they promote instead a cognitive mode centered on emotional connection and empathy and exemplified by the act of imaginative identification. Further, both constitute selves and communities through the logic Richard Brodhead has called "disciplinary intimacy," a process of normalizing the workings of power by routing them through affective relationships, with the result that the hitherto unruly self finds that, in Bill Wilson's words, it "really want[s] to obey."[93] The result, in both cases, is a worldview that treats the individual less as a sovereign entity than as a distinctive node joined to other humans and to the divine by flowing currents of love and sympathy. That self-in-relation sees the realm of the heart and the spirit as more fundamentally real than the material world, and therefore can remain complacent—even skeptical—about conventional political action within that world.[94]

For the middle-class white men of early AA, adopting such a sense of self—even if incompletely—was a transformative experience, since it required a rejection of much that was "normal" for them. As the midwestern pamphlets demonstrate, many of them had hoped that sobriety would allow them to reclaim the hegemonic masculine status they had lost through drinking. But what they discovered was just the opposite: "the AA Way of Life" entailed a conscious and active rejection of many of the traits that helped to constitute that status. To support their commitment to an alternative ideal of masculine selfhood—one that spoke the language of the heart, rather than of the marketplace—they constituted themselves into a close-knit fraternal band. Not a formal and distinct religious sect, like those studied by Max Weber, and not quite a cult, as modern-day critics claim, AA is nevertheless a subculture in the broadest sense of that term: a "social group . . . perceived to deviate from the normative ideals of adult communities." Hardly the spectacular deviance typically associated with the term "subculture," early AAs' freedom to express fear and shame, hope and love (for one another and for God), nevertheless constituted a personal ethic and style generally ruled out of bounds for the self-made, middle-class, white men of their generation.[95]

To the extent that the normative life of self-propulsion had cramped the affective and spiritual dimensions of their lives, and that AA made space for them, early members experienced the life of the self-in-relation as profoundly liberating. The Big Book was careful to note that the 12 Steps were merely "*suggested* as a Program for Recovery" (59; emphasis added), and to acknowledge that "our hats are off" to anyone who "can do the right-about-face" without them (31). But such qualifications were often overshadowed by early members' sense of the profoundness of their transformation and the gratitude that it inspired. As a result, many early AAs came to believe that they had stumbled across a universal truth about the nature of addiction and recovery. Out of their own sense that they had discovered "Utopia . . . right here and now" (16), they promoted the idea of self-will run riot and its antidote, the surrendered self-in-relation, with a zeal that no doubt bordered—and may still border—on the cultish.

As AA grew and diversified beyond its original homogenous membership, it was inevitable that its universalist premises and utopian ideals would be tested and challenged. Perspectives that were radical and transformative for the original members were somewhat less compelling, as we shall see, to some of the people who found their way to AA— or were directed to it by agents of the alcohol and drug industrial complex—in the 1960s and after. The critiques by later affiliates of what they believed to be blind spots in the theories of the surrendered life and alcoholic equalitarianism, along with responses to those critiques by a growing number of traditionalists, generated new energies within AA and across recovery culture more broadly. Because AA's literature had been developed specifically to carry the message of surrender and equalitarianism, it was within the arena of print culture that these energies played themselves out most clearly. It is to the world of print that we now turn.

PART TWO Alcoholics Anonymous and Print Culture

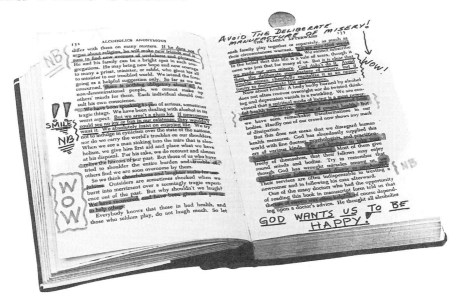

CHAPTER THREE

Reading the Language of the Heart

The clichéd image of an AA meeting features a circle of chairs shrouded in a haze of cigarette smoke, with a totemic coffee percolator gleaming dimly in the background. Within that performative space, orality rules: the community is instantiated by the ritual speech act of "Hi, my name is so-and-so and I'm an alcoholic," consecrated by the incantatory murmur of "thanks for sharing," and finally adjourned with the shared recitation of a prayer. The sacraments of coffee and cigarettes—and sometimes doughnuts or cake—confirm the mouth's centrality in AA culture.

While this stereotypical image has some basis in fact—many, if not all AA meetings, include the elements enumerated above—orality is not the be-all and end-all of AA communication. Attention to real, as opposed to archetypal, meetings reveals a print culture thriving within the fellowship.[1] A variety of books and pamphlets are typically arrayed for sale beside the ubiquitous coffee pot, and in the course of any given meeting, acts of reading intermingle with speech. Groups often display banners bearing the 12 Steps and 12 Traditions and begin meetings by reading them aloud, each participant reading one and progressing around the circle. A standard format "discussion" meeting often begins with a short reading from the Big Book or *Twelve Steps and Twelve Traditions*; less frequently, a selection from AA's *Grapevine* magazine, or from the inspirational volumes *Came to Believe*, *Daily Reflections*, and *As Bill Sees It*, is used for this purpose. In addition to discussion meetings, groups often also sponsor regular "Big Book" or "Step Study" meetings devoted to the exegesis of these canonical writings. Close attention to the text is encouraged—sometimes formally, as in the Valley Central (California) Intergroup flyer shown in Figure 3.1, but more often by informal means. Figure 3.2, for example, shows a page opening of a Big Book annotated according to the "Q. Method," a reading mode passed from sponsor to sponsee that encourages the reframing of Big Book statements as questions that the sponsee answers while working the Steps.[2]

The way AAs treat their Big Books also bears particular notice. Many affiliates bring their copies of the Big Book to meetings with them, and

Figure 3.1. California AA flyer encouraging Big Book reading and annotation.
Collection of Don B. Used by permission.

the attention these volumes receive would gladden the heart of any
teacher of close reading. Pages are routinely filled with highlighting,
annotations, and cross-references—to a sponsor's interpretation, to
other AA literature, or perhaps to Bible verses—that attest, as Figure 3.2
demonstrates, to active, attentive, and repeated reading. These mark-
ings join the phone numbers that AAs often jot down in one another's
books, so that marginalia draws the lived and the written fellowship
into a seamless whole. In contemporary U.S. culture, with its overabun-
dance of printed matter, it is surprising even to find family Bibles so
lavished with attention. Some affiliates fashion protective needlepoint,
leather, woven, or collage dust jackets for their Big Books, as shown in
Figures 3.3 and 3.4. These handmade covers, as well as decorative book-
marks inscribed with AA slogans or Big Book quotations, are perennial
favorites at the raffles that groups hold to cover the expenses of rent and
coffee or to raise money for special events. This affection and reverence

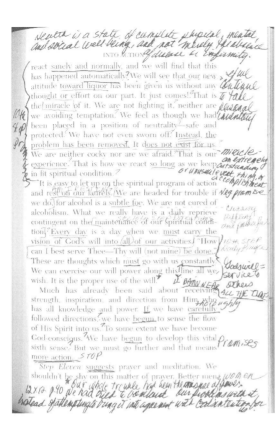

Figure 3.2. Big Book page annotated for Step Study. Private Collection. Used by Permission.

for the Big Book and for AA reading material in general suggests the limits of the prevailing sense of AA as an oral culture.

The growth and development of AA's print culture is the subject of this chapter. That culture deserves study on its merits alone—as the brief description above suggests, it is a substantial and complex one, and its existence challenges current wisdom about the devotional and intellectual life of the fellowship.[3] Rather than comprehensively recounting the history of AA reading and publishing, however, this chapter examines the way that the development of a formal print culture forced the fellowship to reckon with the original "religious rejections of the world" upon which its surrendered life was premised. Reacting against, but also drawing upon, the reading practices of the Oxford Group, early AAs struggled to create a literary culture that would capture the ideals of surrender and equalitarianism at the heart of the "AA Way of Life" and make them available to a far-flung network of desperate alcoholics. But the expansion of the fellowship and its shift from intimate oral com-

Figure 3.3. Big Book cover in leather with image of "Stepping Stones," the home of Bill and Lois Wilson. Collection of Pete K. Used by permission.

munications to impersonal print forms proved complicated. Printed materials forced AA—individual members and the collective—to reckon with a cultural-industrial mode of production that would potentially impact the sentimental senses of both self and community.

At stake in this confrontation, as we shall see, were not merely the form and content of printed texts, but also distribution, sales, and reading protocols. Early AAs cared deeply about the questions of how to write, publish, and read. But print also had a metonymic role in these intra-AA disagreements. Although scholars have focused on AA's rich oral culture, from the group's inception print has been the preferred symbol through which members argue with one another about the organization's nature and purpose. Talking about literature (as AA publications are called in aggregate) is a way of talking about larger, more abstract issues affecting the group as a whole, including its founding premises, expansion and diversification, financial and administrative underpinnings, and perceived distinctiveness (or lack thereof) from the professional, market-based, and "modern" world around it. By attending to AA's print culture, we may better understand both the organization's place within twentieth-century U.S. culture and its internal complexity, which is typically invisible to those outside of it.

THE OXFORD GROUP'S "RELIGIOUS READING"

The early twentieth century found American Protestants wracked by conflicting notions of how to read the Bible. The reading mode es-

Figure 3.4. Big Book cover in needlepoint, ribbon, and fabric. Collection of the author. Used by permission.

poused by mainline Protestant clergy during the period, known as "higher criticism," responded to the challenges that modern archaeology and linguistics, as well as the physical sciences, posed to theology; it was active, critical, and intellectual. Baptist professor of theology William Newton Clarke, for instance, urged readers to "frankly and fearlessly differentiate the Bible into its elements, Christian, Jewish, historical traditional, and whatever they may be [and] set by itself that body of truth which our Savior taught concerning God and religion, and then give glory where glory is due." Only by breaking down the text into issues of history and issues of faith could readers "put the Bible to its true use, as a servant of Jesus Christ."[4] Contrasting this high-minded tradition was a long-lived pragmatic approach—exemplified by social gospel reformer Charles Sheldon's famous question "What Would Jesus Do?"—that looked to the Bible for instruction in personal conduct. A third reading tradition, popularized by the publication in 1909 of the painstakingly detailed Scofield Reference Bible, emphasized the need to parse scripture for timelines, foreshadowings, and clues to the coming millennium.[5]

In keeping with its strategic position outside the established church, the Oxford Group eschewed all these reading modes. Officially, the Group downplayed the importance of reading and study in favor of the active life of good works; one of Frank Buchman's favorite aphorisms was "Study men, not books."[6] But Buchman also described literature as "ammunition for the spiritual bombardment of the nation," and the Group fostered an active reading culture that embraced everything from informational pamphlets to the devotional reader *God Calling* (reputedly a direct transcription of a year's worth of daily messages from on high) and full-length conversion narratives with provocative titles like *For Sinners Only*, *The Big Bender*, and *I Was a Pagan*.[7]

Reading—particularly though not exclusively Bible reading—played an important role in the mystical Oxford Group practice known as Quiet Time, a daily "communion with the Holy Spirit . . . in which God impresses on our minds His counsel."[8] During daily Quiet Time meditation, seekers sought "guidance"—direct communications from God on matters large and small. The communiqués were recorded in special notebooks while the auditors were still in a trance-like state.[9] Guidance was then " 'checked up' with the teachings of the Bible or by conference with others who are also receiving guidance in Quiet Time," to make sure the communications received were genuine and had been understood correctly.[10]

Reading played a key role in the larger Quiet Time ritual, not only because study of the Bible was valuable in its own right, but also because reading calmed the naturally willful spirit and helped to attune the mind to God. Using the Lord's Prayer as an example, the Layman with a Notebook laid out the Group's preferred hermeneutic, which emphasized the need for "dwelling on and thinking out the complete and absolute meaning of each word and phrase with direct application to ourselves. If we are busy people we can take only two or three minutes over each word or phrase, but we could continue to discover in Christ's simple Prayer of Surrender limitless meanings and implications we never thought existed." Intense engagement with the text was necessary, the Layman continued, because "the human mind, being what it is, wanders from concentration [and] invents or remembers a thought of its own." These "thoughts of [our] own" represent the "little piece of self-will . . . which prevents us from receiving the infinite and complete benefits and grace of guidance."[11] Like the Buddhist chant of "om" or the practice of counting the breaths during *za-zen* meditation, engagement with the words on the page provided Oxford Group members with a focal point that relegated the workaday self to the margins of consciousness and opened the channels of divine communication.

Even this brief discussion of Oxford Group reading modes should demonstrate that Group members' use of the Bible set them apart from their more prosaic contemporaries, both liberal and conservative. Guidance itself could be quite pragmatic: the Layman notes that supplicants receive "suggestions as to conduct, solutions to material and spiritual difficulties," and Walter Clark's research has determined that it could include advice on investments, love relationships, and the whereabouts of lost items as well.[12] But the reading that cleared the way for guidance was a mystical practice, a corollary to the Group's ascetic "religious rejections of the world." The words and phrases of scripture were valuable as much for what they *did* as for what they *meant*: like the Middle English mystics, Group members valued the incantatory quality of the text, its ability to dissolve the boundaries between God and the self and thus to allow the joyous surrender of profane physicality to the eternal, infinite, and sacred.[13]

The Oxford Group ideal of reading, then, is perhaps best understood as a version of what religious historian Paul J. Griffiths has called "religious reading," a mode of engagement with texts that predates and directly contrasts the reading practices that have come to dominate the post-Gutenberg era.[14] That debased mode, which Griffiths calls "consumerist reading," sees the text as a series of "limitless signifiers to be arrayed to serve and please" its readers. Accordingly, it treats the book as an "object of consumption . . . relatively unimportant, just as [all] artifacts to be consumed in late capitalist culture are unimportant relative to the process of anticipating, lusting after, and consuming them" (42–45). An alienated mode of production and a profane readerly attitude make consumerist reading a shallow and self-gratifying process, no matter the content of the work that is read.

With "religious reading," by contrast, not the individual's capacity for meaning-making but the text itself is "the object . . . of central importance," and its importance inheres in the fact that it is "intrinsically other than the human, ordered independently of it, and capable of acting upon it" (45). Religious readers seeking to know and to access that supra-human world therefore read with an unusual quality of attention: "as a lover reads, with a tensile attentiveness that wishes to linger, to prolong, to savor and has no interest at all in the quick orgasm of consumption" (ix). Religious reading is intensive, not extensive, focused on a few "stable and vastly rich" texts, which are inexhaustible in their ability to offer "meaning, suggestions (or imperatives) for action, matter for aesthetic wonder, and much else." Not surprisingly, religious reading communities prize memorization, deeming the "incorporation and internalization" of the text into the body the highest sign of learning (41–46).

The readers whose texts and practices Griffiths explores were mystics inhabiting Roman Africa, medieval Europe, and first millennium (BCE) India, and he notes with sadness that both analog and digital communications technologies "share a profound lack of hospitality to religious reading and composition." But while the practice of religious reading in the contemporary world is "hard to maintain because of the power of conformist and consumerist pressures within academia and elsewhere," it is not altogether impossible (59). Given the Oxford Group's sense of itself as a bulwark against the self-same conformism and consumerism, it is perhaps not surprising to find some overlap between its reading practices and the paradigmatic religious reading that Griffiths describes. The Group followed in the path of other mystical sects before it when it refused to "interpret" the Bible during Quiet Time reading and instead simply savored it, working to become sufficiently attuned to it that the voice of the divine would pour through the channel of the inert page and fill mind, body, and heart. Group members' ritualistic engagement with a text disciplined what the Layman with a Notebook called that last "little piece of self-will," and thus facilitated an ecstatic connection to God.

THE BIBLE AND "THE ALCOHOLIC SQUAD"

Both Bill Wilson and Dr. Bob Smith sought release from self-will through the Oxford Group's Quiet Time reading. The summer Wilson spent in Akron it was a daily ritual: Bob Smith's wife Anne "would sit in the corner by the fireplace and read from the Bible, and then we would huddle together in stillness, awaiting inspiration and guidance" (COA, 70). The Bible was Wilson and Smith's primary text—Anne Smith called it "the main Source Book of all" and believed that "no day might pass without reading it"—and the Sermon on the Mount, I Corinthians 13, Psalms 23 and 91, and the Epistle of James were particularly treasured passages.[15] Both men also used popular religious commentaries and study aids to augment their daily Bible reading; as a devotional reader Wilson preferred Presbyterian minister Oswald Chambers's *My Utmost for His Highest*, while Smith was committed to the Methodist periodical *The Upper Room* (*Dr. Bob*, 314).[16]

As they began their work of outreach to other drunkards, Smith, Wilson, and the rest of what came to be known as the "alcoholic squad" of the Akron Oxford Group quickly foisted their reading tastes upon others (*Dr. Bob*, 100). While today it is an AA commonplace that attending meetings is the most important tool for maintaining sobriety, religious reading was paramount while the fellowship was incubating in Akron. In an early report on the group in Akron, Alcoholic Foundation board member Frank Amos wrote that members "must have devotions every morning—a 'quiet time' of prayer and some reading from the Bible and other religious literature. Unless this is faithfully followed, there is grave danger of backsliding." By contrast, "it is important, but not vital, that [the alcoholic] meet frequently with other reformed alcoholics" (quoted in *Dr. Bob*, 131). Accordingly, the Akron pamphlet "A Manual for Alcoholics Anonymous" instructs AAs making 12-Step calls to "supply your patient with the proper literature," including the Bible.[17] In addition, one Akron old-timer recalled that "as soon as men in the hospital could begin to focus their eyes they got a copy of [Emmet Fox's] *The Sermon on the Mount*." Scottish evangelical Henry Drummond's "*The Greatest Thing in the World* [was] another popular book at the time," and that "little nickel book *The Upper Room*" was de rigueur: "They figured we could afford a nickel a day for spiritual reading. . . . We had to read that absolutely every morning" (*Dr. Bob*, 151).

Absent historical records, it is of course impossible to say precisely how such texts were read by early AAs. Most likely, reading modes varied from the fervent to the dutiful. For instance, Dorothy S.M. recalls that "there wasn't a well-equipped bathroom in AA that didn't have a copy [of *The Upper Room*]. And if you didn't see it opened to the right day, you immediately began to suspect them" (*Dr. Bob*, 151). Oxford Group leaders sanctioned a clear and limited canon of texts; their expectations for what and how people would read were clear. Dorothy S.M.'s wry comment implies that perhaps not all the reading that went on in the Akron Oxford Group and its alcoholic offshoot was quite as "religious" as the Layman with a Notebook might have hoped. But it also suggests that there existed a perceived—if not necessarily agreed upon—hierarchy of reading modes, an understanding of right and wrong ways of reading that was acknowledged and, at least to some degree, enforced by communal norms. Among the men who would become the Akron chapter of Alcoholics Anonymous, a belief in "religious reading"—intensive, ritualized, and quasi-mystical—put down deep roots early on.

Bill Wilson's relationship with the New York Oxford Group broke down rapidly upon his return from the summer in Akron. Inspired by his time with Smith and only intermittently able to find work, Wilson attempted to continue his outreach to drunks, throwing his energy into work at Calvary Mission, the program run by Oxford Group minister Sam Shoemaker. A cluster of rather disreputable men soon began to hang around after Oxford Group meetings to talk about their drinking exploits. While the Akron Oxford Group had been eager to participate in alcoholic rehabilitation, the presence of visible inebriates did not sit well with the New York Group's more high-toned members. Late in 1935 Group leaders forbade the drunks living at Calvary to attend the alcoholics-only meeting that had sprung up at Wilson's home, claiming that Wilson and his wife were "not maximum," Buchman's term for not fully committed to the Group's ideas.[18] The disenchantment was mutual. Wilson was observing a high rate of relapse among the men he was working with—including his old friend Ebby T., who had originally introduced him to Oxford Group ideas. Speculating that the Group's "aggressive evangelism . . . would seldom touch neurotics of our hue," he began increasingly to emphasize "Dr. Silkworth's expression describing the alcoholic's dilemma: the obsession plus the allergy" (PIO, 172; COA, 161). The shift in emphasis worked; the hybrid metaphor of "spiritual sickness" seemed persuasive to New York drunks in ways that Buchman's Four Absolutes were not. By the end of 1937, Wilson had decided that Buchman's philosophy was too doctrinaire and too all-encompassing to be of use to the vast majority of alcoholics. A handful of men who called themselves "a nameless bunch of alcoholics" (COA, 165) broke out on its own.[19]

By contrast, relationships between the Akron alcoholics and their Oxford confreres remained strong through the late 1930s. The more homogeneous population of Akron probably played some part in this, as did the Group's relatively deep roots: Buchman's "key man" strategy had been wildly successful in Akron, where the Group had effected the conversion and "cure" of Russell Firestone, heir to the local tire fortune and a notorious drunkard. That very visible success (the Firestone family had sponsored a large conference/party for the Group to demonstrate their gratitude, at which Buchman himself made an appearance) kept them invested in rehabilitating alcoholics for some time afterward.[20] Thus while Bob Smith used the disease metaphor to explain the program to potential prospects, specifically analogizing alcoholism to diabetes, he also described Akron's "non-drinking liquor club" as "a Christian Fellowship" and comported it as such (*Dr. Bob*, 118).

Recruits were screened to determine whether they were truly ready (meaning sufficiently miserable) to change their entire lives, and *Dr. Bob and the Good Oldtimers* recounts several instances where Smith turned prospects away from AA—or threatened to do so—on the grounds that they did not meet this criteria (143, 244, 276). A profession of surrender to God was "demanded" of each alcoholic, and one early member recalled, "You couldn't go to a meeting until you did it." Newcomers were required to obtain sponsors early on. Weekly get-togethers, which included alcoholics, their wives, and non-alcoholic Oxford Group members, were like "regular old-fashioned prayer meeting[s]," beginning with devotional reading, followed by meditation for guidance and group prayer (*Dr. Bob*, 101). The sharing of personal stories was minimal, since, as one Akron old-timer described it, "we already knew how to drink. What we wanted to learn was how to get sober and stay sober" (*Dr. Bob*, 223). Explaining the Akron approach to 12-Step practice, Smith remarked that the slogan " 'Easy Does It' means you take it a day at a time. It doesn't mean that you sit on your fanny . . . and let other people work the program for you" (*Dr. Bob*, 282). This rigor—which reflected both Smith's temperament and Oxford Group thinking—infused Akron AA and the midwestern groups that branched off from it and formed the philosophical framework for the "traditionalist" strain that developed within AA in later years.

Even as the Akron "alcoholic squad" of the Oxford Group continued to thrive, Bill Wilson and the New York group began to debate how they should go about defining their purpose, elaborating their philosophy, and securing the means of survival now that they were an autonomous entity. Their decision to focus on the rehabilitation of drunkards rather than the extermination of sin, coupled with their desire to proselytize to all faiths and to avowed atheists, effectively displaced the Bible from the spiritual, intellectual, and practical center of their organization's day-to-day contemplative life. Finding a book that could instill the same kind of discipline and cultivate the same kind of selflessness as the Bible—finding, in other words, a book that could generate "religious reading" without being literally religious—would prove the first major challenge they faced.

PLANNING THE BIG BOOK

The work of the "nameless bunch of alcoholics" got off to a rocky start. In September 1937, a relapsed affiliate committed suicide in Wilson's house, prompting both cofounders to admit that while their work was going surprisingly well, with about forty members in New York and Akron, it was simply insufficient: "Even within gunshot of this very house," Wilson exclaimed, "alcoholics are dying like flies."[21] He and Smith feared that "at the snail's pace we had been going, it was clear that most of them could never be reached" (COA, 144). The group needed a more effective way to convey their message to the mass audience of suffering alcoholics.

The importance of a common language—its ability to generate recognition and compassion—had been at the center of Wilson and Smith's consciousness from the moment of their first meeting. A badly hungover Smith—corralled into coming to see Wilson by his wife and another Oxford Group member, Henrietta Sieberling—had insisted that he could only spare fifteen minutes to talk to this stranger. Ultimately, their meeting lasted over six hours. Smith recalled later that Wilson "gave me information about the subject of alcoholism which was undoubtedly helpful. [But] *of far more importance was the fact that he was the first living human with whom I had ever talked, who knew what he was talking about in regard to alcoholism from actual experience. In other words, he talked my language*" (BB, 180; original emphasis).

For Wilson as well, the sense of elaborating a vocabulary and a mode of address out of shared experience had proven crucial. The project began with recognition: "I just talked away about my own case until he got a good identification with me, until he began to say, 'Yes, that's me, I'm like that.'" Once that commonality was established, "our talk [became] a completely *mutual* thing. I had quit preaching. I knew that I needed this alcoholic as much as he needed me. *This was it*" (COA, 68, 70; original emphasis). The admission of vulnerability formed the heart of the AA program; it was inconceivable without shared language. It is not a coincidence that in their first years of work Wilson and Smith's name for their ideas about sobriety was "the word-of-mouth program" (COA, 160).

The importance of Quiet Time reading notwithstanding, speech had always preceded print when it came to capturing a drinking alcoholic's imagination and recruiting him to the program. The form of conversation as well as what was said was important: dialogue and self-disclosure captured the spirit of mutuality that animated Wilson and Smith's philosophy. Unlike Gospel Temperance and psychiatry, both of which featured talk from one social level (usually of profession and also implicitly of morality) down to another, one-to-one conversation exemplified the democratic basis of alcoholic equalitarianism. The ability to speak without pretense or calculation was particularly prized, as Akron member J.D.'s recollection of a fellow old-timer makes clear: "You know how crudely Ernie talked. But I would listen to him trying to explain it to me a lot quicker than I would a polished man" (*Dr. Bob*, 140). Although they never would have described it as such, early AAs invested heavily in what philosopher Jacques Derrida has called "the metaphysics of presence," the belief that speech, with its seemingly unambiguous origins in the body and in the present, is inherently more real and more truthful than written communication.[22]

It is not surprising, therefore, that Wilson's first idea for expanding the program's reach was to increase the number of mouths spreading the word. Originally he hoped that philanthropist John D. Rockefeller would provide the seed money. Friends arranged a meeting with Rockefeller in 1937, and Wilson, accompanied by some other New York members, explained their growing program and pitched a grand plan for expanding it through "paid workers [and] chains of hospitals." Though he was impressed by the group, Rockefeller declined to fund it on the grand scale Wilson had hoped, arguing (as Wilson himself would a few years later) that "money would spoil this thing" (COA, 148–49). His parsimony put a quick end to the paid expansion of the word-of-mouth program. A book that explained the program, the cofounders decided, would have to suffice. Rockefeller had set them up with a modest drawing account that would pay them each $30 a month; that would at least begin to cover the costs of writing.

In Akron, however, the idea of a book met a decidedly mixed response, despite Smith's strong support. Some of the Akron affiliates dismissed the idea out of hand on the grounds that it was "a commercial venture" (*Dr. Bob*, 153). "Books and pamphlets could be harmful," others claimed, noting that "the apostles themselves did not need any printed matter" (*PIO*, 180; COA, 145). The cofounders' counterarguments consisted primarily of assertions of print's superiority to oral modes of knowledge transmission. Wilson acknowledged that while it might be preferable "to pass on the message face-to-face, when one could personally observe the other's reactions and be prepared to respond to objections, questions, or confusion," it was simply inefficient to construct a mass movement around such a practice (*PIO*, 196). Further, it could be dangerous, "because the recovery message in which we now had such high confidence might soon be garbled and twisted beyond recognition" (COA, 144). A book could present the fellowship's unique philosophy in a familiar format, and couch it in simple terms accessible to the average reader; it could clarify and codify both what the group was and what it was not. The stability and replicability of print, Wilson and Smith believed, was its strongest selling point, and outweighed its seeming impersonality.

Wilson did not deny the project's commercial dimensions; in fact, he hoped that its sales might generate enough revenue to "enable several of us to become full-time workers and to set up a general headquarters for our society" (COA, 157). He sought to allay the anxieties of the Akronites by assuring them that the price would be modest—about the cost of a bottle of whiskey, since every drunk could afford that much.[23] Thus the book would reach a broad audience, which all agreed was a top priority. As Wilson remarked in a letter to Alcoholic Foundation board member Frank Amos, "I feel duty bound to get the book out, for men everywhere are entitled to know what we know as soon as we can get the information to them."[24] The skeptical Akron members ultimately acceded to Wilson's plans—but only by a one-vote margin (*PIO*, 157). Their questions and objections about the development of a book were really about standardization, centralization, and commercialism—in short, about the creation of a "consumerist" rather than a "religious" reading culture. Their concerns would become a steady refrain as the AA fellowship grew.

During the summer of 1938, Wilson wrote out his own story and an overall introduction to the organization's philosophy entitled "There Is a Solution," and, at the suggestion of Frank Amos, showed them to Eugene Exman, the religion editor at Harper and Brothers and Amos's personal friend. Exman was the perfect reader for Wilson's manuscript. After having passed over in 1929 Lloyd Douglas's popular novel *Magnificent Obsession*—which detailed the workings of an Oxford Group–like religious movement—he published the American edition of the Group's best-selling conversion narrative *For Sinners Only* in 1932, followed by

New Thought minister Emmet Fox's *The Sermon on the Mount* in 1934. Believing that Wilson's work would be well received in the day's expansive religious climate, Exman offered him a contract and a $1,500 advance.

Wilson was elated at the offer. An advance from Harper would solve the organization's cash flow problem, and alliance with an established publisher would ease the logistical difficulties of producing and distributing the book once it was finished. But the Akron contingent's critique of the inherent commercialism of printed matter was fresh in his ears, and after an initial rush of enthusiasm, Wilson decided (over the objections of other New York members and the Trustees of the Alcoholic Foundation) to turn his back on the lure of the marketplace. Even though Harper was legitimate and well intentioned, he argued, "our fellowship should own its own book" (COA, 154). The risk that the workings of a trade press—of the literary marketplace itself—would disable their ability to control their message was simply too great: earning out the $1,500 advance would mean the group started its public life in debt. The group's members would have no say in where and how the book was advertised or sold, nor would they set its price. And as Wilson explained to Frank Amos, he "did not want any man's chance of finding his God and getting over his alcoholism prejudiced by accusations, however ill-founded, that we were too commercial. . . . The very best interests of our work demand that we carry it on [as] independently as possible of money considerations."[25]

While the trustees were shocked and unhappy that Wilson had declined the Harper offer, Exman endorsed Wilson's sense of the book's unique position within the organization, telling him that the special mission of "a society like [yours]" meant that it "ought to control and publish its own literature" (COA, 155). His support helped Wilson convince the board to fund his writing and publishing process through the sale of shares in a joint-stock corporation called "Works Publishing, Inc." While sales of the stock proved sluggish, the "dribble of money" they brought in, combined with a few additional loans and the Rockefeller funds, provided working capital sufficient for Wilson to continue writing, and during the fall and winter of 1938, he began to draft book chapters "from a hastily drawn up list of possible headings" (COA, 159). As he wrote, his ideas were critiqued and revised, typically several times, by members of both the New York and Akron meetings.

In an early address to the medical community, Wilson asserted self-deprecatingly that "the 400 pages of *Alcoholics Anonymous* contain no theory. . . . Being laymen, we have naught but a story to tell."[26] As the discussions of AA pragmatism in chapters 1 and 2 make clear, this anti-intellectual posture was only somewhat disingenuous. Although he was less leery than some of his midwestern counterparts of analytical ability and other "highbrow" vices, from the start Wilson had envisioned the book he was writing as an extremely practical how-to manual; it would eschew both the moralizing of traditional religious appeals and the equally obfuscatory vogue for psychoanalytical diagnoses of drinking as a neurotic symptom. In place of elaborate theories of *why* people drank, it would offer a simple, concrete strategy for *how* to stop drinking. It would be presented in the same frank and friendly language with which one alcoholic addressed another in the word-of-mouth program.

With that end in view, the manuscript hammered on Dr. Silkworth's theory of the obsession plus the allergy—particularly on the image of alcoholism as progressive and irreversible, leading inevitably toward the "twin ogres of madness and death" (COA, 70). Despite such occasional rhetorical flourishes, the chapters for the most part avoided melodrama, relying instead on the rhetorical question-and-answer format found in Oxford Group tomes like *For Sinners Only* and on a narrative voice that Matthew J. Raphael has called a "psychological plain style . . . perfectly serviceable and utterly unremarkable."[27] Tacitly acknowledging that many of its readers might have encountered loftier arguments elsewhere, the foreword stressed that AA was "a useful program for anyone concerned with a drinking problem" (BB, 19), one that aimed simply to "show other alcoholics PRECISELY HOW WE HAVE RECOVERED" (xiii). Wilson took the greatest pride not in the program's originality or its innovative regimes, but in its efficacy. His sales pitch boiled down to the simple "it works—it really does" (88).

This down-to-earth pragmatism shapes not only the book's conceptualization of alcoholism, but also its structural and rhetorical choices. Edmund B. O'Reilly has correctly noted a similarity between Wilson's writing and that of advertising executive Bruce Barton, whose biography of Jesus, *The Man Nobody Knows*, had been a best seller in 1925. Both men relied on a "recipe for effective communication in business that includes conciseness, simplicity, sincerity, and repetition." The primary difference, O'Reilly argues, "may be that Wilson ultimately discovered a product he really believed in."[28] The force of that belief is evident in the first chapter, "Bill's Story," which uses the example of Wilson's life to vividly illustrate both the progressive, addictive nature of alcoholism and AA's spiritual program for recovery. Subsequent chapters follow up with straightforward titles like "There Is a Solution," "How it Works," and "Into Action," which reiterate the recovery message in a plainspoken can-do language. A peppering of rhetorical questions—"Why can't he stay on the water wagon?" (22), "Such a man would be crazy, wouldn't he?" (38), "Where and how were we to find this [Higher] Power?" (45)—lead the reader naturally through the text's argumentative sections.

To enhance the feeling that the reader is participating in a conversational exchange among friends rather than merely perusing a text, the book adopts a direct second-person address that consistently denominates the reader as a "you" to the authorial "we." At points, the narrative voice abdicates the scene entirely, ceding the textual stage to a real-life character in order to "let him tell you about it" in his own words (40, 136). At other times, the frank and friendly prose simply segues into "the rest of the conversation our friend had" (27), which is presented verbatim and framed by quotation marks. These stylistic choices all tend toward the same point: an approximation in text of the dynamics of the person-to-person speech at the center of the program.

Occasionally, Wilson's prose did swerve from the pragmatic into a hortatory mode. One section in chapter 6, for example (known among AAs today as "The Promises"), is an incantatory list of the benefits to be obtained from working the 12 Steps: "We are going to know a new freedom and a new happiness. We will not regret the past nor wish to shut the door on it. We will comprehend the word serenity and we will know peace" (83–84). The first paragraph of chapter 5, which begins, "Rarely have we seen a person fail who has thoroughly followed our path," employs a similarly gnomic tone (58). Such moments were rare, however, and for the most part the text avoids anything that smacks of religiosity, psychology, or any other kind of abstraction.

Therefore, while it is deferential to physicians and psychologists and to the clergy, the Big Book assumes that its reader has been subjected to their theories of alcoholism in the past with no result, and purposefully distances itself from "these sympathetic men." While it freely acknowledges that they were unable to be much help to alcoholics because "we seldom told them the whole truth [or] . . . followed their advice" (73), it also suggests that such professionals' lack of lived experience, and their compensatory surfeit of theory, makes them congenitally unable to aid the alcoholic. "*The ex-alcoholic*," on the other hand, "*can generally win the entire confidence of another alcoholic in a few hours*" because "he is a man with a real answer, that has no attitude of holier than thou." That "real answer" inheres in the principle of alcoholic equalitarianism and manifests itself in lived reality, rather than in vague theorizations about alcoholism's cause or consequences. Unencumbered by tiresome theories, the "real answer" entails "no fees to pay, no axes to grind, no people to please, no lectures to be attended" (18; original emphasis). All that is required is that the listener or reader recognize himself in the narrator's depiction of alcoholic misery. Wilson's stylistic choices throughout the Big Book—rhetorical address, tone, structure—all conspired to make that moment of identification inevitable.

What Wilson called the "backbone of the book" (COA, 159) was chapter 5, "How It Works," which introduced the neatly numbered list of 12 Steps, the logic and simplicity of which delighted Wilson. Many in Akron still endorsed the six-step word-of-mouth regime developed within the Oxford Group, but Wilson came to believe that "this dose was . . . too rich for New Yorkers" (COA, 161). Prideful and stubborn, alcoholics required a more gradual route to surrender. Each of the twelve steps was smaller and more manageable, which made the daunting task of spiritual growth seem like it could be undertaken successfully by anyone with a modicum of common sense. In addition, twelve steps had a quasi-mystical appeal; as Wilson reflected later, while writing, "without any special rhyme or reason I connected [the Steps] with the twelve apostles" and decided that "somehow, this number seemed significant" (COA, 161).

For all his sensitivity to the distinctiveness of the alcoholic case, Wilson's first draft of the Steps nevertheless hewed fairly closely to the alcoholic squad's religiosity: they invoked "God" explicitly, rather than as a "Higher Power" or "God as we understood him," and Step 7 specified that "Humbly ask[ing] Him to remove our shortcomings" must be done "on our knees." But a liberal majority within the New York group, aided by a radical and vocal fringe of atheists and agnostics, persuaded Wilson to tone down this language, arguing that "alcoholics who had tried the missions were forever complaining about this very thing." Playing to his pragmatism, the liberal faction made a strategic rather than doctrinal argument: having experienced for himself the limitations of gospel temperance, how could Wilson condone "the straight religious approach"? Once in the group, "the prospect could take God or leave Him alone as he wished," but forcing it up front would be counterproductive (COA, 163). Because his own conversion experience had been so powerful, Wilson originally resisted any tempering, but the appeals of the more secular members ultimately convinced him. As the manuscript moved through its final stages, he not only toned down the Steps' pietism, but also decided to introduce them in the book as merely a "suggested . . . Program of Recovery" (COA, 167).[29]

While Bob Smith agreed with Wilson's changes, some midwestern affiliates disapproved of them, and this original muting of AA's spiritual dimension would become a bone of contention in later years. But in the moment, the desire for a convincing message with broad-based appeal overrode all other concerns and structured the book's form as well as its content. Chapter 4 enumerated the Steps and explained their order and their relationship to one another. Chapters 5, 6, and 7 examined the rationale behind each Step, instructed readers in how to take it, and explored the likely outcomes. Chapters 8 through 10 described the reactions that family members and employers would likely have to the newly sober alcoholic, and gave advice on how to rebuild relationships strained to the breaking point by years of abuse and neglect.

The final chapter, "A Vision for You," described the way that the book was intended to function, both in the life of the individual readers and as a catalyst for what the cofounders hoped would be a "benign chain reaction" spreading their philosophy throughout the world (COA, 76). It related the story of Smith and Wilson's encounter in Akron and of their tentative outreach to the original "man on the bed." It acknowledged that new members typically felt skeptical about the program until they realized that "the very practical approach to [their] problems, the absence of intolerance of any kind, the informality, the genuine democracy, [and] the uncanny understanding" that the fellowship offered in fact made it "irresistible" (160). The volume's ideal reader, it suggested, would follow a similar path. Taking the book's "clear-cut directions" (29), he would be convinced by its rational arguments, commit himself to sobriety and spirituality, and carry the message to other alcoholics. The chapter concluded on a ringing note: "Thus we grow. And so can you, though you be but one man with this book in your hand. We believe and hope that it will contain all you will need to begin" (162–63).

In his grandest imaginings, Bill Wilson saw the book as a how-to guide not merely for achieving sobriety, but also for cultivating "Utopia . . . right here and now" (16). But as the project progressed, he began to worry that clarity, comprehensibility, and common sense appeal were not equal to such a grand task. The writing dragged as the members in the New York and Akron meetings argued over details; debate over the logistics of the publishing project, as well as over all the intellectual and philosophical issues that fed into it, seemed to dominate every meeting. These heated discussions threw into relief the now-infrequent occasions when a newly sober alcoholic came forward to tell his story, or when an old-timer recounted his own experiences to a newcomer.

As noted above, prayer and guidance remained the hallmarks of group meetings in Akron. But as the New York group had grown, Wilson had come to believe that these personal stories—the vehicle through which one alcoholic realized that another "spoke my language," as Dr. Bob had put it—had become the most convincing argument for the group's approach to alcoholism. While the book paid homage to the importance of such testimony by opening with "Bill's Story," aside from that tale of Wilson's own experiences the working draft contained nothing but theory. Gradually it dawned on Wilson that a book explaining alcoholism in rational, practical, nonjudgmental language was only a start; such straight talk was necessary, but not sufficient, to create the moment in which the alcoholic began to say "Yes, that's me, I'm like that." What was needed was a whole section of true-to-life testimonies, Wilson decided. Personal narratives would "identify us with the distant reader in a way that the text itself might not," and augment the simplicity and organizing power of the book's analytical section (COA, 164). Writing to Smith, he enthused that the collection of first-person "witnesses" would form "the heart of the book," and allow the kind of emotional connection that brought alcoholics together.[30] Sympathetic identification would form a crucible in which plain prose that told "how it works" would be transformed into a mirror in which desperate alcoholics could recognize themselves. Dispatching individual AAs in New York and Akron to commit their stories to paper, Wilson revised the manuscript yet again, this time with an eye to accommodating a second section and explaining how it should work in readers' lives. Hoping that no one would find "these self-revealing accounts in bad taste," he explained in his revised second chapter that "it is only by fully disclosing ourselves and our problems that [you] will be persuaded to say, 'Yes, I am one of them too; I must have this thing!' " (29).

Like the testimonials presented at meetings (sometimes called "leads" or "qualifications"), the twenty-eight Big Book stories "disclose in a general way what we used to be like, what happened, and what we are like now" (58), and do so according to fairly strict generic parameters.[31] With the exception of the one story that treats a female alcoholic's experiences, "A Feminine Victory," and a piece called "The Alcoholic's Wife," every narrator is male, and the stories they tell recount their inscription into the late Victorian heteronormative masculinity described in chapter 2.[32] Most depict the narrator's social background and upbringing, and chart his upward trajectory at work—typically in business or sales, though sometimes as a professional or a tradesman. Many use the First World War as a touchstone, describing either the narrator's service in the armed forces or his frustration at not being able to serve because of age or family responsibilities. Most also describe men's movement into traditional family life, though few detail that life beyond cursory mentions—"a lovely wife came and went" (333), "my boy was going to have the best I could give him" (266), and so on.[33] In aggregate, the narratives present a striking picture of "normal" white middle-class life in the early twentieth-century United States, one characterized by ample opportunity and upward mobility. While a number of narrators mention the hypocrisy of Prohibition and the economic hardships of the Depression (and one touches on the smaller economic slump of 1920–21), as a whole they espouse the official cultural optimism that characterized the early years of the American Century—to the point that one critic has complained that the volume is crippled by its "boosterish tone."[34]

Intertwined with this narrative, however, is its doppelganger: each piece relates the story of the narrator's progressive, debilitating drinking, which acts as a demon to chase him from the edenic American landscape. Tales of home-brewing, speakeasies, and bootleggers; blackouts, failed businesses, and infidelity; hospitalization, incarceration, and family abandonment are interspersed with those of attempts to go "dry" and failed "cures." While these narratives of "what we were like" cannot be called lurid, they are definitely frank and emphasize the uncontrollable nature of the narrators' addiction: "I go back to the hotel and get more gin . . . the indescribable torture has me again . . ." (233);

"each time there was the feeling of regret, inability to understand why, but a firm determination that it would never happen again—but it did—in fact the periods between became increasingly shorter, and the duration of each binge longer" (366); "sometimes decently fed, clothed, and housed, I worked at my business on commission with a large firm; sometimes I dared not appear there cold, hungry, with torn clothes, shaking body and muddled brain advertising what I had become" (376). The result is a decidedly gothic undercurrent running through what are, for the most part, plain-spoken and realistic stories.[35]

Usually right before death or involuntary commitment for "wet brain," the narrator makes contact with Alcoholics Anonymous, which finally offers him a way out of his torment. The stories spend varying amounts of time on this moment of contact. Some simply state "I met that band of life-savers, Alcoholics Anonymous" (248), while others note that the "doctor . . . spent many hours with me telling his experience with alcohol" (301) or that "while in the hospital about twenty men called on me" (331). A few record the narrator's initial critical response to AA's theories—several narrators express frank distaste for the spiritual nature of the group, and some detail failed attempts to practice moderate drinking. All the narratives, however, emphasize the near-magical effect of the moment of identification, of hearing someone else tell a familiar story of drunkenness and of realizing "Yes, that's me, I'm like that." "The Unbeliever" asserts that the recovering alcoholic he meets in a drying-out hospital "g[o]t my confidence when he started to tell what he had gone through. It was so exactly like my case" (199). The "Traveler, Editor, Scholar" explains that because the AAs who visit him tell "of their experiences and how they found the only remedy," they "la[y] the foundation of a very necessary faith" (263). "The Salesman" notes the importance of identification from the other side. He emphasizes that "a very important part" of his story is that he was "almost immediately put to work" by the doctor who helped him get sober, who "sent me to see another alcoholic who was in the hospital" and "tell [him] my story." Expressing a sentiment found throughout the narrative, the Salesman states that the 12th-Step work of carrying the message "is necessary to my continued happiness" (323). By narrating this moment of transformation through identification, each story unambiguously spells out the effect that it intends to have on the reader.

Once embarked on a program of recovery, the narrator typically returns to marital and financial success, regains the respect of his community, and devotes his life to bringing AA's transformative teachings to others in need. "The Backslider's" account testifies to the continuing role that experience-sharing and identification play in recovery. As he makes 12-Step calls on his own, the narrator finds that "the sight of every new alcoholic in the hospital was a real object lesson to me. I could see myself in them as I had been, something I had never been able to picture before" (271). This salutary angle of vision not only inspires his compassion, but also helps him personally, prompting him to stay "mighty close to what has proven to be good for me" (273). More typically, conclusions assert in a general fashion the importance of working within the brotherhood of recovering alcoholics to deepen sobriety and extend it to others: "Today I have Someone who will always hear me; I have a warm fellowship among men who understand my problems; I have tasks to do and am glad to do them, to see others who are alcoholics and to help them in any way I can to become sober men" (264). Like the membership of AA writ large, the narrators vary in the nature and intensity of the spiritual sentiments that they express, but they are unanimous in their endorsement of the AA way of life, with its focus on surrender, alcoholic equalitarianism, and service.

Thanks to a series of coincidences, the book concluded with a meta-commentary on the power of identification and "the help which printed pages could give" (393).[36] Just before going to press, Wilson sent copies of the manuscript-in-progress to physicians and clergy—primarily for comments and criticism, but also in hopes of garnering publicity.[37] One of these copies fell into the hands of a California man who, after reading it "cover to cover" (393), wrote in to share his own story with the New York office. A long-time chronic drunkard, he, like many AAs, had tried a variety of cures with no success. Reading *Alcoholics Anonymous*, however, had changed all that. When "I returned from the sanitarium and your book was here waiting for me[,] I read, more than that I pored over it so as not to miss anything. I thought to myself, yes, this is the only way." The first section of the book "made sense" and he "followed out the suggestions." Most compelling, however, were "the personal stories," which were "very accurate as pertaining to my own experience; any one of them might have been my own story" (393–95). Seeing himself in the mirror of other alcoholics' experiences, the California man believed himself at last to have found a community. He had already loaned his copy of the manuscript to another alcoholic, he wrote, and planned to share it with others at the sanitarium. His story, titled "The

Lone Endeavor," made a thrilling coda to the Big Book, suggesting that distant and isolated readers would indeed be able to enter AA's sentimental subculture via print, "start[ing] out by themselves," as Wilson described it, "with only this book to aid them" (396).

CRAFTING CONFESSIONS

Contemporary critics steeped in the modern "consumerist" aesthetics of the late twentieth century typically fault the personal narratives some AAs call "drunkologues" for the way they privilege sameness and repetition over difference and individuality. For AA narrators, originality and innovation are less important than familiarity with what David Rudy identifies as common "vocabularies of motives."[38] Including not only language but also imagery and narrative conceits, this shared vocabulary leads to a rigorous and tightly defined genre inhospitable to innovation. The reliance on a single genre has played into the perception that AA is a cult. In her anti-recovery screed *I'm Dysfunctional, You're Dysfunctional*, Wendy Kaminer derides AA testimonials as "stultifying," and even more sympathetic critics like Robyn Warhol and Helena Michie have criticized the way their "coherence system" flattens out individual and social distinctions to create a unidimensional "master narrative."[39] These criticisms of form imply that the self-fashioning that takes place through 12-Step narratives is essentially nonliberating and runs counter to the best interests of the narrating self.

This critique overlooks the fact, discussed in chapter 2, that it is not difference that the narrating alcoholic and his or her interlocutors seek, but similarity. AA testimonials seek to cultivate and to express the essential alcoholic self, the self subsumed beneath the destructive fabulations of the modern ego until the acts of surrender and gratitude freed it up. Like the immediacy of the orally delivered "drunkologue," narrow generic parameters facilitate the project of alcoholic equalitarianism; they display the self freed of ego-gratifying flourishes and embroideries. Thus, as Edmund O'Reilly notes, "voicelessness and inarticulateness in [AA] speakers may be valued as markers of powerfully felt, sincere emotions"; conversely, too much polish, suavity, or deviation from traditional norms undercut a narrator's authenticity in the eyes of the audience.[40] The most satisfying narrative form is the one in which the audience members most easily see themselves, not the one whose linguistic vivacity, structural innovation, or other kinds of "originality" distance them from the narrator.

Twelve-Step testimonials are in many ways archaic forms. The spoken counterparts to antique religious reading practices, their three-part structure mimics that of Christian conversion narrative, a genre that began with the Gospel of Paul. Dissenting pietists claimed the conversion genre for their own in the seventeenth and eighteenth centuries, and it reached its height in the United States with the best-selling spiritual autobiographies—some reprints of Puritan classics, others contemporary testimonies—of the early nineteenth century.[41] But the Protestant conversion story was not the only influence on the shape of the stories that appeared in the Big Book.

Once Bill Wilson became convinced that " 'identification' [was] the main, if not the sole route to 'getting the program,' " his enthusiasm for grafting personal narratives onto his practical program meant that he gave no thought to the complexities that might inhere in transforming AA's tradition of oral storytelling to print.[42] Writing had proven fairly easy for Wilson, and when he hit upon the idea of adding a section of stories to the book, he assumed that other AAs would simply transcribe their personal testimonies—as he had—into coherent and readable forms. "The individual stories," he explained to Smith, "should be edited as little as possible."[43] In fact, collecting material for the book's second half proved rather unwieldy. "Getting the stories written in Akron proved difficult," in part because resentment over the commercial dimension of the book lingered. Some members alleged the project was a "racket" cooked up by Smith and Wilson to defraud the group; according to Dorothy S.M., "for a time, we thought the whole Akron group might break up over the book" (*Dr. Bob*, 153). The situation improved when Dr. Bob arranged for an in-house editor of sorts: member Jim S., himself a former journalist, "interviewed members . . . and then helped write their stories" (*PIO*, 200).[44]

The New York group's experience was similarly chaotic. "Since New York had no one comparable to Akron's newsman Jim," Wilson recalled later, "it was thought that each New Yorker with a real record of sobriety could try to write his story himself." But when Wilson and Hank P., the affiliate who worked most closely with him on the book project, "tried to edit these amateur attempts there was plenty of trouble. Who were we, said the writers, to edit their stories?" (*COA*, 164). As tensions mounted, Wilson took Hank P.'s suggestion and hired a professional editor, magazinist, and creative writing teacher named Thomas Uzzell to finish the job. This decision probably made it possible to complete the project, but it also introduced a distinctly commercial element into the gift economy's practice of self-disclosure—and inadvertently confirmed the Akron group's suspicions about the nature of the book project.

Although he published both fiction and nonfiction of his own, Uzzell was primarily a polisher and packager of other people's literary efforts who worked as an editor in at least two branches of the new literary culture that would come to be known as "middlebrow."[45] The first was *Collier's* magazine, one of the monthlies that built a circulation in the millions by mingling advertising with light entertainment between the 1890s and the 1920s; the second was the Book-of-the-Month Club, founded in 1926. In both situations, Uzzell worked to craft literary products that were salable to a mass but middle-class audience. In a letter to Wilson, Hank P. credited Uzzell with the final revisions and polish on "such books as *The Good Earth*, *If I Had Four Apples*, *Outward Room*, and three Book of the Month Club books" before concluding with the somewhat hyperbolic assertion that "in the publishing world there is no one so established and well looked up to."[46] Uzzell had a keen sense of what the literary market would bear, and no prejudices against writing saleable fiction. In one of his two writing textbooks, *Narrative Technique: A Practical Course in Literary Psychology*, he reminded neophyte authors that "these are the days of self-revealment," in which "modern knowledge has lighted many secret places of the heart." Given the cultural climate, he argued, they should see themselves less as artists than as "psychologist[s] with an artistic purpose," using literary "melodrama" to achieve "the narrator's main task [which] is to produce emotion in the reader."[47]

In the months just prior to taking up the Big Book editing job, the "self-revealment" that was uppermost in Uzzell's mind was the sort associated with the popular tabloid magazines of the day; his article dissecting "The Love Pulps" and their appeal to the "sub-mass female reader" had appeared in *Scribner's* in April 1938. Part of a three-part series on "magazines that sell," the article simultaneously celebrated and derided the ability of the pulp confessional to reach an enormous audience of readers who "possess no fertile imagination; [whose] dreams must be written out for them." Cliché and "devotion to convention," Uzzell argued, were the keys to successful love-pulp writing, resulting in "symbols which the reader can easily grasp." These, in turn, "enable the reader to understand a story without working through it."[48] Although he evidenced a typical male modernist's disdain for both the readers and the formula behind the pulps, he admired the technique that pulp writers and editors displayed, and was clearly impressed by their profitability. He brought this appreciation of commerce and craft to the Big Book project as well, telling Hank P. that "you should certainly hold on to the production and distribution of this volume . . . for she ought to go high, wide and handsome, and net those concerned a neat profit."[49] A canny professional and an enthusiastic participant in the Big Book project, Uzzell had ideas about narrative self-disclosure that were quite distinct from the average AA on a 12-Step call.

Of course, even in face-to-face testimony AAs had crafted and shaped their accounts. Akron member J.D. recalled that "we used to have almost a set story" to use with new prospects. At weekly planning meetings, those with longer periods of sobriety would talk "about the mistakes we had made in telling our stories . . . suggest[ing] certain words to leave out and certain words to add in order to make a more effective talk" (*Dr. Bob*, 113–14). But the physical intimacy of the word-of-mouth program, and its tradition of spontaneity—Bill Wilson's "I just talked away about my own case"—allowed them to perceive their personal narratives as pure and unmediated. Because they emanated from surrendered selves, selves that had (in theory, at least) renounced calculation and manipulation along with alcohol, AA stories seemed honest revelations of the speaker's essential and flawed essence. And the immediacy and the imperfections of oral presentation reinforced this perception of the spoken word as inherently and supremely real. It was this deep-seated belief that had led some Akronites to distrust the book from the start. They saw in the transition to print an inevitable warping of the language of the heart, which would have to be manipulated to fit the inhospitable conditions of the marketplace economy. In this they were not far wrong.

Lacking manuscript evidence, of course, we can only guess at the nature and extent of the revisions Uzzell ultimately made to the Big Book stories.[50] According to his grandson-in-law, he routinely boasted in later years to his family that he "basically ghostwrote the whole thing."[51] Certainly his intent included reformulating the stories' heartfelt but probably somewhat incoherent "self-revealment" into meaningful "melodrama," using the tricks and techniques available to the professional litterateur. While his letter assured Wilson and Hank P. that "I spent last evening with the manuscript [and] . . . I found myself deeply moved," he nevertheless felt that something in the raw materials was missing: "The whole book needs the final shaping of a professional hand."[52] Uzzell was willing and able to act as that hand, and Wilson, preoccupied at this point with schemes to finance the book's publication and worn out from arguing over the story edits himself, was happy to let him.

The "final shaping" seems to have been fairly extensive. While Wilson claimed in *Alcoholics Anonymous Comes of Age* that "the story section of the book was complete in the latter point of January, 1939" (164), archival evidence suggests otherwise. Wilson wrote to Frank Amos on 4 January that the story section of the manuscript "has been placed in the hands of Thomas Uzzell"; Amos in turn wrote to fellow trustee Dick Richardson on 21 February to say that "while the main part of the book has been carefully edited the individual stories . . . must still undergo considerable editing."[53] Wilson recollected years later that the editing process was highly contentious, with "the cries of the anguished edited taletellers" causing him "plenty of trouble" (COA, 164). One possible cause of that anguish and trouble may have been seeing their earnest personal testimonies shaped and polished into tiny "melodramas" intended to "produce emotion in the reader."

The Akronites' vociferous commitment to the spoken word, combined with the vexation that surrounded every stage of the Big Book's production, make puzzling the fact that once the book was finally published in April 1939, the Akron members welcomed it with enthusiasm and incorporated it seamlessly into their lives. A variety of factors may have contributed to this situation. The fact that the "commercial" book seemed a dismal failure may have played a role; the 5,000 copies in the first pressrun sat in a warehouse almost untouched for most of the year. In the autumn, stories about AA in the tabloid *Liberty* and the *Cleveland Plain Dealer* sparked an interest, and orders—about sixty a week—began to trickle in. But the figure fell short of Wilson's expectations, leaving him "frustrated, impatient, restless, dissatisfied, and depressed" because the book "wasn't selling" (PIO, 241).

In addition, deteriorating relations with the Akron Oxford Group may have influenced midwestern opinion about the book. "If the alcoholics in Akron had their problems with the Big Book, members of the Oxford Group had even more," and the book was only the last in a string of things with which the Group was taking umbrage (*Dr. Bob*, 154). As the number of alcoholics attending the weekly Oxford Group meeting began to exceed the number of non-alcoholics, tensions had grown on both sides: "We were the main body, and we had the most to say, and we were kind of running the thing," alcoholic member Bob E. recalls. The non-alcoholics, however, typically believed it was their role to advise the former drunkards on the state of their souls and their devotional practice, which rankled the alcoholics. In addition, sitting "in silence, listening for guidance . . . made the drunks very restless" (*Dr. Bob*, 156–57). A month after the Big Book's appearance, that restlessness boiled over: ignoring the strong objections of Oxford Group leaders, alcoholics in Cleveland who had been driving down for Akron meetings set up their own organization, which would "only be open for alcoholics and their families . . . taking the name from the book 'Alcoholics Anonymous' " (*Dr. Bob*, 164). In his cultural biography of Clarence S., the Cleveland member who led that breakaway faction, Mitchell K. credits the Big Book with establishing the sense of identity necessary to make the break. Clarence argued that "now that we've got this book here . . . there was no need to go to the Oxford Group any longer."[54] The book's appearance at this crucial tipping point may have helped midwesterners who were originally skeptical to overcome their antipathy toward it.

With that hurdle surmounted, the Big Book took a central place— alongside the Bible and *The Upper Room*—in a midwestern print culture modeled on that of the Oxford Group. Even as the practice of morning reading and meditation declined in the fellowship as a whole (*Dr. Bob*, 178), it remained central among the groups that were offshoots of the Akron and Cleveland meetings, not only in other midwestern cities, but also in further-flung outposts like Houston (first group established 1940) and Dallas (1942), where transplanted midwesterners began groups modeled on the rigorous cultures in which they had sobered up. Wally P. has noted that strict "Big Book Thumping" AA cultures came into existence early on in Denver and Seattle; Brady S. claims that Little Rock, Arkansas, developed in a similar fashion.[55] Such groups emphasized intensive rather than extensive reading—several early pamphlets published in the Midwest and widely circulated stressed "the necessity of reading and re-reading the AA book"—as well as formal, guided study of the Big Book.[56]

Either a natural or a strategic forgetting of their original suspicion of the printed word—combined with a reading practice that while no longer "religious" in Griffiths's sense of the word was still intensive and devotional—allowed AAs who followed the rigorous version of the Akron program to overlook the traces of professionalism and commercialism that lingered in the Big Book and incorporate it into their ongoing projects of self-surrender. Particularly after Smith's death in 1950, it became a kind of sacred text, valued for the link it provided to the beloved cofounder and to the original energies of the fellowship. That emotional investment led to a kind of fetishization—Wilson encountered considerable resistance to the idea of an updated second edition in the early 1950s, and groused that the text was becoming "more and more frozen" into "something like dogma."[57] When the second edition did appear in 1955, he had to assure the General Service Conference delegates that "'not an iota' of the first part of the text dealing with recovery principles ha[s] been changed."[58]

By osmosis, almost, the Big Book had come to enjoy the same status—the same sense of authenticity and presence—as face-to-face communication. The material form of the book, like its commercial dimension, was canceled out by its transcendent message and its talismanic meaning. Its incorporation into a regime of devotional reading—intensive private and communal study, as well as the public performance and commitment to memory of specific excerpts of sacred texts—allowed the Big Book a place of honor even among those who continued to see the spoken language of the heart as more "real" than other modes of communications. The embrace of this specific book, however, did not completely dispel the suspicion of mass-produced and mass-distributed printed matter, and after the Second World War the tension between Akron and New York returned, transmuted from a battle between oral and printed culture to one between artisanal and cultural-industrial modes of print.

GATEKEEPING THE GIFT ECONOMY

Given Akron's original belief that "even books and pamphlets could be harmful" (*PIO* 180), it is somewhat ironic to note the flood of print culture that came out of midwestern AA in the years following the Big Book's publication. The *Little Red Book* and the pamphlet literature discussed in the previous chapter were central to but not exhaustive of this culture. Cleveland produced the first AA newsletter, the *Central Bulletin*, beginning in the fall of 1942; Chicago followed suit in 1949.[59] Detroit and Minneapolis groups also published informational and inspirational pamphlets that were circulated across North America.[60] Rooted in the rigorous version of "the AA Way of Life," with its full and ongoing surrender to God, spiritual awakening, and service to the AA fellowship, this literature formed the canon that would fuel traditionalist AA in the decades to come.

The midwestern publications were explicitly ecumenical. The Big Book had advocated a "Realm of the Spirit [that] is broad, roomy, all inclusive; never exclusive or forbidding to those who earnestly seek" (46). The authors of *The Little Red Book* concurred, reminding readers that "religious views are things to be dealt with outside of AA. . . . The fact that you believe in a *Power Greater than Yourself* to restore you to spiritual health is all that our program requires." The Chicago pamphlet "Spiritual Milestones" went one step further, noting that "the spiritual life is by no means a Christian monopoly," before going on to praise "the Hebrews," "followers of Mohammed," and those that follow "the eight-part program laid down in Buddhism."[61] But this generous view of the divine was balanced against a clear call to piety—a simmering religiosity that made Bill Wilson nervous.

The authors of *The Little Red Book* were in correspondence with the New York office as early as 1944, when the "book" was simply a series of lecture notes. They seem to have been seeking a stamp of approval for their volume, but secretary Margaret "Bobby" B., writing on Wilson's behalf, noted that "we do not actually approve or disapprove of these local pieces. . . . We keep hands off, either pro or con."[62] Over the next few years the book's audience continued to grow; Wilson noted in 1950 that it was "ha[ving] pretty wide circulation, several thousand copies a year."[63] Sales on this scale were no match for the Big Book—as appendix B shows, its sales were booming in the wake of the war, and in 1950 the thirteenth reprint produced 50,000 copies—but Wilson nevertheless began to worry. He was receiving letters from AAs all across the country asking—or sometimes informing—him about the personalized guides to 12-Step recovery they planned to publish. He explained to one such author that "while a tract like the Minneapolis book has proved rather popular and useful . . . it sets a bad precedent." He mused to another pair of would-be authors that "some of us are beginning to feel that there should be such a thing as standard AA literature," and concluded in another missive that "the Minneapolis Red Book has gone over far. It is, in fact, what purports to be a standard AA text. Actually, it reflects the ideas of a single Group or area, and is the private property, I believe, of individuals."[64]

At the same time that *The Little Red Book* was gaining in popularity, writings from the alcohol studies movement were beginning to dot the AA landscape. The Yale School had begun to distribute its pamphlets for lay readers in the early 1940s, and the volume *Alcohol, Culture, and Society* appeared in 1944 to wide acclaim; the National Committee for Education on Alcoholism began to distribute its own educational pamphlets nationwide, and Marty Mann's *Primer on Alcoholism*, published in 1950, enjoyed strong sales.[65] Founded in 1944, AA's national monthly magazine the *Grapevine* included articles and essays on alcoholism from experts and policy makers outside of AA as well as stories from within the fellowship. As the correspondence above makes plain, plenty of AAs were eager to add to the barrage of print, and publishers—amateur and professional alike—hoped to tap into the market of recovering alcoholics as well. As early as 1955, the General Service Conference discussed the problem of direct marketing to AAs using the contact information available in local directories.[66]

There is no doubt that Bill Wilson feared a free market of AA publications in part out of self-interest. The outstanding shares of Works Publishing, Inc., which had been issued to underwrite the cost of preparing the Big Book and had never earned any dividends, had been bought back from the subscribers in 1940 by the Alcoholic Foundation, effectively returning all Big Book revenue to the general fund of Alcoholics Anonymous. Twenty percent came off the top as royalty payments divided between Wilson and Smith. Wilson's share increased to 15 percent with Smith's death in 1950 (he also earned a 15 percent royalty on all his other writings); conspiracy buffs within AA have long speculated that Wilson's desire to keep control over AA literature was motivated by base hopes for personal gain.[67] Official documents, however, suggest a somewhat more prosaic reason for his concerns about revenue from publishing. Although contributions from the groups around the country were supposed to cover the operating expenses of the New York General Service Office (GSO), "less than half contributed anything," leaving the "constant deficits" incurred by the GSO and *The Grapevine* to be "plugged up with money from the sale" of literature, chiefly the Big Book (COA, 201).[68]

Thus there was cause for concern when the 1951 General Service Conference report noted that "income from the sale of the 'Big Book' and from the sale of pamphlets has declined over the past three years [perhaps] due in part to increased circulation of books and pamphlets from resources other than the [Alcoholic] Foundation." The result was a "disturbing depletion of reserve funds" that posed potentially "serious problems for the future."[69] Big Book revenue—and, to a much lesser extent, income from pamphlet and other book sales—made the expansion of the gift economy possible, funding the distribution of free literature to hospitals and prisons as well as the work of the New York office, which provided information, guidance, and reading materials to new groups. Without that cash flow and the services it provided, Wilson feared, the orderly growth of AA would languish, if not break down completely.

It would be wrong, however, to suggest that financial concerns alone motivated Wilson's growing unease with the alcohol literature marketplace. As he explained in one letter: "The widened book market that our continual growth will certainly bring will present a temptation to many ambitious members to enter the textbook field with their own individual ideas . . . creating a chaotic state in our basic literature."[70] Should different versions of AA philosophy begin to compete among themselves for affiliates' attention, the financial solidity of the gift economy would be undermined and, more important, the essential kinship that joined members together would also inevitably erode. For philosophical as well as economic reasons, Wilson did not want to see literature "reflecting the ideas of a single Group or area" passing itself off as representative of the whole of AA.[71]

His correspondence is never explicit about precisely what local ideas concern him, but the tone of Wilson's letters regarding *The Little Red Book* suggests that he had taken to heart the "liberal" beliefs espoused by the New York members during the writing of the Big Book, and had become leery of too much religiosity. For Wilson, the pietist aspects of midwestern AA of which members were most proud—their focus on surrendered masculinity, rigorous screening of prospects, proactive sponsorship, insistence on an orderly and early working of the Steps, and so on—still resulted in a "dose" that was "too rich" for many alcoholics. In a 1944 *Grapevine* editorial, he observed that "the Twelve Steps of our AA program are not crammed down anybody's throat. . . . The anarchy of the individual yields to their persuasion. He sobers up and is led, little by little, to complete agreement with our simple fundamentals" (*LOH*, 8). This gradualist attitude differed sharply from the midwestern stance, expressed unambiguously in *The Little Red Book*'s dictum that "members do not arrest alcoholism or gain recovery by merely agreeing with the principles of AA philosophy—*They Recover Only If They Live Them.*"[72] To Wilson's mind, the growing tension between these divergent stances risked the "garbling" of the AA message that he and Smith had tried to prevent by developing the Big Book in the first place.

His primary concern was that without the lifeline provided by a clear and coherent AA message, alcoholics might flounder and be lost, and despite his commitment to the anarchic spirit of AA, he believed the organization had a duty to its members—current and future—to maintain and control its essential principles.[73]

The 12 Traditions were Wilson's chief instrument for creating that control, but he also had a specific answer for the potential "chaotic state" he feared would arise from a too-extensive reading culture. The "standard literature" that Wilson had imagined appeared when the 1951 General Service Conference adopted "with complete unanimity" the concept of Conference Approved Literature (CAL)—texts that would be commissioned, authored, and vetted by a newly formed Trustees' Literature Committee within the General Service Conference.[74] Designed to reflect essential AA ideas and history, CAL would also enshrine the principle of the gift economy within the fellowship. Like the Big Book, it would be produced, sold, and distributed by the fellowship itself and priced very reasonably; all profits would flow back to the organization. Thus it would form a stable, unassailable center in what Wilson feared was fast becoming a consumer marketplace of AA and alcoholism literature.

Cognizant that the creation of an official and sanctioned literature might appear somewhat anti-democratic, when it created the category of CAL the General Service Conference carefully stated that it was not intended to "preclude the continued issuance of various printed documents by non-[Alcoholic] Foundation Sources. No desire to review, edit or censor non-Foundation material is implied. The objective is to provide, in the future, a means of *distinguishing* Foundation Literature from that issued locally or by non-AA interests."[75] The Literature Committee would oversee CAL, "review[ing] the material now being released by the General Service Office, to determine what type of material was needed by the Society and to suggest basic elements of policy for a national A.A. literature program."[76] The committee's 1954 policy statement emphasized that new texts would be created through a process intended to be democratic, inclusive, and responsive to the changing fellowship's needs. New publications, the committee explained, would be undertaken when there was

> a definite, expressed need for [them]. If the need is apparent, the general outlines are discussed with headquarters people who are in

touch with AA sentiment worldwide and with Bill. Then a draft is prepared and circulated to six to ten people, sometimes more. Their comments are discussed, analyzed and reconciled and a second draft is prepared. This draft is then circulated to the Trustees and to other AAs throughout the country. The comments and suggestions of these people, representing a reliable cross-section of AA, are incorporated into the final draft that goes to the printer. The important thing is that every effort is made to obtain and incorporate the widest possible range of AA thinking and experience in every item of literature. This is possible and practical only because Service Headquarters [the General Service Office] is literally both a storehouse and clearinghouse of total AA experience with direct access [to] changing currents in AA development throughout the world.[77]

As a result, rather than simply conveying "what someone thinks the movement wants or should be," CAL would be AA literature that reflected "what has actually been the sum total of our experience as a fellowship."[78] Such a centralized, collectively produced print culture, Wilson believed, would be essential to maintaining the alcoholic equalitarianism at the center of AA as the fellowship expanded around the world. In his vision of the "sum total of our experience," the religious rejections of the world that had provided the original foundations for AA sobriety would take their place alongside many other practices.

THE COSTS OF A CULTURE INDUSTRY

Before it became known as Alcoholics Anonymous, the group founded by Bill Wilson and Bob Smith elaborated itself through antimodern communicative modes, specifically the spoken word and the mystical transport of religious reading. Its investment in these practices is not surprising, given the first-century Christian ideals it inherited from the Oxford Group. Suspicion of the impersonality and distorting potential of the printed word and a marked preference for the presence and vitality of speech aligned neatly with the other principles that animated the Group's religious rejection of the world. Mystical communion with the divine facilitated by meditation over a limited canon of sacred texts, needless to say, was also in accord with that rejection.

As AA grew away from the Oxford Group, it evolved beyond these antique attitudes toward print—but it could not abandon them completely. The Big Book took on some of the talismanic properties of the

Bible; reading it became, for some at least, a central part of meditative or devotional practice, even if not a means of connecting directly with the voice of the divine. What had begun as a culture of religious reading became a more conventional culture of intensive reading—few texts, read repeatedly, but for the simple purposes of instruction and inspiration, rather than mystical transport. In the Midwest, this meant a focus on a limited canon that included locally produced literature, which formed the basis for what I have called "traditionalist" AA—pietist, voluntarist, and focused on surrender and service. Increasingly, as we shall see, the print forms through which those ideas circulated came to stand metonymically for the philosophy they expressed.

The New York headquarters of AA also championed a version of intensive reading and, like the traditionalists, its partisans believed that their print culture best served the needs of recovering alcoholics. By erasing individual authorship and the particularity of experience, Conference Approved Literature was uniquely positioned to maintain the universalism at AA's core and thus to carry the message of alcoholic equalitarianism most effectively. Furthermore, CAL made a virtue of necessity, turning the cash transaction involved in selling books and pamphlets to the laudable purpose of sustaining the gift economy.

Because it involved "individual" interpretations of AA and seemed to create a marketplace for competing visions of sobriety, the traditionalist print culture of the Midwest seemed to Wilson and to many members of the General Service Conference to pose a hazard to the future of the fellowship. Because it entailed centralization, revenue generation, and the codification of the language of the heart within public language and stylized genres, traditionalists took the opposing view and deemed CAL the hazard. At stake for each group of print producers was the idealized version of AA as embodied in the original meeting between Wilson and Smith—the moment in which seemingly unmediated language dissolved the barriers that the world erected between individuals and brought them into true proximity to one another and to the divine. The result was the development of two communications circuits, which sometimes overlapped with and sometimes were in tension with each other. These two print worlds remained unified, however, by their distance from the professionally produced literature of the emerging alcohol and drug industrial complex, the origins and intents of which are described in the next chapter.

CHAPTER FOUR

The "Feminization" of AA Culture

ill Wilson's plan to secure AA's financial and conceptual boundaries through the creation of Conference Approved Literature can only be described as a staggering success. Sales of the Big Book during the latter half of the twentieth century grew unceasingly—sometimes spectacularly—from year to year (see appendix B). The high volume of sales allowed the New York General Service Office (GSO) to keep the price of the Big Book low and, through the 1980s, to offer an additional price break on bulk sales of it and other Conference Approved Literature (CAL) to AA groups. Revenues from literature underwrote the substantial growth of the GSO, including a professional staff that wrote and edited the publications that would receive conference approval and then oversaw their distribution.

This professionalization did not mean, however, that AA transformed itself into a full-service publisher or book vendor. Title output remained quite small, thanks in part to the continuing bias within the fellowship in favor of intensive rather than extensive reading, and in part to the time-consuming collaborative authorship and editorial processes required to create CAL. Order fulfillment was also slow: in 1976 it took six weeks to receive materials ordered from the New York office.[1] The fairly small scale of the AA publishing enterprise, its relative awkwardness in book production and order fulfillment, and its continued exclusive focus on alcoholism even as diagnostic and treatment paradigms shifted toward the broader category of "substance abuse" during the 1970s and 1980s—all these contributed indirectly to the development in the 1980s of a larger for-profit recovery culture industry outside the bounds of established 12-Step organizations.

Several factors fed the development of what I call "therapeutic recovery culture." The first and most fundamental was the sheer growth of the addiction treatment industry. In 1963, Sidney Cahn had counted thirty states with specialized alcoholism wards in their hospitals (up from one in 1946) and 120 stand-alone alcoholism treatment facilities throughout the United States. By 1980, a National Institute for Alcohol

Abuse and Alcoholism survey found that the number of alcoholism treatment programs had grown to 4,219 (*SD*, 217, 266). As treatment options expanded and diversified, the population they served became more heterogeneous as well. Most obviously, drug addicts began to appear alongside alcoholics as candidates for treatment. But equally if not more important was the expansion of the disease concept of addiction to include women as well as men.

In AA's earliest days, lingering Victorian notions of gender difference had prompted skepticism among members as to whether women could indeed *be* alcoholics. Those same ideas (most notably the canard of women's "natural" purity and moral supremacy to men) had fed the belief that if women truly were chronic inebriates, they were such degenerates that even AA might not help them. Male AAs' skepticism about female alcoholics seems to have been fed by their wives. As William L. White points out, "the primary fear regarding the involvement of women in AA was of the potential disruptiveness of the sexual dynamic that might emerge" within meetings, a fear cleverly captured in the slogan "under every skirt is a slip." Marty Mann had worked hard to challenge these perceptions and successfully recruited Bill Wilson to her cause; Dr. Bob came around more slowly. Ultimately, however, an argument for gender inclusiveness on alcoholic equalitarian grounds, enhanced by exemplary long-term sobriety on the part of some female pioneers around the country, meant that women were gradually (if sometimes uneasily) absorbed into AA culture.

By 1955, 15 percent of AA members were women, and that percentage grew slowly but steadily through the next decades. In 1968, the year of AA's first formal membership survey, female members made up 22 percent of the total, and by the mid-1980s the figure had settled around the current level of 33 percent (*SD*, 158–61).[2] At the same time that AA was becoming more open to women, the feminist movement was bringing new frankness about women and addiction to clinicians in the helping professions, and federal money that targeted special populations for treatment further incentivized attention to women's addictions. Similar cultural and economic forces worked to overcome long-term and systematic neglect of minority alcoholics and drug addicts, male and female alike. By the 1980s, populations that had for decades stood at the margins of the addiction treatment world had come crowding into the center.

The women, minorities, and multiply-addicted people from all walks of life who flowed out of professional treatment and into AA brought the relative homogeneity of the early fellowship—and with it, some possible gaps in its theorizing of addiction and recovery—into stark relief. New interpretations of the three-part disease and its antidote began to ripple through the 12-Step world, and some of these caught the attention of authors and publishers who, not bound by the idea of alcoholic equalitarianism or the principles of the gift economy, became their eager promoters. By the mid-1980s, the sales potential of therapeutic recovery culture, with its hybrid blend of 12-Step ideas, identity politics, and psychological insights, had sparked a veritable "rage for recovery" that made headlines across the United States.[3]

The previous chapter treated the evolution of AA's spoken "language of the heart" into traditionalist and canonical print forms; this chapter maps that print culture's transition from a cottage industry into a multimillion dollar corporate enterprise. It traces a historical arc that begins in the mid-1950s, when a newly opened treatment center in Minnesota called Hazelden began to publish a popular devotional reader that AA had refused to designate as Conference Approved. Focusing on Hazelden's expanding literary offerings, I trace the development of a new recovery communications circuit rooted in the alcohol and drug industrial complex. This publishing tradition intersected in some places with those of the AA General Service Office and of midwestern AA traditionalists, but was largely independent of and sometimes in tension with them. That tension had to do with the mass production and marketing of 12-Step philosophy, but it was also, and more subtly, a response to the underlying issues of growth and diversity. As the last chapter detailed, the spread of AA ideals through printed matter had become an acceptable, even a proud practice during the fellowship's first twenty-five years. By the last decades of the twentieth century, however, there was a distinct suspicion among some AAs that the new, mass-marketed recovery print forms did not so much "carry the message" as distort and debase it. Their response was to create their own oppositional print culture to preserve what they saw as the true 12-Step message.

PUBLISHING *TWENTY-FOUR HOURS A DAY*

Ed W. and Barry C.'s *Little Red Book* was the first text on the surrendered life to receive wide circulation, but probably the most popular book espousing that ideal was Richmond Walker's daily devotional reader, *Twenty-four Hours a Day*. A wealthy industrialist from Boston,

Walker, like Bill Wilson and Dr. Bob Smith, had stopped drinking when he joined the Oxford Group—in his case, in 1939. Though his abstinence was haphazard until he committed himself to AA proper in 1942, Walker retained a great respect for the Group's teachings; he practiced Quiet Time reading and meditation with the Bible and the Group's daily reader, *God Calling*. Walker wintered in Daytona Beach, Florida, and while attending AA meetings there began to compile a series of index cards on which he transcribed notes, ideas, and biblical passages to inspire him in daily prayer. Other members of his group expressed interest in these writings, and in 1948 Walker compiled them into a small, self-published volume he called *Twenty-four Hours a Day*.

Walker's foreword credits the "universal spiritual thoughts expressed" in *God Calling* as "a basis for the meditations in this book," but his format follows the pattern of more traditional Protestant devotionals like Mrs. Charles Cowman's *Streams in the Desert* (1925) and Oswald Chambers's *My Utmost for His Highest* (1935), devoting a page to each day of the year, with a "Thought," "Meditation," and "Prayer" for each one. Rather than a quote from Scripture, each page begins with an "AA Thought for the Day," typically a set of rhetorical questions designed to emphasize the difference between the alcoholic past and the sober present. The question for 1 January is fairly typical: "When I came into AA, was I a desperate man? Did I have a soul-sickness? Was I so sick of myself and my way of living that I couldn't stand looking at myself in the mirror? . . . *Should I ever forget the condition I was in?*" (original emphasis). Walker's "Thoughts" do not shy away from details: entries frequently mention the financial and marital trouble brought on by alcoholism, as well as hangovers and blackouts, despair and self-loathing, and other "terrible things [that] could have happened to any of us."[4] These states are contrasted to the serenity offered by service and surrender within the AA fellowship.

AA historian Glenn Chesnut has argued that Walker's spirituality owed more to his experiences with Boston's Emmanuel Movement and its inheritor, the Jacoby Club, than to the Oxford Group, and there are flashes of the Emmanuel Movement's New Thought mysticism scattered throughout the text.[5] But for every reference to "the Divine Principle" (10 February) or "the spark of the divine within you" (1 June), there are several pages such as 18 September, which quotes (albeit without attribution) from Psalm 91 to remind readers that "He that dwelleth in the secret place of the Most High, shall abide under the shadow of the Almighty" and urge them to "Dwell for a moment each day in a secret place, the place of communion with God, apart from the world." Walker's text steers clear of any detailed theological discussion and avoids mention of Jesus Christ, sin, and eternal judgment. Its nominal "spirituality," however, is betrayed not only by regular paraphrases and quotes from the Bible, but also by its commitment to the pietist vision of surrendered masculinity that characterized midwestern AA. Like the authors of *The Little Red Book*, much of Walker's rhetorical energy goes to decrying the egotism that lies back of alcoholism and of weak sobriety alike, and he urges meticulous attention to working the Steps—particularly the 12th Step—and to making an ongoing, full-hearted surrender to God.[6]

Walker had been powerfully influenced by Frank Buchman's "anti-materialism," and he developed the AA critique of consumerism more fully than the midwestern authors, drawing heavily on Christian writings to warn his readers against the dangers posed by their continued loyalty to worldly values. Alluding to an image from St. Augustine's *City of God*, the page for 28 January asks, "Do the world's awards bring heart-rest and happiness? Or do they turn to ashes in the mouth?"[7] On 15 May readers are warned that they "cannot serve God and Mammon at the same time," and, quoting Matthew 6:33, Walker instructs them instead to "seek ye first the Kingdom of God and His righteousness and all these things shall be added unto you." The same page invokes the Four Absolutes of the Oxford Group to remind readers that "the first requisites of an abundant life are the spiritual things: honesty, purity, unselfishness, and love. Until you have these qualities, quantities of material things are of little real use to you." The fellowship and peace of mind available in AA, Walker argues, more than make up for material rewards hard won in the competitive world. "Instead of those doubts and fears" that inevitably accompany the competitive life of self-will, "there will flow into our hearts such faith and love as is beyond the power of material things to give, and such peace as the world can neither give nor take away" (8 October). His writings on the threat that seductive consumerism poses to sobriety make vivid and concrete many ideas that the Big Book had touched on only in passing. The sentiment found in the Prayer for the Day for 3 July—"I pray that I may not be held back by the material things of the world"—echoes and reechoes throughout his volume.

Given Walker's deep-seated anti-materialism, the fact that *Twenty-four Hours* played a decisive role in the commodification of 12-Step culture is ironic to say the least. Under the imprimatur of "A Member of the Group at Daytona Beach, Florida," Walker sold his self-published editions via mail order for several years and donated the proceeds to his local group. By 1953, the book had sold out a third printing of 14,000 copies, and Walker was receiving more than 600 orders a month. Unable to keep up with demand, and eager to support the larger work of the New York GSO, Walker wrote to secretary Helen B. "to say that I would be glad to turn over the publishing rights of this book to Alcoholics Anonymous Publishing, Inc."[8] He was eager to make this gift—eager to the point that some pre-sobriety self-will seems to have welled up within him. As orders for *Twenty-four Hours* came in over the next year, he regretfully informed customers that the book was currently out of stock, and suggested that "if you think it would be a good idea to have this book published by the AA Publishing Company, so that all profits would go to the Alcoholic Foundation, we would appreciate your writing [Helen B.] and expressing your approval." In this way, he explained, "you would be assured of a good supply of these books at all times."[9] The GSO received seventy-two such letters, some petition-style, bearing multiple signatures, and many of them explaining that Walker had instructed them to write. LeRoy R. spoke for many when he noted that "I am writing you in regards to a letter that was received from *Twenty-four Hours a Day* [which] stated that they would like for us to write to you pertaining to the publication of these books by the AA publishing company."[10]

Despite this show of popular support, at the 1954 meeting the General Service Conference declined to adopt Walker's book as a piece of Conference Approved Literature. As Glenn Chesnut has pointed out, the Trustees' Literature Committee was deep into the preparation of *The Twelve Steps and Twelve Traditions* and the second edition of the Big Book, and had scant energy remaining to take on new publishing projects.[11] This logistical concern was reflected in the conference report dealing with Walker's suggestion; his offer was rebuffed on the grounds that the GSO might be "flooded with similar requests."[12] An additional sticking point, however, was the book's explicit religiosity. Although the conference report of 1954 did not comment on this issue, Walker apparently received a personal letter stating as much. In an angry response to the chair of the Literature Committee, he expressed his indignation at New York's squeamish secularism. Throwing the committee's language back in its face, he scoffed at the notion that the book's "*religious overtones*" might provoke "*misinterpretation and misunderstanding*," of AA's ecumenism, arguing that "there is no mention of religion in the whole book, for instance, the word 'Christ' or 'Jesus' is never mentioned, nor is it ever advised that we go to *church*. Where then, is the *religion*?" To him, the book's injunctions to prayer and surrender and its quotations from and allusions to the Christian Bible indicated only that "we have a spiritual program—why try to deny it?"[13] For Walker, as for other AA traditionalists, the GSO's denial of the importance of surrender before God was akin to the individual alcoholic's denial of alcoholism, and it could not be reconciled with what *The Little Red Book* and midwestern pamphlet literature described as the "AA Way of Life." The refusal of the conference to absorb *Twenty-four Hours a Day* into the canon of Conference Approved Literature confirmed the worst suspicions many traditionalist AAs harbored about the direction of the fellowship as a whole.

Help appeared from an unexpected quarter, however. Less than two weeks after Walker received the bad news from New York, Pat Butler, president of the Hazelden treatment center outside Minneapolis, informed him that his organization was eager to pick up the publication and distribution of *Twenty-four Hours*.[14] Walker readily agreed. Both the goodwill and the revenue stream that Walker had wished to bequeath to AA redounded instead to Hazelden: a first printing of 5,000 copies sold out within a year, and annual sales steadily climbed. By 1959, 80,000 copies had been sold—which meant, AA historian Glenn Chesnut has argued, that almost half the total membership of AA owned a copy. In the next ten years, sales surged to over half a million; by 1990 they would reach 7 million.[15] What AAs sometimes call the Little Black Book turned out to have very big implications for the world of 12-Step print culture.

"ORTHODOXY" AT HAZELDEN

Hazelden began in 1949 as a "sanatorium for curable alcoholics of the professional class," founded and administered by a group of wealthy businessmen and industrialists who had tried AA after a variety of failed attempts to get sober.[16] From the outset, Hazelden was strongly committed to AA's version of the disease concept and the antidote of surrender: it treated alcoholism as a primary, progressive illness, and advocated a cure that addressed body, mind, and spirit, with an emphasis on the latter. Though it had a strong collaborative relationship with the state psychiatric hospital in Willmar, up until the early 1960s the Hazelden treatment protocol, stated simply, was "intense indoctrination into the AA program" (*SD*, 202). A physician oversaw acute detoxification and provided shots of vitamin B12, but recovering alcoholics handled almost all other aspects of patient care, providing lectures on the Steps and Traditions, running AA meetings, and arranging structured work and recreation. There was no "counseling"; instead the program stressed the rigorous AA fellowship common in the Midwest—early and heartfelt surrender to a Higher Power along with the mutual support to be found in "one alcoholic talking to another over a cup of coffee." The aim of the three-week program was simple: "to implant the AA program and process: abstinence, attendance at AA meetings . . . and familiarity (intimacy) with the Big Book of Alcoholics Anonymous."[17]

When the alcoholism treatment industry began to evolve rapidly in the 1960s, Hazelden changed along with it. Increasingly, attention was paid to dual addictions and "comorbidity" (alcoholism in conjunction with mental illness), gradually moving toward understanding alcoholism within a broad spectrum of "chemical dependencies."[18] The average daily census increased to between forty and fifty patients; the total annual patient population more than doubled between 1960 and 1964 (*SD*, 207). Women, who had been welcomed at a single-sex complex thirty miles away since 1956, arrived on Hazleden's main grounds in 1966. The Fellowship Club, a halfway house in St. Paul for "any man who was homeless, penniless, and friendless because of alcoholism," had tripled in capacity since its opening in 1953; counselors working there saw an increasingly diverse population of alcoholics and addicts.[19] The bulk of Hazelden's activities were still concentrated in its Rehabilitation Division, where the work of sobering up alcoholics and other addicts took place. But it also embarked on an educational mission, establishing in 1965 a Pastoral Training Program that instructed clergy in how to recognize and support alcoholics and addicts; a more broad-based Counselor Training Program followed in 1966 (*SD*, 208).

In response to these changes, the focus of Hazelden's treatment regimen shifted from what William L. White calls a "pure AA" orientation to a "multidisciplinary" one, which drew on the insights of "physicians, nurses, psychologists, social workers, and clergy" as well as "counselors who were recovered alcoholics." President Pat Butler, who had acquired Walker's *Twenty-four Hours a Day* in 1954, had sobered up at Hazelden in 1950; his brother Lawrence had been the first patient when the facility opened the previous year. Butler's successor, however, was not another recovering alcoholic but a psychologist: Dan Anderson, who became vice-president and CEO in 1961, had worked at the Willmar State Hospital since 1950 and been a part-time lecturer at Hazelden since 1957. Anderson appreciated the different ways that "the knowledge of science [and] the knowledge of wisdom and experience" approached addiction, and believed the best treatment "mesh[es] these two kinds of knowing together." Seeking this "dynamic integration" in the treatment of the three-part disease, in the mid-1960s Hazelden began ceding a larger role in patient care to psychiatrists, psychologists, and social workers (SD, 202, 204).

The expansion and enrichment of its treatment protocols served Hazelden well. By 1970, 11,000 patients had been admitted at the Center City facility, and more had been treated at what had become a handful of satellite programs established in nearby St. Paul.[20] The multidisciplinary "Minnesota Model," with its attention to organic, psychosocial, and spiritual causes and manifestations of addiction, was becoming the norm within the industry, and treatment professionals flocked to Hazelden to study its workings like "pilgrim[s] going to Mecca" (SD, 211). The stated mission throughout this period remained "How can we best help the most alcoholics?"[21] Nevertheless, during the 1960s several longtime members of AA who had formed the backbone of the rehabilitation staff departed in disgust, "disillusioned at what they considered the betrayal . . . and the abandonment of AA principles on behalf of psychology." Those that remained redoubled their commitment to Hazelden's version of AA tradition. This tension between what AA historian Damian McElrath calls "orthodox versus unorthodox philosophy"—between individuals committed to a simple, personal, and AA-based approach to addiction treatment and those invested in a dynamic, multifaceted, and expansive approach—would ultimately reshape Hazelden's literary culture.[22]

When it took over the distribution of Walker's *Twenty-four Hours a Day* in 1954, Hazelden had already established a presence for itself in the world of 12-Step print culture. Like other midwestern AAs, Hazelden counselors saw reading and study as key parts of recovery and had worked from the beginning to make the Big Book and related literature available not only to their clients but to any recovering people who needed them. During its first half-dozen years, Hazelden published only promotional materials—a pictorial brochure describing the facility and its services, and a short pamphlet aimed at potential donors titled *Inspiration for Recovery*.[23] But it nevertheless served as an important distributor of 12-Step literature, purchasing books and pamphlets in quantity from the AA GSO and reselling them—at a small mark-up and in plain unmarked wrappers—via direct mail. Unlike the understaffed

GSO, Hazelden enjoyed a manpower surplus in the form of patients on work details, and as a result could provide good customer service—turnaround time on literature orders was typically under a week.[24]

Pat Butler's interest in *Twenty-four Hours a Day* stemmed primarily from his belief in the efficacy of Walker's book. But Butler was also pragmatic; in the mid-1950s, alcoholism treatment was not a particularly lucrative business, and he "thought we could make some money selling a few books."[25] As the sales figures above demonstrate, his instincts were not wrong. As the Alcoholism Movement and AA grew in size and legitimacy during the immediate postwar period, sales of *Twenty-four Hours* increased along with them. The professionalization that had occurred in Hazelden's Rehabilitation Division in the early 1960s rippled through other parts of the organization a few years later; in 1967 the Publishing and Distributing Department was formally incorporated under the Business Division of the center and began to produce original titles.[26] At the outset, these were primarily books and pamphlets that supported the education and counselor training programs and made Hazelden's multidisciplinary approach known to the rapidly expanding addiction treatment industry: urban social and public health workers, trainees in counseling programs, and educators and counselors in schools, correctional facilities, and the workplace. But the inventory of literature for recovering people grew as well during the 1960s and 1970s. By 1969, the catalog offered not only AA Conference Approved Literature, but also the sobriety aids of Ed W. and Barry C. and "Father John Doe"; recovery testimonials by figures like humorist Lewis Meyer and the pseudonymous baseball player Jerry Gray; reprints of nineteenth-century inspirational literature by the likes of Mary Wilder Tileston and William George Jordan; and the works of humanist psychologists Erich Fromm and Paul Tournier.[27] Between 1972 and 1974, the publishing staff jumped from three people to eighteen; it spun off into its own division—known as Educational Materials—in 1975.[28] In that year the catalog—which had been in 1969 a mere three-page folded leaflet offering thirty-three books and fifty-nine pamphlets for sale—ballooned into an illustrated fifty-page booklet, offering hundreds of print and audio titles, not only for addicts and treatment professionals but also for family members affected by addiction.[29]

These changes to Hazelden's literary offerings mirrored shifts in its rehabilitation regime; McElrath describes AA as "alive but not well" within the treatment center at this time. Increasingly, it seemed, "using the Big Book during treatment and referrals to AA as the essential part of an aftercare plan" took a back seat to new therapeutic insights.[30] As a result, the stalwarts of AA "orthodoxy" who remained on the staff and on the board grew more concerned about what they perceived as a drift away from what the 5th Tradition described as AA's "primary purpose." Their unhappiness manifested itself in anxiety about literary production, and in 1972 a Literature Advisory Committee was founded to oversee the production and procurement of new titles and ensure that they adhered to the spirit, if not to the letter, of 12-Step philosophy. Sympathetic old-timers employed throughout the publishing and distribution operation worked to ensure compliance with the Literature Advisory Committee, and their opinions carried great weight. One such individual, production manager Jack V., was described by a colleague as having "almost more power than the Executive Vice-President for Publishing."[31]

A combination of formal and informal mechanisms, then, ensured that Hazelden publications, especially those aimed at treatment professionals, did not stray too far from 12-Step philosophy. Writings on anything other than alcohol or drug addictions were frowned upon, as were "Norman Vincent Peale–type [texts] and 'power within' thinkers," whose books were deemed "unsuitable" for recovering addicts.[32] Books intended for recovering people, furthermore, were uniformly designed to reflect the values of traditionalist AA culture. They were "to resemble prayer books, to be able to be hidden in a pocket, and to be cheap."[33]

The fragile balance of power between those committed to a "pure AA" Hazelden and those with a more expansive, multidimensional, and professionalized vision of the institution shifted in the late 1970s with the rise to prominence of Harry Swift. Although Swift (like Dan Anderson, who had recruited him) was an outsider to 12-Step culture, he was a strong proponent of it and believed that the approach to addiction articulated in AA could be applied with good effect—and a few modifications—to all manner of behavioral and health problems. Trained as a social worker with expertise in family therapy, he had joined the staff at Willmar State Hospital in 1961 before coming to Hazelden in 1966 to become the Supervisor of Social Work. At Hazelden he established the Family Program—first as a lecture, and then as a three-day (1972) and finally a seven-day residential experience—and trained other staff members as facilitators in it. He became the "Administrator"—chief operations officer—in 1976 and president in 1986.[34]

A firm believer in the use of books and reading in addiction treatment,

Swift moved early in his tenure as COO to secure Big Book reading's central place within Hazelden's treatment regimes.[35] But his allegiance to the Big Book did not necessarily make him a proponent of AA's ideal of intensive and "religious" reading. From his position as COO, Swift had a bird's-eye view of the entire Hazelden operation, and he saw the new Educational Materials Division as a key area for growth. "Bibliotherapy" was not yet widespread in the addiction treatment industry, but Swift believed Hazelden's counselor training program could make it happen. "Professionals generally lack understanding of the therapeutic literature and the concepts of Alcoholics Anonymous," he wrote in "Program Management: AA and Bibliotherapy," a pamphlet addressed to addiction treatment professionals. But observing AA at work, and seeing the important role that the Big Book played in its members lives, had led him to an increased appreciation for the role that reading could play in addiction treatment. "Therapeutic reading material," Swift argued, "can be particularly helpful to persons experiencing shame, guilt, anger, and resentment. It provides individuals with a framework for understanding what is happening in their own lives and for finding some solutions to their problems." He urged clinicians to overcome their own ignorance about literature's potential as a therapeutic tool and to recognize that reading materials "should be 'prescribed' in a predetermined manner as part of an individual's overall treatment plan to help a specific situation or condition."[36] Equally important, he set about crafting a literature that addressed those "specifics."

Swift made several new hires in Educational Materials in the late 1970s, including, in 1979, a recent Ph.D. from the University of Minnesota's American Studies program named Karen Casey. While she had no experience in publishing, Casey had joined the 12-Step world as a member of Al-Anon in 1975 and achieved sobriety in AA in 1976. At Minnesota she had written a dissertation about representations of Native American womanhood, and she had been an active, though not militant, member of the progressive campus culture, campaigning for Eugene McCarthy, protesting the Vietnam War, and participating in feminist consciousness-raising sessions and support groups.[37] At the same time that she joined the 12-Step world, Casey had also become an active member of the Unity School of Christianity, a New Thought religion founded in 1889 by Charles and Myrtle Fillmore. Like Swift, Casey was both a firm believer in 12-Step philosophy and a maverick willing to break with some of its traditions. As a young, outspoken woman from a decidedly nontraditional spiritual and political background, she would pose a substantial challenge to Hazelden's lingering AA "orthodoxy."

Casey's first major accomplishment as managing editor of the Educational Materials Division was to bring out *Food for Thought*, a daily meditation book for addictive eaters. The author, "Elisabeth L.," was a member of Overeaters Anonymous; she had grown accustomed to using Walker's *Twenty-four Hours a Day* for her daily devotional reading and just "substituting the word 'food' for the word 'alcohol.' "[38] When that failed to satisfy, she began composing short meditative pieces for her own use; at the urging of friends, she submitted the collection to Hazelden for publication in 1978. The Literature Advisory Committee, however, deemed addictive eating outside the purview of Hazelden's expertise and the project was scuttled. But the manuscript was still rattling around the office when Casey arrived a year later, and it immediately caught her attention because she "knew so many women in AA who struggled with food issues." With a little "arm-twisting," she convinced Harry Swift of the project's virtues; Swift in turn used the somewhat tenuous argument that "people in recovery often become obese" to convince the board that the project meshed with Hazelden's mission.[39] Somewhat reluctantly, the Literature Advisory Committee endorsed the project, and *Food for Thought* appeared in 1980. Casey's instincts about the market for it proved right, and 33,000 copies were sold the first year.[40]

To dispel a persistent loneliness and "feeling of internal dis-ease" that had marked her first years at Hazelden, Casey began writing herself. Her meditations were, initially, a "personal pursuit—a journey" and a kind of spiritual practice; she used the act of writing to draw herself closer to a Higher Power from whom she frequently felt distant. The gender assumptions that colored AA literature were one of the causes of that distance, as Casey found herself increasingly frustrated by the masculinism of the AA literature and culture around her. A Conference Approved pamphlet, "AA for the Woman" (1952, revised 1967), and a reprint of Mary Wilder Tileston's 1884 devotional reader *Daily Strength for Daily Needs* were the only two items in the Hazelden catalog that addressed women specifically.

A new edition of *Twenty-four Hours a Day* had appeared in 1975, lightly revised to be somewhat more gender-inclusive: pages that had previously addressed men specifically were made gender neutral or edited to acknowledge women. The Meditation for the Day of 15 February, for example, had been amended from "the world doesn't need supermen, but super-natural men" to "the world doesn't need super men or women, but super-natural people."[41] Casey found the new edition of Walker's book "helpful in some ways" but still limited; the God it referenced remained, in her mind, "distant, stern, and male." By contrast, "God to me was more than anything a feeling, a presence around me, something to tap into—always accessible, not judgmental; a guide—a 'great spirit' available to us, watching over us, always ready to be turned to. . . . I felt like as women we needed a Higher Power who was not 'Him'—I didn't want any 'Hims' in my book. I had been influenced by the reference to God as 'He'—in my mind there was always a red line through 'He.' " What she intended as a private set of meditations was written in response to that "red line."

Harry Swift urged Casey to publish her writings, arguing that there were likely others who shared her feelings and that Hazelden had a mission to reach out to them; ultimately he convinced her, and she presented the Literature Advisory Committee with a book modeled on *Twenty-four Hours a Day* but addressed explicitly and exclusively to women. Despite Swift's outspoken enthusiasm, the committee's initial response was tepid, with the "orthodox" faction objecting that its gendered focus disrupted the principles of alcoholic equalitarianism on which AA and, by extension, Hazelden rested. CompCare, a chain of for-profit treatment facilities founded in 1969, had been publishing books and pamphlets for niche markets for half a dozen years, but such specialty marketing was not the Hazelden way.[42] "Other than Harry," recalls Casey, the people "in charge of Hazelden didn't feel a need for women's literature. An alcoholic was an alcoholic was an alcoholic—women didn't need a book just for themselves. The general attitude was that there are no differences between us [and] we should not have specific reading materials—it's a kind of exclusion." Production manager Jack V.'s response emblematized this position: "An AA book for women?! Who's going to buy that crap?" he scoffed before storming out of an editorial board meeting. Casey ultimately gathered twenty-five positive external reviews before the committee okayed her project, and even then it took "Swift's *order* to go ahead with the book" to bring the volume titled *Each Day a New Beginning* to publication.[43]

"MEN FIRST, THEN . . . ALCOHOL AND DRUGS"

Like Richmond Walker before her, Casey wrote first and foremost for personal reasons—to deepen and enhance her own spiritual practice.

Only at Harry Swift's urging did she come to see her work as offering similar opportunities for spiritual growth to other women. Despite this avowed personalism, and the fact that her work did not explicitly aim to disrupt the systems of power and privilege that disadvantage women, *Each Day*'s treatment of women's addiction drew on the intellectual and philosophical traditions of Second Wave feminism. Although Casey worked apart from the self-consciously feminist communities discussed in chapter 5, her volume nevertheless moves deliberately to bring women's voices, experiences, and perspectives into a mainstream that had long treated them as marginal.

To acknowledge the feminist dimension of Casey's work, however, is not to say that *Each Day a New Beginning* rejects the precepts of the surrendered life. Quite the opposite: the anonymous epigraph for 1 January makes plain the text's indebtedness to the mystical sense of abjection at the heart of traditionalist midwestern AA: "We don't always understand the ways of Almighty God—the crosses sent us, the sacrifices demanded. . . . But we accept with faith and resignation the holy will with no looking back, and we are at peace."[44] Affirmations of the pleasures of serenity and the human right to happiness abound in Casey's writing, but the vision of life that emerges from the text is in many ways more ascetic—more attuned to the nature and purpose of pain and suffering—than those of Ed W. and Richmond Walker. The page for 20 January notes that "life is enriched by pain," while 24 February explains that "when the anguish is present . . . it is making our spirits whole." On 26 April readers are reminded that "pain is our common denominator as women," and similar sentiments recur throughout the text: "The blows [we encounter] teach us; they are the lessons the inner self has requested" (23 May); "Pain enriches us, prepares us better to serve others. . . . My pain today is bringing me closer to the woman I'm meant to be" (8 November); and so on. This heightened awareness of pain's presence makes the sense of surrender at the center of recovery all the more important.

In addition, *Each Day* preserves intact the anti-intellectualism of earlier AA writings, warning that questioning and protesting the conditions of daily life can too easily become unhealthy exercises of self-will. Like *The Little Red Book*, *Each Day* cautions against the seductions of intellectualism: "Too much thinking [and] incessant analyzing," explains the page for 22 December, "will keep any problem a problem." And 1 May warns that "unless we have faith in a power greater than ourselves . . . we'll 'understand' ourselves in the same ways. We might even use our 'insight' to keep ourselves stuck—to protect ourselves from the risk of change." Just like the midcentury pamphleteers, Casey impresses upon her readers that the psychic activities most appropriate to the surrendered self are acceptance of God's will and gratitude for the ability to know it and carry it out; these are also the only certain paths to sobriety and happiness. Acceptance does not necessarily mean quiescence; the page for 27 August notes that "passive compliance with whatever is occurring need no longer dominate our patterns of behavior." But at the same time, readers are reminded that "fighting an obstacle [or] pushing against a closed door will only heighten our frustration. *Acceptance of what is* will open our minds and our hearts" (16 April; original emphasis). The tangible reward for this letting go, as the page for 20 August makes clear, is serenity and peace of mind: "As we all change into more accepting women, life's struggles ease. When we accept all the circumstances that we can't control, we are more peaceful. Smiles more easily fill us up."

Despite the text's fealty to the deep structures of AA philosophy and its ongoing invocation of AA's Steps, slogans, and fellowship, *Each Day* departs from the principles laid out in both traditionalist and Conference Approved Literature in a number of striking ways—ways related, though not reducible to, men's and women's different experiences of addiction. Casey shares with many avowedly feminist therapists the belief that both the diagnosis of "self-will run riot" and the remedy of the surrendered life are only partially relevant to women.[45] This attention to the social dimensions of the "disease of body, mind, and spirit" entailed crucial revisions to both the disease concept and the accompanying notion of cure.

Casey's most obvious innovation in this regard was to roll back one of the central premises of the disease concept: the idea of alcoholism as a disease unto itself. Instead, she offered—on the book's first page—an explanation of addiction as a by-product of low self-esteem: "For years," she confesses, "I struggled to believe in my worth, my capabilities, my strength." Her lack of a sense of autonomous personhood led her to unhealthy dependence—but a dependence quite different from that typically featured in AA literature. "Because I didn't understand the source of all strength and goodness," she explains, "I turned to men first and then to alcohol and drugs." This radical rewriting of the etiology of addiction bears the traces not only of contemporary humanist psychology, but also of Second Wave feminist consciousness-raising, which focused on understanding the destructive consequences that internalizing patriarchal attitudes had on women.[46] Acknowledging the degree to which society constructs an impossible ideal of femininity and punishes women who fail to live up to it is a central project of *Each Day a New Beginning*. While the book never strays far enough from a traditional AA orientation to suggest that women become addicts because of patriarchy (an argument made by feminist recovery activists like Jean Swallow, whose work is discussed in the next chapter), it nevertheless decisively situates women's addictions within a nexus of social relations shaped by gender and, by implication, by an unequal distribution of power.

Thus Casey argues (albeit indirectly) that contrary to Bill Wilson's original formulations of alcoholic selfhood, it is not an inflated sense of self but its opposite—self-doubt, insecurity, passivity, or what clinicians call "poor ego strength"—that drives women to drink. Contrary to what many feminist critics of recovery have argued, Casey does not treat these psychic characteristics as inherent pathologies. Instead, *Each Day* suggests that hegemonic, heteronormative, mainstream American culture encourages passivity and deference in women, which primes them for addiction. The page for 12 January notes that "most of us were encouraged from childhood on to 'find a husband' [which] keeps us from making those choices tailored to who we are and who we want to be." Similarly, on 31 March: "Most of us were told when we were small girls that we shouldn't be angry," leading to emotional alienation. Instead of developing autonomy and agency, women are taught to aspire to physical attractiveness, and become trapped in the competition and dependence beauty standards create: "Rare is the woman who doesn't long for a svelte body, firm breasts, pretty teeth, a smooth complexion. Rare is the woman who feels content . . . with her total person" (22 March). Encouraged by the most important cultural institutions around them—family, media, peer culture—women identify against their own best interests, stunting their capacity to make informed and intelligent decisions about the deployment of their psychic resources and leaving themselves vulnerable to addiction as a result.

The book's vision of recovery as well as of addiction is tinged by gender-consciousness, with pages asserting that "recovery is choosing to . . . understand our equality as women" (18 January) and "recovery means to learn who we are independent of friends, children, parents, or intimate partners" (23 January). Developing a sense of personhood separate from the identities imputed to women by men and by patriarchal society—one of the central goals of consciousness-raising—is also one of the aims of recovery as Casey depicts it. The page for 23 October draws attention to "how burdened we became, as little girls, with the labels applied by parents, teachers, even school chums" before it notes triumphantly that "our own thoughts and words, our own labels can become as powerful as those in our youth." With this goal of heightened autonomy in mind, entries acknowledge and encourage women's lives outside the home; they assume that women work or attend school, or that they want to do so. In addition, *Each Day* celebrates a newfound sense of female community. In life before recovery, Casey notes in her introduction, "I had been leery of women, assuming they were after my boyfriends, husbands, and lovers. I was always quite certain that women were not to be trusted." This theme of intra-gender competition and distrust is reiterated throughout the book: "We had a friend . . . but could she really be trusted—with our secrets, with our spouse?" (14 February); "We may have secretly hated other women's strengths be-cause we felt inferior" (22 April); and so on. In 12-Step meetings, how-ever, "hearing how much alike we all are eased my anxieties [and] of-fered me the opportunity to love women as sisters" (introduction), and the new perspective offered by recovery allows for the recognition that "other women share our struggle. When we treat our women friends as sisters and fellow pilgrims, we find great joy in our mutual help" (3 December).

Casey's loyalty to the central assumptions of 12-Step philosophy—specifically a humanist conception of the self and the belief, inscribed in Tradition 10, that politics is an "outside issue" not to be addressed within the fellowship—meant that while she acknowledged the struc-tured gender inequalities that affect women's lives, she did not advo-cate for change of those structures. This lack of interest in systemic oppression and a critique of power puts her at odds with activist femi-nism. But her work nevertheless contains a recognizable and explicit critique of the gendered power structures that shape Western culture—a critique insufficient, perhaps, to satisfy more ardent radical or aca-demic feminists, but one that was plenty unsettling to some of Hazel-den's older AA stalwarts.

Their anxiety levels were arguably ratcheted up even further by *Each Day's* reconceptualization of the Higher Power at the center of the 12 Steps. As previously noted, AA literature had from its inception made nodding acknowledgment of non-Christian traditions. But just as its literature had assumed a male audience up to the point at which Casey wrote, AA's default spirituality had been pietist and Protestant, the presence of Catholic members and the New Thought sympathies of the cofounders notwithstanding. Neither Conference Approved nor amateur AA literature had ever depicted a wrathful or judgmental God, but they shared a commitment to a Higher Power that was literally "Higher," located *above* His charges—both cosmologically and noumenologically: God's "creative energy and sense, intelligence and power," *The Little Red Book* noted, "ma[d]e man most insignificant by comparison."[47] Casey's writings, however, looked to dismantle that hierarchy.

Rather than merely acknowledging possible alternatives to a traditional Christian God as her male precursors had, Casey wrote from within one of those alternatives. Her thinking was influenced in part by her graduate study of Native American spiritual traditions. Prior to writing her dissertation, "Portrayal of American Indian Women in a Select Group of American Novels," Casey (like Bill Wilson) had suffered from the "misconception that no 'true intellectual' could possibly believe in a Godly universe." But her study of "[Nez Perce Chief] Joseph and his band of Dreamers" had made her aware that a spiritual belief system could be a source of solace and strength, a force that "foster[ed] both confidence and serenity amidst the turmoil and devastation of oppression." In the introduction to her dissertation she expressed her hope that "non-Indians [will] adopt the spiritual ideas I had come to value and accept."[48]

Casey's study of Native American religions coincided with her entrance into the Unity Church, and the influence of Unity theology is also evident in *Each Day*. An offshoot of Emma Curtis Hopkins's Christian Science Association, Unity has long been one of the largest and most widely accepted New Thought denominations. Its theology and its institutional history are complex, and worthy of longer discussion than I can afford them here. For my purposes, it is sufficient to note that, like many New Thought sects, Unity espouses an idealist cosmology marked by a strong commitment to the idea of the divine within.[49] Although it retains a deeper connection than many other New Thought religions to what cofounder Charles Fillmore called "the Jesus Christ teachings," it eschews conventional notions of sin, the Fall, and the resurrection, believes in "healing by the Christ method . . . [and] affirms the availability of substance, prosperity, and well-being" to all.[50] Unity's devotional practice centers on "affirmation and denial as major techniques" for focusing the spirit. In addition, the sect advocates a distinctive idea of God as simultaneously male and female. Its literature typically uses the term "man" to stand for "human," but the theological center of the creed is what Charles Fillmore called an "Almighty Father-Mother," a God that contained both "the universal Mind principle, which Jesus called the Father [and] a substance that includes the mother or seed of all visible substance."[51]

A version of Unity's in-dwelling "Father-Mother God" is present in the Higher Power that *Each Day* addresses. The page for 8 October notes frankly that "for many of us, invoking God with a male pronoun put an obstacle in the path of our spiritual growth," and stresses the need to move past that impediment. To do so, readers are urged to "pray to a spiritual source that includes everything . . . both sexes, all races, all ages and conditions." To keep the sense of spirituality truly open, Casey avoids ever denominating God with a gendered pronoun, and uses the terms "Great Spirit" and "Creator Spirit" interchangeably with "God" and "Higher Power."

This resistance to a traditionally gendered God set *Each Day* apart from the AA literature that preceded it, but it is possible that the book would not have met the traditionalist resistance it did had Casey's idea of God not also implied changes to other crucial aspects of the 12-Step program. Unity's name derives from its theological idealism—the belief that all beings at all times are part and parcel of the divine; the most important practical manifestation of this belief in *Each Day* is the commitment to the divine within. While assertions like 30 July's "God's presence is within us now and always even though we feel alone," were not on their faces different from the traditional Christian teaching that "the kingdom of God is within you" (Luke 17:21), the degree to which Casey emphasized the oneness of divine and human changed the nature of Step 11's "conscious contact with God." Rather than a supplication of an external and omniscient force, as in Oxford Group tradition, "prayer and meditation" now became a conscious turning inward to the deepest structures of the self. With near relentless intensity, *Each Day* asserted the need to "trust our inner yearnings" (13 February), "let the inner guide direct our behavior" (18 February), and listen to "this special 'inner voice'" (11 August). Step 11's mandate to seek "through prayer and meditation . . . God's will for us" and "the power to carry it out" was transformed into a commitment to "slowing down, going within to our center, listening to the message therein" (17 July).

More than the somewhat recondite concept of the "Father-Mother God," Unity's divine within addressed what Casey believed were the hitherto unaddressed specifics of women's addiction. Affirmations like "recognizing our partnership with our higher power . . . removes all uncertainty about our value to this world" (23 May) and "our actions and decisions are never wrong . . . the design of our lives will pull us back on the track" (14 September) served to recast the divine as a collaborative, nonthreatening, nonjudgmental force. Equally important, they worked to shore up the low self-esteem that lay back of women's addictive and compulsive behavior. For women who had turned "to men first and then to alcohol and drugs," Unity's conception of God, as a web of loving energy within which they and their loved ones were always and irrevocably bound up, offered an appealing alternative to interpersonal dependence, fear, and anger. What Casey called the "gentle and all-encompassing" God of Unity would offer women whose egos had been crushed in destructive relationships—relationships too often sanctioned by patriarchy—an opportunity for meaningful self-love, which in turn would relieve them of the compulsions of addiction.

In a variety of ways, then, Casey's attention to gender challenged some of the fundamental premises of 12-Step philosophy. Although *Each Day* affirmed the importance of alcoholic equalitarianism (e.g., 20 June: "Realizing how much we are like others gives us strength"; 26 August: "Introspection . . . affords us the awareness of how like others we are. How human we are"), the very existence of what Jack V. had called "an AA book for women" suggested that there were limits to the like-ness of alcoholics—an insight being echoed in the professional treatment culture by increased attention to the psychosocial dimensions of addiction and by funding structures that targeted "special populations." In a more roundabout but ultimately more pointed fashion, attention to gender difference also changed the spirituality on offer in *Each Day*. Casey's book removed the traditional masculine God of pietistic Protestantism from the center of AA spiritual practice, and gave voice to the more fluid and mystical divinity of metaphysical religious tradition—a version of the Higher Power that had always been present in AA but had remained largely latent. To compound this heresy, Casey made it clear that the embrace of this Higher Power was prompted by a frankly psychological insight: God could remedy low self-esteem. Finally, by celebrating and endorsing Unity's vision of the divine within, which assumed the oneness of humanity and God, *Each Day* refocused the process of recovery so that the self (albeit a self that was by definition a manifestation of something far larger) was at the center of the cosmos, effectively inverting the critique of self-will and self-centeredness first made in the Big Book and then elaborated in midwestern traditionalist literature. Even an abundant language of abjection and pain could not compensate for the radically revised view of recovery offered by *Each Day a New Beginning*.

Throughout the 1980s, *Twenty-four Hours a Day* remained Hazelden's biggest single seller, but *Each Day a New Beginning* served an important purpose, one that quickly became evident to the Educational Materials Division and, within a few years, to the larger publishing industry.[52] Casey's work opened the door to both conceptual and practical innovations in recovery publishing, demonstrating not only that the antique idea of surrender could be married to contemporary attentiveness to social conditions, but also that a market existed for 12-Step philosophy tailored to different audiences. The results could not help but rankle traditionalist AAs, who saw her refinement of the three-part disease and the antidote of surrender as a sort of bastard child of uppity feminism and banal psychologizing, guaranteed to undermine the spiritual principle of alcoholic equalitarianism. This critique took some time to develop, however. The immediate result of Casey's subtle but striking revision to 12-Step philosophy was a change in the nature and purpose of literary production at Hazelden. In the wake of *Each Day a New Beginning*, more books, different books, and bigger audiences beckoned the Educational Materials Division.

THE TRIUMPH OF THE THERAPEUTIC

The response to *Each Day a New Beginning* took even Harold Swift and Karen Casey by surprise. Contrary to Jack V.'s predictions, the book sold out its initial 10,000-copy printing before it even arrived in the warehouse in 1982; sales that year totaled 250,000.[53] Powered in part by this surprise success—and in part by *Food for Thought*, which for the third year in a row sold around 30,000 copies—in 1983 monthly revenue from Educational Materials increased from $80,000 to $400,000.[54] Sensing that a new day was indeed beginning, Swift quietly dissolved the Literature Advisory Committee.[55]

Hazelden seems to have been driven by a combination of 12-Step evangelism and financial self-interest during this time; it is difficult to determine from the historical record which of those motivations truly drove decision making. "Sure we wanted to make great books and sell the hell out of them," Karen Casey recalls, but "our first priority was to 'carry the message.'"[56] In service, perhaps, to both imperatives, Casey quickly published a second devotional reader, *The Promise of a New Day* (1983; co-written with Martha Vanceburg), and *The Love Book* (1985), a volume of weekly rather than daily meditations. Unlike *Each Day a New Beginning*, which had been published anonymously, both books showcased Casey's name and mentioned her previous publications, including *Each Day*. While Casey was writing, Educational Materials undertook some market research on book-buying habits, and when surveys indicated that people would buy multiple meditation books—for morning and for night, for the bathroom and the car and the office—a stream of new titles poured into the market.[57] An anonymous Hazelden author published *Touchstones*, a meditation book for men in 1986; *Day by Day* included meditations for young addicts; *Today's Gift* addressed the whole family; *The Night Light* featured "serene, reassuring thoughts as we end our day and face the night"; and so on for groups such as the HIV positive, people with chronic illnesses, and people over forty. Ironically, this paradigmatic genre of "religious reading" proved itself uniquely suited to "consumerist" reading practices as well. "I'm not sure why people buy and read more than one" meditation book, Casey observed in an interview, "but they do. Perhaps it's because they are seeking a certain answer and if they don't find it in one book, they buy another."[58] As a result, "potential audiences for meditation books appeared unlimited."[59]

Unlimited, that is, save for the bottlenecks in an antiquated distribution system, and Harry Swift took it upon himself to clear those out at the same time that literary production was being reformed. Hazelden titles had long been acknowledged within the treatment community as well written, carefully edited, and thoughtfully designed and constructed; they also benefited from their continuing association with official AA literature, which appeared alongside Hazelden's own publications in their catalog. Now that Educational Materials was developing a larger inventory of demographically differentiated and attractively packaged literature, it seemed only right to expand beyond old-fashioned direct mail to a highly organized, proactive, and professional sales team. At Swift's suggestion, the Human Relations Department developed a full-fledged business-to-business traveling sales force in 1986. Made up of veterans of Hazelden's Counselor Training Program, it was poised to take advantage of the center's reputation in what had become a white-hot marketplace for addiction treatment.

Positioning themselves first and foremost as advocates of "biblio-therapy," the sales representatives had two primary markets: the federally funded hospitals of the Veterans' Administration and Department of Defense, and the large for-profit hospital chains just entering the addiction treatment field—for-profit health care corporations like Charter Medical, Hospital Corporation of America, and Psychiatric Institutes of America, which included multiple hospitals and facilities under their corporate umbrellas. Speaking with the benefit of Hazelden's experience, sales reps acquainted clinical directors with Educational Materials' products while instructing them on "ways to incorporate literature into their treatment plans."[60] Clinicians could order from a wide-ranging inventory of Hazelden books, pamphlets, and workbooks, now crafted to address different kinds of clients. Their selections were bundled into shrink-wrapped packages, which were given to clients upon check-in. The literature packets typically contained copies of the Big Book, *Twenty-four Hours a Day*, and another meditation book geared to the patient's demographic; workbooks intended to facilitate self-understanding and aid in taking key Steps; and a Hazelden catalog, "so that when people wanted new books when they got out all they had to do was call."[61] Just as early entry into the field of counselor training had made Hazelden the "Mecca" of clinical practice, the advent of this mass distribution system consecrated the center's position within the recovery literature field. It would be wrong to claim that Hazelden monopolized the marketplace for treatment literature, but its position was comfortably dominant; by the mid-1980s gross annual revenue from Educational Materials was over $20 million.[62]

Translating the popularity of its products within the treatment community into sales in the larger world required another adjustment to Hazelden's traditional way of doing business. Booksellers could order Hazelden titles for their shelves, but at only a 20 percent discount off the cover price, not at the trade standard of 40 percent; this made stocking Hazelden books relatively unappealing to retailers. Furthermore, despite ramping up production and distribution to keep pace with the growth of the treatment industry, the center was simply not prepared to produce and distribute books in the quantities necessary to do business with traditional retail booksellers. To redress this problem, in 1985 Educational Materials made a licensing deal—an agreement to produce and distribute, but not to acquire titles—with Winston Seabury, a small religious publisher based in Minnesota. Coincidentally, in the merger mania engulfing the publishing industry at the time, Winston Seabury was almost immediately acquired by Harper and Row.[63] The Hazelden titles were reissued under Harper's San Francisco imprint, and *Food for Thought*, *Each Day a New Beginning*, and *Promise of a New Day* became instant best sellers. "There was hardly any need to market them," said Tom Grady, the Harper San Francisco editor who handled the Hazelden licensed-properties. "The market just sucked them out of us as fast as we could print them."[64] By the late 1980s, with around seventy titles licensed to Harper for trade distribution, literature sales accounted for more than 50 percent of Hazelden's gross revenues, with income from residential treatment lagging at 40 percent.[65]

While this growth was predicated upon a more calculated and corporate approach to publishing than had been the norm at Hazelden in previous decades, it nevertheless was accomplished primarily by playing on existing strengths. Through the mid-1980s, Educational Materials concerned itself with encoding variations on the basic 12-Step message within products aimed at the special populations moving into the treatment industry. That audience was growing rapidly, and portions of it were located in spaces that had hitherto been outside Hazelden's reach, but its defining features remained primarily the same: readers of Hazelden literature were, with few exceptions, alcoholics and addicts. Drawing on AA insights, Hazelden had long recognized the importance of addressing what early AAs and Al-Anons called "co-alcoholism," and had distributed Al-Anon literature (at the center and through the catalog) since it began to be published in the 1950s. During the 1970s, Harry Swift had helped to develop a Family Program that drew on Al-Anon principles to address the fact that when the chemically dependent person "stop[s] drinking or using other drugs . . . the structure of the whole family must be reorganized completely."[66] But while other treatment centers had made conscious decisions in the late 1970s to begin to see "codependents" as patients in their own right—with an eye to consecrating their condition as a discrete and reimbursable medical condition—Hazelden's rehabilitation focus had remained on the addict. This conservative attitude had prevailed in Educational Materials as well as in Rehabilitation. In 1980 the catalog offered some pamphlet literature on family issues for professionals, including the volume by Swift (written with Terrence Williams) cited above and a smattering of publications from other treatment centers on "The Recovery of Chemically Dependent Families" (Johnson Institute) and "Alcoholism: A Family Illness" (Smithers Foundation). But the Educational Materials Division defined codependency as "not in accord with the Twelve Step program and philosophy" and therefore did not publish in that area.[67]

As a result, Hazelden had passed on two manuscripts submitted in the early 1980s that extended the disease concept of addiction to children of alcoholics, Claudia Black's *It Will Never Happen to Me* and Janet Woititz's *Adult Children of Alcoholics*. Black self-published her book and sold 500,000 copies, then licensed the book to Random House for sales of over 2 million. Woititz's volume was picked up by Florida's Health Communications Incorporated and sold over 2 million copies during a forty-eight-week sojourn on the *New York Times* best-seller list.[68] Then, in 1985, Los Angeles–based publisher Jeremy Tarcher had another surprise best seller with Robin Norwood's *Women Who Love Too Much*. Like Black and Woititz, Norwood utilized the disease concept and invoked the history of 12-Step organizations as a way to explain women's unhappy relationships—even reprinting a midcentury chart detailing the downward spiral of alcoholism that had been a fixture in many local AA publications.[69] But she pushed the idea of disease one step beyond the Adult Child paradigm, arguing that for a variety of reasons besides parental alcoholism, certain vulnerable women became addicted to destructive relationships. The addiction Norwood hoped to counter consisted of "obsessing about a man and calling that obsession love, allowing it to control your emotions and much of your behavior, realizing that it negatively influences your health and well-being, and yet finding yourself unable to let go."[70] This redefinition of obsessive behavior as a form of emotional "addiction" proved extremely compelling; Women Who Love Too Much groups dedicated to using the 12 Steps to end their "addictions" to men sprang up around the country, and Norwood's book sold over 2.5 million copies.[71]

The popular ratification of 12-Step-derived ideas led Swift and Casey to remark once again that pent-up demand for the recovery message existed outside the traditional treatment milieu, and that as the leading professional disseminator of that message, Hazelden had an obligation to meet that demand—through literary production if not through clinical practice. They argued that to refuse to enter the codependency marketplace was, in effect, to abdicate responsibility. Thus in 1986, over the heated objections of Rehabilitation Division staff, Hazelden published Melody Beattie's *Codependent No More*, which had previously been rejected by twelve trade publishers.[72]

Beattie, a former alcoholic and heroin addict as well as a recovering codependent, defined her addiction even more expansively than Norwood: codependents "let another person's behavior affect" them and, as a result, become "obsessed with controlling that person's behavior."[73] Although the book spoke routinely of codependence as a state that arose from close relationships with addicts, it followed Norwood's lead in arguing that not just intimacy with addicts, but all manner of life experiences could trigger codependency, including "relationships with emotionally or mentally disturbed persons . . . with chronically ill people . . . [with] children with behavior problems . . . with irresponsible people," and so on (34). In short chapters, the book provided case studies of codependent behavior, detailed the characteristics of codependency, and offered suggestions for how to understand and combat it through variations on 12-Step philosophy. It included a number of quizzes and checklists intended to help readers determine if they were codependent, and each chapter ended with a series of "activities" intended to prompt further self-scrutiny and aid in behavior modification.

That the Rehabilitation Division would object to *Codependent* should come as no surprise: Beattie's volume accurately reflected the complete integration of therapeutic discourse into what had been Hazelden's "pure AA" milieu. Beattie located her understanding of codependency in her own experiences in Al-Anon, and urged her audience to join 12-Step programs. She referenced spiritual issues by evoking, as Karen Casey had, a New Thought–style God who "is in each of us and speaks to each of us" (93), urging readers to "trust that Someone greater than ourselves knows, has ordained, and cares about what is happening" (63). Surrender and acceptance were important for the codependent just as they were for the addict, and Beattie reminded her readers repeatedly that "we don't have final say on much of anything; God does" (169). But despite its invocation of 12-Step ideas, *Codependent*'s primary reference points were therapeutic. The bulk of Beattie's sources were writings by addiction-treatment and family therapy professionals, and she drew as well from humanist psychologists Albert Ellis and Fritz Perls, popular self-esteem guru Nathaniel Branden, motivational coach

Wayne Dyer, and, in one chapter, David Schwartz's 1959 power-of-mind classic *The Magic of Thinking Big*. She believed that self-esteem issues were the root of all problems, arguing that "our low self-worth or self-hatred is tied into all aspects of our codependency" (121 and passim), and she advocated an emphatically psychodynamic solution, which entailed, first and foremost, "finish[ing] up business from our childhood" (104) and "nurtur[ing] and cherish[ing] that frightened, vulnerable, needy child inside us" (106).

The images of active fellowship that underpinned the Big Book and *Twenty-four Hours a Day*, and which had been recast in *Each Day a New Beginning* as invocations of sororal community, were noticeably absent in *Codependent*. Addressing both men and women, Beattie showed none of Karen Casey's interest in pointing out the ways that social structures and gender norms contributed to low self-esteem and interpersonal dependence. Instead, she presented both the problem of codependency and the solution to it as strictly psychological issues. Individuation and autonomy were Beattie's goals, and she concluded the book by noting that "through my experience with codependency, I found my *self*. . . . I hope I have helped awaken you to your *self*" (233–34; original emphasis). In the same spirit, *Codependent*'s acknowledgments page bore the remarkable inscription, "This book is dedicated to me." Although Beattie mobilized a recognizable language of disease and spirit, love and letting go, it is difficult to imagine a more thorough inversion of the 12-Step philosophy codified by Bill Wilson and Bob Smith in the 1930s.

It is ironic, then, that it was Beattie's iteration of 12-Step philosophy —the one routed through classical American success literature and the family therapy and humanist psychology of the 1960s and 1970s—that brought the idea of recovery into the center of the U.S. literary and cultural mainstream. The Hazelden mail-order edition of *Codependent No More* sold 76,000 copies its first year, then jumped into the stratosphere in 1987 when the Harper/Hazelden edition appeared, with sales of over 300,000. In 1989, Hazelden entered into a licensing agreement with mass-market publisher Ballantine, the better to allow its "mission to reach the broadest possible base . . . in drugstores, groceries, and discount outlets."[74] By 1990, Beattie's book had spent more than two years on the *New York Times* best-seller list, with sales of over 4 million. A 1989 follow-up volume, *Beyond Codependency*, debuted on the *Times* list and stayed there for more than twenty weeks.[75] At the peak of her popularity in 1990, Harper San Francisco had around 100 Hazelden titles under license, but Beattie's two volumes alone generated more than half of Harper/Hazelden's revenue of $9 million. The same year, the Educational Materials Division grossed over $27 million in annual sales. Revenues from publishing were so extensive, according to Harry Swift, that he worried that the IRS might seek to revoke Hazelden's status as a not-for-profit corporation.[76]

Selling this hybrid version of recovery—the 12 Steps in combination with other, more familiar American ideas about the self, the causes of suffering, and the means to happiness—to people who were not themselves addicts or even closely connected to addicts turned out to be a good business decision for Hazelden. In 1991, the bottom fell out of the addiction treatment industry as managed care began to dry up insurance payments to residential treatment programs. Literature that crossed over into the mainstream marketplace not only "carried the message" in unprecedented ways, but also provided a financial cushion during what was a catastrophic time for the industry as a whole. Although even Hazelden's rehabilitation unit had vacant beds for the first time in decades, its financial position remained strong enough that it could purchase the backlists of two of its main competitors, CompCare and Parkside, when they collapsed in the early 1990s. By the middle of the decade, the Educational Materials Division had become accustomed to thinking of itself as a revenue-generating part of the Hazelden enterprise. It became increasingly professionalized, with an international literature distribution center, a subsidiary rights department, profit and loss statements on individual titles, and a system of executive bonuses.[77] That new corporate mindset placed a premium on actively cultivating new markets and developing new product lines to meet their needs. While books and pamphlets continued to occupy center stage, electronic production became the new growth area. Attempts at Internet marketing were unsuccessful, but videos dealing with addiction and recovery proved increasingly popular.[78] Well suited both to addicts with little formal education and to harried clinical staff, Hazelden's low-budget docu-dramas came to take the place of "bibliotherapy" in the outpatient clinics and prisons that, by century's end, had become the vanguard of addiction treatment.

Members of the conservative AA old guard that had objected to "an AA book for women" lingered on the treatment side of Hazelden, continuing to voice their "suspicion and mistrust" of the Educational Materials

Division through the 1990s.[79] While their complaints occurred during and were related to the expansion and diversification of Hazelden and of alcoholism treatment generally, it is important to establish that they were not explicitly complaining about opening up 12-Step culture to broader and more diverse populations. Rather, traditionalists objected to what they perceived as the dilution of AA spirituality by therapeutic ideas, to the fracture of alcoholic equalitarianism by attention to diversity, and to the conscious marketing of and profiting from the transformative gift of 12-Step ideals. Though Hazelden remained a nonprofit organization, its professionalization—emblematized in the evolution of Educational Materials into a full-fledged recovery communications circuit integrated into the larger circuit of commercial trade publishing—meant that it was no longer a privileged adjunct to the anti-market community of AA. Administrators' attempts to return it to that status were half-hearted and, in any case, futile. Within Hazelden proper, Damian McElrath has observed, "it was too late to restore the spirit of smallness."[80] Outside of the treatment center's grassy precincts, however, and beyond the reach of the professional therapeutic community, that spirit was taking on new life.

"A WEAK CUP OF TEA"

Traditionalists on the Hazelden staff were not the only members of AA concerned about a possible erosion of the fellowship's core principles during the 1980s and 1990s. At scheduled roundtables and open microphone question-and-answer sessions at the annual General Service Conference, delegates wrestled with how to live up to AA's Responsibility Pledge—"When anyone, anywhere, reaches out for help, I want the hand of AA always to be there—and, for that, I am responsible"—as they accommodated a flood of referrals from treatment centers and the criminal justice system. Sheer numbers were a part of the problem, but AAs were also concerned that individuals remanded to the program by judges, parole officers, or physicians would not recover within it because they did not really meet Tradition 3's baseline requirement for membership: "a desire to stop drinking."

Accompanying these logistical concerns were uncertainties about how to handle the cultural diversity of the newcomers. Though rarely tied explicitly to class, gender, or race, anxiety about the presence of individuals who fell outside AA's white, middle-class demographic mainstream infused the delegates' questions and complaints about multiply addicted people, people who used a lot of profanity and/or had criminal records, the mentally ill and homeless, and so on. The solutions posed in annual meetings typically reiterated the importance of alcoholic equalitarianism in such situations: AA had an obligation to help anyone who was an admitted drunk. Beyond that, there was extensive discussion of how to create better links between treatment centers and local AA groups, how to model strong sobriety, and how to encourage sponsorship so that people knew what AA was "really" about. Most groups, it seems, improvised responses to the situation as best they could. For some AAs, however, such reactive suggestions fell short of the mark. Traditionalists took it upon themselves to create a literature and culture of their own, one whose form, content, and distribution methods reiterated the pietist values of the "AA way of life" discussed in chapter 2. Their lectures and publications disparaged what they saw as the special interest groups, psychological insights, and commercialism that characterized the therapeutic recovery culture of the alcohol and drug industrial complex—a culture, they believed, that despite its nominal commitment to the 12 Steps, threatened to supplant the true "AA way of life."

While the traditionalist subculture that arose in the 1980s and 1990s was a response to changes within AA as a whole, it was rooted in long-standing discontent with the GSO and its perceived attempts to shape reading practices through Conference Approved Literature. After the fracas over Walker's *Twenty-four Hours* in the mid-1950s, agitation against the GSO's policies appeared to die down for several years, but it flared up as membership grew and diversified. A 1965 GSO survey of literature use had revealed that a substantial minority of AA groups used non–Conference Approved Literature in meetings—24 percent used *Twenty-four Hours a Day*, 17 percent used *The Little Red Book*, and a handful used other traditionalist publications.[81] Now, as groups responded to a massive influx of newcomers, the appeal of that canonical literature to some members of the fellowship seemed to increase. The annual General Service Conference became a literary battleground.

Conference delegates fielded repeated requests to certify *Twenty-four Hours a Day* as Conference Approved or, failing that, to create a meditation book that resembled it. Delegates also requested that the Literature Committee consider a facsimile edition of the first edition of the Big Book, a concordance to the Big Book, and a special pocket edition of the first, expository section of the Big Book. They raised complaints about there being too much literature and about too much specialization within the literature.[82] In 1980, when a specially convened Literature Task Force presented its annual report, "so many Conference members lined up at the floor microphones" to register their questions and opinions "that the session ran overtime" and had to reconvene on another day (11).

Partially in response to this pressure, and partly out of their own concern that treatment-center rhetoric was beginning to infiltrate AA, the General Services Conference toughened its stance regarding literature and its uses. During a time of "squabbles [within] our fellowship, within groups, among AAs in and out of the field of alcoholism" (1974, 6), CAL—with its polite acknowledgment of diversity, carefully noncommittal spirituality, and collaboratively achieved picture of the alcoholic experience—seemed to assume a more important role than ever. As a result, the conference promoted CAL with a zeal bordering on obsession, and, in the face of apparently nonconforming behavior, reiterated again and again that distinctions between CAL and non-CAL should be made clear—with labeling, with differentiated displays—in individual meetings, as well as in intergroup and area offices.[83] The conference never went so far as to disallow the use of non-CAL works in meetings, and a 1978 statement in the GSO's newsletter, *Box 4-5-9*, reaffirmed that designating some texts as CAL "does *not* mean the Conference disapproves of any other publications. . . . What any A.A. member reads is no business of G.S.O., or of the Conference, naturally."[84] Nevertheless, the GSO's preferred parameters for the use of literature at AA meetings seemed clear from floor actions like "AA groups [should] be discouraged from selling literature not distributed by the General Service Office and the *Grapevine*" (1977, 43) and presentations featuring statements like "AA's literature is another way of keeping our message from becoming diluted or distorted" (1986, 16).

The discussion of literature during this period was colored by the Conference's relatively liberal stance toward both spirituality and diversity. In 1968, for the first time, it acknowledged that *Twenty-four Hours* had been denied CAL status in 1954 because of its explicit religiosity. In a later presentation on CAL, a speaker implicitly criticized Walker's book by asking, "What does a newcomer think when he or she comes to an AA meeting for the first time and someone opens and chairs the meeting out of a meditation book, perhaps even referring to his or her own Higher Power by name?" (1986, 15). Readers eager for a daily devotional were encouraged instead to use the 1967 anthology of Bill Wilson's writings entitled *As Bill Sees It*.[85] A volume of short essays by AA members about their spiritual experiences, *Came to Believe*, was published in 1973; a devotional reader, *Daily Reflections*, was finally published in 1990. But that same year, a "pamphlet on the spiritual aspects of AA" was tabled on the grounds that "there is not sufficient need for it at this time" (11).

Instead of additional publications on spiritual topics, what the fellowship needed was a more diverse literature. The first response to the growing heterogeneity within the fellowship had been 1976's pamphlet "Do You Think You're Different?" which actively inscribed a variety of alcoholics—old and young, black and Jewish, etc.—within the discourse of alcoholic equalitarianism. In the same year, a third edition of the Big Book included forty-three personal stories, with some specifically intended to speak to young alcoholics, members of the military and the working class, women, and African and Native Americans. In 1977, the conference had approved the revision of CAL publications (although not the original portions of the Big Book) to avoid the exclusive use of masculine pronouns (1977, 37). Pamphlets addressing younger and older alcoholics, the clergy, the incarcerated, Native Americans, gays and lesbians, and African Americans had been appearing for some time.[86] This diversification was painstakingly slow; no activist would consider the workings of the Trustees' Committee on Literature a progressive powerhouse.[87] But a recognizably multicultural stance was discernible by the late 1980s, when a Trustee's report noted that while "we have created pamphlets to reach" some previously marginalized alcoholics, like "the young, women, and lately . . . Native Americans," there are "still others whom we do not reach as effectively as we should [such as] black, Hispanic, Native American, handicapped, aged, and lately, Russian alcoholics" (1988, 27). Conference Approved Literature was still vested in the idea of universal alcoholic selfhood, and had no interest in the way social position might complicate the premises of the three-part disease. But during the 1980s and 1990s it began consciously to acknowledge and affirm the increasingly diverse constituency of AA.

It would be incorrect to say that many AAs believed that changes in literature and in literature policy were themselves degrading to the fellowship. Instead, Conference Approved Literature and attitudes toward it came to emblematize a larger decline, one that was evidenced not only by therapy-speak and identity politics, but also by the fact that while more people were coming to AA, fewer seemed to be getting and staying sober there than had been the case in earlier years.[88] Describing the fellowship's fallen state in the mid-1970s, Tom P. Jr. wrote that there were currently "three ways to work the program of Alcoholics Anonymous":

1. The *strong* original way—proved powerfully and reliably effective over forty years.

2. A *medium* way—not so strong, not so safe, not so sure, not so good, but still effective.

3. A *weak* way, which turns out to be really no way at all but literally a heresy, a false teaching, a twisting and corruption of what the founders of Alcoholics Anonymous clearly stated the program to be.[89]

AAs who favored the latter—what Tom P. Jr. called "the weak-cup-of-tea approach"—typically "cop out and stay copped out on most of the 12 steps." In fact, he fulminated, a "more accurate term than 'weak AA' for [their] practice is 'copped-out and watered-down AA' or COWD AA for short." To emphasize his contempt for that stance, he illustrated his article with an image of a black and white cow gazing meekly out at the reader (Fig. 4.1).

Faced with this state of affairs, Tom P. challenged his fellow alcoholics to embrace once again what he called the "strong original . . . [the] undiluted dosage of the spiritual principles" with which AA had begun.[90] The ongoing struggle over CAL made clear that literature was a key example, if not an actual cause, of "COWD-ness" and "dilution." Traditionalists committed to what *The Little Red Book* had called the "AA Way of Life," and what Tom P. Jr. called the "*strong* original way" began to develop their own print culture in response—one that built on the midcentury canon of the surrendered life, circulated by hand and direct mail, and aimed specifically to counter what its partisans believed were toxins leaching into the fellowship from outside.

Not all the traditionalist literature published in this period was overtly ideological. The commonplace books of Walter S. and Mose Yoder, for example—small stapled collections of edifying sayings, prayers, and verse, culled from AA meetings and the storehouse of American folk wisdom, privately published and sold for a few dollars—simply offered a selection of inspiring thoughts to aid in private meditation or perhaps to enliven a meeting. Yoder's compendium of *Grateful Thoughts* (Fig. 4.2), collected over thirty-seven years in AA, reflected his belief that when alcoholics "get out of the drinking business and into the thinking busi-

the program. A more inclusive, more accurate, and more descriptive term than "weak AA" for this practice is "copped-out and watered-down AA," or COWD AA for short.

With the passage of time, a definite evolution has taken place in AA in the respective popularity and acceptability of the strong and COWD approaches.

In the first years of their existence, the COWD AAs tended to feel obliged to defend and sing the praises of their "heterodox" approaches and even to chide the strong AAs a bit for being rigid and holier-than-thou. The strong AAs, for their part, tended to be more relaxed and tolerant, less strident, less defensive. After all, their method was obviously safer since it involved taking more of the medicine. And it was obviously the original and genuine article as the Big Book eloquently attested.

But this juxtaposition of attitudes came to have a peculiar effect in a movement which prided itself on its good-natured

13

Figure 4.1.
The "COWD AA" from Tom P. Jr., "Gresham's Law and Alcoholics Anonymous," 1976. Courtesy of 24 Communications, Inc.

ness" it was important for them to have simple, uplifting ideas to focus on because "as a man thinks, so is he. The two greatest things I have to work on [are] cultivating my thinking and purifying my thoughts. An idle mind is the devil's workshop." Similarly, Walter S. noted with pride that his Bright Star Press publications, like *Handles to Hang on to Our Sobriety* and *Stinkin' Thinkin': (Thoughts For)*, could "be tucked into the pocket for a moment of meditation."[91] The familiar, anonymous snippets that filled their pages, combined with their drastically simple material form, embodied the ideals of surrendered selfhood at the center of 12-Step philosophy without editorializing on the topic.[92]

Other forms of traditionalist literature were less circumspect in their criticisms. In a few cases, authors frankly stated their antipathy toward what was perceived to be the overly liberal AA of Conference Approved

```
                (I MUST)

Accept the knowledge that I am an
     alcoholic.
Accept the fact that I shall always be
     allergic to alcohol.
Accept the fact that I can never again
     become a social drinker.
Accept the fact that I .must constantly
     be on guard.
Accept the fact that it is not of my
     doing, but a higher power that keeps
     me sober.
Accept the fact that I must live this
     program daily.

Accept the new and wounderful world
     around me though the fellowship of
     A.A.
Accept the fact that it has helped me
     to help myself, to achieve a contented
     sober life in which alcohol has no
     place.
          Accepting these truths,
          I SHALL KEEP MY SOBRIETY

_____

          "BY THE GRACE OF GOD".
          THE UNDESERVED REWARD.

Time wasted in getting even can never be
used in getting ahead.

Ulcers are something we get from mountain
climbing over mole hills.

Lack of alcohol does not constitute
                "sobriety"

Get in the middle of the bed,
It's the guy on the edge who
always falls out.

A.Λ. can not be bottled.

A.A. meetings keep me stimulated.

God is my Doctor.  A.A. meeting is my
     medicine.

Learn to listen.   Then listen to learn.

What you seek you will not find unless
     you share it.

Don't let the grammer of A.A. wear off.
```

Figure 4.2. Page opening from Mose Y., Grateful Thoughts, *ca. late 1970s. Courtesy of Chester H. Kirk Collection on Alcoholism and Alcoholics Anonymous, John Hay Library, Brown University.*

Literature and the General Service Office. In 1985, an Akron entity called "Carry the Message, Inc." (CTM) exploited a weakness in the Big Book copyright and published a facsimile edition of the original 1939 edition. The volume was explicitly intended to counteract what the preface described as the GSO's "insidious gradual eroding away from our original, primary purpose of carrying the message." "Significant legal exchanges" between the GSO and CTM were required to convince the latter to cease publication.[93] Another facsimile was brought out in 1992 by a group calling itself Intergroup World Service (IWS), which intentionally priced its volumes far below the GSO's retail price. A legal settlement led to IWS ceasing publication in 1995, but another maverick house, Anonymous Publishing, continues to publish its own edition today. In a similar vein, unauthorized translations of the Big Book that emphasized the surrendered life began to appear outside the United States—in Mexico, Canada, and Europe—during the late 1990s, the work of traditionalist members who believed that the GSO's position of spiritual neutrality—like its ownership claims to intellectual property—violated the spirit of the fellowship.[94]

Most traditionalist publications fall somewhere between these extremes. Probably the largest body of traditionalist literature in circulation today takes the form of what might best be called sobriety guides—books and workbooks intended to move readers through the Steps, to deepen their understanding of the Big Book, and, above all, to increase the quality and the durability of sobriety by aiding them in the surrendered life. Sobriety guide authors are deeply invested in AA's oral traditions. Their publications typically derive from or are intended to work in concert with talks by seasoned members, who travel the U.S. offering workshops on how to implement the insights they have committed to print; audiotapes of their talks form an important complement to their printed works. Sobriety guides are not monolithic—some, for example, make an explicit case for Bible study while others are more ecumenical —but their authors generally share the characteristics associated with the midwestern, midcentury version of AA, and incorporate reprinted pamphlet material from that place and time alongside original writing, charts, and diagrams.[95]

The audience for this kind of traditionalist publication—both its size and its demographic make-up—is difficult to ascertain. It is most likely, however, that it has grown since the late 1990s, when the Internet began to provide traditionalist authors and their partisans an efficient means of communication and a highly visible platform. Web sites like Silkworth .net (<www.silkworth.net>), AA Big Book Study Group (<www.aabbsg .org>), The Primary Purpose Group (<www.ppgaadallas.org>), and GSO Watch (<http://aagso.org>), to name only a few, promote traditionalist authors alongside *The Little Red Book* and *Twenty-four Hours a Day*. While such sites differ in the degree of vitriol that they hurl at the dominant AA culture, all of them tout amateur publications as counterweights to a cultural moment in which "the 'Language of the Heart' has gotten all tangled up with drugs, pop psychology, clinical terminology, and emotionalism."[96] Traditionalist publications provide a way to resist that entanglement and, according to AA historian Mitchell K., during the 1990s they also helped to support the creation of a "growing movement . . . [of] 'underground' meetings." As in early midwestern AA, admission to these meetings is carefully controlled: they "are not advertised; and attendance at them is by invitation only. One has to be 'sponsored' into them . . . [and they] are open for alcoholics and their families only." This rigor, Mitchell K. argues, counteracts official AA's misplaced "desire to help the greater number of people," which has "led to lower expectations and to diluting of the message to make it more palatable."[97]

Mitchell K.'s own book, *How It Worked*, is not a sobriety guide per se, but a biography of his sponsor, Clarence S., founder of the first Cleveland AA chapter and a longtime critic of Bill Wilson and the GSO. It concludes with an extended exultation over the fact that the number of traditionalist publishers and audiotapers is on the rise, supported by the Internet and by a growing sense of historical consciousness among many AAs. Such growth is essential, Mitchell K. believes, to preserve the essence of a fellowship that has been "watered down" and "diluted" by the mandate "to become all things to all people," and is administered by "high salaried employees" located in a "headquarters office space [characterized by] high rentals, expensive books and therapeutics." Urging amateur authors and historians to resist this bureaucratic centralization by locating, saving, and publishing old documents relating to "the AA program, its history, its growth, and . . . HOW IT WORKED," the volume concludes with the reminder that "THE TRUTH IS OUT THERE."[98] Elevating traditionalist print culture to the level of "TRUTH," this reference to the popular crime-conspiracy television program *The X-Files* also suggests the degree of beleaguerment and persecution that some AAs felt as they watched their equalitarian community of the gift evolve into just one more mass-marketed discourse of the self in the last decades of the twentieth century.

MEN AND WOMEN, MASCULINITY AND "FEMINIZATION"

For the bulk of AA's members in the 1970s and 1980s, the demographic, philosophical, and cultural changes that rippled through the fellowship as it responded to changes in the alcohol and drug industrial complex were issues to be taken in stride, best grappled with via the slogans "Easy does it" and "Take what you like and leave the rest." Traditionalists committed to "the AA Way of Life," however, felt differently, and William L. White has observed that during this period they "began to refer to the burgeoning mountains of commercialized literature, tapes, and paraphernalia as 'recovery porn' " (*SD*, 278). The turn of phrase is a telling one. Commonsense understandings of pornography typically see it as a male-dominated form of commercial cultural production, one that exploits women for the pleasure of men. Viewed in its historical context, however, the notion of "recovery porn" seems to invert that understanding. Like much of the traditionalist critique, it obliquely links aggressive and self-interested women to a machine-like, profit-obsessed marketplace, and suggests that the two have worked together to exploit and degrade a pure and vulnerable body—in this case the body of surrendered masculinity at the heart of the AA fellowship.[99] Complaints against recovery porn crystallized traditionalists' outrage at what they saw (and in some cases, still see) as the "feminization" of AA culture that occurred with the growth and diversification of the 1970s and 1980s, changes that registered to them as a falling away from original spiritual purity into a debased therapeutic and commercial mode that lacked rigor and efficacy.

AA traditionalists were not the first group of relatively privileged white men to decry the feminization of their culture. Indeed, the phenomenon has been observed by scholars looking at the shift from artisanal to industrial modes of cultural production in a wide range of periods and places.[100] Typically, as modes of cultural production shift and become more professional and rationalized, more massive and more lucrative, the rate at which women participate in production increases slightly. At the same time, the men displaced from their creative and gate-keeping roles in the old production scheme mount a critique of the new productive modalities, decrying the low quality of the new cultural goods. Over time—and usually not a long time—the presence of real women and the sense of declining quality blur into one another. In an essay tellingly titled "Mass Culture as Woman," Andreas Huyssen defines "feminization" as the intertwined material and conceptual processes by which "mass culture [becomes] somehow associated with women while real, authentic culture remains the prerogative of men." The result of that association is a discourse in which women become both the cause and the symbol of cultural degradation.[101]

By the 1980s, it seems likely that even the most traditionalist men in

AA had moved beyond seeing women as the fellowship's "most un-welcome minority" (*Dr. Bob*, 241), but their more enlightened attitudes toward individual women did not stop them from buying into the time-honored discourse of feminization. Concern about what one confer-ence report called the "mass-produced" addicts flooding out of treat-ment centers and into AA meetings was echoed by concern about an expanding, changing, and "mass-produced" 12-Step literature, one that talked more about self-esteem than about a Higher Power, elevated "special interests" over alcoholic equalitarianism, and circulated in a clearly commercial marketplace.[102] Individual traditionalists may not even have thought about the fact that much of that literature was pro-duced by and for women. But their shared anxieties about commercial-ization and (for lack of a better word) therapeuticization nevertheless expressed themselves through gendered metaphors: the "emotional-ism" and the "weak cup of tea"; the "watered-down" and "tangled-up" meetings; even Tom P. Jr.'s cartoon cow. These images gestured to, without explicitly naming, an amorphous feminine presence that threatened to engulf and destroy everything in its path.

The appearance of this traditionally masculinist discourse among sur-rendered men who, as chapter 2 detailed, in many ways bucked the hier-archies of gender upon which normative masculinity relied is important for several reasons. First, it demonstrates the extent to which, despite the desire to repudiate their habits of "domination [and] dependence" (*12/12*, 117), AAs remained indebted to deeply ingrained conceptualizations of gender—and to hierarchies constructed through and around gender—to explain their world. When faced with change in the organization, they defaulted to the discourse of feminization to explain it, suggesting the limits of their individual or collective ability to imagine and/or to truly dismantle the hegemonic masculinity that they believed had entrapped them in what the Big Book called lives of self-propulsion (BB, 60). Al-though they were keenly aware of the limits of those lives, awareness did not translate automatically to the desire or the ability to renounce its privileges—especially when calls to do so were perceived as coming from outside, rather than from within the fellowship.

This lingering commitment to a traditional masculine selfhood may also help to explain the continued importance of amateur print culture within the AA fellowship. Authorship, with its implicit control of public discourse, has long been a means of confirming male prerogatives, and the cultivation of an "underground" print culture became a key way for traditionalists to combat what they felt to be their displacement from the center of AA's conceptual world. Unsurprisingly, traditionalist authors are (to the best of my knowledge) exclusively male. Assuming the role of author and publisher became a way to re-center the AA world in male experience for some; reading and organizing meetings around a tightly circumscribed canon seems to have served a similar function for others. Like many creators of oppositional print cultures, traditionalists reveled in low-tech print forms that simultaneously countered the divisive logics of professionalism (in both the alcohol and drug industrial complex and in the for-profit publishing world that aided and abetted it) and reflected their own sense of disenfranchisement.[103] In this case those critiques were made by the reiteration of the importance of alcoholic equalitarianism and the gift economy to AA as a whole.

Although they came at the problem from a completely different angle and were motivated by nearly opposite concerns, AA traditionalists shared the perspective of the disease critics discussed in chapter 1: in the seemingly endless expansion and mutation of 12-Step culture lay the potential for great harms. For a core group of men within AA, writing, publishing, and reading were acts of conscious resistance to the broad, multifaceted, and highly profitable culture of recovery that had grown out of and around AA. Understanding better the roles of the women who, traditionalists implied, shaped and had a stake in that culture, and tracing the communications circuits through which their ideas flowed, is the project of this book's third section.

PART THREE

Politics and Spirit

CHAPTER FIVE

The Varieties of Feminist Recovery Experience

n September 1983, the *Feminist Bookstore News*, a San Francisco–based bimonthly publication distributed to women's and feminist booksellers, featured a cartoon illustrating the bathroom graffiti in a typical feminist bookstore (Fig. 5.1).[1] Depicted were a few retail axioms ("sales ÷ inventory = turnover"; "sales × cost of goods = replacement costs") and a bundle of quips on the feminist workplace grind like "Independent bookstores run in the red; lesbian bookstores run in the lavender." But the place of honor at the center of the cartoon was occupied by a notable exception to this site-specific graffiti. In the space between the roughly sketched toilet and lopsided doorframe appeared the bold pronouncement "I like sober dykes!"

At first blush, the inscription of recovery sentiment on the radical space of a feminist bookstore bathroom wall seems somewhat anomalous, but to any habitué of the feminist scene of the early 1980s, it would have made perfect sense. Addiction and recovery emerged as pressing concerns for a wide range of feminists during this time, and women's bookstores were some of the first alcohol-free social spaces in the feminist community.[2] Furthermore, in a time when few trade presses published about addiction and recovery at all, much less about *women's* addiction and recovery, women's bookstores offered hard-to-find publications by feminist therapists, recovering incest survivors, and cross-addicted lesbians (to name just a few), works whose authors deviated sharply from standard treatment center and 12-Step rhetoric to offer a highly charged antipatriarchal perspective on the issues. Together these publications formed a cornerstone of what I call "post-12-Step recovery": theorizing about the nature of addiction and recovery that criticized aspects of 12-Step culture even as it built upon its central insights. Sober dykes had a place on the walls of feminist bookstore bathrooms because in 1983, to like sober dykes—or to be a sober dyke—was not merely to state a personal preference, but also to take a feminist stand.

By the end of the decade, however, as what seemed to be a pandemic of process addictions began to compete with concerns about women's alcoholism and drug abuse, a growing chorus of critics had emerged to

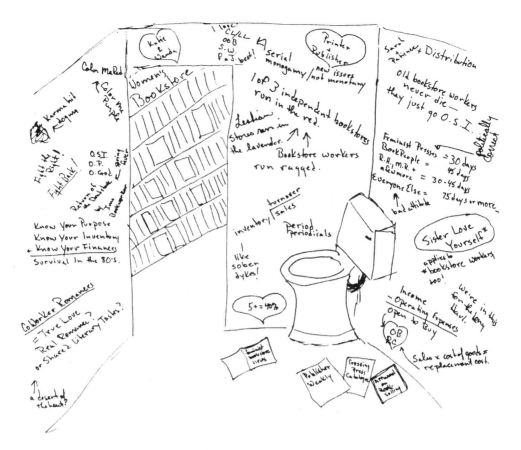

Figure 5.1. Carol Seajay, "I like sober dykes!" cartoon, Feminist Bookstore News,
September 1983. Courtesy of San Francisco Public Library.

challenge the validity of feminist recovery. Writing in the gay and lesbian magazine *Out/Look* about the growth of 12-Step organizations like
Overeaters Anonymous and Sex and Love Addicts Anonymous, Ellen
Herman wondered whether "addiction programs sap our political vitality." Susan Faludi urged her readers to recognize that the "leaders
of the codependency movement" had helped to orchestrate the 1980s
backlash against feminism by "exhort[ing] their female patients to picture and even treat themselves like little girls." Most insidiously, Elayne
Rapping argued, recovery culture had appropriated the concerns of Second Wave feminism in order to gut its political analysis: " 'Dysfunctional' replaces 'patriarchal'; 'toxic' replaces 'oppressive'; and so on.

And all the ways feminists have taught the world to judge sexist acts and thoughts are here incorporated in ways which take out the political sting and demand for change, and replace them with ideas about 'addiction' and 'disease' and 'giving oneself up to a Higher Power' who will make things right if we only believe." While they acknowledged that some women might actually have psychological problems that needed to be addressed, feminist critics of recovery's chief concern was with recovery's "depoliticizing" effects, manifested in its suggestion to unhappy women that they should seek "not to change society but simply to change themselves."[3]

Few observers are so foolish as to blame the recovery movement outright for the "postfeminist" turn of the late 1980s and 1990s.[4] The roles played by internal differences within the women's movement, as well as by powerful external forces like economic constriction, the rise of cultural conservatism, and the culture-wide backlash against the perceived excesses of the 1960s are all too obvious to ignore. Nevertheless, for many scholars who have mapped the evolution of U.S. feminism beyond its heyday in the 1970s, recovery has a unique status. On the one hand, the turn toward recovery seems a logical fulfillment of the signal insight of the women's liberation movement, namely that "the personal is political."[5] Yet at the same time, recovery can appear a perversion of that slogan's promise, a recasting of the loaded questions of systematic power imbalances and social control such that they appear to be merely personal neuroses or unhappiness. In part because it still bears the traces of feminist consciousness-raising, but seems *not* to push its devotees toward collective action for social change, recovery has become a favorite scapegoat, seen as a narcissistic consumer lifestyle that lured women away from the movement and/or a corrupting virus that undermined it from within.[6]

With an eye to understanding both their political and depoliticizing dimensions, this chapter explores the varieties of women's recovery discourse developed by different fractions of the feminist community during the 1980s. Women's addiction and recovery were causes taken up by a wide-ranging cross section of feminists—liberal and radical, straight and gay, white and of color—during the decade.[7] As in the broader Alcoholism Movement of midcentury, proponents of various approaches overlapped with, intersected, and contradicted each other in their struggles to advance their views and to help women whom they believed to be in need. Feminist recovery advocates' consciousness of the political nature of their work, and, indeed, their very definitions of "politics," varied according to their understandings of addiction. Equally important, however, were their social locations—their relative race, class, and educational privileges as well as, in some cases, their ties to the professional addiction and recovery industry. All of them, however, saw their work as contributing to the expansion of equality, freedom, and justice for women; none repudiated the broad demands for that expansion that the organized feminist movement had made during the 1960s. Why, then, did their critics condemn the recovery culture they had created as "depoliticized"?

The best answer to this question lies in the specifics of different activists' practices. Liberal, radical, and women of color feminists who advocated in favor of recovery drew upon (and resisted) the ideas and institutions of 12-Step and therapeutic recovery culture in different ways and to different degrees, depending on their distinctive theorizations of the female self and women's community. The aggregate meaning of women's recovery culture cannot be understood apart from these discrete innovations.

BECOMING VISIBLE:
THE WOMEN'S ALCOHOLISM MOVEMENT

In 1978, when the family of former first lady Betty Ford staged an intervention and had her hospitalized for addiction to alcohol and valium, she became the most visible casualty of what was perceived at the time to be a hidden epidemic of women's alcohol abuse sweeping the United States. While alcohol researchers had long believed that women drank significantly less than men (with significantly lower rates of alcoholism as a result), that perception began to shift in the 1960s, partly due to the efforts of pioneering researchers and partly thanks to general shifts in American gender roles and relationships. Thus in 1965, Dr. Marvin Block of the American Medical Association's National Committee on Alcoholism suggested that, contrary to popular opinion, "there are as many female as male problem drinkers and alcoholics" in the United States.[8] Thanks to Block and to the other researchers and lobbyists who made up what came to be known as "the women's alcoholism movement," much of the 1970s was devoted to finding, quantifying, and recruiting to treatment what journalist Marian Sandmaier called "the invisible alcoholics"—the millions of women who ostensibly hid their drinking problems because they feared a double standard that stigmatized women's alcoholism more harshly than men's. Almost exclusively white, educated, and middle class, the professionals in the women's alcoholism movement enacted a clear politics of liberal feminism, deploying their own expertise and relative privilege in the service of institutional and policy changes that would result in "sexual equality or, as it is sometimes termed, gender justice."[9]

A large part of this project entailed dismantling the Victorian gender ideologies that had long made it impossible to gather information, much less to talk about women's drinking, and replacing them with more dispassionate empirical information. While researchers disagree as to whether and/or to what extent women's drinking (problematic or otherwise) actually increased from the mid-1960s onward, no one can dispute the fact that it became more visible.[10] Sandmaier counted a mere twenty-eight scholarly articles on women and alcohol published in English between 1929 and 1970; during the decade of the 1970s, however, 126 such articles appeared.[11] Despite the exponential growth in the number of alcoholism treatment programs between the 1950s and 1980s (discussed in the previous chapter), in 1982 a scant twenty-three treatment programs in the United States offered specialized services for women. Ten years later that number had more than doubled. The number of government agencies, task forces, special commissions, and lobbyist groups proliferated accordingly. The National Council on Alcoholism established a special office devoted to Women and Alcoholism in 1976, and its initiative inspired the founding of such groups as the National Coalition for Women's Alcoholism Programs (mid-1970s), the National Women's Congress on Alcohol and Drug Problems (1980), and the National Association of Women in Alcoholism and Other Drug Dependencies (1988).[12] Their combined work did not confirm Block's suspicion that the incidence of alcoholism in women was equal to that in men, but over time it did suggest that of the estimated 10 million alcoholic/problem drinkers in the United States, approximately one-third were women—even though women constituted less than 20 percent of the population in treatment facilities.[13]

The foot soldiers of the women's alcohol movement were drawn from various parts of the alcohol and drug industrial complex rather than from liberal feminist organizations like the National Organization for Women. That they identified with liberal feminism's desire for the equitable treatment of women, however, is suggested at one level by their choice of Susan B. Anthony, a recovering alcoholic and the great-niece of the nineteenth-century women's suffrage advocate of the same name, as one of their most visible spokeswomen.[14] Gender equity, in various different forms, was also the substance of their agenda. The movement's aim for alcoholic women was a gender-specific version of what Marty Mann had accomplished at midcentury with the National Council for Education on Alcohol: a reduction in the stigma surrounding women's drinking that would make it as easy and effective for women to seek help as it was for men. This humanistic drive to improve the lot of alcoholic women was leavened by a more self-serving (though perfectly reasonable) professional-middle-class desire for legitimation in the workplace. Like their colleagues in the health and education fields, the liberal feminists who made up the women's alcoholism movement sought to dispute the chauvinist perception that their area of professional expertise—in this case, "alcohol and drug abuse in women"—was "a 'non-field.' "[15]

Their work to achieve these linked goals fell along two lines. First, researchers and policy analysts sought to demonstrate the masculinist biases that had long skewed research on the causes, manifestations, and progression of alcoholism, obscuring women's experiences and thus limiting their opportunities for prevention and/or treatment. Into the 1970s, the typology of drinking derived from E. M. Jellinek's study of the self-reported drinking histories of a handful of middle-aged white male members of AA (see chapter 1) was still widely used to determine who and what counted as "alcoholic." Other standard metrics used to gauge the severity of drinking problems—such as DWI citations, trouble at work, arrests for public brawling—had grown out of the Jellinek scale. They posited the male experience of work outside the home and convivial, bar-based drinking as universal. Such measurements, women's alcoholism movement activists believed, would never capture the experience of female problem drinking, which (for heterosexual white women, in any case) was more likely to be home-based and solitary.[16] Until the analytical tools used to capture information about drinking improved to become genuinely gender-neutral and/or to reflect the differences in men's and women's physiological and social lives, women's alcoholism movement researchers argued that ideology, rather than science, would continue to shape understandings of women's drinking.

Ideological debunking, in the form of stigma reduction, was the women's alcoholism movement's second and more far-reaching goal. "People of both sexes and all social classes," Sandmaier reported, believe it is "worse for a woman to be drunk than a man," and this gendered double standard conspired to make women alcoholics the agents of their own invisibility.[17] Work to disable it extended and amplified the midcentury project of promoting the disease concept, and focused just as it had on generating media messages that would change public opinion.

But stigma reduction was a clinical as well as a public relations issue, since shame-inducing treatment would hardly invite increased participation by women. The most obvious and yet probably the most profound innovation in this regard was simply to increase sensitivity on the part of treatment professionals, who needed "to convey a nonjudgmental attitude of openness, patience, and ease" in order to reassure women alcoholics that it was acceptable for them to ask for help.[18] A host of other innovations followed from this basic insight into the need to make treatment more woman-friendly. The creation of single-sex treatment groups was the most obvious one, but feminist clinicians also advocated for programs that incorporated family member participation, offered childcare and job placement assistance, and incorporated parenting workshops, sex education sessions, and assertiveness training alongside more traditional individual and group therapy and 12-Step meetings. The shared goal of all these was to undo the constellation of forces— which, contrary to 12-Step logic, women's alcoholism advocates saw as resolutely social and psychological—that had contributed first to women's drinking and then to their covering it up.

As they fought to create diagnostic and treatment protocols that attended to real rather than to idealized women's lives, women's alcoholism movement activists stumbled repeatedly over one particularly disturbing commonality among female alcoholics, namely their experience with childhood sexual trauma. In part because of ideological biases similar to those that constrained women's reporting on their drinking behavior, statistics on sexual trauma are notoriously difficult to obtain and subject to chronic underreporting. In 1953, Alfred Kinsey's *Sexual Behavior in the Human Female* had reported that 5.5 percent of adult women in the United States had experienced sexual contact with a male relative while they were children; many researchers believed at the time that this (along with some of Kinsey's other claims) was wildly exaggerated. In 1979 and 1980, however, a handful of studies found that between 12 and 54 percent of problem-drinking and alcoholic women reported instances of childhood sexual trauma; when asked about adult rape as well, the number zoomed to 74 percent—far higher than the rate that supposedly held for the general population. These findings corroborated research outside the addiction treatment world, where feminist social workers and community activists alike were beginning to agitate for greater attention to childhood sexual abuse.[19] These overlapping agendas created a conceptual synergy, and although no large-scale, controlled studies emerged to verify the link between sexual abuse and addiction, within a few years most liberal feminist recovery advocates had come to endorse researcher Sharon Wilsnack's claim that "experiencing incest, rape, or other sexual abuse may increase a woman's risk for subsequent alcohol abuse [as] alcohol or other drugs may be used in an attempt to reduce feelings of guilt, shame, anger, and loss of self-esteem that are common among victims of sexual abuse. . . . The pain and low self-esteem resulting from sexual abuse may drive some women . . . into overtly self-destructive use of alcohol or other drugs."[20] Sexual abuse and the psychic damage that flowed from it thus became key parts of an emerging but murky picture of "female alcoholic personality syndrome."

As psychologist Harriett Braiker admitted, however, a definitive diagnostic category that captured the specifics of women's addiction "remain[ed] elusive" despite "repeated attempts to capture [its] essence." As qualitative and quantitative researchers, treatment providers, and policy makers vied for how best to reveal and to assist the hitherto invisible alcoholic, it became clear that "the only agreement on what constitutes the female alcoholic personality centers on a poor self-concept and low self-esteem, although it is unclear whether such traits are the result or the cause of problem drinking."[21] But just as midcentury alcohologists had been unfazed by the imprecision of the disease concept, so members of the women's alcoholism movement did not quibble over precisely how low self-esteem figured into women's drinking lives. Like the three-part disease, it was a diagnosis that felt true. Some of this theory's key presumptions (e.g., gender biases run deep and can be profoundly damaging to women; men's sexual predation is more common than has hitherto been acknowledged) resonated with many of the core insights of the women's movement, and this common-sense appeal was enough to make it viable for dissemination through articles in the popular press and coverage on the TV talk show circuit.

Thus as cause, as effect, and often as a little of both, low self-esteem became the centerpiece of the women's alcoholism movement's diagnostics, accompanied by a belief that efforts to combat it should center on the equally expansive concept of "empowerment." Reducing stigma would empower women to seek treatment, and treatment in turn would empower them to face the issues that had disempowered them and driven them to drink in the first place. For the professionals who staffed the treatment and policy communities, stigma reduction and empowerment would best be achieved by the creation of equitable diagnostic and rehabilitative opportunities for women. Feminist recovery advocates operating outside the alcohol and drug industrial complex, however, theorized the dyad of cause and cure in quite different ways, typically in light of their own—or their communities'—experiences of addiction.

"I AM A COMPETENT WOMAN AND HAVE MUCH TO GIVE OTHERS"

Women for Sobriety (WFS), founded in 1975 by Jean Kirkpatrick, is a woman-centered antidote to Alcoholics Anonymous and a grassroots expression of the liberal feminist desire for equity that animated the women's alcoholism movement. "For too long," Kirkpatrick argued, "programs for alcoholics have been designed by men, administered by men, dominated by men, and applied to women."[22] She believed this bias had contributed to her own inability to remain sober in AA, an experience that led her to conclude that because male-dominated programs did not reflect the realities of women's alcoholism, such programs were worse than useless for women alcoholics, whose failure to find meaningful counsel within them only compounded the sense of shame and guilt instilled in them by drinking, driving them into a deeper cycle of alcohol abuse and despair.

The first woman at the University of Pennsylvania to win the prestigious Fels Prize for public policy research, Kirkpatrick completed a Ph.D. in American Civilization in 1970. Her thesis, "The Temperance Movement and Temperance Fiction, 1820–1860," was, ironically, completed between drinking binges and suicide attempts. Kirkpatrick had begun attending AA near her hometown of Quakertown, Pennsylvania, before she began her graduate study and after she was fired from an elementary school teaching job in Kansas for coming to work drunk. She stayed in the program for three years before returning to a life of progressively worsening drinking combined with prescription drug abuse during the late 1960s. While living in Quakertown and trying to dry out after completing her Ph.D., she returned to AA but soon left it, disgusted by what she felt to be its counterproductive paternalism. Her list of complaints about AA no doubt resonated with many feminist recovery activists. "The men were set in their ways and ideas, they dominated the meetings, their stories were often lurid and contained an ego element of bragging, their descriptions of women were very often chauvinistic . . . and their constantly calling me a 'gal' began to grate on my nerves. I found that with every meeting I attended, I had a great desire to go out and get drunk."[23]

The only mitigating factor, Kirkpatrick discovered, was the satisfaction she got from talking to Ruth, the only other woman in her group. Watching Ruth struggle with her sobriety and with the chauvinism of AA (she acted as the secretary for the group and fended off leering inquiries into how her drinking affected her private life), Kirkpatrick decided that "women alcoholics needed something more [than AA], something special, because alcoholic women feel that they have failed . . . as wives, as mothers, as daughters, as women. . . . [They] carry great burdens of guilt from the feeling of this failure which society . . . our culture . . . continually reinforces." As a result, she resolved to "give up on AA, although I would help Ruth when I could. She began to rely on me and I found that my talking to her helped me."[24] Women for Sobriety was the result of that sororal impulse, which is further elaborated in Kirkpatrick's description of the organization: "Women for Sobriety groups provide acceptance and nurture, they provide kinship and identification; they provide supportive love, help, and care; they are nonjudgmental; they reinforce faltering self-esteem; they provide a place to be rid of anxiety; they provide friendship with others of the same mind and circumstances; they provide a place of trust; and they provide a forum for those women who need to talk and relate."[25]

In her writings, Kirkpatrick makes no bones about the ways in which AA and the treatment profession that grew out of it treat women as a "second sex," but WFS nevertheless retains some key 12-Step principles. Most notable of these is the emphasis on mutual help, as illustrated above, but WFS also affirms AA's sense that alcoholism is a terminal illness that is progressive, all-encompassing, and arrested only by abstinence. Kirkpatrick also advocated coming to terms with alcoholism through a series of stages not unlike AA's, which WFS breaks down as "admission . . . surrender . . . acceptance."[26] She framed this process as a reality check rather than as a spiritual process, however, arguing that "in AA, the alcoholic is taught that he or she is powerless over alcohol, while in WFS she is taught that she has a disease that she can control by not drinking. AA's *powerlessness* then leads to the surrendering of the problem to a higher power (i.e., God); WFS's *control* leads to thinking about why she drank."[27] This emphasis on thinking and control sets WFS apart from its older masculinist counterpart.

Reflecting its rejection of AA's founding principles, the first of WFS's 13 Steps deliberately inverts AA's Step 1—and sounds the theoretical party line to which most feminist recovery advocates adhere. The statement "I have a drinking problem that once had me" signifies a decisive break with an unhappy past and announces a newly empowered status that is the grounds for both personal well-being and efficacy in the world. With that sense of empowerment comes a new and productive relationship to the community, acknowledged in the claims of Steps 12 and 13: "I am a competent woman and have much to give others" and "I am responsible for myself and my sisters."[28]

Within WFS, a woman's claim to power rests in her ability to analyze the thoughts, feelings, and behaviors that contributed to her destructive drinking; its middle steps focus on developing that ability. In contrast to the anti-intellectualism of AA, where the slogan "Your best thinking got you here" mocks the limits of self-analysis, WFS makes thinking central to recovery, impressing upon its members the need to think about "*why* we turned to alcohol to cope with life's problems."[29] This thinking transpires through meditation, diary-keeping, and small group meetings where members share their current experiences and states of mind "in hope of understanding the motivation or faulty thinking" behind their drinking, so that it "can be recognized for what it is, and positive thinking and positive action may take place instead."[30]

Both singly and together, women in WFS engage in rational, compassionate self-scrutiny rooted in the foundational feminist insight that women's experiences in the world, alcoholic and otherwise, are different from and, historically, more constrained than men's. In her writings, Kirkpatrick discusses the ways that modern feelings of alienation and loneliness can drive drinking for both men and women, but she gives greater emphasis, unsurprisingly, to the fact that "through the ages women have been viewed as inferior to men, second-class citizens."[31] The result is conflicting messages about how to nurture and be nurtured, perfectionism perversely combined with learned helplessness, and above all a constant sense of guilt and failure, of never being good enough. Women drink both to help them in their quest to meet the impossible expectations set for them by society—to accentuate their femininity; to cope with the boredom of being housewives; to relax sufficiently to meet their husbands' sexual demands—and they drink to numb their resentment at having to meet those expectations or to blunt the pain that they feel when they fail to do so.[32] While not quite the consciousness-raising practiced within the women's liberation movement, wfs's emphasis on analytical thinking with attention to the social construction of male and female roles serves a similar function, namely to lead women to see that their feelings of inadequacy and unhappiness stem from the distorted expectations placed on them by a male-dominated society, *not* from any failings of their own. Having acknowledged gender's structuring power, they become free to elaborate a plan for evolution beyond its constraints.

This rational-seeming practice, it should be acknowledged, is nevertheless shot through with a distinctly spiritual message. wfs's 8th Step states that "the fundamental object of life is emotional and spiritual growth," which results in "inner peace and calm, a knowing [of] one's place in the scheme of the universe, of feeling a relationship to all things and to something greater than ourselves."[33] Like Karen Casey, Jean Kirkpatrick had become a follower of the Unity Church while she was struggling for sobriety, and she exhorted members of wfs to acknowledge both "the divine within" and the "power of mind." The line between recognizing the degree to which the internalized dictates of a male-dominated world shape behavior and using one's thoughts to change reality is a fine one in her writings. In *Turnabout* she explains that "the whole program of Women for Sobriety is based upon the concept of our thoughts creating the world in which we live"; *Goodbye, Hangovers* concludes with a chapter on "Mind Control for Life Control."[34] Six of wfs's 13 Steps, which Kirkpatrick called "the six keys to a lifetime recovery," suggest a deep allegiance to New Thought ideals: "Negative emotions destroy only myself" (Step 2); "Problems bother me only to the degree that I permit them to" (Step 4); "I am what I think" (Step 5); "Love can change the course of my world" (Step 7); and "The past is gone forever" (Step 9).[35] Through journal-writing, meditation, and the daily repetition of positive affirmations, members of wfs work at modifying their world and their lives through their thoughts.

The only scholar to study wfs in depth, sociologist Lee Ann Kaskutas, observed nothing mystical in the wfs group meetings she attended, and she makes no mention of Kirkpatrick's ties to Unity. As in aa, the character of WFS groups may vary from place to place; it is possible that the group Kaskutas observed was a particularly secular one. In addition, even at her most New Thought–ish, when Kirkpatrick invokes the "law of compensation" or argues that "we have the faculty of being able to transport ourselves where our minds take us," her statements about the power of mind sound more like exercises in cognitive therapy than attempts to get in tune with the mystical vibrations of the universe.[36] It is quite possible that scholars have overlooked the spiritual dimensions of WFS because they are almost completely obscured by its pragmatic tone. For Kirkpatrick, however, it is clear that the spiritual dimension of recovery was key—and was intimately tied to redressing low self-esteem. "Feelings of self-esteem," she argued, "must be based upon images of ourselves, and my experience has shown that most women have little concept of themselves" beyond what society has foisted upon them.[37] The constructive re-self-fashioning that WFS offers requires creating new self-images and then thinking them into reality, a mental labor that was simultaneously an act of feminist critique and a mystical practice.

After its founding, WFS grew gradually and somewhat erratically, chiefly as a result of Kirkpatrick's writing (in venues like *Women's Day* and *Vogue* as well as in the professional addiction treatment press) and public appearances. Although Sharon Wilsnack and Linda Beckman's canonical *Alcohol Problems in Women* (1984) makes no mention of WFS in its overview of the field, by 1990 there were between 250 and 300 groups, with approximately 5,000 members. By 1996, however, those figures had declined: the number of groups was down to 125 and membership was estimated at 1,000; Kaskutas described WFS at that time as "relatively hidden from the therapeutic and academic communities."[38] This downward trend seems to have reversed itself in the past decade, despite Kirkpatrick's death in 2000. An on-line community with bulletin board and chat features was created in 1998, and that, combined with a phone support tree and several hundred face-to-face meetings around the world, allows WFS to claim currently that "several hundred thousand women us[e] our program."[39]

In its early years, however, the radical feminist recovery advocates who distanced themselves from the women's alcoholism movement and its allied 12-Step organizations seem also to have been largely unmoved by (or unaware of) WFS. The organization goes unmentioned in writings about addiction and recovery in journals like *Sinister Wisdom* and *Quest: A Feminist Quarterly*. Unlike AA's cofounders, Kirkpatrick created a centralized organizational structure; WFS members pay a set fee at each meeting and leaders follow a short training course in order to become certified.[40] This perceived hierarchy and formality may have seemed off-putting to grassroots-oriented activists, especially when taken in combination with WFS's limited gender critique (i.e., willing to point out inequality and support women in getting out from under it, but not interested in fomenting plans for broad structural change). Kirkpatrick's commitment to using the power of positive thinking to change the negative self-images gleaned from a chauvinist culture would have seemed thin gruel indeed to the radical activists that the next sections of this chapter explore.

Like the women's alcoholism movement, then, and for some of the same reasons, the equity-focused Women for Sobriety was not assimilated into the broader feminist and women's health movements that grew out of more radical 1970's feminist activism. The movement's organizations—clinics, shelters, day care and rape crisis centers, to name just a few of the most visible—responded to the needs of regular women and, in doing so, transformed the institutional and policy fabric of the nation. Even if the resulting institutions have ended up assimilated into the mainstream service economy, scholars see them as one of the key legacies of the women's liberation movement.[41] Woman-centered addiction treatment seems of a piece with these other innovations, yet is rarely discussed as part of the history of feminist institution-building.

Laura Schmidt and Constance Weisner have argued that women's alcoholism and addiction remained at the margins of organized feminism because of a clash between "dry" and "wet" perspectives among liberal feminists. Professionals inside the alcohol and drug industrial complex marked out the "dry" perspective, which emphasized drink cessation and treatment. Their struggle to make women visible within the clinical and legal discourses of alcoholism and to obtain equal access to appropriate services for women alcoholics was probably seen as valuable by some feminist treatment providers who worked in publicly funded, community-based clinics. But "wet" sentiments were strong within the National Organization for Women and other groups that had been influenced by the civil rights and antiwar movements. In those circles, both the disinhibition and, to a lesser extent, the impaired social functioning brought on by alcohol and drug abuse could easily be construed as gestures of protest against an uptight "straight" world, and distrust of formal, professionalized, bureaucratic organizations, particularly those funded by the government, was an article of faith. Schmidt and Weisner argue that some specific campaigns within the women's alcohol movement, like those that focused on alcohol's differential impacts on men and women, or on the health risks of drinking during pregnancy, could be seen as reinforcing normative gender roles. Along with the overarching mandate for increased "sensitivity" to women's issues in treatment, such programs could be read simply as fronts for new and more subtle attempts to control women's lives. Deep skepticism about the nature and purpose of sobriety, and about whose interests were served by sobriety promotion, flowed naturally from feminist questioning of patriarchal authority. Since the proponents of Women for Sobriety and the women's alcoholism movement seemed ultimately more committed to alcoholism than to feminism as such, they had "limited success in becoming part of the 'big picture of women's issues'" during the 1980s.[42]

Schmidt and Weisner's "dry" versus "wet" theory goes a long way toward explaining the disinterest many feminists outside the treatment community seem to have shown for the equity-focused activities of the women's alcoholism movement and Women for Sobriety. But a "wet" feminism, logically, should have had no interest in addiction and recovery, and, as evidenced by the *Feminist Bookstore News*'s bathroom graffiti, such was not the case. Quite the contrary: as the rest of this chapter makes clear, while liberal feminists were advocating for gender reforms within the addiction treatment world, their radical counterparts were developing their own theories of addiction, along with programs intended to disable it at the grassroots. Their thinking along these lines was bold and ambitious; upon examination, it seems reasonable to argue that it was not disinterest in addiction and recovery as such, but investment in these homegrown ideas about their origins, effects, and remedies that accounted for grassroots feminists' coolness toward their liberal counterparts.

SOBER DYKES AND OUR FRIENDS

The discovery of a hidden epidemic of women's drinking during the 1970s was paralleled by similar revelations of rampant alcohol abuse in gay and lesbian communities. Bars had for many years played crucial roles in the development of those communities: alcohol may have helped many to blunt the pain of a sexual identity constructed as "deviant"; it facilitated flirtations and sexual encounters that, too often, had to remain quick and/or clandestine. It is no accident that the event that signaled the beginning of the Gay Liberation Movement, an uprising by gay and transgender men fed up with police harassment, took place at the Stonewall Inn, a gay bar in New York's Greenwich Village. For much of the twentieth century, bars incubated the gay and lesbian relationships (romantic and otherwise) that were outlawed in "polite" society.[43]

Given alcohol's visible and highly charged position in gay and lesbian life, it should not be surprising to find that gay men and lesbians were among the special populations identified by the treatment community as in need of attention in the 1970s and 1980s. Activists within the community and, to a lesser extent, academic researchers took it upon themselves to quantify the extent of alcohol abuse among gays and lesbians and to devise treatment programs free of the homophobia and bias that characterized the mainstream addiction establishment. Like research and advocacy around the disease concept and women's alcoholism, the early exploration of gay and lesbian drinking generated both anecdotal and flawed empirical evidence, whose weaknesses were only sometimes acknowledged by activists eager to draw attention (and funding) to a public health issue that had long been swept under the rug. In part because information circulated through gay and lesbian community-based media and personal networks, rather than through "official" scientific channels, erroneous claims were often amplified rather than contested and ascended quickly to the status of truth.[44]

The prime example of this occurred with the publication in 1975 of Lillen Fifield's study of gay/lesbian drinking habits and alcohol abuse, *On My Way to Nowhere: Alienated, Isolated, and Drunk—An Analysis of Gay Alcohol Abuse and an Evaluation of Alcoholism Rehabilitation Services for the Los Angeles County Gay Community*. After surveying a self-selected sample—bartenders and patrons at gay bars, recovering gay alcoholics, and habitués of the L.A. Gay Community Services Center (the funding agency for the study)—Fifield reported that "31.4% of the total Los Angeles county gay and lesbian population show signs of alcoholism or heavy drinking," with 10.4 percent in the " 'crisis or danger stages of alcohol consumption and in need of alcoholism services.' "[45] Journalist and activist Randy Shilts repeated Fifield's findings in the national gay and lesbian magazine *The Advocate* the following year, and, despite the flaws in the data collection (e.g., self-reporting by people likely to abuse alcohol, the aggregation of male and female accounts, no control group), the idea that one-third of gays and lesbians were or would soon be crippled by alcoholism was soon accepted as fact. As the conservative backlash of the 1980s and then the AIDS epidemic began to threaten gay and lesbian communities, the one-in-three figure became a powerful emblem for a community under siege, and breaking out of denial to move toward recovery became a political act.

One of the key figures within the lesbian community to be energized by the perceived epidemic was Jean Swallow. Born in North Carolina into a family with a history of alcoholism, Swallow identified as an alcoholic, a survivor of childhood sexual abuse, and a codependent. During the 1970s she worked as a journalist and published fiction and poetry in small lesbian/feminist publications. She got sober after moving to San Francisco late in the decade "with the help of [the] women who loved me, but not with an organized group."[46]

In sobriety, Swallow began to see her own experiences of addiction and codependence replicated throughout the communities that lesbians had carved out for themselves across the United States during the 1970s. A self-described "book fiend," she looked for reading material that addressed lesbian addiction and codependence, but could find very little. At the urging of her partner, Sherry Thomas, one of the owners of the San Francisco publisher Spinsters Ink, in 1983 Swallow published the anthology *Out from Under: Sober Dykes and Our Friends*, the first book by and for lesbian addicts. She saw the book as "a road-map and a vision, a sharing and a song," and intended it to raise consciousness, "spark some discussion," and create a "lesbian wave effect" in response to what she perceived to be a crisis for both individual lesbians and the larger lesbian/feminist community. "Since I came to this feminist movement almost ten years ago," Swallow explained, "I have repeatedly heard talk . . . that we must throw off the messages of patriarchy if we are to be free. That is as true today as it ever was. What we must recognize is that substance abuse is part of the patriarchy. . . . It is a lie. It is every bit as much a lie as sexism, capitalism, racism, and homophobia [and has] the same effects on us: low self-esteem, anger, depression, hopelessness, and loss of purpose. There is a major difference, though. Sexism, racism, and the rest of them are done to us; we do the substance abuse to ourselves" (x–xi). And the extent of this self-damage was grievous indeed: citing an unspecified study that further inflated Lillen Fifield's statistics, Swallow argued that "the lesbian community [is] 38% alcoholic, 30% problem drinkers. For a lesbian, those statistics mean you either are one or you love one" (ix). Addressing both addiction and codependence was an essential task if the lesbian community hoped to survive the assaults of the 1980s intact; Swallow intended *Out from Under* as the beginning of that housekeeping project.

The anthology consisted of thirty-two pieces, including both creative (fiction, poetry, song lyrics, memoirs) and journalistic (essays, interviews) writing. Swallow had solicited contributions through flyers mailed out to gay and lesbian community centers, women's bookstores, and other convivial gathering spots, and her democratic approach netted a wide range of contributors. Some pieces had appeared previously in lesbian journals, others were parts of longer works in process, and still others were by first-time authors. Each dealt explicitly with the process of recovery (rather than recounting days of drinking and drugging), and each concluded with the author's answer to this question: "If your lesbian community were clean and sober, what would it look like?" A short bibliography of sources dealing with alcohol, addiction, and codependence—from scholarly journals, from 12-Step and treatment publishers, and from lesbian and gay community organizations—rounded out the volume.

The contributors to *Out from Under* did not share Women for Sobriety's antipathy toward Alcoholics Anonymous. A few talked about feeling marginalized or closeted in 12-Step meetings, but several others noted that they had found AA/Al-Anon meetings or literature useful. None, however, had found AA sufficient to their needs as lesbians, not necessarily because it was homophobic (though a few reported as much), but because Bill Wilson and Bob Smith's "three-part disease" failed to capture what they believed to be the ineluctably social dimensions of lesbian addiction. Like Kirkpatrick and the therapists who worked within the women's alcoholism movement, Swallow and her collaborators talked about drug and alcohol abuse as the side effect of a larger problem rooted in biased sex and gender relations. They drank to blunt the pain of being a lesbian in a hostile culture, to create the mindset necessary to act on taboo sexual desires or to endure unwanted heterosexual sex, and to facilitate admission into an underground social scene. Addiction was intimately related to lesbians' social marginalization, they agreed, but their critique went beyond a liberal feminist interest in addiction's connections to self-esteem to argue that "alcoholism/drug addiction is one of the most powerful, political, oppressive tools that exists . . . [to] keep the masses down" (86).

This focus on oppression, rather than inequality, differentiated radical feminist recovery advocates from their liberal coevals in research, treatment, and policy. Two theories of addiction as a tool of oppression circulate throughout *Out from Under*. The first strikes a bold, almost paranoid note. "On a political level, I think people are forced to become addicted," states Misha Cohen, identified as an herbal healer and anti-imperialist activist. "Alcohol and heroin and methadone . . . exist to keep people under control" (75). Her sentiments are echoed by antiviolence advocate Nina Jo Smith, who argues that for years, "alcohol has been used as an instrument of colonization and control to quell resistance. . . . As women we have been 'targeted' by the liquor advertising industry in the last ten years [because] women and gays are rising" (130).

More common than these explicitly conspiratorial sentiments (which echoed anti-drug and anti-alcohol discourse circulating within the Black Power and American Indian Movements) is a somewhat softer-edged critique derived from radical feminism's interest in "interior colonization," the process whereby women identify against their own best interests with the values of the dominant capitalist, patriarchal, and heterosexist culture.[47] "Cultural conditioning keeps wimmin [*sic*] from valuing themselves and each other," argued artist Abby Willowroot, and social messages promoting alcohol consumption are "designed to keep wimmin consuming in order to feel better about themselves and boost the economy" (123). Therapist JoAnn Gardner-Loulan's contribution concurred with this vision: condoning alcohol meant condoning a system that ran counter to women's interests. "Buying into the culture of alcohol and drugs is buying into instant pain release [and] the ultimate capitalism. Capitalism says if you buy this, you'll feel better, as opposed to doing your healing work on your own" (101). Expanding on Willowroot's theory that "alcoholism is just another word for womyn-hating [*sic*]," therapist Suzanne Balcer observed that lesbian and feminist activists "have been fighting oppression without identifying the tools of oppression. . . . We have to stop using tools 'they' have given us and come up with our own healthy, powerful tools" for both personal pleasure and political change (123, 83). One of the by-products of women's misplaced faith in the "tools 'they' have given us" was low self-esteem—"a goal for all should be [its] development and enhancement," counseled Balcer (81). But more so than their liberal counterparts, the radical contributors to *Out from Under* affirmed the connection between psychic and social issues, and saw the elimination of individual cases of low self-esteem as intimately linked to a deepened understanding and contest of oppressive social forces.

Beyond this general theoretical principle, *Out from Under* did not attempt to provide a thoroughgoing and unified theory of addiction or recovery; its anthology form, which self-consciously mixed genres and voices, would have cut against such a monolithic viewpoint in any case. While the contributors were unanimous on the need for a structured program of abstinence, they suggested that the structure could be achieved through commitment to exercise, meditation, or a health food diet. A support network was crucial, but might take the form of a counselor, therapy group, or friendship community. Detoxification and treatment were generally seen as important steps toward sobriety, but formal 12-Step groups or treatment programs that traded in the racism, classism, and homophobia of the mainstream or straight world could easily compound the sense of alienation that fed addiction, rather than relieving it. Contributors had similarly diverse perspectives on the spiritual dimension of recovery: some discussed at length the roles yoga, martial arts, or a retreat to nature had played in their sobriety, while others remained silent on the topic.

In one important way, however, all the pieces in *Out from Under* referenced a central concern of traditionalist AA. Swallow's prompt to each contributor to end her piece with a consideration of what a clean and sober lesbian community would look like was an attempt to raise the same issues that midcentury midwestern authors had broached when they contrasted "AA Sobriety" to "sobriety, period." For those middle-class white men, the realm beyond dryness was a spiritual one in which lonely autonomy and aggression were replaced by brotherly love and the noncompetitive community of the gift. In their clean and sober projections, the *Out from Under* contributors acknowledged that despite the foundation of sisterly solidarity that undergirded the lesbian/feminist community, divisions existed within it that needed healing by flows of love. Sobriety would mean "there would be less fighting" and "everyone would be able to take care of herself and each other without having anyone be the victim" (70, 78). The disappearance of the emotional distance caused by "the cold grip of a chemical prison" (33) would allow collective action to flower. "As lesbian women, we aren't working together on issues that are important to all of us," argued fundraiser Lonnie Schilling. "We aren't able to [because] the alcohol puts space between us" (137). Rather than being riven by the drama of addiction and codependence as it was at present, in recovery the lesbian community could "turn its full attention on its oppressors" and fight "for justice in our lives as passionately as we have fought for life itself" (186, 133). As in AA, although through different mechanisms and with entirely different ends in mind, the greatest satisfaction of sobriety was the merger of the individual self with the broader, unified, and affectively charged collective. Lesbian recovery was thus a personal and psychological project, but also one that, by dint of the psyches involved, was profoundly collective and public. It was *Out from Under*'s sense of the lesbian self as constituted through that community and in fundamental opposition to the dominant society that led Swallow to "claim recovery as a political act, as a new tool, as part of the politic of the lesbian community."[48]

For Swallow personally, as for many of the radical feminists who shared her sentiments about addiction and recovery, writing and publishing on the topic were ways of putting that political tool into action. The texts that resulted raised individual consciousness and, equally if not more important, circulated information that many activists believed mainstream America preferred to suppress. The *Feminist Bookstore News*, which regularly promoted addiction, abuse, codependence, and recovery titles as crucial for consciousness-raising, advocated this line of thinking, as Figure 5.2 demonstrates.[49] Feminist bookstores, the *News* argued, had a duty to make hard-to-find women's recovery titles available to lesbian and feminist communities, not only to promote women's sobriety but also to remain actively engaged in the fight against a "straight" world that would like to see women drunk and their bookstores bankrupted.

This sense of mission shaped Swallow's writing career in the wake of *Out from Under*'s success. Despite her full-time job as a medical administrator, she traveled frequently to feminist bookstores and conferences on lesbian recovery, speaking and reading about her own recovery and leading writing workshops for others grappling with addiction and codependence. Swallow longed for sufficient financial resources to quit her day job, but when she was approached by Doubleday to write a trade book about women and recovery shortly after *Out from Under* appeared, she declined. While she believed such a book would be a useful and original contribution, she felt called "to stretch myself as a writer," having come to believe that the complexities of lesbian addiction and

Figure 5.2. Bulbul, "Somebody wants us drunk" cartoon, Feminist Bookstore News, *September 1983. http://www.bulbul.com. Courtesy of San Francisco Public Library.*

codependence were such that she needed to "learn to do different forms, different ways to get at the truth." With this in mind she continued to work within the feminist print culture underground, serving as poetry editor for the journal *Common Lives/Lesbian Lives* but increasingly turning her own attention to fiction.[50]

The result was *Leave a Light on for Me,* published in 1986, a thinly disguised autobiographical novel about a group of Bay Area lesbians whose lives are marked by the struggle to come to terms with their alcoholism and childhood sexual abuse. The novel dutifully recounts the inter- and intrapersonal struggles of addiction and codependence, and captures nicely a particular historical moment in San Francisco's gay and lesbian community. Printed in an edition of 15,000 copies, it sold well among the women whose lives it sought to depict, but its impact beyond that demographic niche seems to have been negligible.[51] This tepid response was not unwarranted: Swallow's papers attest to the fact that she worked hard at fiction writing, drafting careful character sketches and plot outlines meant to create a unified and dynamic story, but her language rarely sings and the characters' insights into their "issues" feel somewhat mechanistic.[52]

Thus while the novel was reviewed respectfully in the lesbian press, it was not treated, as *Out from Under* had been, as a work that cleared out conceptual space for a whole new discussion. This may have been the result of Swallow's limited abilities as a fiction writer, but it is also possible that it had nothing to do with the specifics of *Leave a Light on for Me*. A few years before it appeared, another novel about women's recovery had stolen onto the scene, redefining the terms—and the marketplace—for literary treatments of the topic. Jean Swallow's fictionalized accounts of addiction, abuse, and recovery, no matter how precise or heartfelt, were no match for Alice Walker and *The Color Purple*.

"HEALING DARKNESS" IN THE COLOR PURPLE

Alice Walker's *The Color Purple* is perhaps the most important feminist recovery text to appear in the early 1980s, despite—or perhaps because of—the fact that it says nothing about alcohol or drugs. At one level, the novel focuses on individual recovery from sexual abuse; at a higher level it takes on what literary and cultural critic bell hooks has called "healing darkness": the process of individual and communal recovery from the spiritual and psychic wounds that sexism, racism, capitalism, and imperialism have inflicted on people of color, particularly but not exclusively women.[53] This recovery project, what hooks describes as the work of reclaiming "the whole self that existed prior to exploitation and oppression," originated in the anticolonialist and black liberation struggles that began in the 1950s and was explored by a variety of African diasporic writers and activists during the tumultuous decades that followed.[54] Its most popular and influential American expression, however, appeared in the 1980s alongside feminist writings on recovery from alcoholism, drug addiction, and sexual abuse.

Published in 1982, *The Color Purple* is generally seen as a turning point in Walker's already successful career as an author and activist. A native of rural Eatonton, Georgia, she had attended Spelman College beginning in 1961 before going on to graduate from Sarah Lawrence in 1965. At the urging of her teacher, poet Muriel Rukeyser, she published her first volume of poetry, *Once*, upon graduation. After traveling to Africa for several months, she returned to the South to teach and to facilitate voter registration, marrying white civil rights lawyer Mel Levanthal in 1967. For the next seven years, supported by short-term teaching jobs at schools ranging from Tougaloo to Wellesley College, Walker wrote fiction, essays, and poetry that explored white racism, black sexism, and their complicated interrelationships with unusual frankness. Her work was hailed as bleak but ground-breaking by both African American and feminist critics.

Literary critic Tuzyline Jita Allan aptly describes the project of Walker's earliest fiction as an attempt to capture "the mule-of-the-world stage in the development of black female consciousness." That sense of self, she argues, leads black women, "feeling partly responsible for white society's emasculation of black men [, to] offer themselves in atonement, their self sacrifice demanding from them total submission to male desire."[55] As a result, Walker's first novels, *The Third Life of Grange Copeland* and *Meridian*, offer stark portrayals of sexual and domestic violence, loneliness, and female self-negation—sparked only intermittently by glimpses of a "new black woman who recreates herself out of the legacy of her maternal ancestors."[56]

Allan argues that these dark literary explorations of the way oppressive social structures play out in black women's lives, coupled with Walker's personal experience of racism and sexism as part of an interracial couple living in the black power–era South, led the author to become disenchanted with both the organized white feminism and the confrontational race politics that played out during the 1970s. In response, toward the end of the decade she began actively to cultivate a distinctive and life-affirming theory of race and gender relations she called "womanism." Strongly rooted in the values of the black folk community, and keenly aware of what it has taken for that community to survive, the womanist self is characterized by curiosity, audacity, and, most important, love. The womanist "loves music. Loves dance. Loves the moon. *Loves* the Spirit. Loves love and food and roundness. Loves struggle. *Loves* the Folk. Loves herself. *Regardless*."[57] Although womanism is first and foremost a distillation of black folk values, it is also a reaction against the extremes of white feminism (specifically its separatism) and black nationalism (specifically its patriarchalism), both of which Walker had begun to experience as profoundly alienating. She began to formalize her ideas about an alternative road to empowerment in 1975 when, depressed and in the middle of a divorce, she found herself increasingly drawn to mystical spiritual traditions (tarot reading, telepathy, transcendental meditation, paganism) and to what she called the "religion [of] love." After a dozen years at the cutting edge of radical politics, Walker believed she was ready to turn her life and her writing away from "violence and what it could do" and toward "show-[ing] good people who struggle—and survive."[58]

The result of that turn was *The Color Purple*, a novel that charts one woman's transformation from an abused "mule of the world" into one who "loves herself. *Regardless*." The novel unfolds as a series of letters from the protagonist, Celie, to God, and scholars have interpreted that stylistic choice as evidence of Walker's conscious decision to "signify on" the epistolary novel form—that is, to appropriate, adapt, and tacitly critique it, thus claiming it for a distinctly African American use.[59] Read within the context of the broader feminist recovery movement, the novel can also be seen as signifying on the classic 12-Step narrative structure of "what we were like, what happened, and what we are like now." That form was likely also a familiar one to Walker, as her companion during the years she was writing the novel, Robert Allen, was a recovering alcoholic.[60] Like a 12-Step testimonial, the novel narrates Celie's journey from a place of spiritual darkness into a full and happy humanity. But as Walker tells that personal story, she also reveals the deep structures of racial, gender, and economic oppression that give it shape and meaning. Calling attention to the structuring forces elided in traditional white 12-Step narratives, *The Color Purple* suggests the inherently political dimension of black women's spiritual self-recovery.

While the typical 12-Step narrative expends the bulk of its energy recounting "what we were like," Walker depicts the constellation of wounding forces from which Celie must recover with remarkable efficiency. The novel's first page inaugurates the reader into a horrific scene of father-daughter incest. Celie's mother, described as "half-dead [from] all these children," has spurned her husband's sexual advances, leaving Celie to do "what your mammy wouldn't." Walker spares few details of "Pa's" (he is later revealed as her stepfather) rape of the fourteen-year-old girl: "First he put his thing up gainst my hip and sort of wiggle it around. Then he grab hold my titties. Then he push his thing inside my pussy.

When that hurt, I cry. He start to choke me, saying You better shut up and git used to it."[61] His routine abuse of her is made all the more monstrous by the fact that he impregnates Celie twice, each time taking the babies and, she believes, killing them in the woods. She consents to sex with him, however, in order to keep him away from her younger sister, Nettie.

A scant few pages later, Celie becomes the subject of new forms of intimate violence and degradation. "Pa" convinces their neighbor Mr. —— to marry her, persuading him with the argument that Celie is "ugly . . . but she ain't no stranger to hard work. And she clean. . . . She'd come with her own linen. She can take that cow she raise" (9). For a time, Nettie comes to live with Celie and Mr. —— to escape "Pa's" threats, but Mr. —— forces her to leave when she doesn't respond to his sexual overtures. At the same time, he "beat[s Celie] like he beat the children" (23) and subjects her to systematic marital rape: "git up on you, heist your nightgown round your waist, plunge in . . . like he was going to the toilet on you" (81). The novel's first few sections establish male power and female vulnerability as the hallmarks of Celie's world. Through her eyes and voice, Walker establishes a picture of a black patriarchy bent on exploiting women's bodies and breaking their spirits. As Celie prepares for another beating from Mr. —— she says, "I make myself wood. I say to myself, Celie, you a tree" (23). Her story of "what we were like," in other words, is a story of the dehumanization of black women at the hands of black men, who, in the post-slavery era have adopted the roles (raping, whipping, selling) that had hitherto been the privilege of white men.

But Walker's primary concern in the novel is less the depiction of "what we were like" than of "what happened," of the ways in which Celie overcomes the harms visited on her thanks to the interventions of a coalition of loving and empowered women. After Nettie leaves Mr. ——'s house, she moves to Africa to work as a missionary, but her place in Celie's life is filled by a variety of other "sisters," her "amazon" (71) daughter-in-law Sofia and Mr. ——'s lover, the blues singer Shug Avery, chief among them. From these two nontraditional women Celie learns the linked skills of resistance and self-love, which replace simple endurance ("I make myself wood") as her mode of engagement with the world.

Sofia is her first teacher in this regard. When her husband, Mr. ——'s son Harpo, complains to Celie that he can't make Sofia obey him, Celie parrots back the lessons she has learned from the male culture around her and suggests that he beat Sofia into submission. He is unsuccessful, and when Sofia discovers that it was Celie who encouraged his quest for patriarchal supremacy in their household, she is furious—until Celie confesses that it is jealousy of Sofia's ability to fight that motivated her. Uncertain how someone could *not* fight, Sofia asks Celie what she does when she gets angry. "I can't even remember the last time I felt mad," Celie responds. "After while every time I got mad . . . I got sick. . . . Then I start to feel nothing at all. . . . Sometime Mr. —— git on me pretty hard. . . . But he my husband. I shrug my shoulders. This life soon be over, I say. Heaven last all ways" (43–44).

Sofia's response to this classic story of resignation and self-negation is to suggest that Celie "bash Mr. —— head open. Think bout heaven later" (44), and shortly thereafter, Celie puts this lesson to use. When Mr. ——'s father, Old Mr. ——, pays a call and talks negatively about Shug Avery, whom Celie has come to admire, she "drop a little spit in Old Mr. —— water" when he isn't looking, then fantasizes about how "next time he come I put a little Shug Avery pee in his glass. See how he like that" (56–57). This sequence of events signals the beginning of Celie's self-recovery, as she rids herself of the norms she has internalized from the abusive men in her life and begins to recognize, and act upon, her own righteous anger.

More so even than Sofia, it is Shug Avery who models the honesty, creativity, and audacity that Walker had come to believe were the keys to black women's survival, and she teaches Celie by precept and example how to define herself in terms of sexuality, gender, and spirit. When she learns about Celie's childhood sexual abuse and her brutal marital relations with Mr. ——, Shug licenses Celie to rewrite her sexual history, declaring "you still a virgin" (81) and offering a long overdue anatomy lesson. First by masturbating, then by becoming Shug's sexual partner, Celie begins to claim the sexuality that her abusive circumstances conspired to deny her. Her emerging lesbian identity is symbolized within the novel by her casting off, at Shug's suggestion, the cumbersome and ill-fitting dresses traditional for a woman of her age and station and adopting pants instead. The pants also become the agent of Celie's economic liberation: they become popular first within the family and then, when Shug wears them on tour, in the larger world. Bankrolled by Shug, Celie sets up "Folkspants, Inc." in her dining room, employing other women to cut and sew while she designs pants for the mass market.

These various examples of female empowerment pave the way for the novel's central lesson: the need to ground the self's disparate freedoms —psychic, sexual, economic—in a spiritual existence that affirms, rather than denies, blackness and femaleness. Shug is once again Walker's spokeswoman. She narrates her own journey to such a spirituality when, about midway through the novel, Celie learns that Mr. —— has hidden years' worth of letters that Nettie has written to her from Africa and that her "Pa" was not her real father, but a man who married her mother after her real father was lynched by whites because his store encroached on their business. As literary critic Lauren Berlant has suggested, the revelation of the letters and of the lynching shift the referential framework within which the novel operates, allowing Walker to complicate and add nuance to the vision of "what happened" that takes up the novel's first half and to open it to an exploration of spirituality.[62]

Celie's response to the revelations about her husband's and her "father's" duplicity is to become angry at God. She stops writing her letters to him and writes to Nettie instead. "The God I been praying and writing to is a man," she tells Shug, "and act just like all the other mens I know. Trifling, forgetful, and lowdown" (199). This theological insight is elaborated when Shug and Celie find the letters from Nettie that Mr. —— has hidden, and those documents become part of the substance of the novel. As the text shifts between Celie's and Nettie's letters, Walker moves beyond the richly depicted local context, the space of black men's sexual brutality and black women's sustaining love, and sketches a global history of racial oppression and colonialism, which the novel makes plain are the forces that have conditioned and enabled the violence against women that its earlier chapters had so vividly depicted. Nettie's letters about tribal African religion and folkways (including the practices of scarification and female circumcision) and their desecration by British colonials not only provide the back story to the history of slavery, racial apartheid, and patriarchal domination in the United States, but they also make clear the role that the white church has played in facilitating and legitimating that history. This far-reaching indictment of the linked forces of whiteness, capitalism, and patriarchy informs the spiritual counsel Shug offers to Celie when she makes her complaints about God: a black woman's life will never be enriched by the God "that's in the white folks' bible," and so she must labor instead to find the "God [who] is inside you and inside everybody else" (201–2).

Walker's commitment to this spiritual liberation, which she sees as both the foundation and the abiding challenge of womanist self-recovery, is evidenced by the amount of time Shug spends discussing it. For much of the novel, Shug makes the defiance of soul-killing convention look easy, a question of attitude captured in the matter-of-fact statement "why any woman give a shit what people think is a mystery to me" (208). Her spiritual development is the only aspect of her unconventional life that seems ever to have been marked by disillusionment or doubt, and it is the only dimension of her personality explored in much detail. Describing her own spiritual evolution, she explains that she, too, had once unthinkingly believed in a "big and old and tall and graybearded and white" God until she realized that the Bible was "just like everything else [white people] make, all about them doing one thing and another, and all the colored folks doing is getting cursed" (201–2). As a result, she turned away from the organized church. "My first step from the old white man," she explains to Celie, "was trees. Then air. Then birds. Then other people. But one day when I was sitting quiet and feeling like a motherless child, which I was, it come to me: that feeling of being part of everything, not separate at all. I knew that if I cut a tree my arm would bleed" (203).

What Walker calls Shug's "paganism" dismisses the white male God found in church, but, more important, it connects her spirituality to life-giving pre-colonial African experience via the African worship of the "roof-leaf" plant, which Nettie had discussed in an earlier letter.[63] Shug's recognition of her spiritual kinship to a tree inverts Celie's earlier, degraded experience of "mak[ing] myself wood" by affirming African American connections to Africa—connections that the trauma of the Middle Passage and the dehumanization of enslavement attempted to sever, and that the internalization of white values conspires to obscure. Because paganism predates the experience of the colonization and exploitation of African peoples, Walker suggests, it has the capacity to become the self-affirming spirituality that can make black women whole, can allow them to be "part of everything, not separate at all."

Thus Shug urges Celie to "git man off your eyeball"—to rid herself of the white patriarchal spirituality she has internalized. "Whenever you trying to pray, and man plop himself on the other end of it, tell him to git lost." In his place, "conjure up flowers, wind, water, a big rock" (204). Such creative reconceptualization of the divine transforms the shame and fear-inducing white male God foisted on enslaved Africans by Western culture into one that is authentic to them, tied into both their rich pasts and their everyday encounters with the natural world. The result is a non-anthropomorphized God, a beneficent "it" that suborns beauty, wonder, and sexual pleasure. As Shug notes, rather than seeking obedience and deference, this God "love[s] everything [we] love" and is "always trying to please us" (203). More so than her claims to her own anger, sexuality, or labor, Celie's ability to finally "chase that old white man out of my head" and notice the freely given gifts of a genuinely loving God— like "a blade of corn (how it do that?)" or "the color purple (where it come from?)"—signals her successful project of self-recovery (204).

As in an AA narrative, then, Walker's version of "what happened" is a spiritual transformation. But while AA constructs the spirit as a realm apart and a refuge from the larger world of political and economic competition, for Walker the nature of black experience means such a separation is neither possible nor desirable. Within the African American community, she suggests, the spirit cannot be understood apart from the brutal history of racial oppression and colonialism. More important, the recovering spirit cannot be separated from the other spirits in the black community. This is true even, or perhaps especially, for those unrecovered souls within that community who compulsively re-enact the oppressor's domination on individuals more vulnerable than themselves. What Walker names as the womanist commitment to the "survival and wholeness of entire people, male *and* female" means that, even more so than in AA, the decolonized and recovered self has an obligation to "carry the message" to those who still suffer.[64]

This crowning insight is driven home in the novel's "what we are like now" conclusion. When Celie and Shug leave him to take up housekeeping together in Memphis, Mr. ——'s years of self-hatred, rage, and violence finally catch up to him, leaving him "shut up in the house . . . like a pig," tormented by ghosts and the sound of his own heart (231). Nurtured back to sanity by his son Harpo, he emerges newly humbled and apologizes to Celie for the way he has treated her. Her immediate response is vindictive: "I see he feeling scared of me. Well, good, I think. Let him feel what I felt" (230). But Mr. —— shares his own spiritual journey with her, including both his sorrow at the way his anger affected her and all his children and the peace that has come to him with the realization that "us here [on earth] to wonder" (290). His admission that "the more I wonder . . . the more I love" prompts Celie to concede that "he got a lot of feeling hind his face," and to extend her own heart out to him and suggest "let's us be friends" (280, 290).

In that moment of acceptance and forgiveness, a great peace sweeps over her: "*I be so calm*," she realizes, "and then I figure this the lesson I was suppose to learn" (290; original emphasis). Coached first by Sofia and Shug and then by a man who was originally her tormentor, Celie has successfully completed the womanist project of "comprehend[ing] and transform[ing] alienating experiences and oppressive social structures" into frameworks for self- and community-love.[65] Her recovery is a return to wholeness, a healing of the fractured sense of self and world that hallmarks the black experience of diaspora. The salutation in Celie's final letter suggests the successful integration of disparate parts of her life through love: "Dear God. Dear stars, dear trees, dear sky, dear peoples. Dear Everything. Dear God" (292). From its grim opening, the novel has moved to a nearly impossibly happy ending, tracking Celie's triumphant movement from isolated, abused child to "part of everything, not separate at all."

THE COMMUNITY AND THE SELF

A broad spectrum of feminist activists put forth an equally wide-ranging set of post-12-Step ideas about addiction and recovery during the late 1970s and early 1980s. Their visions were resolutely social, rejecting the idea of addiction as a disease in and of itself and seeing it instead as a symptom of a larger problem, namely women's disempowered position within a social fabric designed and controlled by men. Following from this etiology of addiction was an adamantly egalitarian recovery ideal, which rejected the masculinism that had passed itself off as universalism within older 12-Step organizations and treatment programs in order to center on the specifics of women's experience. Albeit to different degrees, feminist recovery advocates all saw sobriety maintenance as a communal rather than an individual project, and they cast that project (although again, to different degrees) as part of a broader struggle for equality and justice in the face of long-standing asymmetries of gendered power. Particularly when compared to the universalizing spiritualism of Alcoholics Anonymous, which cast questions of socioeconomic order as "outside issues," this take on recovery cannot help but seem political. What, then, has fueled feminist critics' suspicion of recovery, their sense that the desire to end addiction and to heal from trauma inevitably also means to turn away from the structural analysis of power and the organized effort for social change?

A relatively narrow framework of analysis is in part to blame. Feminist criticism of "the recovery movement" has looked almost exclusively at Adult Children of Alcoholics and Codependents Anonymous, with a dash of Women Who Love Too Much thrown in for good measure. Elayne Rapping, for example, argues that books by therapists Robin Norwood, Melody Beattie, and John Bradshaw "laid the theoretical groundwork" and formed the conceptual center of women's recovery culture. In doing so, she overlooks the writers and activists of the 1970s and early 1980s whose work cleared the space for those later authors.[66] Rooted in depth psychology and family systems therapy, neither of which foreground analysis of gendered structures of power and their effects on the self, these groups also borrowed the 12-Step commitment to the 10th Tradition of having "no opinion on outside issues." What is surprising is not that such therapeutics-driven groups are not "political," but that ostensibly feminist cultural critics like Rapping, Wendy Kaminer, and Susan Faludi would overlook the range of feminist theorizations of addiction and recovery that preceded and continued to exist alongside of them.

If a narrow slice of the recovery movement is one reason why "recovery" can seem depoliticized, a narrow definition of "politics" is another. Recovery's feminist critics, by and large, argue from a perspective largely unconcerned with institutional reform. Thus while the liberal feminists who advocated for expanded and improved addiction treatment options for women saw the changes to the system made by the end of the 1980s as major successes, such reforms have been deemed largely irrelevant by recovery's critics. AA's increasing openness to women (and members of the LGBT community) is also rarely counted as "politics," despite the fact that the increasing visibility of women-only meetings and the gender-sensitive emendations to Conference Approved Literature discussed in the previous chapter were the direct result of women's protests.[67] Similarly, the creation of Women for Sobriety has not been seen as a "political" or "feminist" victory, even though as a successful women-only organization it threatened AA's monopoly on the mutual-aid-for-addiction market, and thus may have exerted evolutionary pressure on AA's masculinist status quo. Like the creators of the feminist organizations that Myra Marx Ferree and Patricia Yancey Martin have studied, feminist recovery advocates' greatest achievement, in the long run, was to infuse the dominant discourse in preexisting bureaucratic organizations with an awareness of gender and power, and, in doing so, to humanize and democratize them.[68] A profound suspicion of institutions, however, informs the critiques of feminist recovery critics, predisposing them to overlook such reforms as negligible. Indeed, as Elizabeth Morrissey has argued, to the extent that making addiction treatment more hospitable or responsive to women encourages women to enter treatment, and thus to assume a "sick" or depoliticized role, liberal reforms are actually counterproductive.[69]

The methodologies and epistemologies through which feminist critics have constructed recovery as an object for analysis, then, are part of the reason they see that recovery culture as depoliticized. Casting a broader historical and conceptual net complicates that construction, and reveals recovery as a cultural field within which diverse women articulated the range of political traditions—liberal, radical, or woman of color—that together constituted Second Wave feminism. Undertaking this complication of women's recovery has been my largest intention in this chapter.

But historicizing women's recovery advocacy and attending to the intentions of the women behind it can go only so far in contesting the claim that recovery discourse contains logical and rhetorical moves that shift its adherents' attention away from public, collective, and structural social problems and toward the inner world of the self. Rapping, Kaminer, Faludi, et al. are correct when they note that by the end of the 1980s, increasing numbers of women, including self-identified feminists with track records as civil rights, anti–Vietnam War, pro-choice, and Gay Liberation activists seemed drawn to explain their unhappiness through a personal language of pain, healing, and individual responsibility rather than through a collective narrative of oppression and struggle. Both the nature of this shift and some of its largest implications are captured neatly in the evolution of Women for Sobriety's 13th Step. The original, written around 1978 (and quoted earlier in this chapter), read, "I am responsible for myself and my sisters." A few years later, anxious to make clear that WFS stressed "personal responsibility . . . rather than any dependency on others," Kirkpatrick revised it to state simply "I am responsible for myself and my actions."[70] The focus on gender-specific solidarity was replaced by an interest in individual agency; the collective ceded ground to the self. Why, precisely, did this happen?

Part of this inward turn resulted from the changed circumstances within which feminists found themselves as the 1980s unfolded. As the political climate and the economy shifted under Ronald Reagan—whose presidency saw the defeat of the proposed Equal Rights Amendment, a major backlash against affirmative action, and the systematic dismantling of the funding structures and government institutions of the Great

Society (to name just a few of its accomplishments)—some feminists withdrew from active engagement with politics. While some critics have viewed this turn as a defeatist retreat, others have characterized it as a strategic decision, a reflection of the fact that the conditions for creating change were simply not right.[71] Given the political tenor of the times, some women came to believe that "change was better achieved through personal and cultural transformation" than through traditional movement politics because, as one former activist put it, "women are not going to make changes until we have the integrity of our own containers intact." This belief—that if you truly want change, "you've got to start with yourself"—departed sharply from the collectivist focus that had developed within the women's liberation movement of the 1960s and 1970s even as it retained the movement's commitment to the idea that "the personal is political." This subtle but important shift seems to have resonated with a broad cross-section of women in recovery.[72]

Among those who came to advocate passionately for this stance was Jean Swallow, and her post–*Out from Under* writings persuasively demonstrate the way recovery prompted the turn away from movement-based and toward personal politics that feminist recovery critics have seen as "depoliticization." Although it was written before the codependence boom took hold, *Out from Under* contained a fair bit of discussion of "co-alcoholism" in families of origin and in lesbian relationships. As Swallow probed deeper into her own co-alcoholism and childhood history of sexual abuse for her fiction writing, she became increasingly convinced that her alcoholism had simply masked a larger lack of "emotional sobriety"—the state that one *Out from Under* contributor had described as "learning to be sober around your emotions, learning that there are no more big deals. . . . Accepting what is."[73] This insight caused her to reevaluate her political commitments, and she came to see the years she had spent at meetings, demonstrations, and rallies as simply variations on her bar-going habits. Both were attempts at what she called "getting off the planet," strategies for evading what was truly wrong in her world.[74] "As my battle with what I have been taught as a child becomes more clear," she wrote, "I see how much more treacherous, how much more damaging, demanding, and deadly those lessons were and how much harder they are to change than my overt struggles with political patriarchy, how almost easy political change seems compared to the slippery morass of invisibility and denial with which I continue to play out and honor the lessons of my abusive childhood."[75]

Conceptualized in this way, political activism was a community-sanctioned form of codependence, a means to continue denying where the true impediments to freedom lay. Speaking at a lesbian recovery conference in 1986, Swallow urged her audience to confront the oppressor that lurked within, which might easily take the form of too-passionately held theoretical and political positions: "In your town it might be the pornography debates; in mine it might be racism. I heard in Chicago, it was separatism; in Iowa City it was class. These are wars too. And they have devastated women."[76] Overcommitment to such abstractions was emotional insobriety, an indication of both the individual's and the community's reluctance to face its true psychic and spiritual needs.

The greatest of those needs, Swallow concluded, was love, specifically the love that had been denied to lesbians as they were growing up in abusive families. "As a small girl-child, were you supposed to be alive?" she asked her audience. "Did you have any control over what happened to you? Did you have any choices?" Only when they admitted that the answer to these questions was "no" would women be free to admit the pain they were in, to "feel it [and know] you won't die from it." Breaking through the denial of this pain was a precondition for individual and community healing: "All that pain that we carry around, that the little girls inside us carry around, if we express it, we can heal ourselves." Starting with these inner children and working outward, Swallow argued, was the only viable political action left for a lesbian feminist community besieged from the outside and straining from within. "If we don't learn to love again," her talk concluded, "we'll never get anything done."[77]

Jean Swallow in no way withdrew from public life: she continued to lead writing and recovery workshops and to do public readings from her works, and she became a leading advocate for alcohol- and chemical-free spaces within the lesbian feminist community.[78] But her politics, like that of many feminists in recovery, became during the 1980s a politics of personal change. By the time a follow-up volume to *Out from Under* appeared in 1992, Swallow had declared, "I march in no more demonstrations. . . . I have given up trying to get justice here [and begun] to appeal to a higher authority. . . . I go to church and I pray."[79] Unlike its predecessor, which had devoted an entire section to "The Politics of Our Addictions," *The Next Step: Lesbians in Long-Term Recovery* contained no analysis of the gendered and sexed political economy of alcohol and drugs. Instead, in selections with titles like "The Goddess Loves All

Creatures," "Life on Life's Terms," and "The Hidden Dancer," it focused on spiritual growth and healing from childhood abuse.

Few ideas associated with recovery have been as derided as the "inner child," and it is tempting to lay Swallow's turn from the rigors of interior colonization to the banalities of our wounded little girls at the feet of the treatment industry therapists with whom that image is usually associated. While she never used AA to deal with her alcoholism, during the mid- to late 1980s Swallow did attend workshops with codependence gurus Claudia Black and Sharon Wegscheider, among others.[80] A history that uses Swallow's life metonymically and asserts that the original, oppression-focused feminist vision of recovery fell victim to the platitudes of profit-mongering apolitical therapists would be simple and satisfying to write. An honest accounting of the turn toward healing the wounded self through love, however, must acknowledge that the idea was first popularized—within the feminist community as well as in the larger marketplace—not by apolitical therapists but by Alice Walker's *The Color Purple*.

Given the far-reaching, even militant nature of Walker's womanist critique of how class, gender, imperialist, and race politics merge to fuel abuse and dysfunction in the black community, it may seem counterintuitive to treat *The Color Purple* as part of the depoliticizing dynamics of recovery, much less to cede it a central role. Attention to the novel's publishing and reception history, however, demonstrates its capacity in this regard. Ironically, the novel's critical and commercial success deracinated its message, and Walker's narrative of the specifics of "healing darkness" within the African American community came to be read instead as a universal story of the power of forgiveness and self-love.

Though Walker had earned strong reviews for her first books, their sales had been unspectacular, and while some of her champions (male and female) within the publishing world believed prior to its publication that *The Color Purple* would do substantially better in terms of sales, their enthusiasms were not widely shared.[81] Harcourt, Brace, Jovanovich, Walker's publisher, did not even send advance copies out to readers. Nevertheless, propelled by strong reviews, the book became a "modest best-seller" in the fall of 1982.[82] Sales surged the following spring when Walker won both the American Book Award and the Pulitzer Prize. Her race and gender, however, combined with the novel's subject matter, continued to make executives leery about the book's sales potential. Editor Susan Ginsburg of paperback publisher Pocket

Books had negotiated the purchase of paperback rights over the objections of Pocket's president, Ron Bush, who strongly believed there was no market for a book about a poor black woman in the early twentieth-century South. As a result, rather than appearing in a mass-market edition after winning the Pulitzer, as might have been customary, the novel went into Pocket Books' relatively new quality paperback imprint called Washington Square Press.

Twenty-first-century readers may be hard-pressed to remember a world without quality paperbacks, the attractive, larger-format paperbound books that occupy the market niche just between traditional hardbacks and the mass-market paperbacks sold on racks at newsstands and convenience stores. Although they had existed in one form or another for decades (primarily for classroom use), in 1983 quality paperbacks were coming into their own, poised to remake a book industry in decline. Inflation, market stasis, corporate mergers, and a 1980 Internal Revenue Service ruling that had made excess inventory into a taxable asset caused contractions across the publishing industry in 1980.[83] The two bright spots in the picture were innovations designed to create new readers: the moderately priced and attractively packaged quality or "trade" paperback and its retailing counterpart, the shopping mall–based chain bookstore.[84] Both aimed to attract the attention and the purchasing power of the middle-class female consumers who made up the bulk of the book-buying public.

Needless to say, the vast majority of those consumers were white, and it was to them that *The Color Purple* was marketed and sold. From before the novel was published, the sentiment within the industry had been that if there was a niche for it, it was as a woman's book, addressing feminist rather than black issues. The early reviews in the popular press ratified that opinion. In the *New York Times*, Mel Watkins dutifully inserted it into the category of "powerful novels" by the likes of Toni Morrison, Gayl Jones, and Toni Cade Bambara that "dramatize the theme of conflict between black men and women," but the bulk of his review discussed the "poignant tale of women's struggle for equality and independence" and its "theme of female oppression."[85] Just so at Washington Square Press: *The Color Purple* was a woman's book "important enough for a universal market," according to Susan Ginsburg, a book most definitely not "just for the African American market." This colorblind reading of the novel carried the day, and over a million quality paperback copies sold by early 1984. By the next year, when publishers reflected on the ways chain stores and quality paperbacks were remaking the industry, *The Color Purple* had become a favorite object lesson, a leading example of how to reach a new kind of suburban, middle-class, female consumer—an audience that, it went without saying, was majority white.[86]

Walker's subject matter has always been black women, whom she finds "the most fascinating creations in the world," and *The Color Purple* was meant to have black women as its audience as well. "If I write books that whites feel comfortable with," Walker explained in an interview shortly after the novel appeared, "I have sold out."[87] Yet clearly, with sales of over 6 million copies, white women were quite comfortable with the book. This suggests that they were able to overlook Walker's critique of the interlocking structures of imperialism, capitalism, and whiteness over and against which Celie's recovery is achieved and, in so doing, to overlook the ways they themselves were implicated in those structures.[88]

White women's long-standing will to blindness regarding the specifics of black women's oppression no doubt facilitated such a reading, which became even more likely after Steven Spielberg's successful movie adaptation of the novel in 1985. As black feminist critic Jacqueline Bobo has observed, Spielberg (like Walker's white supporters at Harcourt Brace and Washington Square Press, though to a greater extent) "felt the novel was not about race exclusively [but] 'about human beings . . . about the triumph of the spirit—and spirit and soul have never had any racial boundaries.' " His version of the story eliminated some plot elements, added others, and recast the narrative as a whole to emphasize what he saw as its "Dickensian" and "heart-tugging" qualities.[89] White readers who came to the novel after seeing the film, or who encountered the mass-market paperback edition emblazoned with images and promotional materials from it, would have found themselves quite comfortably insulated from Walker's most trenchant criticisms.

Lacking empirical evidence, of course, it is not possible to say definitively how the novel was read by its millions of fans. But it seems a safe guess that the average white female reader, finding the novel in a suburban mall or shopping plaza and lacking the cultural literacy and historical background to decode its distinctive significations on 12-Step narrative form, probably absorbed its vision of recovery fairly uncritically. To such a reader, Celie's transformation was not a process of interior decolonization but a simple embrace of acceptance, forgiveness, and the healing power of love—lessons that could be put to use in any life. Not surprisingly, those lessons came to form the center of the "depoliticized" recovery culture that feminist recovery critics came to despise.

Both Swallow's and Walker's visions of self-love and healing reflected the specific experiences of the communities that shaped those selves. Removed from those communities, and the histories of struggle and oppression through which they defined themselves, those visions lost their political resonance. Read as a universally appealing "woman's novel"—rather than as the *black* woman's novel that Walker intended— *The Color Purple* offered a template for healing the self and the world through love, an agenda for change conveniently free of the "politics" that, during the 1980s, had come to seem both divisive and ineffectual to many feminist activists.

THE POLITICS—OF LACK THEREOF—OF FEMINIST RECOVERY

As the previous chapter demonstrated, changes in the publishing traditions and the economics of treatment centers like Hazelden helped to drive the late 1980s phenomenon that *Publishers Weekly* called "the rage for recovery." The addiction and codependence best sellers (and would-be best sellers) of authors like Karen Casey and Melody Beattie are generally credited with sparking this publishing trend, and it is almost certainly true that without their spectacular and surprising sales New York trade publishers would have remained skeptical of recovery's viability as a category. The appearance of *The Color Purple*, however, coincided with that of many of these nonfiction titles, and just like *Each Day a New Beginning*, its content and form influenced the recovery and "spiritual wellness" titles that proliferated throughout the decade. Alice Walker's novel demonstrated that a market existed for a post-12-Step recovery literature—for writing that treated hitherto stigmatized topics like addiction and abuse with attention to both their social dimensions and the transcendent power of the human spirit.[90]

Along with the writings of Karen Casey, Jean Swallow, and others who focused more narrowly on addiction, Walker's novel helped to create the women's recovery culture that so discomfited AA traditionalists and the disease critics discussed in chapter 1. Sold through therapists' networks, conferences, and weekend retreats as well as the dozens of "sobriety boutiques" that sprang up around the country, books that went beyond a classic 12-Step message to stress the importance of forgiveness and self-love generated millions in sales and spun off oceans of "recovery porn": workbooks, journals, tapes, calendars, stuffed animals, coffee mugs, and so on.[91] The market for all these products, according to industry observers, was made up almost exclusively of well-educated and relatively affluent white female baby boomers, women whose lives, whether they called themselves feminists or not, had been indelibly stamped by the insights and demands of Second Wave feminism.[92] For the consumers of recovery culture, as for the varied activists and authors whose work fed into it, thinking about addiction and trauma, about wounding and recovery, was a way to extend the thinking about gender and power that had begun in the late 1960s—even if many card-carrying feminists did not recognize it as such.

At the end of the day, perceptions of whether or to what degree women's recovery is "political" seem to have as much to do with how politics is being defined, and by whom, as with the substance of recovery itself. The idea that "the personal is political" was embraced by both the liberal and radical feminist wings of the Second Wave, but each emphasized different elements of the deceptively simple phrase and thus arrived at slightly different interpretations. Liberal feminists interpreted it to mean that "the personal *is* political" and thus deserving of attention and reformist energy equal to that focused on the "impersonal" realms of labor, government, and finance, which had historically been dominated by men and, not coincidentally, singled out for attention by male activists in the New Left and civil rights movements. Working against the default devaluation of women's experiences as merely private or personal, the liberal feminist recovery advocates of the women's alcohol movement and Women for Sobriety drew attention to research and treatment biases that assumed a male addict whose addiction played itself out in public. As a remedy, they called for attention to the ways addiction factored into women's experiences as wives, mothers, survivors of sexual assault, and so on, and demanded that treatment professionals give the same respect and attention to addiction's impact on historically private areas of life as they did to its more visible and public costs, like unemployment or incarceration. Purging treatment discourse and institutions of their long-standing bias in favor of masculinist definitions of addiction, like creating new discourses and institutions centered on women's experiences, was therefore a significant achievement for personal politics.

For radical and women of color feminists who saw addiction and other forms of dysfunction as the results of interior colonization, recovery was also a political act, albeit one with a somewhat different valence. Rather than highlighting the ways in which "the personal *is* political," radical and womanist thinkers emphasized that "*the personal* is political." This slight shift placed the focus on the oppressive circumstances within which the female self is constructed, and in doing so implicitly argued that personal change is always already political, since it attempts to undo a preexisting psychological indoctrination. Far from being apolitical because it is *merely* about the self, for feminists invested in a vision of the psyche as a contested terrain, recovery is political precisely *to the extent* that it is about the self. Bell hooks makes this position plain with her claim that "living as we do in a white supremacist capitalist patriarchy that can best exploit us when we lack a firm grounding in self and identity, choosing 'wellness' is an act of political resistance."[93] If psychological and spiritual wellness and wholeness, the substance of sobriety, are states that the dominant culture seeks to disallow its subalterns, then to claim them is in effect to foil the dominators' attempts at conquest and to win a space of freedom for the self.

For liberal activists invested in the remaking of social institutions, freeing the psyche is perhaps a useful first step, but not more. At the same time, for radicals who believe that the most potent structures of oppression work within the mind rather than outside it, institutional reform can seem like just so much shuffling of the deck chairs on the *Titanic*. Most feminists genuinely committed to the betterment of women's lives work somewhere between these two poles, but it is the voices at the extreme ends of the spectrum that have tended to resound most strongly. Given this range of feminist definitions of "the political," not to mention the wide variety of recovery discourses aimed at women, it is not surprising to find that there is little consensus among scholars and critics as to how to view women's investments in the pursuit and maintenance of sobriety (in all its forms) during the 1980s. Recovery can be read as a political choice—or as a retreat from politics. Perhaps more important, proof of its political-ness or lack thereof seems often to be a matter of assertion rather than demonstration.[94]

Rather than attempt some definitive determination of recovery's feminist politics, what I have tried to show here is the complex relationship between feminism, broadly defined, and an equally capacious recovery culture. What I am calling "post-12-Step recovery"—indebted to the 12-Step original but also infused with a critical perspective sensitive to the social standpoint of the recovering self—evolved out of that relationship during the 1980s. Post-12-Step discourses that focused on racialized experiences of addiction also evolved within African American and Native American communities during this period, but their size and their impact on the broader cultural mainstream were negligible compared to that of the women's recovery culture that emerged from Second Wave feminism.[95] The appearance of this culture should be of interest not only to historians of recovery as such, but also to any scholar seeking to understand popular feminism and gender politics in the wake of the Second Wave. Whether its ultimate forms were "depoliticized" or not, the mass-marketed recovery of the late twentieth and early twenty-first centuries owed as much to the insights of feminist thinkers as it did to those of Bill Wilson and Bob Smith, and it popularized those ideas— from the tangible presence of a gendered double standard to the more abstract concept of interior colonization—far beyond the precincts of women's centers and lesbian coffee houses. Rather than feminism's evil other, post-12-Step recovery's hybrid discourse of spiritual seeking and self-love was its offspring, and a key tool through which average American women pondered questions of gender, self, and power. Whether this should be read as a success or a failure for organized feminism remains an open question.

CHAPTER SIX

Oprah Winfrey and the Disease of Difference

The writings of Karen Casey, Melody Beattie, Jean Swallow, and Alice Walker all contributed to the women's recovery culture that seemed to saturate the American scene during the late 1980s, but if there is one name that is synonymous with the "rage for recovery"—that stoked that rage at its inception, showcased its defining texts, and became its biggest and most enduring spokesperson—that name is Oprah Winfrey. The central figures that this book has thus far treated were innovators in the realm of print culture; their success in its less glamorous corners put pressure on mainstream trade publishers to open up their lists to recovery ideas, with profitable results for all concerned. Fresh ideas and good timing accounted for part of that profit, but cross-media synergy was also a factor: word of mouth and hand-selling, along with distribution through professional addiction treatment networks, played key roles in spreading recovery ideas, but so did television talk shows. Indeed, as Elayne Rapping has argued, no cultural force did more in the 1980s and 1990s to "place the truths of recovery in our collective hearts and minds and make sure they stay[ed] there" than daytime television programming aimed at women.[1] For good or ill, no television personality has been identified more closely with those "truths of recovery" than Oprah Winfrey.

But as the link between Winfrey and recovery has hardened into a matter of common sense, the details that might make that relationship meaningful have been proportionally obscured. What, precisely, has led observers to see *The Oprah Winfrey Show* as a "bully pulpit for recovery"?[2] *Oprah* did feature its fair share of addicts and codependents, sober and otherwise, during the late 1980s. Its first nationally syndicated season (1986–87), for example, showcased Adult Children of Alcoholics, Women Who Love Too Much, Credit Card Junkies, Negative Addictions, Fundamentalists Anonymous, Addicted Spouses, Religion Addicts, Cocaine Prostitutes, Obsessive Lovers, and Young Adult Alcoholics.[3] And at the height of the rage for recovery, in 1989–90, Winfrey devoted a program each month to addiction, creating a highly visible platform for experts such as Claudia Black, Janet Woititz, and John Bradshaw. But Phil Donahue, Sally Jessy Raphael, Ricki Lake, and a dozen other talk show doyennes, as Rapping notes, hosted similar if not identical programs without becoming synonymous with recovery. What accounts for this difference is what happened when the rage for recovery died down. While others moved on, Winfrey moved deeper, innovating on a host of existing conventions to create a personal recovery discourse that she placed at the center of her multimedia empire.

Two considerations prompted her decisions in this regard. First, rather than simply showcasing recovery discourse on her show, Oprah Winfrey believed in it. Though she has never formally identified as a member of a 12-Step group, Winfrey embraced recovery as a result of her experiences as a survivor of childhood sexual abuse and compulsive overeating, issues she battled for years in private before "hitting bottom" and subsequently reordering her life according to spiritual principles during the early 1990s. When her own recovery process turned her inward to meditate on the nature of forgiveness and gratitude, she found herself called to share her vision of the recovered self and life, and to use the vast array of media at her disposal—both electronic and print culture—to do so. Thus by the dawn of the new millennium, Winfrey had come to embody a recovery ideal that, while it drew upon the ideas and practices of a host of other recovery advocates, was distinctly her own—and seemed to be everywhere.

This chapter charts the development of that ideal out of Winfrey's experiences and across her media properties, paying particular attention to the ways in which she has linked recovery to ideas of social justice. To assert such a linkage may sound silly: as the feminist critics in the previous chapter made clear, when taken out of the context of discrete identity-based communities, recovery's personalist tendencies seem to militate against collective social action. Surely the tendency toward deracination and banality observed within the women's recovery culture of the 1980s would only be exacerbated by the mass-marketed and highly commercialized nature of Winfrey's enterprise. Close attention to Winfrey's evolving recovery discourse, however, suggests otherwise. While no one could find her views unproblematically progressive, they do make a recognizable argument for social justice, one premised on a philosophy similar to that of AA precursor Frank Buchman's "world-changing through life-changing."[4]

If the comparison of the effusive and spiritual Winfrey to the ascetic evangelical Protestant Buchman sounds counterintuitive, it should not. In many ways, Winfrey's is the most "religious" version of recovery to receive widespread attention since Bill Wilson's "alcoholic squad" split from the Oxford Group in 1937. Where it differs is in its theology. To a base of 12-Step and feminist/womanist insights, Winfrey has added a significant dose of New Thought religiosity, foregrounding the mystical spirituality that has hovered in the background of recovery culture from the time that Wilson and Dr. Bob attended weekly "spook sessions" together. New Thought's belief in the divine within, the power of thought to shape reality, and the interconnectedness of human, divine, and cosmic life—all the things that fascinated Wilson and Smith, Richmond Walker, Marty Mann, Karen Casey, and Jean Kirkpatrick (to name just a few)—have become for Winfrey the organizing and central principles of recovery rather than simply its grace notes. For her, the antidote to the three-part disease lies in the recognition that "I am Creation's daughter. I am more than my physical self. I am more than the job that I do. I am more than the external definitions I have given myself. . . . Those roles are all extensions of who I define myself to be, but ultimately I am Spirit come from the greatest Spirit. I am Spirit."[5] Like other addicts before her, Winfrey had a life-changing experience when she became willing to acknowledge fully the spiritual dimension of the self. Where she differs from them is in her desire—and her ability—to create a mass program to inculcate that same awareness in others, and to foment the individual and collective transcendence of social difference. More so even than the womanist recovery advocates with whom she shares many concerns, Winfrey envisions recovery as a socially significant act.

A comprehensive accounting of how Winfrey has elaborated her recovery ideals across over twenty years worth of television shows, thousands of pages of magazines, dozens of made-for-TV and feature films and documentaries, and constantly updated web pages is neither conceptually nor logistically feasible. Not for nothing has media studies scholar Eva Illouz described Winfrey's Harpo, Inc., multimedia corporation as "tentacular."[6] In acknowledgment of this fact, after tracing Winfrey's own journey to recovery and her development of an explicitly New Thought–inspired recovery message for *The Oprah Winfrey Show*, this chapter turns to examine one bounded area where that message was conspicuously and fulsomely displayed: the original incarnation of Oprah's Book Club, which existed between 1996 and 2002.[7] Better than any other facet of the sprawling Harpo empire, this latter-day example

of recovery print culture displays the ways that Winfrey and her audiences have worked toward a vision of recovered selfhood and, more
important, a recovered human community. Through their reading and
discussion of books, individuals joined together to create and promote
the flows of divine and interpersonal love that Winfrey argues are the
only forces capable of healing the disease of "difference" and bringing
health and light into a troubled world.

"OPRAH'S STORY"

During the first few years of *The Oprah Winfrey Show*, the stories of
addicts, codependents, and abuse victims appeared regularly within a
heterogeneous mix of programming, rubbing shoulders with relationship and beauty advice, self-help and homemaking, interviews with celebrities and trauma victims, and, occasionally, explorations of social
issues. Addiction and abuse stories made for dramatic, engaging television, and their narrative heft was enhanced by Winfrey's apparently
effortless ability to relate to her guests and sympathize with their struggles. Her willingness to explore the nature of these taboo subjects and
to empathize with and respect people from outside the white, middle-
class mainstream earned her plaudits from media studies scholars who
celebrated her show's disruption of the polite conventions of broadcast
television.[8] At the same time, television critics who focused on more
practical matters agreed that Winfrey's knack for sympathetic interaction and comfort with therapeutic language were what allowed her to so
quickly surpass her chief competitor, Phil Donahue, in the ratings. Neither set of commentators, however, seemed aware of the fact that Winfrey may have felt at home discussing addiction, dysfunction, and recovery for personal reasons.

While she has never identified herself explicitly as a recovering addict, Winfrey positions herself as such in her accounts of her struggles
with compulsive eating and dieting, issues that seem to have consumed
much of her adult life. Her battle with food became a topic on her show
soon after it went national. In fall 1988, to celebrate the fact that she lost
sixty-seven pounds on a liquid diet, she hauled a wagon loaded with an
equal amount of pig fat across the stage of *The Oprah Winfrey Show*
while the audience cheered. But she soon began regaining the weight,
and as the pounds increased so did a familiar sense of despair. By the
following spring, she was twenty pounds heavier; a year later, she had
put on fifty more. At the Daytime Emmy Awards in 1991 she prayed

silently that Phil Donahue would win the Best Talk Show Host award so that she would not face the embarrassment of standing up in her too-tight dress.[9]

Following this disastrous relapse, Winfrey devoted three years to working with personal trainer Bob Greene to change her diet and exercise habits and, more important, her relationship to "my drug, which was food" (19). She narrates this personal reform project in *Make the Connection*, the best-selling 1996 nutrition and diet book she coauthored with Greene. Just as "Bill's Story" opens the Big Book with a classic account of "what we were like, what happened, and what we are like now," so "Oprah's Story" begins *Make the Connection* by narrating the ways that "weight consumed my life" (18) until she found a way to be free of her obsessive relationship to it.

The book maintains a certain distance from the 12 Steps. It promises only "Ten Steps to a Better Body" and, at one level, seems to reject recovery-inflected weight loss programs out of hand. Overeaters Anonymous is never mentioned, but Winfrey does briefly describe—and dismiss—a program called Diets Don't Work, a "12-Step compatible" regimen that prods clients to "get at their root issues with food" through group work and self-scrutiny.[10] Although the confessional aspect of the program is powerful ("Stood in a room in a bathing suit and admitted that I was 200 pounds. That was hard" [17]), Winfrey decides that after "two days in a room with 30 other people, all of us trying to rediscover ourselves[,] I discovered I needed another approach" (11). Despite her disenchantment with Diets Don't Work, the "other approach" she chooses bears a striking resemblance to a traditional 12-Step program.

While Winfrey's diet and exercise travails are well known to anyone who has ever glanced at a supermarket tabloid, "Oprah's Story," recounting her lifelong struggle with obsessive, unhealthy eating, is nevertheless a grueling read. Her list of diets and exercise plans is a long one. She was an early advocate of the Atkins diet, as well as "the Scarsdale diet . . . the crazy banana, weenie, and egg diet . . . Weight Watchers . . . Diet Workshop . . . Diet Center, and later Nutri-Systems [and] the Beverly Hills Diet" (5). Describing an incident where she smeared frozen hotdog buns with maple syrup and ate them before they could fully defrost, she notes that "looking back, I see no difference between myself and a junkie, scrambling for a needle and whatever dope might be around. Food was my dope" (9). The parallel is reiterated several times in "Oprah's Story."

Shifting between Winfrey's voice in the present and the diary she kept in the years before she met Greene, the narrative veers between moments of white-knuckle resolve—"I will not eat, drink, or consume anything that will prevent me from reaching my goal" (15)—and wretched abjection—"I'm carrying fat around. It's overcoming me . . ." (16). Awareness that she has a problem does not in any way help her to control that problem. Instead, Winfrey's fluctuating weight becomes "symbolic of how out-of-control I was" (1). Like so many Big Book narrators, she mistakenly believes that what she needs is more self-control, and the excerpts from her diary center obsessively on attempts to will herself into thinness: "I've got to bring it to an end . . . ," "I'll show them . . . ," "It is possible and I will . . ." (13–15).

Somewhat predictably, "Oprah's Story" also includes a moment of hitting bottom. In a diary excerpt from 1991, Winfrey recounts that on vacation she "gained eight pounds, bringing me to an all-time whopping 226 pounds. So big, disproportionate, fat in the face. Unable to move freely. . . . I don't know this self. My body has betrayed me, or has it just acquiesced? I don't know who this is waddling through the airport. I caught a glimpse of myself reflected in the store window. I didn't recognize the fat lady staring back at me" (17). This episode of misrecognition proves transformative. Momentarily distanced from herself, Winfrey realizes that "sometimes I can feel the connection between my own fears and the weight. So what am I afraid of? That's the question. The answer can set me free" (17). The mental process set in motion by her encounter with her own reflection is the same as the one prompted by the 4th Step inventory, the move to "feel the connection" between addictive behavior and deeper emotions like fear and anger.

Winfrey has often spoken of her life as a triumph over adversity: raised in rural Mississippi, she has overcome poverty, race and gender bias, and a host of other obstacles to live a highly publicized version of the American dream.[11] She typically invites observers to see her as victorious, not surrendered, and the conclusion to "Oprah's Story" can be read in that light. Soon after her encounter with her reflection in the airport window, she tells us, she began working with Greene on her diet and physical condition, and the chronological end to her story is her successful completion of a marathon in 1994. But while she describes her marathon finish as "a proud and joyful moment" (31), the true conclusion of "Oprah's Story" is a notably humble, almost somber one. It features a set of familiar caveats about the ongoing nature of recovery, the need to "look after yourself every day" and to acknowledge, even relish, human imperfection and weakness. "I still work out every day," Winfrey acknowledges, and "I try to stay in the low to mid 150s . . . but to stay there, I have to work incredibly hard. With my current schedule that's not always possible. And that's okay, I've accepted that." This acceptance of her own limitations forms the core of Winfrey's changed —recovered—life, and the narrative stresses that "the biggest change I've made is a spiritual one. It comes from the realization that taking care of my body and my health is really one of the greatest kinds of love I can give myself" (32).

"Oprah's Story," particularly its conclusion, suggests the baseline vision of recovery with which Winfrey would become identified—a blend of traditional 12-Step as well as therapeutic insights that by the early 1990s had become familiar to a wide audience. Like so many feminist recovery advocates, she identified the precipitating factor behind her addiction as low self-esteem, an issue she has been quoted as saying is "the cause of most of the problems in the world."[12] But her solution lay less in consciousness-raising or in conventional psychodynamic therapies than in the realm of the spirit.

In the chapters following "Oprah's Story," *Make the Connection* outlines a series of commonsensical diet and exercise strategies that culminate in Step 10's "Philosophy of Daily Renewal," a form of spiritual practice that echoes the injunctions of Steps 11 and 12: to use "prayer and meditation to improve our conscious contact with God" and, "having had a spiritual awakening as a result of these steps . . . to practice these principles in all our affairs." Addressing the three dimensions of the strange illness of addiction—body, mind, and spirit—Daily Renewal "confirms what is truly important to you" and facilitates "your soul speaking to your heart, your heart translating to your mind, and your mind giving your body directions" (226). By using exercise, journal writing, meditation, affirmations, and other rituals to focus on "your true desires" and minimize the importance of "events and circumstances [that] seem to challenge" them, seekers concretize their weight loss goals and, more important, practice the ambitious project of "living in the moment [and] finding joy in your life" (227, 230). At its core, Daily Renewal is a ritual for recognizing the falsity of negative ideas—for instance, ideas about the self as fat and/or otherwise stigmatized—and focusing on the true self and its desires. By participating in it and becoming attuned to that higher reality, followers of *Make the Connec-*

tion do not merely improve their own lives, but also become better at "expressing love." And love, Bob Greene concludes, is the highest and most enduring reality of all, the ultimate reason "why we're here" (240).

In her introduction to the chapter on Daily Renewal, Winfrey describes how working with Greene on her mind-body-spirit health has "changed my life [and] freed [me] from my own personal prison" (225). "I've spent a lifetime being afraid," she explains, acknowledging that her weight became a way to "anesthetize" the fear (224). This self-numbing allowed her to avoid the pain of being in the moment, but also ensured that she would know little joy and express little love. The culmination of her work with Greene, therefore, was not merely her slimmer body and healthier eating habits; as in traditional 12-Step practice it was a recognition of the falsity of her fears and the liberating reality of the love that replaced them. Freed from the fears that for years had literally weighed her down, and embarked instead on a loving and spiritual way of life, Winfrey determined to share her insights with others.

FEAR, LOVE, AND OTHER POWERS OF MIND

Unlike cynical intellectuals Bill Wilson and Karen Casey, Oprah Winfrey had an easy time with the spiritual dimension of recovery. Raised in a religious family, Winfrey has never shied away from frank talk about spirituality.[13] During the early part of her career she spoke routinely to interviewers about her churchgoing life, favorite Bible passages, habits of prayer and meditation, and abiding personal faith. "There's only one way I've been able to survive being raped, molested, whipped, rejected, . . . fat and unpopular," she told *McCall's* in 1987. "As corny as it sounds, my faith in God got me through."[14]

African American religious tradition has played a key role in Winfrey's life—she was brought up a Baptist and attended all-day Sunday School, and she credits the techniques she mastered in the Baptist Training Union for much of her performative style. "Whenever she is feeling down," one biographer explains, "Oprah reaches for her Bible and cues up Aretha Franklin's 'Amazing Grace' on the stereo."[15] But like Alice Walker, Winfrey has also distanced herself from the black church and what she calls "the very narrow view" of religious faith that she grew up with, one in which the image of "God [as] a man with a long white beard and a black book checking off the things you can do" was intended to "keep you under control."[16] In its place she has embraced a hybrid faith, one whose roots, perhaps, lie in the black church, but whose distinctive and quite visible flowers reflect the influence of New Thought teachings.[17] Her explanations of her success refer frequently to the power of the divine within: "I believe in the God force that lives inside all of us," she has stated, "and once you tap into that, you can do anything."[18] Along with this belief, New Thought's essential idealism—the belief that all God's creation is divine and good, and that what seems sick, evil, or bad is in fact just misperception that the practice of faith will dispel—has played a key role in the development of Winfrey's recovery ethos.

It is difficult to say precisely when or how Winfrey became a follower of New Thought, but the most careful accounts of her religious development suggest that it occurred around the time *The Oprah Winfrey Show* went national in 1986. Winfrey was supposedly "very active" in the Bethel AME Church while living in Baltimore during the late 1970s, and she joined Trinity United Church of Christ once she moved to Chicago in 1983. But she "never completed membership classes" and eventually stopped attending, a change Trinity pastor Jeremiah Wright attributes to her growing interest in New Thought: "She now has this sort of 'God is everywhere, God is in me, I don't need to go to church, I don't need to be a part of a body of believers, I can meditate, I can do positive thinking' spirituality. It's a strange gospel. It has nothing to do with the church Jesus Christ founded."[19]

The first few seasons of *The Oprah Winfrey Show* would seem to bear out Wright's suspicions. Guests during the late 1980s included a smattering of New Thought practitioners, including dream interpreter Gayle Delaney, mental healers Bernie Siegel and Louise Hay, and power-of-positive-thinking advocate Robert Fulghum.[20] In a lengthy 1989 profile in the *New York Times Magazine*, Barbara Grizutti Harrison announced to the world that Winfrey believed in "a metaphysical theory . . . partaking of Eastern religion and Western religion and of what is called New Age," a description substantiated by Winfrey's claim that her faith centered on "discernment" of "what the Universe put [me] here to do." Somewhat disjointedly, she continued, "I've been blessed, but I create the blessings. . . . Most people don't seek discernment [but] I hear the voice, I get the feeling. . . . I am highly attuned to my Divine self."[21] Despite the clear commitment to esoteric spirituality Winfrey articulated in the article, however—or perhaps because the clear intent of

Harrison's profile had been to ridicule that commitment—for the next several years New Thought ideas appeared only infrequently on *The Oprah Winfrey Show*.[22]

In 1992, however, a shift toward the spiritual began to be apparent. In the spring of that year, Marianne Williamson, then the pastor of Detroit's Church of Today, an outpost of Unity Church, appeared twice on the program. Like Winfrey, Williamson does not identify as an addict, but she acknowledges that her faith was founded and shaped in Alcoholics Anonymous, which she attended for unspecified reasons during a period of unhappiness and soul-searching that lasted for many years. Williamson took the disease concept in a somewhat different direction than Bill Wilson and Bob Smith, however, deciding that it was "my personality in general [and] my negativity" that were "as destructive to me as alcohol is to the addict." In light of this insight, she began to work the 12 Steps in hopes that "a power greater than myself could turn me around."[23] Soon after her turn to a Higher Power in AA, Williamson discovered the metaphysical best seller *A Course in Miracles*, which simultaneously "suggested that I surrender the fight completely" and "unleashed huge amounts of hopeful energy inside me" (xv).[24] In 1983 she began to teach seminars on *A Course in Miracles*, believing that other white, middle-class Baby Boomers like herself had "slipped into a barely camouflaged vortex of self-loathing" and would benefit, as she had, from "the spiritual journey [of] relinquishment, or unlearning, of fear and the acceptance of love back into our hearts" (6, xviii). These teachings came together in her book *A Return to Love*, which urged readers toward the same path as Bob Greene's *Make the Connection*, a spiritual way of life Williamson described as "mind training in the relinquishment of a thought system based on fear, and the acceptance instead of a thought system based on love" (18). Williamson appeared on *Oprah* to promote *A Return to Love* the week before it was published; Winfrey later called the book "one of the things that changed my life forever."[25]

The host was not the only one so moved; the unprecedented amount of viewer mail generated by Williamson's appearance prompted Winfrey to invite her to return in June to answer lingering questions about the relationships among fear, faith, and love. The dialogue that ensued saw Williamson and Winfrey join together and call on the audience to use their collective mental powers and pray for the "miracles" necessary to turn around the lives of guests who had suffered from illness, unemployment, marital strife, and so on. Such change could easily be effected, Williamson explained to the rapt audience, if "[we] withdraw our faith from the negativity and finite belief system of this world and . . . instead open ourselves to the faith that God has the power to break through this limitation [and offer us] infinite possibilities as opposed to the finite possibilities that we see now." As they echoed and reinforced the personal changes that Winfrey had begun to make in her work with Greene, Williamson's visits, as Janice Peck has argued, inaugurated a new "framework for making sense of the problems addressed on [Winfrey's] show," one that mobilized New Thought's belief in the essential nonreality of suffering and hardship as both an explanation of the world and an agent for change within it.[26]

The following season, this idealism was brought more sharply into focus by a series of "Conversations with Oprah," in which Winfrey interviewed a handful of "poets and thinkers and crusaders [who] are truly enlightened," including author Maya Angelou, mind-body healer Deepak Chopra, and psychiatrist M. Scott Peck, author of the New Thought classic *The Road Less Traveled*.[27] Chopra, who is trained both in Western and in Indian Ayurvedic medicine, focused on the degree to which the mind can control cellular behavior and "metabolic pathways" and thus enable weight loss, cure disease, and even stave off death. What he called the "quantum worldview" (so called because it disrupts traditional understandings of the relationship between mind and matter) was elaborated in varying ways by his fellow interviewees.[28] His argument that contemporary Americans' obsessive focus on "space-time events [and] trivial, mundane things . . . interferes with our connection to the spirit" was recapped by M. Scott Peck, who noted that both the world's rewards and its obstacles existed not for themselves but "to teach you holiness."[29]

Speaking in a somewhat more down-to-earth register, Maya Angelou made the same claim. Discussing how Winfrey could best negotiate the stress of being pilloried in the tabloid press, Angelou reminded her, "You're not in that." The reality created by the paparazzi, she explained, "has all and everything to do with the perpetrator," but bore no necessary resemblance to the reality in which Winfrey herself lived; therefore it would not affect her unless she permitted it to do so. Drawing on her own history of childhood sexual abuse, Angelou argued that the ability to distinguish between such false and true realities was a necessary survival strategy, a tactic that could shield the self from the routinized degrada-

tions, cruelties, and disenfranchisements meted out by impersonal social structures and hateful individuals alike—torments Angelou likened
to being "pecked to death by ducks." Angelou argued that such "pecking," which could take the form of slander, rape, or comments about
being overweight, could have real effects because "words are things. . . .
They stick on the walls . . . they go into your clothes and finally into your
very body." But the material reality of words was trumped by a higher
spiritual reality: the knowledge that "God loves me," Angelou asserted,
would moot the reality of wounding words and defuse their power. Freed
from that negative reality, the believer would be able to love herself or
(since Angelou allowed that self-love was not always easy) at least to
"approve of [her]self for living."[30]

For all three guests, as for Bob Greene and Marianne Williamson, the
cultivation of the capacity for love was essential, a commitment that
went beyond the merely therapeutic to enrich not only the individual
and the family, but also the world. "Think about love; talk about love,"
urged Chopra. Love "gets rid of everything [negative] because love is the
ultimate truth." Similarly, Peck argued that love was a "technology of
reconciliation" that could "cure . . . racism, bigotry, and hate."[31] Winfrey occasionally played the skeptic to these claims, asking Peck how he
could "solve the problem of . . . racism with [mental] discipline" and
challenging Chopra as well: "What about poverty? What about if you
can't pay your light bill?"[32]

Her guests responded in two ways. First, they emphasized the power
of changed perspectives. Once people relinquished their spurious commitments to "money . . . power . . . fame" and the life of "pecking" that
went along with them, they would be freed up to focus instead on "the
divinity inside" and "take pleasure in the smallest moments."[33] Second,
they would benefit almost immediately from ripple effects. Their individual reorientations would spark similar changes throughout family
and community networks, since ever-increasing numbers of people
would alter their behavior in order to attain the peace of mind they
observed in those who had exchanged fear and its accompanying destructive habits for love. Chopra brought these two elements together
when he invoked the example of Martin Luther King, who he argued was
the most famous of twentieth-century Americans to live—and to inspire
others to live—by his dreams. "What we experience as the physical world
at any one point . . . in time," he argued, "is the collective dream of a
people that is manifesting itself as physical reality at a certain point in

history. . . . We can change those physical realities if we all . . . put our attention to it."[34] The civil rights movement was one such manifestation.

The ratings for the "Conversations with Oprah" episodes were not especially high, but they appear to have fertilized the seed that Marianne Williamson's appearances the preceding spring had planted in Winfrey's mind.[35] The 1993–94 season featured several episodes centered on the importance of cultivating positive thoughts, with Winfrey drawing her audience's attention to "Only Good News," "Random Acts of Kindness," and "Angels Around Us," among other things. Williamson returned mid-year, and her message of changing the world through faith and positivity was reinforced by the appearance of Larry Dossey, like Deepak Chopra a pioneer in mind-body medicine and healing through prayer.[36] These episodes were interspersed among more traditional talk show exposés ("Human Encounters with Aliens," "I Raised a Rapist," and "Husbands Who Work with Brazen Hussies Are Lured into Illicit Relationships; Wives Vent Frustration"), but their intermittent appearances suggested that a theme was beginning to crystallize at Harpo studios.[37] By the fall of 1994, circumstances beyond the boundaries of Winfrey's show had pushed that theme to the fore.

"MY SHOW IS A MINISTRY"

When she debuted nationally in 1986, Winfrey's only competitors had been Phil Donahue and Sally Jessy Raphael. Within a season she had bested them in the ratings, and she held her own against newcomers Geraldo Rivera and Morton Downey Jr. when they appeared a few years later. In the early 1990s, however, a blizzard of new talk shows appeared, whose young hosts, sensational topics, and production designs aimed to create maximum conflict and disruption among the guests and the studio audience. By the spring of 1993, Winfrey was facing competition from twenty nationally syndicated programs, each regularly treating topics like "When Your Best Friend Is Sleeping with Your Father," "Get Bigger Breasts or Else," and "Women Who Marry Their Rapists."[38] While she continued to lead the field both in market penetration and in ratings, her overall share of the audience dropped an unprecedented 7 percent between 1993 and 1994.[39]

In "Oprah's Story," Winfrey discussed the ways her anxiety over ratings fueled her compulsive eating, and it may have been a desire to break out of that cycle (what she had described to M. Scott Peck as her "disease to please") that led her to rethink her show's content.[40] Rather than battle it out within what critics were calling "the talk show wars," chasing ratings with increasingly salacious and negative programming, she decided to reorient her entire program to reflect her own growing spiritual commitments.[41] Thus the beginning of the 1994 season found Winfrey explaining to her audience that her growing sense of connection "to the bigger picture of what God is" had come to influence her thoughts on programming. She explained in an interview that in 1993 she had "asked [God] for freedom. . . . And this year I asked for clarity." As a result of that prayer, she had "become more clear about my purpose in television and this show."[42] This heightened sense of purpose meant she had realized that "I've been guilty of doing trash TV and not even thinking it was trash. I don't want to do it anymore."[43] Contrasting herself to her upstart competitors, whose greedy eyes were fixed on the bottom line and the lowest common denominator, she declared that "the time has come for this genre of talk show to move from dysfunctional whining and complaining and blaming. I have had enough of people's dysfunction. I don't want to spend another hour listening to somebody blaming their mother. . . . We're all aware that we do have some problems and we need to work on them. What are you willing to do about it? . . . That's what our shows are going to be about."[44]

Having reoriented her life around love and acceptance rather than fear and negativity, Winfrey now wanted her show to do the same, and the 1994–95 season moved her New Thought–based recovery sensibility to the forefront. As she discussed her plans for the season, she reiterated once again her commitment to New Thought's idealism: while the "trash pack" of other talk shows disseminated "false values" of exploitation, immorality, and crass materialism, her own program would offer content that was uplifting, meaningful, and hence "true." Or as she explained in another interview, "I feel that my show is a ministry—we just don't take up a collection."[45]

Winfrey's commitment to remaking her show along spiritual lines was evident at every level. She fired her long-time producer and friend Debora DiMaio, who had urged her to stick with "talk show basics, namely tough, hard-edged topics . . . such as women who want sex with their stepsons."[46] With DiMaio's departure, Winfrey took on a greater role in determining program content, and not only the substance of *The Oprah Winfrey Show* but also its production specifications changed: participation by rowdy audience members and dysfunctional guests declined and the show took on a more staid look, with more taped features and studio interviews.[47] Programs on scandalous or outré topics did not disappear completely: the 1994–95 season featured a program on "Women Who Smelled Bad at Work" as well as "My Child Tried to Kill Me—What Now?"[48] But such content was increasingly marginal. Air time that had been given over to such salacious features went instead to a growing roster of New Thought experts.

Marianne Williamson again led the field, appearing in December 1994 to urge the audience to use prayer to banish their "thoughts of attack . . . thoughts of guilt . . . of grievances . . . of judgment . . . of criticism . . . of anger" and "open the way for light to come in" to their lives. Her argument that "internal power is greater than the power of the external" was echoed across the season by *Celestine Prophecies* author James Redfield, *Care of the Soul* author Thomas Moore, and positive thinking advocate Stephen Covey.[49] In addition, programs showcasing positive thinking, gratitude, and forgiveness went from occasional to regular features: "Thank You Day," "How to Forgive When You Can't Forget," "Dreams Really Do Come True," "Day of Compassion," "Would You Know a Miracle If You Saw One?" and similar programs aimed to cultivate a heightened awareness of the mystical forces at work in the world and to remind audiences of the many things in life for which to be grateful.[50]

The spiritually enhanced *Oprah Winfrey Show* proved successful. Winfrey won daytime Emmy Awards in 1994 and 1995, and in 1996 received broadcasting's highest honor, the George Foster Peabody Individual Achievement Award. This positive reception increased her commitment to creating "television that inspires us to make positive changes [and acts as] a light in people's lives."[51] The 1997 season began with the announcement of the philanthropic "Angel Network," through which viewers could contribute to "The World's Largest Piggy Bank" or connect with local chapters of Habitat for Humanity to build houses for the homeless. Winfrey's own ongoing spiritual journey continued to feed into the show: in January 1998, she found herself the subject of a lawsuit brought by the National Cattleman's Beef Association, a Texas trade group that argued she had caused a precipitous drop in beef prices with a show that discussed mad cow disease. Her faith was challenged and deepened by the experience, which she told her audience "she began to see . . . as a metaphor for life's trials." As a result, "I kept asking God, 'What is the deeper meaning of this?' [And then] I became calm inside myself and I thought, *'The outside world is always going to be telling you one thing, have one impression—accusatory, blaming, and so forth. And you are to stand still inside yourself and know the truth, and let it set you free.'* "[52]

With the beef trial reconfirming for her the importance of internal reality over that which "the outside world" tried to impose, Winfrey began the 1998 season with her most ambitious spiritual project thus far, a complete regimen of "Change Your Life TV" intended to help audiences prepare for the coming millennium. She urged her fans to fully activate the power of mind in their lives, explaining that "Changing your life . . . [is] about really changing the way you think, the way you see your life, the way you see your family, your children, your relationships."[53] The new season of *Oprah* would help audience members to effect that change in their lives in two ways. First, they could attend to the insights of a group of motivational and inspirational experts who would appear regularly on the show: therapist John Gray, Yoruba Priestess and New Thought minister Iyanla Vanzant, prosperity consultant Suze Orman, and spiritual counselor Gary Zukav.[54] Assisted by occasional visitors like Williamson, medical intuitive Caroline Myss, and simplicity advocate Sarah Ban Breathnach, the Change Your Life team counseled the audience on how to use positive affirmations to reduce fear and shame, smooth relationships by practicing acceptance and forgiveness, and maximize the presence of divine love in everyday life by clearing away material and psychic clutter and aligning themselves with the intentions of the universe. The team members' insights were reiterated in a five-minute daily segment entitled "Remembering Your Spirit," which focused on the ways regular people (and occasional celebrities) worked at the project of spiritual growth, which Winfrey described as "going inside, removing yourself from the chaos, confusion, and the noise of the world and finding a way to bring peace to yourself."[55]

In her 1989 interview with Barbara Grizutti Harrison, Winfrey had commented that "most people don't seek discernment; it doesn't matter to them what the Universe intended for them to do."[56] Ten years later, her position had shifted, becoming significantly more democratic. Change Your Life TV, she explained to *Jet* magazine, was meant to cultivate the capacity for discernment in every individual. Its aim was to help people—especially those whose life circumstances militated against it—to "connect with the importance of listening to what their soul's desires are and remembering to incorporate those desires into their lives."[57] Although she rarely moved to critically interrogate the forces that might interfere with such listening and incorporating, Winfrey's focus on reconnecting with the soul's heretofore alienated desires (what *Make the Connection* had called "true desires") and rejecting what was false, counterproductive, and/or imposed from without resembled in some ways the decolonization at the heart of womanist self-recovery. By "remembering [their] spirit[s]," individuals spoke truth to the powers that conspired to make them forget or deny those spirits in the first place. Urging her audience in this direction was Winfrey's response to the 12th Step's injunction to "carry the message."

While there is little reason to doubt the sincerity of Winfrey's spiritual transformation or to assume that she sought to share her insights with her fans in anything other than good faith, the fact that her promotion of this New Thought–inflected recovery ideal was also a canny business strategy cannot be ignored. In his "Conversation with Oprah" in 1993, Deepak Chopra had mentioned in passing one of the central pillars of New Thought's prosperity gospel—the belief that the power of mind determines financial as well as spiritual well-being. People should stop seeking after external things like money and power, he counseled, because "what we really need to seek in life are the real things, like peace . . . harmony . . . laughter . . . knowledge . . . love. And when we do that, then the external things also come."[58] While Winfrey herself rarely harped on this particular version of the power of mind, the turn in her fortunes in the wake of her decision to commit herself to doing spiritual work suggests that it was certainly operant in her life.[59] Her self-consciously uplifting message helped *The Oprah Winfrey Show* to avoid the censorious gaze of the civic watchdog group Empower America, which in 1995 began a major public campaign to end "trash talk" on TV by pressuring advertisers, networks, and industry executives to regulate and de-fund offending programs. Even after that furor died down, Winfrey's "soul-branding"—the creation of "an aura of positive feeling and receptivity" by "address[ing] society's appetite for higher values"— remained a key means by which she differentiated herself from her talk show competitors.[60] It gave her a platform from which to address an older, whiter, and more affluent audience (the same cohort of female baby boomers that precipitated the rage for recovery) and thereby to attract more advertising dollars. Equally if not more important, it served to unify the various parts of what was becoming a multimedia empire.

Over the course of the 1990s, Harpo Inc. grew from a relatively undistinguished (save for the phenomenal success of *The Oprah Winfrey Show* itself) television production company into what then-CEO Jeff Jacobs called "an intellectual property company" that " 'multi-purpos[es] our content' for various outlets."[61] That evolution began with an interactive web site in partnership with America Online in 1995; that site became, in the fall of 1998, the stand-alone Oprah.com, a multi-tiered portal inviting viewers to "expand their relationships" with Oprah and the "Change Your Life" TV experts and "use the information and resources provided by" the program and its web site.[62] The Oprah.com site dropped the "Change Your Life" slogan in 2001 to accommodate the appearance of *O, the Oprah Magazine*, with its new motto, "Live Your Best Life: Your mission is true happiness. Your purpose is your destiny."[63] In addition to branding the web site and magazine, "Live Your Best Life" also served as the tagline for an ongoing series of live "personal growth summits" Winfrey hosted around the country. Along with the slogan, Harpo's electronic, print, and live formats all shared content and underwriters. Their meditations, affirmations, and inspirational narratives and images worked simultaneously to help audience members fulfill their "mission" and "purpose" and to distinguish Winfrey's properties from what she had taken to calling the "mental poison" of most television.[64]

It was within this trajectory of combined economic expansion and spiritual growth that Oprah's Book Club first appeared. While Winfrey continued to enjoy unsurpassed ratings and industry acclaim during the course of the 1990s, cynical media critics had begun sniping at her spiritual message fairly early on. The inception of Change Your Life TV increased the vitriol, generating acid remarks like the *Chicago Sun-Times*'s "You don't [change] your life by watching TV—you [change] your life by turning off the TV and going back to school." Journalists, especially at the influential papers in the major media markets, seemed to take snide glee in the fact that *The Oprah Winfrey Show* was "losing about a million viewers each time a 'Change Your Life' segment was aired."[65]

The negative press was no match for Winfrey's commitment to her own and to her audience's spiritual growth; nevertheless, the flood of positive coverage that followed her announcement of the book club in September 1996 must have come as a relief. The press could not admire the book club enough, and by the end of the year editorials praising Winfrey for promoting reading and cultural uplift had appeared in almost every major newspaper. Her plan to sell book club selections in Starbucks and donate the proceeds to literacy education (announced at the end of the club's first season) was similarly hailed as an example of bold civic leadership. Engaging, perhaps, in their own version of thought-as-power, secular critics declared the iconography of the book strong enough to neutralize the New Thought–inflected recovery message of Change Your Life TV. It is ironic, therefore, that the club proved to be one of the most consistent and coherent incubators of that message.

THE METAPHYSICAL CLUB

Between the fall of 1996 and the spring of 2002, Oprah's Book Club worked something like this: approximately every six weeks, Winfrey announced the selection of a new title on the air—usually, though not exclusively, a work of recent fiction—and solicited readers' letters in response to the book.[66] A select few letter writers then joined Winfrey and the author to discuss it, often over a meal. Taped highlights from this conversation, interspersed with Winfrey interviewing the author, a montage of the author's thoughts on his/her creative process, and studio audience members' comments were among the elements featured on the book club broadcasts; readers could also discuss the book on a dedicated bulletin board on the Oprah.com web site. Although it began as one segment within the larger program, the book club quickly expanded to fill the whole hour-long *Oprah Winfrey Show*. Occasional features like trips to the locales where the books unfolded were added for variety's sake, but the core of the club remained unchanged over its history: taped excerpts of Winfrey, her guests, and the author discussing plot, characters, themes, and other elements they liked and disliked about the book. At the center of these discussions was a consideration, often tearful, of how the incidents or characters in the books resonated with the readers' own lives.

As noted above, press coverage of the book club was overwhelmingly positive, and Winfrey received breathless praise from journalists and academics alike for inviting a mass audience to experience the complexities of authors like Toni Morrison, Bernhard Schlink, and Rohinton Mistry. The few critics who were less than enthusiastic about the club, on the other hand, argued that while there were notable exceptions, the bulk of the book's selected titles fit too comfortably within the narrow and uninspiring genre of women's melodrama. Though intending to do just the opposite, this criticism begins to suggest the distinctive power of the fiction featured on Oprah's Book Club. The problem with Winfrey's selections was not simply that most of the authors and protagonists were women, D. T. Max complained in the *New York Times*, but that they were unrealistic women. In defiance of decades of demographic and social change, hardly any of them were in the paid labor force, and their stories unfolded almost exclusively in small towns. Depicted at a distinctive remove from the contemporary knowledge economy, "Winfrey's fictional landscape is one in which people are loving, hating, thinking," Max argued, but "almost never working." The result was a profoundly unrealistic set of texts, disconnected from the complexities of modern women's lives. Striking a similar note, *Slate* critic Chris Lehmann argued that instead of addressing contemporary realities, Winfrey's "therapeutic canon" concerned "tales of lurid family abuse, tales of the individual struggle of redemption, and—God help us all—tale upon tale of three generations of women absorbing life's hard knocks in a small town."[67] Critics who sought to counter this critique typically invoked the politics of multiculturalism as they did so, arguing that the club and its readers materialized the lives (and reading practices) of poor women and women of color, whose experiences were often rendered invisible by the workings of white male literary gatekeepers.[68]

Both the club's critics and its defenders, however, missed a crucial point: rooted as they were in Winfrey's New Thought convictions, the club's selections (and, as we shall see, its modes of reading) were intended to demonstrate an essential idealism—a commitment to the belief that it is ultimately not the realms of work or social interaction that are truly real, but the realms of "loving, hating [and] thinking" and of "abuse [and] redemption." The club positioned fiction as a unique means of transport to those realms, in part by framing the act of authorship as a mystical process of connecting to the ephemeral world. The image of the book as a highly charged mystical object, and of reading as a nonrational practice that connected the material world to its metaphysical counterpart, was established in the club's first episode, during which author Jacquelyn Mitchard described her novel *The Deep End of the Ocean* as having originated in "a dream I had three years ago." As she explained to Winfrey and the assembled guests, "I woke my husband up about 5:00 that morning to tell him about this wonderful story," but soon after she began work on the novel, "he got cancer and he only lived a few months." After his death, "everyone who loved me kept telling me . . . 'think about security. . . . Don't think about dreams anymore,'" but she persevered with the novel as a way of honoring her dead husband's spirit.

Juxtaposing the realist advice she had received to her "dreamy" book project, Mitchard affirmed the veracity of New Thought's idealist world-view: the believer's sense that true desires are meant to be fulfilled. Furthermore, the existence of an intimate connection between material and spirit worlds was manifest in the fact that Mitchard "finished the book exactly two years to the day after Dan died."[69]

Throughout the course of the book club, this sense of authorship as a mystical practice and of the book as an enchanted object framed the readings of specific texts. Winfrey's questions to authors laid down the terms of the discussion—"did the characters . . . visit you, like little people in your house, or little people in your head?"—and few authors challenged it.[70] Typically, authors explained their work with statements such as "the story was so large in me that there were times I felt like I couldn't keep up with it"; "I start writing a book and somehow [the characters] emerge from—from someplace"; and "It was like a flower. . . . I had never imagined it, but I thought it was beautiful."[71] Toni Morrison, frequently invoked as an exemplary guest in the club, is more accurately viewed as an exceptional one: each time she appeared on the show, Morrison would draw attention to the writer's craft, with comments such as "I love to hear it when [people] say . . . 'I had to read every word.' And I always wanted to say, 'Yeah—and I had to write every word.' "[72] While approvingly noted by Winfrey and the guests, Morrison's commitment to the labor of writing did not carry over to other episodes.[73] More often, books were treated not as material objects but as the products of efflorescent forces that periodically surged into the workaday world through the portal formed by the author and her word processor. The club's enchanted books invited a similarly nonrational reading. Toni Morrison was again an exception that proved this rule, urging frustrated readers of *Paradise* "to have an intellectual response to the issues being debated here" and promising that it "may be easier than you think." In every Morrison episode, Winfrey and her guests praised the author's intellection, noting her rich, allusive language and puzzle-like plots, which required careful note taking and multiple readings. But the club's aim was not the cultivation of such "intellectual response," even with a heady author like Morrison. In direct contrast to the author's suggestion, Winfrey exhorted readers of *Paradise*, "Don't read this book just with your head!"[74] Unintentionally echoing AA's midwestern traditionalists, she suggested that a too-cerebral analysis could in fact detract from what made the reading experience truly valuable: in this case, the dissolve of interpersonal boundaries that precipitated out of direct emotional engagement.

Winfrey had learned that reading had such power as a result of "growing up [with] a sense of loneliness." Francie Nolan, the protagonist of Betty Smith's *A Tree Grows in Brooklyn*, had been the solitary teenage Winfrey's friend: "There was a tree outside my apartment, and I used to imagine it was the same tree. I felt like my life was like hers."[75] The importance of such identification only increased for her as she grew older. Like Smith's novel, Maya Angelou's *I Know Why the Caged Bird Sings* helped Winfrey break down the feelings of isolation that resulted from her experiences with childhood sexual abuse. The emotional connections engendered by reading created a sense of community that compensated Winfrey for what she felt was the affective sparseness of her childhood, the alienation that came with growing up as a "little Negro child . . . unloved and so isolated" and that led as a result to low self-esteem.[76]

Tapping into the mystical, imagined community manifested in literature had been an early way for Winfrey to undo feelings of both social and spiritual isolation. Accordingly, it became the starting point for book club reading. Winfrey actively solicited acts of identification within the club, urging would-be guests to explain how the book touched them in their letters to her. Similar questions guided the on-air discussions as well, as she asked guests, "Did you see yourself?" or "[Was] this story . . . like your own in any way?"[77] The readers who answered those questions in compelling ways were the ones chosen to appear on the on-air book club. Their discussions explored the transformative power of identification, which they framed as a simultaneously cognitive, therapeutic, and mystical process, one capable of changing the self and, by extension, the world.

"THERE IS NO DIFFERENCE"

Though no empirical research has yet documented precisely how many of Winfrey's viewers read along with the club during its six-year existence, retail and library records suggest that the number was in the millions. Generalizing with any precision about the experiences of these readers is difficult; as a host of historians of reading have demonstrated, individuals derive wildly varying meanings from the texts they encounter. Both individual idiosyncrasy and cultural norms of what counts as "good" or "bad" reading shape the reader's encounter with the meanings that an author (not to mention genre, language, and the mechanisms of book marketing) encode in a text. As a result of these complex variables, speculating about the experiences of the millions of people who read along with Oprah's Book Club is a risky proposition.[78]

What can be documented, however, is the reading Winfrey encouraged and showcased on the air, an interpretive mode that began with the act of empathetic identification and moved from there to the cultivation of "openness"—a state of affective transcendence that merged the self with the wider world. The basic assumptions of this affect-driven reading are well known. A bare-bones version of it can be seen in the reading for psychological validation ("I liked this character; I could relate to her") that occurs in most high school and college classrooms. Such reading forms the basis for what Wayne Booth has called "ethical criticism," a mode of textual engagement in which "one serves one's 'self' in part by *taking in* the new selves offered in stories." Such imaginative incorporation of the unfamiliar into the self, Booth argues, is the basis not merely of Western democracy, but also of the moral sense, and a similarly capacious intention can be clearly seen in the reading for "openness" encouraged by Oprah's Book Club.[79]

On the televised episodes of the book club, Winfrey encouraged her guests to use the emotional connection inherent in identifying with a literary character as the first in a multistage process. "Opening" themselves to others would reveal the essential unreality of the destructive social and political hierarchies that had marked their lives and begin the process of replacing them with harmonious flows of love and kindness. Regularly discussed during book club episodes, openness was simultaneously a cognitive, an emotional, and a spiritual state, premised on the New Thought belief that "the dualism of . . . soul and body" was a fiction, one that the exercise of faith would resolve into "an indivisible and inseparable unity."[80] Readerly identification revealed the falsity of that dualism at both the psychic and the social levels. As they dissolved the divides between mind and body, club readers also healed the rift between self and cosmos: through the mystical medium of the book, their own sense of woundedness and alienation became a transformative empathy capable of reshaping the larger world.

One of the club's first episodes, devoted to Ursula Hegi's *Stones from the River*, exemplified the journey Winfrey hoped readers would make: into the narrow confines of individuated selfhood, through a critical engagement with society, and finally into a transcendent space of affective union, a state characterized by the dissolve of difference. Hegi's novel tells the story of Trudi Montag, a dwarf who works in a library and hides Jews from the Nazis in wartime Germany. When a guest named Kathleen noted that Hegi's novel "opened [my] eyes to the differentness of being a dwarf," Winfrey concurred: "It's expanded me. . . . I think I'm pretty open-minded . . . but it opened me up in a way."[81]

Because self-reflection was a crucial element in the pursuit of openness, club discussions could sound decidedly solipsistic at times. Midway through the Hegi discussion, Winfrey compared Trudi Montag's attempts to stretch her diminutive body to her own childhood identification with Shirley Temple, revealing that "I remember . . . putting a clothespin on my nose with two cotton balls trying to get my nose . . . to point up" (15). But contrary to what critics of the club's "therapeutic" reading have suggested, this turn to personal experience was not merely narcissistic. Identification drew readers more deeply into their individuated selves by equating their own experience with that of others. But that rudimentary point-to-point comparison then reversed itself: readers "opened" out into the larger world when they recognized the ways in which *both* sets of experiences were structured by similar and similarly divisive social hierarchies. Winfrey's Shirley Temple reverie ended with her reflection that "you can't change who you are. . . . that's how I identified . . . that's what slavery did to black people, is to teach us self-hatred for the way we looked" (15). By naming the social institutions and mores that create and enforce hierarchy (antisemitism or slavery, "lookism" of all kinds), readers served to speed them on their way to dissolution. At the close of the *Stones from the River* episode, Winfrey noted that once she "open[ed] . . . up to a new way of thinking" she recognized that "[even] if you are a dwarf, then . . . there is no difference between yourself and myself" (13). Reflecting the insights of feminist and womanist recovery, Winfrey acknowledged that social differences and hierarchies were real and had the power to wound. Her New Thought faith, however, led her away from that acknowledgment, to a version of AA's alcoholic equalitarianism, which dismissed that divisive reality in order to focus on a greater human sameness.

The second stage in the process of opening—the moment where reading prompts a recognition that social hierarchies affect all members of the human community—bears some scrutiny. The *Stones from the River* episode was fairly typical in the way it noted issues of social inequality; it was unusual in the kind of action it countenanced. A guest whose Jewish parents had lived in Germany during the war recounted that "when the Nazis marched into [her father's] office . . . and told him Jews cannot be attorneys anymore . . . most of the secretaries went along with it, and yet, one stood up and she said, 'Why? Why are you doing this?' . . . They still did it, but at least she said, 'It's not all right' " (10). In this instance, the act of opening yourself to others, of extending your subjectivity to include them, became the grounds for social action, for refusing to cede power to an oppressive political regime. Winfrey and the guests agreed that after reading *Stones* it would be hard to just "do that phony little laugh thing" when they heard an offensive joke or to "seeth[e] inside [because] you don't like" the injustices that you see in the world (11). Having "opened" themselves to Trudi Montag, they would take her resistance to the Nazis as a model for future action.

The formulation of such concrete plans to resist unjust or immoral behavior in the world, however, was infrequent in the club. Typically, Winfrey and her guests simply acknowledged the hierarchical divisions of society that their reading had brought to light and then moved past them into the utopian space of "no difference." The final book club episode of the 1996–97 season, devoted to Maya Angelou's memoir *The Heart of a Woman*, demonstrated this dynamic. Staged as a dinner and pajama party at Angelou's home, the program built on ideas the poet had articulated in her 1993 appearance on the show, unfolding as an unstructured discussion that touched on a variety of social ills, including sexualized violence (one guest, like both Winfrey and Angelou, had been a victim of childhood sexual abuse) and urban crime (*Heart of a Woman* treated Angelou's response to her son's involvement with a gang). As Winfrey and her guests celebrated Angelou's willingness to address such troubling issues, the author explained that "I had to tell the truth" about them because "to tell the truth liberates."[82]

But after acknowledging the existence of a divisive, violent social reality, Angelou's elaboration on truth-telling pushed the discussion away from any additional consideration of those conditions—away, for instance, from the material conditions that might produce urban gangs or the sexual politics that suborns incest. The truth that liberates, in this case, was less a detailed report on worldly conditions than a reference to what transcended those conditions—the "truth," in other words, not of a materialist but of a metaphysician. Telling the truth for Angelou was important insofar as it "reminds human beings, all of us, that [we] are more alike than we are unalike. . . . Nothing human can be alien to me" (4–5). Elaborating on the falsity of the differences created by the social world, Winfrey chimed in, "Don't you believe . . . that the heart of every woman—and man, too, for that matter . . . really is the same? That's what I try to tell people" (5).

Such transcendent human sameness, host and guests all agreed, was difficult to recognize during what Angelou called "these lean and mean and terrifying days." Winfrey attributed part of this problem to the legacy of racism, asserting that "there's a whole generation of people, particularly in [African American] culture, who never learned to say, 'I love you,'" a sentiment with which Angelou concurred. Further elaborating on key tenets of womanist self-recovery, she went on to assert that those who had themselves suffered as a result of these stringencies had a special duty to work to end them. "In order to change," Angelou instructed her audience, "you have to . . . say, 'It stops here. The cruelty stops here. The silences stop here. From me on, there will be kindness. From my mouth on, there will be tenderness. From my throat, there will be softness.'" The conscious decision to allow love—rather than fear or anger—to drive one's interactions with the world respected the "truth" Angelou had previously established, the truth of humanity's interconnected and divine nature. Winfrey consecrated her guest's injunction to act on this truth when she followed Angelou's speech with her customary toast, "Here's to books." "Opened" by their identification with Angelou's insights, she and her guests had connected to a spiritual truth that both transcended and could potentially change their lived reality, which all agreed was a world of "cruelty . . . silences . . . and hard words" (9).

Not every guest on the book club elaborated the idealist tenets of "Live Your Best Life" as eloquently as Maya Angelou, but most provided something similar. Even Toni Morrison, who resisted incorporation into the discourse of the enchanted book, was swept up in this dynamic. Early in the episode dealing with *The Bluest Eye*, Morrison talked explicitly about the racism that dominated the period in which she wrote the novel (1965–69) and excoriated the "hierarchy of race" that structured protagonist Pecola Breedlove's life.[83] As in the Angelou episode, however, once the issue of racism was introduced, it was quickly removed from the material realm and redefined as a lack of love. By the end of the broadcast, the sexually abused and outcast Pecola was recast as suffering "the ravages of an unloved life" (16), and guests were enjoined to bring more love into the world as a way to right social wrongs.

Glossing her own representation of the consequences of institutionalized racism, poverty, and patriarchy, Morrison observed that "the most important thing is . . . do your eyes light up when your child walks into the room?" (9).

Given the high percentage of mothers in Winfrey's audience, such an endorsement of the transformative power of maternal love is not surprising. But at issue in these discussions of love was not simple familial affection and respect, but the love M. Scott Peck had called in his "Conversation with Oprah" a "technology of reconciliation." When readers allowed love to replace fear as the structuring power in their lives, the cruelty and disenfranchisement encoded in social and material reality would cease to be real for them. Instead, paraphrasing Angelou's 1993 admonition to Winfrey about how to deal with the tabloid press, they would say, "I'm not in that." Thousands of individual decisions to choose love rather than to buy into the structures of oppression would have a cumulative effect far beyond the lives of individual readers or their immediate families, ultimately replacing a cold and unjust society with one that was warm, loving, and equitable. Winfrey articulated her ambitions for her life-changing program when she claimed, at the close of *The Bluest Eye* episode, that "it will change the world if everybody read[s] this book!" (18).

Many of the practices promoted on *The Oprah Winfrey Show* and in other Harpo media were intended to help cultivate this world-changing love, but book club reading—perhaps because it was simultaneously personal and social—was perhaps the most powerful.[84] While it is important to emphasize that the reading experiences of the millions of individuals who read along with Winfrey's selections remain largely unknown to scholars, the specific pedagogy Winfrey sought to instill in her readers is available via the televised episodes of the book club. There, just as in the dialogues she engaged in with New Thought experts on her show and web site, and in the editorials and commentary in her magazine, she "carried the message" to her audience, inviting readers to take the spiritual path she had chosen for herself.

For Winfrey, the crucial element of the changed life was seeing through the superficial differences erected by a divisive social reality in order to identify with and embrace those who, at first blush, seemed "other." Indeed, book club readers who were disinclined to interpret texts in this way earned Winfrey's scorn. To one guest's remark that he "d[id] not have compassion" for a character in Andre Dubus's *House of Sand and Fog,*

Winfrey snapped, "Would you give us a break here, George?" In the episode devoted to Barbara Kingsolver's *The Poisonwood Bible*, an African American audience member claimed that she "really dislike[d]" one of the novel's Anglo-American main characters "because she got everything that I want. She got my African husband and my homeland," to which Winfrey replied testily, "OK. It's just—it's just a book."[85] Perhaps more than anything else, this impatience with outliers who could not be recuperated into her idealist community demonstrates Winfrey's commitment to creating what she hoped would become a world of "no difference."

RECOVERY CULTURE AND THE
NEW SENTIMENTAL POWER

A thorough understanding of Oprah Winfrey as a recovery innovator —and indeed, of recovery's place in twenty-first-century American culture and life—requires attention to her relationship to *The Color Purple*, the novel Winfrey claims told "my story" and "changed my life."[86] In various interviews over the years, she has recounted the story of how she read the novel in one sitting soon after it came out in 1982, then went to the local mall and bought up all the copies to give to her friends. "I couldn't have conversations with women who hadn't read *The Color Purple*," she told *Life* magazine.[87] Winfrey went on to star as Sofia in Steven Spielberg's 1985 film adaptation of the book, receiving an Academy Award nomination for her performance; she claims that acting in the film "changed me because it was the first time that I knew what love was."[88] In 2005, she co-produced the successful Broadway musical based on the novel.

But while she convincingly embodied Sofia on the big screen and talks frequently in interviews and on her TV show about race, racism, the history of slavery, and the importance of honoring ancestors, Winfrey seems quite consciously to have chosen not to adopt Sofia's (or Shug Avery's) version of womanist self-recovery as her own. As she sought to heal the damage done by childhood sexual abuse and a lifetime of food addiction, Winfrey, for a variety of reasons, looked less to the narrative of decolonization Alice Walker had written than to the story of personal transformation via forgiveness, faith, and love that the "colorblind" book industry had marketed. She elaborated out of her reading of the novel an expansive recovery program dedicated to eradicating self-loathing and fear by building trust in divine love. As the book club episodes make plain, this vision of recovery acknowledges the existence and pain of racially specific wounding (as well as wounding specific to gender, class, sexuality, nationality, and disability), but uses that acknowledgment primarily as a stepping stone to a universal and transcendent vision of the self and the world. Like the alcoholic equalitarian AAs whose testimonies fill the pamphlet "Do You Think You're Different?" Winfrey has come to believe that investment in what her New Thought faith prompts her to call "the external definitions I have given myself" is in fact counterproductive.[89] For her, personal recovery and meaningful engagement with the social world require the abilities simultaneously to see difference—blackness, womanhood, wealth—and to see past it to shared and vulnerable humanity. It was toward this all-encompassing and quite utopian vision that the televised episodes of the book club ultimately urged their audiences.

Perhaps not surprisingly, this perspective has earned Winfrey the scorn of some progressive critics. Their ire results in part from the promiscuous growth of the Harpo media empire, which has expanded in near-uncanny concert with Winfrey's spiritual rhetoric. That the two things should grow apace is actually not unusual: New Thought advocates have long advanced their faith through pamphlets and books sold directly to believers rather than through the creation of formal and hierarchical institutions; indeed, this combination of decentralization and frank commercialism has been one of the reasons the New Thought enterprise has been seen as disreputable by critics in and outside of more established religions. Winfrey's delivery of the New Thought gospel through television, the Internet, and a glossy monthly magazine is the logical extension of what Richard Huber has sneeringly called the "post-office ministry" of early twentieth-century New Thought preachers.[90]

Progressives' complaints with Winfrey, however, are less about the form of her delivery than its idealist substance and the powerful political economy that underpins it. As a hypercapitalist entrepreneur, Winfrey has been criticized by black feminist critics and their white allies because she does not use her bully pulpit to address the workings of what womanist recovery advocate bell hooks calls "white supremacist capitalist patriarchy."[91] Instead, Patricia Hill Collins has argued, the star has carved out a niche for herself by purveying slickly packaged spiritualism that ignores the persistence of racial inequality in the United States in favor of an "individualistic ideology of social change that counsels her audiences to rely solely on themselves."[92] Addressing more specifically Winfrey's habit of simultaneously encouraging her

fans in their efforts at personal and community uplift while unabash-
edly celebrating her own wealth, Tarshia Stanley argues that Winfrey
appears to "do many good deeds for the weak with one hand and cycles
the system that would make them weaker with the other."[93] Although
they stop short of calling her a race traitor, these critics suggest that
Winfrey's mass-marketed and universalizing spiritual solutions to social inequalities undermine her credentials as a progressive force for
racial justice.

Marrying issues of race to those of class structure, Janice Peck, a
white Marxist critic, takes this critique a step further, reading the way
Winfrey has distanced herself from what she has called the "militant
thinking" that accompanies "black power and anger" as an analogue
for her larger disdain for progressive politics.[94] Despite her experiences
with a class- and race-stratified society, Peck argues, or perhaps because
of her success in appearing to obviate that stratification, the talk show
host has become a "cultural icon for the neoliberal era," an advocate of
personal transformation rather than meaningful governance, and a
clear beneficiary of the late twentieth century's regressive tax policies
and media deregulation. In this formulation, Winfrey's belief in the
corrosive power of self-hatred and her corresponding embrace of spiritual "empowerment" not only emblematizes but has also helped to
promote and legitimize the anti-progressive ideology of the Reagan-
Bush-Clinton era. Her lived and discursive commitment to an ethics of
self-scrutiny and personal responsibility—to what she calls "excellence"
and Peck calls "the enterprising self"—aligns Winfrey seamlessly with
the political status quo. Worse than mere bread and circuses, *The Oprah
Winfrey Show* and its satellite properties work to speed the degradation
of the social contract and to justify the growing inequality upon which
post-Fordist global capitalism is premised.

Although it has its own unique shadings, Peck's withering criticism
of Winfrey stands metonymically for the left's quarrel with recovery
culture as a whole. That complaint is structured along the same lines as
the feminist critique of recovery discussed in the previous chapter, but,
as sociologist Craig Reinarman's version of it makes plain, it does not
limit itself to questions of class, gender, or racial particularity:

> There is in all group meetings an unremitting focus on "personal
> recovery." Even awareness of social conditions is actively shunned,
> along with any mentalities, modes of discourse, or actual efforts to

change social reality. . . . There is a "we" mentality in 12-Step groups that seems to stem from the mutual help and "united we stand" values. Yet there is no systematic analysis or ideology reaching beyond the self. . . . Rather than transforming private troubles into public issues or at least linking the two, 12-Step ideology tends to sever this link or to transform what might be understood as public issues into private troubles.[95]

Resting on a clear-cut opposition between individualistic and class-based, humanist and materialist worldviews and theories of social change, this logic marks recovery's person-centered and spiritual strivings as deeply suspect. And there are good reasons to suspect them.

By constructing social difference as largely imaginary and, worse, as inimical to the development of a sober and surrendered self-in-relation, recovery—whether advocated by midwestern AAs in their pamphlet literature or by Oprah Winfrey in her book club selections—militates against other logics of transformation or interpersonal connection. Recovery's personalism, emotionalism, and claims to universality, while radically revelatory to adherents, cut against the development of the forms of connection recognized as "radical" by the traditional left: class or gender solidarity, for example, or a shared sense of racial or ethnic identity. As a result, what seems most transformative to recovery's adherents simply cannot be assimilated into the logic of transformation that prevails among progressive critics within and outside the academy. While love, faith, and divine energy may seem to their partisans to dissolve the disease of "difference," to those who take their stand on material grounds they promise nothing so much as the erosion of the constituent fibers of the social fabric, which will leave only atomized and private individuals in its wake.

But this refusal to traffic in traditional radical concepts does not mean, as Patricia Hill Collins claims, that Oprah Winfrey "counsels her audiences to rely solely on themselves," or that, as Reinarman would have it, "there is no systematic analysis or ideology reaching beyond the self" within recovery culture. As this book's excavation of it has made clear, recovery culture in all its incarnations is founded on a distinctly critical view of the possessive individualism that has hallmarked the life of the twentieth- and twenty-first-century United States, and it invites the development of selves and communities oriented to quite different values. The tradition of sponsorship in the 12-Step community, like mentoring within Winfrey's world, explicitly pushes the individual beyond the boundaries of the self (and perhaps more radically beyond those of the heteronormative family) into tutelary and inspirational relationships that evade the common categories of late capitalist social organization. But such interventions are decidedly not materialist or structural and their effects, as a result, may be diffuse, idiosyncratic, and hard to observe; experts have not yet developed a reliable metric for assessing whether or to what degree "world-changing through life-changing" actually works. Absent evidence to the contrary, radical critics may dismiss recovery out of hand simply because its rhetoric and practice focus on personal and spiritual rather than social-structural transformation. But just because a set of critical tools and vocabulary are not readily cognizable does not mean they do not exist; a more nuanced assessment of recovery must take into account the kinds of individuals it seeks to produce, as well as the nature of the communities that they combine to form.

Oprah's Book Club's castigation of a loveless world, like the principle of alcoholic equalitarianism in which it originated, is a call to transform individuals isolated by the cold and calculating workings of modern market society into selves-in-relation, to remake possessive individualists into a community of the heart. Such communities are simultaneously powerful and entropic. They exist in the realm of the social, and, as the discussion of racial and sexual politics in the book club make plain, material and political-economic relations may be among the things with which they concern themselves. But they may also retain a belief—one present in all the articulations of recovery this book has catalogued, but most pronounced in Oprah's Book Club—that the things of this world are ultimately less real, or at least less important, than matters of the spirit.

Within AA and throughout the 12-Step culture that developed in its wake, this belief manifested itself in the 10th Tradition's prohibition against incorporating "outside issues" into the rhetoric and practice of recovery. Bill Wilson framed that decision as a practical one, albeit with a metaphysical dimension: taking up social questions could distract individual AAs and the organization as a whole from the "primary purpose" of spiritual growth into sobriety. Oprah Winfrey's relative disinterest in taking up hard questions of social inequality may have a practical dimension, too. After all, she is the host of a mainstream talk show and needs to appeal to a wide audience in order to retain that status.

But as a believer in New Thought doctrines that cede primacy to the spiritual and devalue the material, she may also be driven by simple matters of epistemology. Universal health care, government support for the inner city, the de facto apartheid of America's public education system—the things toward which Winfrey's left-liberal critics might wish that she would direct her energies—may ultimately seem less real to her and to many members of her audience than divine love.[96] For individuals committed to such an idealist worldview, advocacy for change is a matter of insisting on that higher reality. The interpretive community formed by Oprah's Book Club and around other Harpo outlets, like that formed within early AA or among sober lesbian feminists in the mid-1980s, forms a space within which the belief in that reality can flourish.

Although the United States has long nurtured progressive communities of faith, since the ascendancy of the religious right during the 1980s interest in and tolerance for idealist and spiritualist subcultures by the champions of progressive politics has declined precipitously.[97] An important exception to this distancing and dereliction, and one that may help those outside of recovery culture to understand and even to appreciate its worldview, can be found in the work of some feminist historians and literary critics of antebellum sentimental culture. I suggested at the end of chapter 2 that the surrendered men of mid-century AA were usefully understood as inheritors of the sentimental tradition; explicating the idealism at the center of Oprah's Book Club in that tradition's light throws the continuities between the two cultural formations into yet sharper relief.

The middle-class white women who read and wrote sentimental literature during the early nineteenth century, Jane Tompkins has argued, organized their worlds via "sentimental power," the belief, derived from biblical typology, in the primacy of spirit and in loving human relationships as the earthly manifestation of God's will. This evangelical Christian epistemology informed distinctive and logical "attitudes toward the family and toward social institutions; a definition of power and its relation to individual human feeling; [and] notions of political and social equality," all of which were premised on the notion, inscribed throughout the Bible and especially in the story of Jesus Christ, that "it is the spirit alone that is finally real."[98] From within this idealist worldview the denizens of antebellum sentimental culture elaborated the morals, rhetoric, and hermeneutics necessary to organize and maintain a compassionate and humanist engagement with a rapidly changing and perilously unequal social world. While that engagement was expressed in countless daily behaviors and practices, it found its most elaborate articulation in the print culture of the period, most notably didactic fiction like Harriet Beecher Stowe's *Uncle Tom's Cabin* and Susan Warner's *The Wide, Wide World*, but also in professional and amateur poetry, commonplace books, and diaries. Adherence to the set of beliefs enumerated in that literature, Tompkins argues, cannot be assimilated to traditional notions of political action, but it nevertheless had truly revolutionary implications. Sentimental power energized the abolition movement in Britain and in the United States and sparked a host of other reform efforts as well; equally if not more important, its less tangible workings helped to redefine gender roles and relations and to shape the deep moral structures of a nation convulsing under the shift from market to industrial capitalism.[99]

Neither Oprah Winfrey and the members of her book club nor any other exponents of recovery ideals have been dignified by the passage of time in the way antebellum authors and their audiences have been. This may be one reason why scholars seeking to rebut the highbrow criticisms of Winfrey enumerated above have not discussed her as an inheritor of the tradition of sentimental fiction, but instead have tried to read into the club some version of progressive secular politics—arguing for instance, that Winfrey challenges the existing power structure by disrupting its literary hierarchies, a move analogous to some recovery activists' claim that participation in 12-Step groups may lead to heightened environmental consciousness.[100] Both these claims may be true to a certain extent, but they dodge a larger and thornier problem, namely, how to conceptualize and make sense of utopian energies that resist conscription into the familiar secular and materialist politics that are the stock in trade of contemporary progressives.

The freeing up of such utopian energies, as the evidence presented above should make clear, has been Oprah Winfrey's goal since the early 1990s; the power of healing and love were articulated across her media properties over the course of the decade and crystallized within her book club. Her aim was recovery that began with the individual but encompassed the globe—the creation of a world freed from the disease of "difference" via the exercise of the imagination, the heart, and the spirit. Whether this reformist program was effective or not remains open to debate, but Winfrey's success in reaching an ever-widening audience suggests that her version of "world-changing through life-changing" has resonated and continues to resonate with millions of fans. Like that of most of the other proponents of recovery surveyed in this volume, the specificity of the conceptual categories that work to order Winfrey's world has been overlooked—in part because such a program for reform is threatening, in part because it is "other" to the forms of analysis and evaluation common within the academy, but also for the simple reason that it has been hidden in plain sight.

Recovery as a "Populist" Culture

The first thing to bear in mind (especially if we ourselves belong to
the clerico-academic-scientific type, the officially and conventionally
"correct" type, "the deadly respectable" type, for which to ignore
others is a besetting temptation) is that nothing can be more stupid
than to bar out phenomena from our notice, merely because we are
incapable of taking part in anything like them ourselves.
—William James, The Varieties of Religious Experience, 1902

The intellectual and cultural history of 12-Step recovery and its offshoots, as I noted in the introduction, is largely unknown to many otherwise well-educated academics and professionals. When it is known, it is
frequently misunderstood. While one book cannot capture the range
and complexity of recovery experience and writing across the twentieth
and twenty-first centuries, I have tried in this volume at least to gesture
both to what seem to be the canonical texts of 12-Step, therapeutic, and
post-12-Step recovery and to the networks of readers, publishers, and
distributors that allowed them to come into being. I have spent less time
attempting to explain why these scores of titles and millions of readers
have been largely absent from progressive academic accounts of popular
culture. By way of conclusion, I want to address that question by looking
briefly at a notorious example of writing about addiction and recovery.
James Frey's *A Million Little Pieces* may or may not be true—but its
meditations on recovery literature suggest some of the reasons why
recovery culture as a whole, despite its size, complexity, and longevity,
has seemed to fall outside the bounds of legitimate scholarly inquiry.[1]

During the fall of 1992, when he was twenty-three years old, James
Frey was a patient at Hazelden.[2] His arrival at the clinic was ostensibly
presaged by an extended crack binge that had brought to a head more
than ten years of addiction to alcohol and "cocaine . . . in every form that
it exists . . . pills, acid, mushrooms, meth, PCP and glue."[3] The substance of *A Million Little Pieces* is Frey's resistance to Hazelden's version
of the 12-Step cure, a choice articulated in a ringing pledge Frey makes
to his counselor upon his release: "I'm gonna stay clean . . . if for no

other reason than to be able to come back here and show your self-righteous ass that your way isn't the only way" (307).

Frey's refusal to be conscripted into the discourse of disease and surrender takes various forms in his book; the most instructive incidents (and perhaps the ones most likely to have occurred) are those that involve his encounter with and rejection of the official literature of 12-Step recovery. Frey encounters three different books during his time at Hazelden. The first is the Big Book, which he finds on his nightstand upon arriving on the ward, and the second is a Hazelden "First Step workbook," an illustrated, interactive text whose story and questionnaire are meant to help patients arrive at the First Step admission that their addiction is out of control. In contrast with these touchstones of the recovery canon is a third volume, the *Tao te Ching*, a copy of which Frey receives from his brother early in his stay at the treatment center. Frey's engagement with the three texts is meant to explain his journey both to sobriety and to the mature writerly aesthetic that ostensibly informs *A Million Little Pieces*. It sketches out the cultural field against which he intends to define himself and, in so doing, gestures to the reasons that so much of the recovery movement—and the long spiritual and emotional tradition of which it is a part—has been invisible to academic eyes.

The 12-Step literature, not surprisingly, is the object of Frey's scorn. He derides the Big Book as "very simple. If you do what the book says, you will be cured. . . . If you join the club, you're the lucky winner of a lifelong supply of bullshit Meetings full of whining, complaining and blaming. . . . As with most testimonials like this that I've read or heard or been forced to endure, something . . . strikes me as weak, hollow and empty" (71). Disgusted, he throws the Big Book, along with a Bible, out his window into the rain. When they mysteriously reappear in his room the next day, he "carr[ies] them to the Bathroom and stuff[s] them in the garbage can beneath the used razors, the brown Q-Tips and the dirty snot rags. If I could . . . I would stuff them into the toilet and I would shit on them" (85). The First Step Workbook fares no better. Designed for low-level readers, it tells the story of an alcoholic named Joe in "simple words and . . . simple pictures consisting of empty outlines of figures and places. . . . The idea, I am guessing, is that while spending time filling in the pictures, I am supposed to grasp the horror of Joe's story and then relate that horror to situations in my own life. If Joe is out of control, I must be out of control as well" (178). Instead of coloring in the images and answering the questionnaire at the end of the booklet, Frey spells out across each page "I DON'T NEED THIS BULLSHIT TO KNOW I'M OUT OF CONTROL. When I am finished I review my work. Each page looks perfect and I like it" (179, original emphasis).

The *Tao te Ching*, by contrast, appeals to Frey. Unlike the "thick, worn blue" cover of the Big Book (70) and the First Step "children's coloring book" (149), the *Tao* is "a small thin paperback. The title is written across the front in simple white type against a black background." This pared-down aesthetic carries over into the book's contents, "a series of short poems numbered one through eighty-one" that inspire Frey to rhapsodic heights: "The words and the words together and the meaning and the context are simple so simple and basic so basic and true and that is all that matters true" (160–61). While his African American roommate plays the clarinet, Frey realizes that the *Tao* "calms me without effort" and "fills in the blanks of my strategy for survival" (230). Unlike the "simple words and . . . simple pictures" of official recovery literature, the austere yet resonant simplicity of the *Tao* provides both a usable guide to sobriety and the foundation for a mature aesthetic.

Whatever else it may be, *A Million Little Pieces* is the story of how James Frey aspires to modernism—the story of how the *Tao*'s minimalist, heady aesthetic (its testosterone quotient conveniently boosted by its proximity to African American jazz) triumphs over its flat, formulaic, and, above all, feminized competitors, with their "whining, complaining, and blaming . . . testimonials" and their "empty outlines of figures and places."[4] Simultaneously "weak, hollow, and empty" and verbally and emotionally excessive, these grotesque literary forms seem to have lives of their own, as evidenced by the Big Book that returns out of the rain to plague the man who would reject and rise above it. Escaping the aesthetic gravity of such texts requires acts of conceptual, if not literal, violence. Recapping the dynamic that Sandra Gilbert and Susan Gubar observed among male writers in the early twentieth century, Frey rises to the challenge by scribbling over and metaphorically shitting on the pages that offend him with their insipidity.[5]

As James Frey goes, so goes much of America's cultural elite. More graphically, perhaps, than some better credentialed commentators, Frey's reckonings with these three texts suggest why recovery remains a largely unknown phenomenon among literary critics, cultural historians, and cultural studies scholars of the contemporary United States—even those who claim an interest in popular culture. The culture of recovery is flat, simple, and repetitive, spiritual rather than cerebral, aphoristic rather than truthful, and earnest rather than ironic. In his disdain for these qualities, Frey is not alone. Travel the groves of academe or peruse the pages of leading cultural journals, and it becomes quickly apparent that Frey's investment in the existential, aesthetic, and performative style Ann Douglas has termed "terrible honesty" is shared by many, if not most, of the cultural gatekeepers in the academy and the belles-lettristic press.[6]

Douglas's sweeping overview of the de facto official culture of the contemporary United States begins to suggest why this might be. Growing out of the working-class urban cultures of white ethnics and people of color in the early 1900s, the "mongrel" ethic and aesthetic of terrible honesty, she argues, liberated the nation's culture from the tyrannical white Victorian matriarchs who had held sway over it since the previous century. While those pious prudes of the Gilded Age had sought to protect "themselves and their readers from what cannot be borne," Douglas explains, "the moderns sought it out; the 'horrors of life' and the compromises that purport to mask them were the subject matter of the post-war generation" (33). Desire, rage, and the will to power became the subject and substance of cultural expression, manifesting themselves in jazz, cinema, and skyscrapers as well as in a host of literary forms.

The ethos of terrible honesty not only changed aesthetics, but also reshuffled the criteria by which cultural expressions would be valued. No longer was "high" or legitimate culture that which confirmed the middle-class Christian ideals of the WASP elite, and "low" or disreputable culture anything that failed to do so. Instead, admittance to the canon of official culture was open to any and all who could meet the aesthetic and existential mandate for "accuracy, precision, and perfect pitch and timing" (8). Cultural products, like personalities, would be evaluated by their perceived authenticity. For the moderns, Douglas suggests, virtue—in both life and art—consists of adopting a "discourse of disbelief that claims a monopoly on self-knowledge and shreds the 'pretty' in the interests of the true" (54).

One might think that our own postmodern age, with its investment in surfaces, playfulness, and ironic detachment, might have left behind this early twentieth-century commitment to what Douglas calls "the arts of exactitude" (35), but such is not the case. As Kimberly Chabot Davis has observed, the theoretical architects of postmodernism continue—redouble, even—modernism's disdain for the aesthetic, moral, and epistemological values of matriarchal Victorian culture, seeking to reveal the constructed nature of both "the 'pretty' " and "the true" by self-reflexively "calling attention to their own aesthetic and narrative constructions." Like their modernist precursors, Davis argues, postmodernists privilege hardness, rejecting the notions of organic form, beauty, and sympathy that shaped that earlier era's aesthetics and morals.[7] Together, these two masculinist modes have become the official literary and artistic culture of the twentieth and twenty-first centuries. They are enshrined in university syllabi and discussed in all the reputable journals, and inform at every level the personal styles of the individuals who inhabit those precincts of American culture we recognize as "elite," "stylish," or "hip."

The democratic impulse within terrible honesty, its skepticism of received wisdom and the status quo, has at one level made for a refreshing opening of the cultural canon, which now acknowledges the experiences and expressions of women, the working class, and people of color. Especially in the wake of the progressive movements of the late 1960s, scholars informed by Marxist theories of class struggle and, to a lesser extent, by ideas of identity politics prevailed upon the academy to recognize "popular culture"—the texts and experiences from the vernacular "margins" of society—alongside offerings from its more erudite realms. This democratization of the canon means that in any Introduction to American Culture class today, students are as likely to encounter African American stories of conjure practices as they are to read the sermons of Puritan divines, or to scrutinize the songs of the young European immigrants who agitated for the first labor unions alongside of, and with the same intensity as, the policy statements of their bosses. The result has been an outpouring of rich, exciting scholarship that recognizes the pluralistic nature of the American experience. At the same time, however, this democratization has resulted in a further calcification of the conceptual categories through which we evaluate that experience.

I say this because the popular culture that has destabilized the old American canon is not just any culture created by nonelite people. What has come to count as popular culture is terribly honest culture: texts and practices, beliefs and institutions that oppose the values and the forms of that old Victorian matriarchy and the class- and race-stratified, liberal Protestant world for which it stood. The culture of the class-conscious working class, of disenfranchised youth, people of color, the sexually transgressive—all these have been welcomed into the academic study of popular culture.

Texts and actors like those described in this book, however, have fared less well. As noted in the previous chapters, while there has been some effort to rehabilitate the sentimental culture of Victorian women (and, to a lesser extent, men), progressive literary and historical critics have shown scant interest in excavating contemporary cultural forms that perpetuate a moral vision of the world, that treat language as a transparent medium, that draw meaning from the antiquated realms of spirit and affect.[8] These present-day articulations of the values of late nineteenth-century genteel culture still seem in some way disreputable, dishonest. As James Frey's treatment of recovery print culture makes clear, the lingering phantoms of the genteel tradition tend to prompt disgust rather than stimulating inquiry.[9]

But as this book has attempted to demonstrate, just because recovery culture fails to conform to academic notions of "the popular" does not mean that it is not "popular" in the layperson's sense of that term—widespread, well known, and enthusiastically integrated into everyday life. Recovery's adherents number in the millions; it is a diverse and multifaceted cultural formation, with an intellectual history and an evolving aesthetic. What it lacks is the discernible political valence that would allow it to be easily incorporated into the analytical and value-conferring frameworks of the academy. My sense is that there are many other widespread but similarly elusive cultural formations—popular cultures that do not quite meet the established criteria of "the popular" because their politics are opaque, fluid, or incoherent.

Because it is both a widespread cultural formation and one that resists easy recuperation into the definitions of the popular that prevail within the academy, I have taken to calling recovery a "populist" culture. The term captures accurately the scale of the phenomena in question; more important, it serves also to connote a degree of anti-elitism, but one with a decidedly indeterminate and labile politics. As the preceding chapters have attempted to demonstrate, recovery culture makes a pronounced and distinctive critique of the modern world and its dominant institutions; it offers its adherents strategies for negotiating their ways in that world, and even for effecting change within it. As such it cannot be called apolitical, save by those who define politics through the narrow liberal prism of electoral participation or its radical counterpart, the inculcation of revolutionary consciousness. Nor can recovery culture fairly be pigeonholed as inherently reactionary, as has been argued by a number of critics cited in previous chapters of this book and elsewhere.[10]

Rather, the emotional foundations of populist culture mean that its politics may move in any—or many—directions. As Timothy Aubry and Kimberly Chabot Davis have pointed out in their astute readings of contemporary popular fiction, identification with strangers may be the first step toward the building of meaningful, even utopian community, with affect opening up opportunities for coalition building in ways that ideological or strategic appeals are incapable of replicating.[11] At the same time, however, as the history of populism in the United States and abroad makes plain, that same investment in affect can produce particularly stubborn xenophobia, paranoia, and cultural entrenchment. Lawrence Grossberg nicely sums up these prospects, noting that "affective relations are, at least potentially, the condition of possibility for the optimism, invigoration, and passion which are necessary for any struggle to change the world," even as they can also "position people in ways which make them particularly vulnerable to certain kinds of appeals [and] can easily be articulated into repressive and even totalitarian forms."[12] Recovery culture as a whole has yet to evolve into either of these positions—though no doubt the process of recovery has pushed some individuals in one (or both) directions; it is possible that, like much populist culture, it will remain fairly politically inchoate.

I believe, however, that despite both aesthetic obsolescence and political indeterminacy, such populist cultures—particularly those intertwined, as recovery is and always has been, with faith-centered institutions and practices—require serious and sustained attention from scholars and critics. In my research for this volume, I have encountered far more people to whom versions of recovery culture offer a meaningful way of looking at the world than I have people who are swayed by the aesthetics and politics of terrible honesty. They are my students, the staff members at the schools where I have worked (as well as the donors to those schools), family members, friends, tradespeople, miscellaneous riders on public transportation, and more. Although it is in many ways a foreign tongue to me, the language of the heart resonates powerfully for them. The beliefs that lie back of that language, the cultural forms through which it is transmitted, the bonds that it forges among speakers and listeners, writers and readers—all these merit the cultural elite's most careful consideration.

Alcoholics Anonymous Membership

Beginning in 1951, the annual General Service Conference report included information on AA membership. However, data gathering and reporting were not always consistent in the early years. For instance, for much of the 1950s, conference reports announced membership totals for the previous year, rather than the year of the report itself. In some years, "Loner" members (those who declare membership in AA to the GSO, but do not affiliate with a particular meeting or group) in the United States and Canada were also included in tabulations of area and regional membership. The number of members in hospitals and prisons was reported routinely but never broken down by location, so how those figures count toward national and international totals is ambiguous. The table below represents the most accurate figures available from annual conference reports and other sources for AA membership in the United States and Canada, overseas (the rest of the world), and worldwide (all countries), but the data may not be definitive. Total worldwide membership is greater than the sum of the United States and Canada plus overseas due to Loners, Internationalists (the AA membership category for people who move from place to place and therefore do not identify with a particular meeting or group, such as expatriates or members in the merchant marine or armed forces), and institutional groups whose subtotals are not given here. All figures are from the conference report for the year specified unless otherwise noted.

TABLE A.1. ALCOHOLICS ANONYMOUS MEMBERSHIP

Year	AA Membership, United States & Canada	AA Membership, Overseas	AA Membership, Worldwide
1935[1]	2	n/a	2
1940[2]	n/a	n/a	2,000
1945[3]	n/a	n/a	15,000
1951[4]	n/a	n/a	120,000
1955[5]	103,496	14,687	136,195
1960	112,899	16,420	151,606
1965	144,426	36,846	217,967
1970	179,478	63,000	297,077
1975	330,621	107,127	502,733
1980	444,547	362,772	868,171
1985	702,311	575,681	1,351,793
1990	978,982	762,046	1,793,834
1995	1,223,017	516,015	1,790,528
2000	1,258,940	666,413	1,990,504
2007[6]	1,308,712	616,899	1,989,260

[1]General Service Conference Report 1951, 10.

[2]COA, 192–93.

[3]Kurtz, *Not-God*, 113.

[4]Table shifts years to allow recognition of first General Service Conference, held in 1951. Conference Report 1951, 10.

[5]General Service Conference Report, 1956, 57–58. In this conference report, total membership is greater than the sum of the North American and overseas membership because it includes members in hospitals and prisons in unspecified locations.

[6]"Estimates of AA Groups," http://www.aa.org/lang/en/subpage.cfm?page=74.

Reprintings and Distribution of *Alcoholics Anonymous*

AA historians agree that the first edition of the Big Book was reprinted sixteen times, with minor emendations: figures were updated; typographical and usage errors were corrected; and some slight changes in language were made. The exact figures for each successive printing are a matter of some dispute; archival evidence in not definitive on this question. Table B.1 shows one historian's calculations of the size of successive printings of the first edition. Subsequent editions in 1955, 1976, and 2001 completely revised the second section of personal stories, but aside from updating figures, made no further changes to the first section.

TABLE B.1. REPRINTS OF THE FIRST EDITION OF
ALCOHOLICS ANONYMOUS

Printing	Date	Copies Printed
First	April 1939	4,730
Second	March 1941	5,000
Third	June 1942	5,000
Fourth	March 1943	5,000
Fifth	January 1944	5,000
Sixth	June 1944	5,000
Seventh	January 1945	5,000
Eighth	February 1945	20,000
Ninth	January 1946	20,000
Tenth	August 1946	25,000
Eleventh	June 1947	25,000
Twelfth	n.d.	25,000
Thirteenth	n.d.	50,000
Fourteenth	n.d.	50,000
Fifteenth	n.d.	50,000
Sixteenth	n.d.	50,000
		TOTAL: 349,730

Source: Art Sheehan, "*Alcoholics Anonymous* First Editions."

TABLE B.2. NORTH AMERICAN DISTRIBUTION HISTORY OF *ALCOHOLICS ANONYMOUS*

Year[1]	Regular	Non-Current	Spanish[2]	French[3]
1955	19,015	9,838	106	n/a
1960	24,533	42	n/a	n/a
1965	29,900	n/a	813	n/a
1970	54,725	n/a	1,059	n/a
1975	176,274	n/a	2,760	n/a
1980	369,980	n/a	5,790	n/a
1985	696,300	n/a	10,900	11,358
1990	691,583	n/a	27,200	10,882
1995	498,718	n/a	39,882	7,018
2000	413.519	n/a	37,349	6,823

Note: The term "distribution" is used in the General Service Conference reports to indicate numbers of Big Books sold as well as those given away.

[1]The conference reports for a particular year report the distribution figures from the previous year.

[2]The conference report of 1955 notes that "as a service to Spanish-speaking groups, Headquarters assumed responsibility [this year] for printing 500 copies of a Spanish edition of the first section of the Big Book which had originally been translated and mimeographed privately" (17). The 1962 conference report noted that a new translation of the first part of the Big Book, plus Bill's and Dr. Bob's stories, was

Paperback[4]	Large Print	Abridged "Pocket"	Total Big Books Distributed
n/a	n/a	n/a	28,959
n/a	n/a	n/a	24,575
n/a	n/a	n/a	30,713
n/a	n/a	n/a	55,784
n/a	n/a	n/a	179,034
n/a	n/a	n/a	375,770
n/a	n/a	n/a	718,558
432,388	9,007	n/a	1,171,060
404,754	18,256	95,266	1,063,894
346,579	23,083	116,359	943,352

being prepared by a group in Mexico. The report for the following year inaugurates regular reporting on sales of the Spanish-language edition of the Big Book, but without mentioning which version is being counted.

[3]The conference report of 1985 (reporting on literature distributed in 1984) is the first to mention distribution of *Gros Livre des Alcooliques anonymes*. A "composite" volume in French, incorporating parts of the Big Book, *Twelve Steps and Twelve Traditions*, and *Alcoholics Anonymous Comes of Age* was under discussion as early as 1961.

[4]A paperback edition of the Big Book was distributed for the first time in 1986 (Conference Report 1987, 54).

NOTES

Introduction

1. Klein, "Bill Clinton: Who Is This Guy?," <http://nymag.com/news/features/40563>. Additional discussion of Clinton playing the role of "Family Hero" amid addiction-related dysfunction appears in Maraniss, *First in His Class*, and of course in Clinton's memoir *My Life*.

2. Connor, "Newser's Book," <http://www.nydailynews.com/news/us_world/2007/10/28/2007-10-28_newsers_book_ford_saw_clinton_as_a_sex_a.html>. The issue is discussed, for example, in two articles titled "Is Clinton a Sex Addict?" by Laura Miller and Wendy Kaminer, as well as in Levin, *Clinton Syndrome*.

3. Connor, "Newser's Book."

4. Moskowitz, *In Therapy We Trust*, 277.

5. Bush's discussion with Graham is featured prominently in his campaign biography, *Charge to Keep*, 135–37. Craig Unger's *Fall of the House of Bush*, by contrast, asserts that the image of Graham convincing Bush to take the pledge was manufactured by his public relations team during the presidential campaign. On the machinations of this manufacture and the events for which it was meant as a smokescreen, including Bush's destructive drinking behavior and his conversion by the decidedly nonpatrician evangelical preacher Arthur Blessitt, see especially the chapter "Prodigal Son," 79–99.

6. Romano and Lardner Jr. "1986: A Life-Changing Year."

7. Brisbort, "Dry Drunk," <http://www.americanpolitics.com/20020924Bisbort.html>.

8. O'McCarthy, "Is Bush a 'Dry Drunk'?," <http://www.buzzflash.com/contributors/03/03/10_drunk.html>.

9. Articles on Bush as a dry drunk and/or as having relapsed back into alcoholism appeared in a variety of left online publications like *Counterpunch*, *In These Times*, *Salon*, *Conspiracy Planet*, *Prison Planet*, and *SFGate.com*, as well as in more centrist tabloid outlets like the *National Enquirer* and *Breitbart.com*. The latter was notable for spreading Venezuelan president Hugo Chavez's critique of Bush as "an alcoholic, a sick man with a lot of hang-ups" ("Chavez Extends," <http://www.breitbart.com/article.php?id=060921201049.4stienzo&show_article=1>).

10. AA World Services, "Estimates of AA Groups and Members," <http://www.aa.org/lang/en/subpage.cfm?page=74>.

11. Judit Santon, personal communication to the author, 10 September 2001.

12. Al-Anon Family Groups, "Introduction," <http://www.al-anon.alateen.org/pdf/mediakit/mkintro.pdf>; OA information from Alexis Kerschner, personal communication, 17 July 2008. Narcotics Anonymous's "Basic Information" notes that in 2007, there were over 43,000 meetings worldwide, <http://www.na.org/basic.htm>.

The total of 645,000 comes from assuming an average of 15 people per meeting (the figure used by Al-Anon and OA as "average") and multiplying.

13. Karen G., email to the author, 8 August 2008. Appearance and growth of CODA, as well as criticisms of the group, are discussed in chapters 1 and 4.

14. *Statistical Abstracts*, 128.

15. Roebuck et al., "DATStats: Results."

16. AAWSO, "AA Preamble," <http://www.aa.org/lang/en_pdfs/smf92_en.pdf>.

17. The evolution and some of the workings of the General Service Office are discussed in chapters 2 and 3. AA's service structure is detailed in *The AA Service Manual*.

18. When I use the terms "recovery movement" and "recovery culture" in this book, I do so to designate the aggregate of the three different modes of recovery—12-Step, therapeutic, or post-12-Step. In addition, I use the term "recovery movement" largely as a matter of writerly convenience, not to impute to recovering people or recovery organizations the sense of urgency that the term "social movement" frequently has for scholars in the social sciences. As Alfred Katz (*Self-Help in America*) and Robin Room ("Alcoholics Anonymous as a Social Movement") have argued and as the chapters that follow make clear, for a variety of reasons 12-Step organizations and their offshoots are for the most part not organized with the goal of critiquing or advocating for changes to social policy, institutional practice, or the workings of the state, though some critiques and advocacy work may be byproducts of the recovery process. Feminist scholars of self-help Verta Taylor and Marieke Van Willigen ("Women's Self-Help") have argued that while they do not necessarily "constitute a concerted social force for political change," self-help groups should nevertheless be considered social movements because they "typically develop an ideology or set of beliefs and values that identifies injustices in the system . . . and a set of strategies and tactics that specify goals and processes of social change" (124). Although the feminist recovery organizations discussed in chapter 5 of this book fit this description, and the followers of Oprah's Book Club described in chapter 6 perform a version of this cultural work, the 12-Step and therapeutic recovery organizations that preceded and informed them explicitly rule out such practices, meaning that "the recovery movement" or "recovery culture" in aggregate does not meet even Taylor and Van Willigen's loose criteria for a "social movement."

19. The AA General Service Office calculates that, since AA was founded in 1939, 542 organizations have been granted permission to adapt the 12 Steps and 12 Traditions for their own needs. However, it is unknown how many of those organizations are still in existence. Amy Filiatreau, email to the author, 3 August 2007.

20. For overviews of this dynamic, separated by decades but both reflecting on how it hamstrings the field of alcoholism research, see Ron Roizen, "Great Controlled-Drinking Controversy," and Brook Hersey, "Controlled Drinking Debates." Recent attempts to push past this dilemma are chronicled in the "Effectiveness and Outcomes Research" section of volume eighteen of *Recent Developments in Alcoholism*, which seeks to refute what section editor J. Scott Tonigan describes as the impression that "AA outcome research is a tower of Babel and that empirically based statements about the desirability and benefit of AA cannot be made" (352). Despite shared belief

that rigorous study of AA is both possible and worthwhile, Tonigan and the other authors in his section admit that a host of factors continues to conspire to make it difficult to gauge—or even to define—the program's effectiveness. These include self-selection into AA and ease of exit from it, regional and group variations in the program, the clash between AA's alcohol-only focus and the realities of poly-addiction, and, above all, lack of researcher familiarity with AA's core principles.

21. On the medicalization of deviance generally, see Peter Conrad and Joseph Schneider, *Deviance and Medicalization* (which includes a chapter on AA). On recovery and its connections to this trend, see, for example, Levine, "Discovery of Addiction," Reinarman, "12-Step Movements and Advanced Capitalist Culture," and Valverde, *Diseases of the Will*.

22. On deriving identity from participation in the recovery movement, see Denzin, *Alcoholic Self*, Irvine, *Codependent Forevermore*, and Rice, *Disease of One's Own*. On the specific role of narrative, see Carole Cain, "Personal Stories," Jensen, *Storytelling in Alcoholics Anonymous*, O'Reilly, *Sobering Tales*, and Warhol and Michie, "Twelve-Step Teleology." While all of these make use of ethnographic research to some extent, the ethnographic turn is particularly evident in Rudy, *Becoming Alcoholic*, and in Brandes's excellent *Staying Sober in Mexico City*.

23. Warhol and Michie, "Twelve-Step Teleology," 329.

24. On this phenomenon, see, for example, Giddens, *Modernity and Self-Identity*, 70–109, and Wuthnow, *Sharing the Journey*.

25. AA promotes historical research and the collection of local and area histories through its publications "The AA Archives," "The Archives Workbook," "Archives Guidelines," and "The Oral History Kit." I use the term "AA historian" to designate authors who are largely self-taught and do not make their living as historians—they are "amateurs" in the true sense of that word, from the Latin *amator*, "lover of." Two exceptions to this rule are Ernest Kurtz (Ph.D., American Civilization, Harvard, 1978) and Glenn Chesnut (D.Phil., Religious History, Oxford, 1972). Despite their training, however, neither author aims his writing about AA history at an audience of professional historians. While the academic studies mentioned above have helped me significantly in the preparation of this book, without the help of the AA historians named here, this project would simply not have been possible.

26. Roizen and Room are the rare sociologists of alcoholism who can break from studying usage patterns and "paths to treatment" and consider historical issues in some depth. See, for example, Room, "Alcoholism and Alcoholics Anonymous in U.S. Films, 1945–1962" and "Alcoholics Anonymous as a Social Movement," and Roizen, "American Discovery of Alcoholism, 1933–1939" and "Paradigm Sidetracked, 1940–1944." Raphael's *Bill W. and Mr. Wilson*, the most astute biography of AA cofounder Bill Wilson, situates him and the larger organization in turn of the century American literature and culture. Rotskoff's *Love on the Rocks* looks at the growth of AA and Al-Anon in the context of evolving ideas of gender and family during the Cold War era. Although William L. White writes primarily for the professional addiction treatment community, his work (for example, *Slaying the Dragon*, on which I have relied heavily here, and *Drunkard's Refuge*, coauthored with John W. Crowley) is detailed and nuanced enough that it transcends the disciplinary divide. Less successful examples of

the historicizing impulse can be found in Elayne Rapping's *Culture of Recovery* and John Steadman Rice's *A Disease of One's Own*, each of which posits a fairly monolithic version of the "the sixties" as the origin of the codependency craze of the late 1980s. Rod Janzen's *The Rise and Fall of Synanon*, by contrast, considers that organization as part and parcel of the social fabric of the 1960s and 1970s.

27. AA's publications are discussed in the chapters that follow. Most 12-Step organizations publish some account of their origins along with an outline of how their program works as well as informational pamphlets and, in some cases, journals or workbooks. The number and variety of publications closely correlates with the size of the organization. A large organization like Al-Anon, for instance, publishes a history, *Lois [Wilson] Remembers*; an overview of the organization, *The Al-Anon Family Groups*; a collection of personal testimonies, *From Survival to Recovery*; and three volumes of daily meditations, along with a number of other topic-specific book-length titles. Narcotics Anonymous offers an eponymous "Basic Text" as well as *Miracles Happen: The Birth of Narcotics Anonymous in Words and Pictures*; *It Works, How and Why: The 12 Steps and 12 Traditions of Narcotics Anonymous*; and a daily meditation book. Other programs follow suit.

28. Margaret Jones, "Rage for Recovery." In *Selling Serenity*, his account of his work as an editor for the recovery lifestyle magazine *Changes*, Andrew Meacham notes that market research by HCI, the publisher of *Changes*, revealed HCI's readers to be "baby boomers in their 30s and early 40s—80% of whom were women with an above-average education and income, 57% of whom were divorced" (79).

29. Two general critiques of the recovery movement that devote whole chapters to its excessive print culture include Rapping, *Culture of Recovery*, and Kaminer, *I'm Dysfunctional*. Like many of the criticisms triggered by the "rage," these authors focused almost exclusively on Codependence or Adult Children of Alcoholics groups, with occasional gestures to AA but relatively little interest in the differences among organizations or theories of addiction and recovery. Harriet Goldhor Lerner's "Problems for Profit" takes a similar approach. For more wide-ranging views of recovery/therapy and print culture, see Wendy Simonds's study of women's self-help reading, *Women and Self-Help Culture*.

30. Foucault, *Discipline and Punish*, 211.

31. Darnton, "What Is the History of Books?"

Chapter 1

1. All citations noted parenthetically in the text.

2. Public policy statement on addiction from the American Society of Addiction Medicine, quoted in Graham and Schulz, *Principles of Addiction Medicine*, 1485.

3. Fingarette, *Heavy Drinking*, 3.

4. Sontag, *Illness*, 100–102.

5. Peele, *Diseasing*, 3–5. Original emphasis.

6. *Celebrity Rehab* (VH-1, 2008–present) features a group of B- and C-list celebrities in an addiction rehabilitation program overseen by addiction medicine specialist Dr. Drew Pinsky. *Intervention* (A&E, 2003–present) showcases the stories of ad-

dicts whose family and friends have decided they need to be remanded to treatment and stage interventions to persuade them of this; the process is captured on film.

7. A part of this historical trajectory is the move, during the 1960s and 1970s, to collapse the traditional distinction between alcohol and drug addiction (presumed to have different causes and trajectories, and to affect different classes of people) into the blanket category of "substance abuse." I have touched on that issue when it is germane within this chapter, but for the most part have tried to focus specifically on alcohol advocacy and policy unless otherwise noted.

8. For an overview of the internationalization of alcohol and drug policy informed by the disease concept, see Robin Room, "Addiction Concepts and International Control." The spread of Alcoholics Anonymous is documented in AAWS's *Alcoholics Anonymous: 70 Years of Growth*.

9. Roizen, "Great Controlled-Drinking Controversy," 246.

10. Rush, quoted in William L. White, *Slaying the Dragon*, 3. Original emphasis.

11. American Temperance Society corresponding secretary Justin Edwards, quoted in Dannenbaum, *Drink and Disorder*, 38.

12. Crothers, quoted in Crowley and White, *Drunkard's Refuge*, 19. On the history of the inebriety movement, see also Tracy, *Alcoholism in America*.

13. Gusfield, *Symbolic Crusade*, 7, 8, 4.

14. Quoted in ibid., 107, and in Asbury, *Great Illusion*, 112.

15. Valverde, *Diseases of the Will*, 52.

16. Agnes Spark, M.D., quoted in William L. White, *Slaying the Dragon*, 89.

17. Asbury, *Great Illusion,* 105–11. On this topic see also the chapter "The Wets Strike Back," in Kerr, *Organized for Prohibition*, 160–84.

18. Valverde, *Diseases of the Will*, 96.

19. On links between the liquor interests and the Communist conspiracy, see Gusfield, *Symbolic Crusade*, 151–55. For examples of conservative fulmination against these conjoined menaces, see William D. Upshaw's *Bombshells for Wets and Reds* and *The Christian Crusader* newsletter of the Texas Drys, Chester H. Kirk Collection on Alcoholism and Alcoholics Anonymous, John Hay Library, Brown University, Box 15.

20. This history is documented in a variety of sources; two particularly cogent examples are Roizen, "Great Controlled-Drinking Controversy," and Room, "Sociological Aspects of the Disease Concept of Alcoholism."

21. See William L. White, *Slaying the Dragon*, 23–31, and Crowley and White, *Drunkard's Refuge*.

22. Baylor's theories are laid out in his *Remaking a Man* (1919); Peabody's appear in *The Common Sense of Drinking* (1931). On the Emmanuel Movement and/as New Thought religion, see Greene, "Emmanuel Movement, 1906–1929," and Cunningham, "Emmanuel Movement: A Variety of American Religious Experience." On the Emmanuel Movement, Baylor, Peabody, and their places in the history of addiction treatment and of AA, see William L. White, *Slaying the Dragon*, 101; Mel B., *New Wine*, 117–26; and Dubiel, *Road to Fellowship*.

23. Peabody, "Psychotherapeutic Procedure," 111, 116.

24. Johnson, *Alcoholism Movement*, 70.

25. Menninger, *Man against Himself*, 170. Further citations are noted parenthetically in the text.

26. Quoted in William L. White, *Slaying the Dragon*, 97.

27. Weijl, "Theoretical and Practical Aspects of Psychoanalytic Therapy," 202.

28. Blum and Blum, *Alcoholism: Modern Psychological Approaches*, 90.

29. Johnson, *Alcoholism Movement*, 223.

30. Buchman, *Remaking the World*, 5.

31. The Keswick movement, named after the county in the Lake District in England where the meeting takes place, is a late nineteenth-century Protestant perfectionist tradition, similar to the evangelical fervor of the Second Great Awakening in the United States.

32. Buchman, *Remaking*, 4.

33. The group settled on the name Moral Re-armament in 1938, then assumed its current incarnation, the global youth leadership program "Up with People," in 1965.

34. Walter Clark, *Oxford Group*, 92; Cantril, *The Psychology of Social Movements*, 146. Buchman's life is detailed in Garth Lean, *On the Tail of a Comet*. A fairly scathing depiction of "the Buchmanites" in action—in Akron, Ohio, no less—appears in Ruth McKenney, *Industrial Valley*, 54–59. My thanks to Ernest Kurtz for bringing this source to my attention.

35. Walter Clark, *Oxford Group*, 108.

36. Ibid., 119.

37. The Layman with a Notebook, *What Is the Oxford Group?*, 29, 21.

38. AAWS, "The Twelve Steps of Alcoholics Anonymous," <http://www.aa.org/en_pdfs/smf-121_en.pdf>. Original emphasis.

39. Towns was a Georgia farm boy turned insurance salesman and failed stock speculator. Under the auspices of the State Department, he traveled to China during the 1908 Opium Wars and claimed to have cured 4,000 addicts with his tonic of prickly ash bark, hyosycamus, and belladonna, which was followed by liberal doses of castor oil until the patient proved his or her return to health by producing "a stool that consists of green mucous matter." Towns did not conceptualize addiction as a disease, but he did believe that ongoing exposure to addicting substances (alcohol and narcotics alike) deformed cell structure and development and created cravings, hence the need for violent purgatives. The U.S. government and the medical establishment were beginning to lose faith in the Towns cure by the 1920s, according to David Musto, but he maintained his quite luxurious and exclusive drying-out facility through midcentury. See William L. White, *Slaying the Dragon*, 84–87, and David Musto, *American Disease*, 79–82.

40. Silkworth, "Alcoholism as a Manifestation," 1–2.

41. Ibid., 3, 2.

42. Lobdell, *This Strange Illness*, 71. On the medical community's skepticism, see, for example, Haggard, "Critique of the Concept of the Allergic Nature."

43. Kurtz, "Disease Concept," 10. Original emphasis.

44. Unless otherwise noted, citations to *Alcoholics Anonymous* throughout this volume are to the 4th edition, 2001. As chapter 3 makes clear, the Big Book has two

parts: the first an expository overview of the AA program and the second a collection of personal narratives. The various editions of the Big Book have distinctly different story sections, but the first part (including "The Doctor's Opinion") has been largely unchanged over time, save for a few silent corrections of grammar and typographical errors and the updating of figures (e.g., first edition: "In one western city and its environs there are eighty of us . . ."; 2nd edition and after: "In one western city and its environs there one thousand of us . . ."). What Matthew J. Raphael calls the "petrification" of the first section of the Big Book was a source of some irritation to Bill Wilson, who, while struggling to update the selection of personal stories in 1952, remarked that "I am assured by many that I could certainly be excommunicated if a word [of the first section] were touched" (*Bill W. and Mr. Wilson*, 152). For a thorough cataloguing of the silent edits to the first part of the Big Book, see "Big Book Changes," <http://www.barefootsworld.net/aabigbookchanges.html>.

45. Kurtz, "Disease Concept," 20.

46. For biographical information on those early AAs whose stories have appeared in the Big Book, see "Authors of Stories from the Book *Alcoholics Anonymous*," <http://silkworth.net/aabiography/storyauthors.html>.

47. Room, "Sociological Aspects," 49.

48. Keller, "On Defining Alcoholism," 253.

49. Johnson, "Alcoholism Movement," 409.

50. Valverde, *Diseases*, 103.

51. Johnson, "Alcoholism Movement," 58.

52. Ibid., 129.

53. Valverde, *Diseases*, 101.

54. Jellinek, "Outline of Basic Policies," 105.

55. Jellinek, "Phases of Alcohol Addiction," 683. Original emphasis.

56. Jellinek, "Phases in the Drinking History," 7. One hundred and fifty-eight questionnaires were returned, but of those, sixty had to be discounted on the grounds that they were filled out incorrectly or were by women. On the role Jellinek's problematic data played in the development of a backlash against the disease concept, see Roizen, "Great Controlled-Drinking Controversy."

57. Jellinek, "Phases in the Drinking History," 7.

58. Further refinements appear in Jellinek's 1960 book, *The Disease Concept of Alcoholism*.

59. Room, "Sociological Aspects," 56–57.

60. Page, "E. M. Jellinek and the Evolution of Alcohol Studies," 1627.

61. Jellinek, "Notes on the First Half Year's Experience," 280–82.

62. Milgram, "Summer School of Alcohol Studies."

63. Mann's biographers, Sally and David Brown, note that although she joined AA in early 1939, she "slipped"—returned to drinking—three times between then and December 1940; thus, some might say her sobriety dates to 1940 (*Mrs. Marty Mann*, 131).

64. Brown and Brown, *Mrs. Marty Mann*, 156.

65. Kurtz, *Not-God*, 119.

66. Mann, "Formation of a National Committee," 354.

67. *Pass It On*, 319–20; Kurtz, *Not-God*, 118–20.

68. Johnson, "Alcoholism Movement," 312.

69. On the *Primer*'s appearance in the *BOMC News*, see Brown and Brown, *Mrs. Marty Mann*, 220. On the BOMC's subscriber base in this period, see "Harry N. Abrams interview," <http://www.aaa.si.edu/collections/oralhistories/transcripts/abrams72.htm>.

70. Brown and Brown, *Mrs. Marty Mann*, 229, 246.

71. Room, "Sociological Aspects," 69.

72. Brown and Brown, *Mrs. Marty Mann*, 209, 230–32.

73. Ibid., 300.

74. On alcoholism in Johnson's family, see Randall B. Woods, *LBJ: Architect*, 5–44.

75. Wiener, *Politics of Alcoholism*, 28.

76. Ibid., 28.

77. Quoted in ibid., 3.

78. It is important to note that of that $795 million, only 6 to 7 percent came directly from the federal government. The rest was from state matching grants, out of pocket payments, and, as we shall see, third-party reimbursements.

79. As Jay Lewis notes in "The Federal Role in Alcoholism Research," by far the largest share of federal dollars flowed to treatment—approximately a billion dollars of the $1,328,500,000 that the NIAAA distributed between 1971 and 1980. Although "preventive activities [were] lumped budgetarily with treatment," they "were funded at lower levels than even research and training" (392–93).

80. Gomberg, "Special Populations"; Schmidt and Weisner, "Emergence of Problem-Drinking Women," 318–21.

81. "Capitalism Plus Dope" (<http://marxists.anu.edu.au/history/usa/workers/black-panthers/1970/dope.htm>) was written by Michael "Cetewayo" Tabor of the Black Panther Party in 1970. A synthetic history of radical indigenous and ethnic agitation against addiction has yet to be written. Mark Sanders briefly surveys the Afrocentric anti-addiction programs of the Nation of Islam, the African American Survivors Organization, Free-n-One, One Church-One Addict, and Glide Memorial Church in his "Response of African American Communities." Additional discussion of Glide Memorial's remarkable recovery program can be found in David Smith et al.'s "Cultural Points of Resistance." Two other Afrocentric programs that have received scholarly attention are Cleveland's Iwo San (a Swahili term meaning "House of Healing"), a residential program for women and children (discussed in articles by Mary S. Jackson), and the Engagement Project of Los Angeles, a single-session counseling program organized around the seven principles of African and African American life that Maulana Karenga calls the Nguzo Saba (discussed in Douglas Longshore et al). For overviews of the growing awareness of the need for culturally sensitive alcoholism treatment among Native Americans, see Maggie Brady, "Culture in Treatment," and Don Coyhis and William L. White, "Alcohol Problems in Native America." Exemplary programs that build on indigenous cultural values include the White Bison "Wellbriety" movement, of which Coyhis is a founder, and the Sacred Circle of Life approach described by Michael Tlanusta Garrett and Jane J. Goodman in "Mending the Broken Circle."

82. Treatment professionals drifted toward seeing alcoholism and drug addiction as versions of the same problem for much of the 1970s and 1980s. In 1987, the American Medical Association formalized the merger of the two, declaring that all "drug dependencies, including alcoholism, are diseases" (Meacham, "AMA Declares"). The dissolve of the distinction between the two was symbolically concretized in 1989 when the National Council on Alcoholism changed its name to the National Council on Alcoholism and Drug Dependence. On disputes among researchers about the legitimacy of the disease concept and its treatment models, see Roizen, "Great Controlled-Drinking Controversy," and Peter Nathan, "Human Behavioral Research." It is also at this point that allegations begin to surface that researchers with competing interpretations of alcoholism were being pushed out of the field as apostates, a phenomenon documented by Room in "Sociological Aspects" (63) and by Andrew Meacham, whose *Selling Serenity* discusses rumors that conflicts between abstinence and controlled-drinking proponents may have escalated into murder (18–23).

83. Weisner and Room, "Financing and Ideology," 172–73.

84. Holder, Lennox, and Blose, "Economic Benefits," 64, 63.

85. Weisner and Room, "Financing and Ideology," 173.

86. Wiener, *Politics of Alcoholism*, 125.

87. Schmidt and Weisner, "Developments in Alcoholism Treatment," 369–78.

88. Quoted in Weisner and Room, "Financing and Ideology," 173.

89. Weisner and Room, "Financing and Ideology," 176.

90. Ibid., 173.

91. On this phenomenon see, for example, Trice and Sonnenstuhl, "Contributions of AA," and William L. White, *Slaying the Dragon*, 163–77 and 274–75.

92. Kirk Collection on Alcoholism, New Box 7, New Box 6.

93. Ibid., New Box 1.

94. Ibid., New Box 2.

95. "Let's Be Friendly" was the title of a pamphlet published by AAWS in 1958.

96. Information on the founding of Narcotics Anonymous and Pot, Pills, and Cocaine Anonymous from William L. White, *Slaying the Dragon*, 239, 279; on the founding of Overeaters Anonymous, "Between the Sheets," <http://www.shutitdown.net/text/oa.html#15>; on Nicotine Anonymous, "A Brief History," <http://www.nicotine-anonymous.org/admin/prod_images/brief%20history%20of%20nicotine%20anonymousrevised.pdf>.

97. Schaef, *Co-Dependence*, 24.

98. Gamblers Anonymous, "History," <http://www.gamblersanonymous.org/history.html>; Debtors Anonymous General Service Board, "History of Debtors Anonymous," <http://www.debtorsanonymous.org/about/history/htm>. The "Emotions Anonymous" homepage (<http://www.emotionsanonymous.org>) defines "emotional difficulties" as "depression, anger, broken or strained relationships, grief, anxiety, low self-esteem, panic, abnormal fears, resentment, jealousy, guilt, despair, fatigue, tension, boredom, loneliness, withdrawal, obsessive and negative thinking, worry, compulsive behavior and a variety of other emotional issues." Information on the Augustine Fellowship from "Sex and Love Addicts Anonymous," <http://www.

slaafws.org>. Absent from this list is Parents Anonymous, a support group for child-abusing parents founded in 1969 that originally made use of 12-Step principles but has since become a professional lobbying and therapy organization. For the history of PA, see Barbara Nelson, *Making an Issue of Child Abuse*.

99. Room, " 'Healing Ourselves and Our Planet,' " 717.

100. Workaholics Anonymous, "The History of Workaholics Anonymous," <http://www.workaholics-anonymous.org/page.php?page=history>; Hepatitis C Anonymous, Inc., "HCV Hepatitis C Anonymous," <http://www.hcvanonymous.com/default.htm>; Clutterers Anonymous, "What Is Clutterers Anonymous?," <http://www.clutterersanonymous.net>.

101. Jellinek's role in excluding women from the category of "alcoholics" merits mention here. He notes in "Phases in the Drinking History" that fifteen women alcoholics completed the *Grapevine* questionnaire, but that "these were excluded from the analysis because on the one hand the number was too small to be analyzed separately, and on the other hand the data differed so greatly for the two sexes that merging the data was inadvisable" (6). Because women's experience might complicate emerging theories of alcoholism, it was simply excluded. On women in midcentury AA, see McClellan, " 'Lady Tipplers' "; Rotskoff, *Love on the Rocks*, 67–69; and William L. White, *Slaying the Dragon*, 158–63.

102. Wilson, *Lois Remembers*, 172.

103. Rotskoff, *Love on the Rocks*, 149–93.

104. Haaken, "From Al-Anon to ACOA," 335.

105. Rice, *Disease of One's Own*, 59, 5.

106. Adult Children of Alcoholics Anonymous, "Early History," <http://www.adultchildren.org/lit/EarlyHistory.s>.

107. This definition of CODA via affiliates' "common problem" is taken from Leslie Irvine, *Codependent Forevermore*, 29. Since the publication of Irvine's book in 1999, the organization has shifted its self-definition to center on a "common *purpose*," which their "Preamble" describes as "develop[ing] healthy relationships." See "Welcome of Co-Dependents Anonymous," <http://www.codependents.org/foundation-docs-welcome.php>.

108. Rice, *Disease of One's Own*, 53. See also Irvine, *Codependent Forevermore*, 17–24.

109. Cermak, *Diagnosing and Treating*, viii; Schaef, *Co-Dependence*, 6. Both original emphasis.

110. Cermak, *Diagnosing and Treating*, 63–64.

111. Meacham, *Selling Serenity*, 177–203.

112. Room, " 'Healing Ourselves and Our Planet,' " 717.

Chapter 2

1. Arthur Cain, "Cult or Cure?" 48.

2. Synanon, a California-based closed therapeutic community aimed primarily at narcotics addicts, was founded by former AA member Chuck Dederich in 1958, but became notorious during the mid-1970s, when Dederich declared it a religion. Synanon's demands of its residents became more and more intense—extending to va-

sectomies for men, abortions for women, and mandatory divorce—and the group also ran afoul of the IRS during that period. Dederich and two associates pleaded no contest in 1980 to the charge of attempting to murder an attorney involved in a lawsuit against the organization. The Seed, a treatment program for juveniles based in Ft. Lauderdale, Florida, was founded in 1970 by recovering alcoholic Art Barker and premised on Synanon's "confrontational" tactics; to avoid a Senate investigation into its treatment protocols in 1976, some of Barker's followers spun off the adolescent treatment program called Straight, Inc. Reputedly Nancy Reagan's "favorite" drug treatment program, Straight folded in 1993 under the weight of abuse lawsuits. On Synanon, see Janzen, *Rise and Fall of Synanon*; on the development of "tough love" therapeutic communities derived from Synanon, see Szalavitz, *Help at Any Cost*. An impressive array of anti-Seed and anti-Straight testimony and documentation can be found on the web site "$traights Dot Com" (<http://www.thestraights.com/>), maintained by Wes Fager.

3. Trimpey, "Of Course It's a Cult!," <http://www.positiveatheism.org/rw/ofcourse.htm>, original emphasis; Trimpey, "Recovery Group Disorders Are Real," <http://www.rational.org/html_member_area/reasons_cancel.html>.

4. Bufe, *Cult or Cure?*; Peele, Bufe, and Brodsky, *Resisting 12-Step Coercion*. The site called "AADeprogramming" (<http://www.aadeprogramming.org>) was the creation of the pseudonymous "Apple" in 1999. "Orange Papers" (<http://www.orangepapers.org>) was founded in 2001 by the individual known as "Agent Orange." Trimpey's quote is from "Recovery Group Disorders Are Real."

5. Valverde, *Diseases of the Will*, 96–104. On the broader historical turn see Warren Susman, " 'Personality' and the Making of 20th-Century Culture."

6. Rudy, *Becoming Alcoholic*, 16, quoting Lewis Coser, "Greedy Organizations." For a similar argument, see also Norman Denzin, *Alcoholic Self* and *Recovering Alcoholic*.

7. Max Weber, "Religious Rejections of the World," 323–62, and, on disenchantment, "Science as Vocation," 129–68.

8. Max Weber, "Religious Rejections," 329.

9. Galanter, *Cults*, 211–17. Since 1948 AA has strictly limited monetary contributions to the group; at present, both annual and testamentary gifts are limited to $3,000. Circumstances leading up to this decision are discussed in *12/12*, 160–65; details appear in the pamphlet "Self-Support."

10. The term "AA Way of Life" is used throughout *The Little Red Book*, discussed below, to designate this state. I use the term "equalitarian" rather than the more common "egalitarian" because the former was more common in the eighteenth- and nineteenth-century Christian traditions (discussed below) on which alcoholic equalitarianism builds.

11. Room, "Alcoholics Anonymous in U.S. Films," 376–79. Room uses data from the 1946 *Grapevine* questionnaire discussed in the previous chapter to deduce that in 1939, AAs had a mean age of about 45.

12. Rotskoff, *Love on the Rocks*, 110; Rumbarger, " 'Story' of Bill W.," 767–74.

13. Rumbarger, " 'Story' of Bill W.," 775; Rotskoff, *Love on the Rocks*, 109, quoting Pfister and Schnog, *Inventing the Psychological*.

14. Kimmel, *Manhood in America*, 9.

15. Lears, *No Place of Grace*, 12.

16. From "Invictus" (1875), by British poet William Ernest Henley (1849–1903). Detailed treatments of the workings of this hegemonic masculinity in the period appear in Bederman, *Manliness and Civilization*; Hoganson, *Fighting for American Manhood*; and Nelson, *National Manhood*.

17. Sandage, *Born Losers*, 2.

18. The most thoughtful of the various Bill Wilson biographies is Matthew J. Raphael's *Bill W. and Mr. Wilson*. See also Cheever, *My Name is Bill*; Hartigan, *Bill W.*; and Thomsen, *Bill W.*

19. Raphael, *Bill W.*, 61, quoting *Pass It On*, 81.

20. On Wilson and Smith's conservative politics, see *PIO*, 97, and *Dr. Bob*, 127. On AA as a conservative and communitarian response to the Great Depression, see Shlaes, *Forgotten Man*, 230–31, 360–61.

21. Wilson, "Testimony before the Special Subcommittee," quoted in Lobdell, *This Strange Illness*, 61.

22. Parsons, *Manhood Lost*, 55.

23. Lears, *No Place of Grace*, 53.

24. Kurtz, *Not-God*, 209, 216.

25. Max Weber, "Religious Rejections," 347. Further citations are noted parenthetically in the text.

26. An additional shaping spiritual force, felt particularly keenly in Akron but ramifying through AA as a whole, was present in the actions and person of Sister Ignatia, the registrar of St. Thomas Hospital in Akron and the "angel of Alcoholics Anonymous." On Ignatia's influence, particularly her commitment to "unremitting surrender," see Mary Darrah's fascinating biography *Sister Ignatia*.

27. Quoted in Lean, *Tail of a Comet*, 97.

28. Ibid., 99. On evangelical trends in this period, see William McLoughlin, *Revivals, Awakenings, and Reform*.

29. Layman with a Notebook, *What Is the Oxford Group?*, 29. Further references are cited parenthetically in the text. Given that he worked primarily among college-age men, it is perhaps unsurprising that the chief form of morbidity that concerned Buchman was "impurity." A scandal arose at Princeton in 1922 after Buchman conducted a series of meetings that he alleged revealed that "eighty to ninety per cent of all youths in the adolescent stage have sexual problems, and many of them are troubled by secret sins affecting their sex life" (81, 103–4). The Oxford Group's Victorian obsession with sexual impurity definitely did not carry over to AA, as Raphael points out (*Bill W.*, 127–31). Perhaps because of Wilson's own history of philandering, the Big Book talks frankly about sex, noting that "many of us needed a overhauling there," but making clear that this is not because of "impurity" so much as the fact that "we [had] been selfish, dishonest, or inconsiderate" (BB, 68).

30. Lean, *Tail of a Comet*, 121.

31. Quoted in Driberg, *Mystery of Moral Re-Armament*, 68.

32. Buchman in fact was known for his taste for the good life, which he indulged at the expense of his patrons. See Walter Clark, *Oxford Group*, 50, 101–4.

33. Max Weber, "Religious Rejections," 332.

34. Antze, "Symbolic Action in Alcoholics Anonymous," 175. As AA grew, its official position on conversion changed to acknowledge that more gradual "spiritual awakenings" might ultimately achieve the same effect as dramatic "spiritual experiences." In the second edition of the Big Book, the original language of Step 12 ("having had a spiritual experience as the result of these steps . . .") was amended to its present form ("having had a spiritual awakening . . ."), and the appendix "Spiritual Experience," which discussed the differences between the two terms and stressed that neither way was more correct than the other, was added. On tensions between "awakening" and "experience," see Kurtz, *Not-God*, 99, 132.

35. An abundant literature traces the historical and theoretical construction of the hegemonic male body as clearly and firmly bounded, governed by the invisible workings of rational thought rather than by the messy material exchanges (eating, drinking, elimination) associated with corporeal pleasure. Peter Stallybrass and Allon White, relying on the work of Mikhail Bakhtin, trace this conceit to antiquity, when visual art began to differentiate between an idealized "classical" body (usually male) and its opposite, the (typically female) "grotesque." "The classical statue," they argue, "has no openings or orifices, whereas grotesque costume and masks emphasized the gaping mouth, the protruberant belly and buttocks, the feet and the genitals. . . . The grotesque body is emphasized as a mobile, split, multiple self, a subject of pleasure in processes of exchange; and it is never closed off from either its social or eco-systemic context. The classical body on the other hand keeps its distance" (22). On the perceived threats posed to the hegemony of this self-contained and unmarked body by various social forces in contemporary American life, see among others, Bordo, *Male Body*; Robinson, *Marked Men*; and Pfeil, *White Guys*.

36. On the tradition of the *unio mystica*, see, for example, Riehle, *Middle English Mystics*, and Beckwith, *Christ's Body*.

37. Wilson, "Basic Concepts," quoted in Antze, "Symbolic Action," 158.

38. A voluminous body of literature by scholars and by AA historians treats the question of spirituality and/or religion within the fellowship. The most detailed discussion, and one of the few to situate AA's spiritualism within U.S. religious history, can be found in Kurtz, *Not-God*. Glenn Chesnut, Richard Dubiel, and Dick B. have also written at length on the issue. Scholars outside of AA who have tried to parse the difference between AA "spirituality" and religion proper include David Rudy and Arthur Greil ("Is AA a Religious Organization?"), A. Javier Trevino ("Alcoholics Anonymous as a Durkheimian Religion"), and Linda Mercadante (*Victims and Sinners*), to name just a few.

39. Pittman, *AA the Way It Began*, 174. Pittman argues that Catholics accounted for over 50 percent of the members in Akron, for example. Bill Wilson expressed this point in a 1940 letter, arguing in his typically pragmatic fashion that "many Catholics would feel they could not be interested" in an explicitly religious group. "Since there are plenty of alcoholic Catholics," Wilson continued, "why deprive them of their chance by being dogmatic?" (*PIO*, 173).

40. Chesnut, "Classic Protestant Liberalism and AA," <http://hindsfoot.org/ProtLib.html>. On Wilson's later flirtations with Catholicism, see Raphael, *Bill W.*, 161–64.

41. The term "seeker" is from Leigh Schmidt, who uses it to describe the open,

questing mindset he chronicles in *Restless Souls*. The definition of " 'true' spirituality" is from Peter Washington, *Madame Blavatsky's Baboon*, 9.

42. Wilson, *Lois Remembers*, 2. On connections between Swedenborg, New Thought traditions in general, and homeopathic medicine in particular, see Ahlstrom, *Religious History of the American People*, 486, and Robert Jones, "Development of Medical Sects." An issue deserving of further study in this regard is the influence of Bill Wilson's mother, Emily, on his thinking during AA's formative years. Trained as an osteopathic physician in Boston during the 1900s, she would have been exposed to a wide range of mind-body-spirit medicine ideas. Her relationship with her son, however, remains largely unexplored.

43. Wilson, *Lois Remembers*, 84. In *New Wine*, Mel B. argues that *Science and Health* served as a model for the Big Book (104).

44. On Dr. Bob's attendance at Camps Farthest Out, see Dick B., *Dr. Bob and His Library*, 58. A brief description of the Camps' mission, including its history of intercessory prayer, can be found at the Association of Camps Farthest Out, Inc., "How It All Started," <http://www.acfona.org/index.asp?pageId=34>. A box of Dr. Bob's personal effects in Brown University's Hay Library contains a carefully maintained clipping file documenting New Thought lectures in and around Akron, as well as publications from Theosophical and Unity Church publishers from around the Midwest. Dr. Bob Archives, John Hay Library, Brown University, Box 2. The cofounders' abiding investment in New Thought mysticism is borne out as well in the list of "Books Early AAs Read" compiled by Bill Wilson's secretary Nell Wing and reprinted in Bill Pittman, *AA the Way It Began* (192). It includes a range of classic Mental Science, Divine Science, and positive thinking titles by laymen and clerics as well as William James's *Varieties of Religious Experience*. Indeed, only three examples of non–New Thought reading—two books by comparative religions scholar Lewis Browne and journalist A. J. Russell's collection of Oxford Group conversion stories—appear on Wing's list.

45. James, *Varieties of Religious Experience*, 78. Further citations are noted parenthetically in the text.

46. Max Weber, "Religious Rejections," 325.

47. Ibid., 330.

48. Mel B., *New Wine*, 101–16.

49. Raphael, *Bill W.*, 81–83.

50. James, *Varieties of Religious Experience*, 57.

51. Emma Curtis Hopkins's "Christian Science" was a rival to Mary Baker Eddy's church of the same name. On the relationships and tensions between the two Christian Sciences, see Satter, *Each Mind a Kingdom*, 79–105. On connections between High Watch and AA, see Harbaugh, "Sister Francis and the Ministry of High Watch."

52. Gilbert, *Men in the Middle*, 108. For an excoriation of the feminization of piety, see Douglas, *Feminization of American Culture*; more dispassionate accounts can be found in Bederman, " 'The Women Have Had Charge of the Church Long Enough,' " and Reynolds, "Feminization Controversy." An exploration of male religiosity in the face of this feminization is Lippy, *Do Real Men Pray?*

53. Precise origins of much of the midwestern pamphlet literature are difficult to

determine. In Akron, the pamphlets "A Guide to the Twelve Steps of Alcoholics Anonymous," "A Manual for Alcoholics Anonymous," "Second Reader for Alcoholics Anonymous," and "Spiritual Milestones in Alcoholics Anonymous" were written by Evan W. between 1941 and 1947, at the behest of Dr. Bob, who feared that the Big Book might seem daunting to readers with lower levels of education than AA's original members. At around the same time, a group in Chicago produced "Impressions of AA," "Alcoholics Anonymous: The Long Haul," "AA Is a Tender Trap," "Alcoholics Anonymous 'Willingness,' " "It's All in the Mind," "Out of the Fog," "The Devil and AA," and "AA God's Instrument." Unlike the Akron pamphlets, these are all (with the exception of "Impressions") transcriptions of talks. The Chicago Area AA Service Office confirms the publication dates of the last three of these as 1943, 1948, and 1954 (from a talk given in 1943), but otherwise dates of original talks and of initial publication are unknown. Colloquialisms, references to popular culture, and in some cases mentions of the Traditions suggest 1945–1955 as the likely window for publication.

54. Max Weber, "Religious Rejections," 329.

55. This juxtaposition is made most explicitly in "Tender Trap," 3 and passim.

56. "Devil," 13; "Trap," 4.

57. "Willingness," 5.

58. "Haul," 10; "Trap," 6.

59. "Willingness," 8.

60. On the distinctive practices of Dr. Bob's group, especially the importance of prayer, see *Dr. Bob*, 117–18, 137–42, and Mitchell K., *How It Worked*, 55–58.

61. Pittman, foreword to the fiftieth anniversary edition of *The Little Red Book*, xiv. Further citations are noted parenthetically in the text. The volume was originally titled *The Twelve Steps* but referred to casually as "the little red book"—red because of its cover, and "little" to distinguish it from the first edition of the Big Book. The fifth printing, the first of two in 1949, was the first to be officially titled *The Little Red Book*. For a transcript of Ed W. and Barry C.'s original 1942 outline, see "Ancestor of the Little Red Book"; for a discussion of the evolution of Ed W.'s ideas from the 1946 to the 1949 editions of *The Little Red Book*, see "First Edition of the Little Red Book," both by Glenn Chesnut.

62. "Trap," 18; "Fog," 8.

63. "Haul," 16 (emphasis added); "2nd Reader," 12 (original emphasis); "Instrument," 12; "Milestones," 15; "Trap," 16.

64. Rotskoff, *Love on the Rocks*, 12 and passim.

65. Ehrenreich, *Hearts of Men*, 17–28; "Haul," 11 (original emphasis).

66. The loquacious author of "Out of the Fog" is the exception, and even his discussion of his improved domestic life is fairly circumspect: "I still quarrel at home, though I've learned in the last months that somebody has brains and judgment in my house and it isn't myself. . . . I've finally found out the true value of a give-and-take gal—and I don't mean one that gives you chloral hydrate and takes your billfold. For months now, in the Blank domicile nothing heavier has been hurled than the milder form of insults" (13–14).

67. Max Weber, "Religious Rejections," 329.

68. "Instrument," 11, 8.

69. Max Weber, "Religious Rejections," 329, "Instrument," 12.

70. "Haul," 19–20; "Willingness," 7, 9; "Trap," 19–20.

71. "Willingness," 11.

72. I take the term "self-in-relation" from the writings of literary historian Joanne Dobson, who sees this mode of subjectivity as an inversion of the values associated with the self-made man. A product of the same rapacious capitalism, but one that sought to counter rather than to capitalize on its logics, Dobson argues in "Reclaiming Sentimental Literature" that the self-in-relation takes "intimacy, community, and social responsibility [as] its primary relational modes," and "affiliation on the plane of emotion, sympathy, nurturance, or similar moral or spiritual inclination" as its primary aim (267). The term "self-in-relation" is also used by feminist psychologists Carol Gilligan and Mary Belenky and their colleagues at Wellesley College's Stone Center for Research on Women (see Jordan et al., *Women's Growth in Connection*). I use the term in Dobson's sense, however, because the Stone Center scholars' reliance on a psychodynamic rather than a historical construction of selfhood is at odds with my interests here.

73. Bateson, "Cybernetics of 'Self,'" 323–24.

74. Franklin, *Autobiography*, 94–105. Among the many interpretations of self-help tradition that trace this history and either tacitly or explicitly inscribe AA within it are Decker, *Made in America*; Huber, *American Idea of Success*; McGee, *Self-Help, Inc.*; and Starker, *Oracle at the Supermarket*.

75. The enumerative nature of the Steps does make them appear similar to works like Carnegie's *How to Win Friends and Influence People* (1936) and Hill's New Thought classic *Think and Grow Rich!* (1937), which respectively offered lists like "Six Ways to Make People Like You" and "13 Steps to Riches." Further scholarship is needed to determine whether and to what extent these works and others like them impacted the cofounders' thinking.

76. The literature treating the development of equalitarian sentiment within evangelical Protestantism and the theological, reformist, and aesthetic implications of that sentiment is far too vast to enumerate fully here. For general treatments of the evangelical church, see Campbell, *Religion of the Heart*, and Carwardine, *Transatlantic Revivalism*; on evangelical religion in the United States, see Hatch, *Democratization of American Christianity*, and Noll, *Rise of Evangelicalism*. For the influence of the doctrine of Christian equalitarianism on social reform, see, for example, Elizabeth Clark, "'Sacred Rights of the Weak'"; Crane, "Suggestions toward a Genealogy"; David Brion Davis, *Problem of Slavery in Western Culture*; and Goodman, *Of One Blood*.

77. Fisher, *Hard Facts*, 100. More discussion of the epistemological and aesthetic implications of this worldview can be found in Agnew, *Worlds Apart*; Camfield, "Moral Aesthetics of Sentimentality"; Hendler, *Public Sentiments*; Meyer, *Instructed Conscience*; and Tompkins, *Sensational Designs*, to name just a few.

78. The original man in the bed was Akron attorney Bill D. His story appeared in the second and fourth editions of the Big Book under the title "Alcoholics Anonymous Number 3," and is discussed in *Pass It On*, 153–54, and in "Bill D–: AA Member Number 3," <http://www.scratchinpost.net/barefootbob/aabilld-aa3.html>.

79. Alexander, "Alcoholics Anonymous," 9. Reprinted in pamphlet form shortly thereafter and still in print, Jack Alexander's article became a key outreach tool.

80. AAWS, "Do You Think?," 77. Original emphasis.

81. Hyde, *Gift*, 45.

82. Ibid., 47.

83. Wilson argues in *Alcoholics Anonymous Comes of Age* that "in reality I [was] not the author of the Traditions at all. I had merely put them on paper in such a way as to mirror principles which had already been developed in AA group experience. AA's General Headquarters, its Trustees, and its staff had actually made the formulation of these vital principles possible" (204). However, since Wilson crafted the language of the Traditions and was their primary promoter during this period, I refer to him as their author.

84. Kurtz, *Not-God*, 100. Pointing out that "a good percentage of those newly sober had worked in sales," Kurtz argues that once they were sent back out on the road, "strange cities and lonely rooms often brought back the old fears, so in new places they sought out alcoholics to whom they could give their program in order to keep themselves sober."

85. Dealings with Rockefeller and the establishment of the Alcoholic Foundation (later the General Service Board) are discussed in *Pass It On*, 181–90, and in *Alcoholics Anonymous Comes of Age*, 147–53.

86. Lender and Martin, *Drinking in America*, 75.

87. Contemporary reports on the Washingtonians quoted in Milton Maxwell, "Washingtonian Movement," 415–20.

88. AAWS, "Twelve Traditions," <http://www.aa.org/pdf/products/p-28_thetwel tradofaa.pdf>.

89. On the various nineteenth-century fraternal temperance orders and their rituals, see Furnas, *Life and Times of the Late Demon Rum*, 95–115, and Fahey, *Temperance and Racism*, 2–15.

90. While liberal at one level, this "live and let live" stance could have distinctly illiberal consequences. That tendency is clearly seen in the way that some AA groups, guided by local custom in their attitudes toward nonwhite alcoholics, suborned racism. Oscar W. recalls that an African American woman in Cleveland was told by members of the Lake Shore Group that "she could be in AA but she had to attend a different group" (*Dr. Bob*, 247). Similarly, some members at the 1952 Conference asserted that they did "not believe it 'safe' to have colored people attend our meetings" (Conference Report 1952, 14). In a special session on "Interracial and Foreign Language Groups" at the 1953 General Service Conference, Bill Wilson framed the question of nonwhite participation in AA thus: "With whatever personal persuasions we have, each of us wants these good people to have, as far as possible, exactly the same opportunity we had. But we do have a lot of different customs and situations in different parts of this country, and this is no place to get up and tell ourselves how very broadminded we are. The sole question is this: how can each locality, from the point of view of its own customs, afford a better opportunity to colored people to get well?" Responses from the delegates varied, but most favored separate meetings for nonwhites, arguing variously that people of color would not be able to relate to white

people (and vice versa) and that African Americans (or Native or Mexican Americans) were not "true" alcoholics (Conference Report 1953, 24). For more extensive treatment of this question, see Rotskoff, *Love on the Rocks*, 118–20. For discussion of exceptions to this rule, see Chesnut, "Early Black AA" (<http://hindsfoot.org/Nblack1.html>) and *Lives and Teachings of the AA Old Timers*.

91. Lears, 45, 6. Further references are cited parenthetically in the text.

92. AAWS, "Do You Think?," 27.

93. Brodhead, *Cultures of Letters*, 13–47.

94. On this epistemological bent within antebellum sentimental culture, and its effect on rhetoric and politics, see especially Camfield, "Moral Aesthetics of Sentimentality," and Dobson, "Reclaiming Sentimental Literature."

95. Thornton, "General Introduction," 2. On subcultural identity as an essentially narrative and symbolic project, see Dick Hebdige, *Subculture*.

Chapter 3

1. Examples in the text are not intended as either a random or a representative sample of AA reading practices; they are simply my observations from various meetings.

2. The Origins of the Q. Method are obscure. One practitioner estimates it originated around 1950; there are no written materials (workbooks, study guides, etc.) involved in it. Instead, it focuses on the act of inscribing questions and answers in the Big Book itself as a means to focus and concentrate attention on the Steps. (Pam C. interview with the author, March 2009.)

3. Some of the aspects of AA's print culture and reading practices that I do not discuss here include the history of the monthly magazine, the *AA Grapevine* (founded 1944); the development of local and regional newsletters and their role in creating a sense of identity and shared community; and the practice of institutionalized collaborative authorship within AA's General Service Office. Any and all these would be rich sites of inquiry for scholars of print culture, communications networks, and sociologists of knowledge as well as for those interested in the history of addiction and recovery. I sketch a beginning outline of AA's print culture in "Print Culture in the AA Fellowship."

4. Quoted in Timothy Weber, "Two-Edged Sword," 108.

5. Sheldon, *In His Steps*. On general bible-reading habits, see Gutjahr, *An American Bible*.

6. Quoted in Walter Clark, *Oxford Group*, 109.

7. Quoted in Pittman, *AA: The Way It Began*, 126. Matthew J. Raphael notes in *Bill W. and Mr. Wilson* that it was "the quest of the historical Jesus"—one of the aims of higher criticism—that "moved the Oxford Group to emulate, as far as possible, the practices of first-century Christians," and goes on to argue that because AA was inspired by the Group, it "may also be said to have sprung from the root of biblical Higher Criticism" (13–14). There is little in Oxford Group literature or reading practices, however, to suggest that members were interested in uncovering empirical information about what theologians call "the Jesus of history"; the Group's focus was decidedly on "the Christ of faith."

8. The Layman with a Notebook, *What Is the Oxford Group?*, 68. In a pamphlet

entitled "The Quiet Time" (<http://www.aabibliography.com/pdffiles/quiettimerose.pdf>), author Harold Rose listed reading "the Scriptures" as the first and foremost means of connecting with "the Holy Spirit in Attentive Prayer."

9. Russell, *For Sinners Only*, 93.

10. Layman with a Notebook, *What is the Oxford Group?*, 69. Needless to say, the notions of guidance and of "checking" have been seen by some as problematic. Walter Clark, who attended Group meetings as a college student, notes that "what 'comes to' the listeners ranges all the way from profound spiritual insights and self-revelations to absurd trivialities" and points out that when the leader of a meeting received guidance that contradicted that of another member, "the ensuing altercation was hardly an edifying spectacle for the rest of those present" (29–30).

11. Ibid., 47, 69, 72.

12. Ibid., 67, and Walter Clark, *Oxford Group*, 29.

13. Riehle, *Middle English Mystics*, 13–23.

14. Griffiths, *Religious Reading*. Further citations are noted parenthetically in the text.

15. Anne Smith is quoted in Dick B., *Good Morning!*, 68. On preferred selections from the Bible, see "Dr. Bob's Required Reading List," in Pittman, *AA the Way It Began*, 197. AA historian Dick B. has written extensively and enthusiastically on the importance of the Bible to early AAs. See especially his *Good Book and the Big Book* and *James Club*.

16. Wing, *Grateful to Have Been There*, 31–32.

17. Alcoholics Anonymous of Akron, "Manual," 3.

18. Wilson, *Lois Remembers*, 103.

19. Wilson notes in the same passage that "from this phrase it was only a step to the idea of 'Alcoholics Anonymous,'" a name that emerged only as the group began to search for a title for their book.

20. Raphael, *Bill W. and Mr. Wilson*, 100–101.

21. Bill Wilson, "How the Big Book Was Put Together," <http://www.barefootsworld.net/aabook1954.html>.

22. The implications for Western philosophy of the metaphysics of presence and its corollary, "logocentrism," are the subject of *Of Grammatology*; the terms are introduced on pp. 43–44. See also Culler, *On Deconstruction*, 89–110.

23. Interview, Vinnie M.

24. Bill Wilson to Frank Amos, 26 September 1938. Alcoholics Anonymous Archives, AA World Service Office, New York, Box 59.

25. Ibid. AA did engage in a joint publishing venture with Harper some years later, when the trade publisher brought out an edition of *12 Steps and 12 Traditions*.

26. Bill Wilson, "Three Talks to Medical Societies," 39.

27. Raphael, *Bill W. and Mr. Wilson*, 123, 125.

28. O'Reilly, *Sobering Tales*, 105, 104.

29. The "radical" and "liberal" terminology is Wilson's own; he refers in this section of COA to the Akron-style pro-religionists as "conservative" as well. An additional endorsement of the more gradual approach came from a New Jersey psychiatrist named Dr. Howard, one of the several medical professionals to review the

manuscript prior to publication. "He pointed out that the text of our book was too full of the words 'you' and 'must.' He suggested that we substitute whenever possible such expressions as 'we ought' or 'we should' [in order] to remove all forms of coercion" (COA, 167). Raphael documents the textual emendations between the original manuscript, the prepublication multilith edition, and the published first edition in *Bill W. and Mr. Wilson*, 120–22.

30. Bill Wilson to Dr. Robert Smith, June 1938. Alcoholics Anonymous Archive, Box 59, Folder B.

31. All citations to first-person Big Book narratives in this section are to the first edition, Works Publishing, 1939.

32. Florence R. of New York, the author of "A Feminine Victory," was the first woman to get sober in AA, but her sobriety did not last and she died of alcoholism (*SD*, 158). The story "An Alcoholic's Wife" was written by Marie B. of Akron and was included in the volume as "an early forerunner of today's [Al-Anon] Family Group development" (COA, 164). Neither narrative appeared in later editions of the Big Book.

33. A notable exception to this rule is "My Wife and I," which centers on how the narrator's drunkenness imperils the businesses he runs with his wife, whom he describes as "an able, well-educated woman who had an unusual gift of common sense and far more than the average business vision, a true helpmate in every way" (287). Similarly, in "Another Prodigal Story" the narrator refers to his wife "at the store, working" (357) at what is later referred to as "our business" (361).

34. Robertson, *Getting Better*, 73.

35. Raphael notes the presence of Edgar Allan Poe's gothic imagination in Bill Wilson's own life and writings (*Bill W. and Mr. Wilson*, xi–xii, 151–58); these are similar, though fainter echoes.

36. A number of AA historians allege that Wilson's secretary Ruth Hock was the actual author of this story. See Pittman, *AA: The Way It Began*, 181, and the silkworth.net author biography entitled "Biography: 'The Lone Endeavor,'" <http://silkworth.net/ aabiography/patcooper.html>. The "Memoirs of Jimmy," by Jim B., a member of the original New York group, however, accord with the official accounts; <http://www.aabib liography.com/jim_burwell_aahistory.html.> "The Lone Endeavor" was removed in the second printing of the Big Book because the AA offices lost contact with the author and could no longer vouch for his sobriety.

37. In a letter to Alcoholic Foundation trustee Bernard Smith discussing the second edition of the Big Book (14 June 1954), Wilson notes that the prepublication multilith contained "the text, plus five of the original twenty-eight stories." Alcoholics Anonymous Archives, Box 75, Folder D.

38. Rudy, *Becoming Alcoholic*, 44.

39. Kaminer, *I'm Dysfunctional*, 72; Warhol and Michie, "Twelve-Step Teleology." Writing from a poststructuralist point of view, the latter authors critique the AA narratives for their attempts to "elide social and cultural differences" and "to uphold the fiction of the unified self" (328, 332).

40. O'Reilly, *Sobering Tales*, 145.

41. Brereton, *From Sin to Salvation*, 4–12.

42. Kurtz, *Not-God*, 89.

43. Bill Wilson to Bob Smith, June 1938, Alcoholics Anonymous Archives. All correspondence regarding Big Book stories are from Box 59, Folder C, unless otherwise noted.

44. Jim S.'s own story appeared in the first edition under the title "Traveler, Editor, Scholar."

45. Ohmann, *Selling Culture*, 1–10, 118–74.

46. Hank P. to Bill Wilson, 5 January 1939.

47. Uzzell, *Narrative Technique*, xxix, xix.

48. Uzzell, "Love Pulps," 41.

49. Quoted in Hank P. to Bill Wilson, 5 January 1939.

50. *Pass It On* states simply that the original draft of Wilson's 12 Steps "has been lost"; the same fate seems to have befallen the stories.

51. Interview, Louis Kauffman.

52. Quoted in Hank P. to Bill Wilson, 5 January 1939.

53. AA's official history also errs in crediting Uzzell as the editor of the entire Big Book. Box 59, Folder C, contains brief correspondence between Wilson and Hank P. and a Peekskill, New York, woman named Janet Blair, discussing her editing of the first part of the manuscript during early February 1939.

54. Mitchell K., *How It Worked*, 136.

55. Wally P., *But, for the Grace of God*, 98, 102, 110, 184; Buddy S., "How AA Got Started in Arkansas," n.p.

56. This citation from "AA Sponsorship . . . Its Opportunities and Its Responsibilities," by Clarence S., Cleveland Central Committee, 1944; reprinted in Mitchell K., *How It Worked*, 243. Similar wording appears in Akron's "Manual for Alcoholics Anonymous," 8. The "Little Rock Approach" required that new prospects read the entire Big Book within three days of getting sober (Buddy S., "How AA Got Started in Arkansas").

57. Kurtz, *Not-God*, 356n67. Wilson expressed similar ideas in correspondence with Trustee Bernard Smith and in assorted other correspondence. Alcoholics Anonymous Archives, Box 75, Folder D; Box 28.

58. Conference Report 1955, 32.

59. Wally P., *But, for the Grace of God*, 79.

60. "An Interpretation of the Twelve Steps," published in Detroit in 1943, is also often called "The Detroit Pamphlet." However, because a version of it was reprinted there soon after, it is also called "The Washington DC Pamphlet." For details on its publishing and distribution history, see the "Note" by Glenn Chesnut at his electronic edition, <http://hindsfoot.org/Detro.html>. The importance of "If Drinking Isn't Fun Anymore—Alcoholics Anonymous," published in Minneapolis around 1946, is cited in Wally P., *But, for the Grace of God*, 132.

61. *Little Red Book*, 40–41; "Spiritual Milestones," 14–15.

62. Quoted in Pittman, foreword to the fiftieth anniversary edition, xiii.

63. Bill Wilson to Ed W., 15 November 1950 (not the Ed W. who wrote *The Little Red Book*). All citations to correspondence regarding outside literature in this section, AA Archives, Box 26, Folder 10.21.

64. Bill Wilson to Clem L., 28 February 1950; to Mr. and Mrs. Einer M., 5 July 1949; to Ray H., 21 December 1950.

65. NCEA Pamphlets from this era included "What Is an Alcoholic?" "Why This Committee?" "What Can I Do?" "Book of Etiquette," "Lecture Service," "Services," and "Reading Matter," all dated 1946. Dr. Bob Archives, John Hay Library, Brown University, Box 2.

66. Conference Report 1955, 34. Wilson addresses this issue in his 1950 letter to Ray H. as well, noting that if Ray H. proceeds to write a book for AAs, he may find that his "publisher may be hellbent to use the AA Group Directory" for direct-mail solicitations. "From time to time publishers try this only to come a cropper. This is because they have no idea how smitten AAs are on the subject of commercialization and unauthorized use of this confidential document. Unfailingly, such attempts do more harm than good. The conventional open market is best" for the sale of 12-Step literature, Wilson concludes.

67. Conference Report 1951, 12. For conspiracy theories, see, for example, "Documents Concerning AA History" at the GSOWatch web site, <http://gsowatch.aamo .info/aaws/index.htm>.

68. Over the years, the GSO has tried a variety of strategies to break its addiction to revenue from literature sales, including a host of schemes to increase group contributions. None of these, however, have generated revenue that even approaches that earned on the Big Book, and funds from publishing are routinely used to cover other operating expenses.

69. Conference Report 1951, 12.

70. Bill Wilson to Ed W., 15 November 1950 (not the Ed W. who wrote *The Little Red Book*).

71. Bill Wilson to Ray H., 21 December 1950.

72. *Little Red Book*, 78. Original emphasis. In fairness, it should be noted that the Big Book employs similar language, reminding readers that "half-measures availed us nothing" (59) and that "the spiritual life is not a theory. *We have to live it*" (83, original emphasis). When Wilson fulminated about the book becoming "more and more frozen" (see note 57 above), it may have been the result of a desire to bring the original text more in line with his new appreciation of gradualism.

73. Given the welling up of discussions about race and the desirability of integrating AA meetings (see chapter 2, note 88 above), it is also possible that Wilson was concerned about the long-term effects for AA should local or regional racist practices begin to pass themselves off as representative of AA as a whole. If beliefs such as it is "difficult . . . getting colored people to understand alcoholism except as a moral issue or sin" (Conference Report 1952, 14) worked their way into the fabric of AA philosophy, the principle of alcoholic equalitarianism and the entire premise of the gift economy would be permanently undermined.

74. Conference Report 1951, 15. The composition and role of the Literature Committee are discussed in *AA Service Manual*, S55–S57.

75. Conference Report 1951, 15. Original emphasis.

76. Conference Report 1952, 12.

77. Conference Report 1954, 13.

78. Conference Report 1961, 11.

Chapter 4

1. Conference Report 1976, 25.

2. On gender bias in early AA, see *Dr. Bob*, 241–47, and Brown and Brown, *Mrs. Marty Mann*, 122–30.

3. Margaret Jones, "Rage for Recovery."

4. Richmond Walker, *Twenty-four Hours a Day*, 15 April. Walker's volume uses dates rather than page numbers; further citations noted parenthetically in the text. The original text used the term "desperate man" in this entry; the current edition reads "desperate person." On the revision process leading to this and another similar changes, see note 41 below.

5. "Richmond Walker and the Twenty-four-Hour Book," <http://hindsfoot.org/RWfla1.html>. Richard Dubiel's *Road to Fellowship* likewise notes that Walker's emphasis on fellowship and service are due to the lingering influence of the Jacoby Club on the Boston AA culture in which Walker was steeped (132–35).

6. One lyrical example can stand for many of Walker's pages. The meditation for 3 January prompts the reader to acknowledge that "I need God's help. His spirit shall flow through me and, in flowing through me, it shall sweep away all the bitter past. I will take heart. The way will open for me." The day's Prayer materializes the attitude of the surrendered self with the supplication, "I pray that I may be taught, just as a child would be taught. I pray that I may never question God's plans, but accept them gladly."

7. Augustine, *City of God*, Book 21, chapter 5: "Then there are the apples of Sodom which grow indeed to an appearance of ripeness, but, when you touch them with hand or tooth, the peel cracks, and they crumble into dust and ashes." <http://www.clerus.org/bibliaclerusonline/en/bsq.htm/>.

8. Walker to Helen B., 27 June, 19 September 1953. All correspondence cited in this section, Alcoholics Anonymous Archives, AA World Service Office, New York, Box 73, Folder C.

9. Walker to John R., 1 September 1953.

10. Leroy R. to Helen B., 28 October 1953.

11. Chesnut, "Richmond Walker and New York," <http://health.groups.yahoo.com/group/AAHistoryLovers/message/1999>.

12. Conference Report 1954, 22.

13. Walker to O.K. P., 18 February 1954. Original emphasis.

14. Walker to Alcoholic Foundation, 25 May 1954.

15. McElrath, *Hazelden*, 90, 138; Chesnut, "The Earliest Printings," <http://hindsfoot.org/rwcvphot.html>; Margaret Jones, "Rage for Recovery," 17.

16. McElrath, *Hazelden*, 25. On the history of Hazelden see also Spicer, *Minnesota Model*, and McElrath, *Quiet Crusaders*.

17. McElrath, *Hazelden*, 39.

18. Spicer, *Minnesota Model*, 119–22.

19. On women at Hazelden, see McElrath, *Hazelden*, 108–15; on Fellowship Club, 60–67.

20. Ibid., 144.

21. Ibid., 146.

22. Ibid., 126, and McElrath, *Further Reflections*, 25.

23. McElrath, *Hazelden*, 52.

24. Interview, Mark Crea.

25. Ibid.

26. McElrath, *Hazelden*, 138.

27. Hazelden Catalogue, 1969. My thanks to Damien McElrath for providing me with this document.

28. Interview, Ruby Rott; McElrath, *Further*, 31.

29. Chester H. Kirk Collection on Alcoholism and Alcoholics Anonymous, John Hay Library, Brown University. Box label "Hazelden Foundation Pamphlets," file "Catalogues, May '75–Holiday '85."

30. McElrath, *Further Reflections*, 6–7, 17.

31. Interview, David Spohn.

32. Interview, Harry Swift.

33. Interview, David Spohn.

34. Interview, Harry Swift; McElrath, *Further Reflections*, 43.

35. McElrath, *Further Reflections*, 7.

36. Swift, *Program Management*, 14, 11, 15.

37. Unless otherwise noted, all information regarding Karen Casey and quotations from her are from an interview with the author in December 2005.

38. Interview, Elisabeth L.

39. Interview, Harry Swift.

40. Interview, Elisabeth L.

41. It is not possible to determine when, precisely, the decision was made to undertake these changes and who oversaw them. The entire text was edited with an eye to gender-sensitivity as well as to updating Walker's sometimes anachronistic turns of phrase. Typically, changes were small: "Any man can fight the battles of just one day" became "Anyone can fight the battles of just one day" (31 July), "Queer birds" became "odd ducks" (9 February). Others, however, were more elaborate. For instance, the original entry for 1 June, which adumbrates "some things I don't miss since becoming dry," included "facing my wife at breakfast and looking at my breakfast. Also composing the alibi and sticking to it. Also trying to shave with a hand that won't behave." The revised edition reads, "facing my loved one at breakfast. Also composing the alibi and sticking to it. Also trying to shave or put on make-up with a shaky hand."

42. See, for example, John Michael's *Sober, Clean, and Gay*, Chaney Allan's *I'm Black and I'm Sober*, and the remarkable *Twelve Steps for Everyone . . . Who Really Wants Them* (by "Grateful Members") which uses gender neutral pronouns throughout.

43. McElrath, *Further Reflections*, 33. Emphasis added.

44. Karen Casey, *Each Day a New Beginning*. Like Walker's book, Casey's contains

no page numbers, so citations are to the date on a given page. Further citations noted in text.

45. See, for example, Bepko, *Feminism and Addiction*; Covington, *Helping Women Recover*; and Kasl, *Many Roads, One Journey*.

46. Mid-twentieth century "Second Wave" feminism (sometimes designated "Women's Liberation") is so called to distinguish it from what scholars retrospectively have recognized as a "First Wave" of agitation for women's suffrage that began in the late eighteenth century. The role of consciousness raising in Second Wave feminism is discussed at length in Alice Echols, *Daring to Be Bad* (1989), especially 83–89 and 382–89.

47. *Little Red Book*, 42.

48. Casey, "Portrayal of American Indian Women," 6, 14. Contemporary scholars of Native American spirituality may find much to quarrel with in Casey's treatment of her subject. While the introduction to the dissertation foregrounds the importance of "Indian spirituality," it never really explains what is meant by the term, nor does it provide much by way of example. Casey does not differentiate among tribal groups or historical periods, and relies almost exclusively on Anglo-Americans' writings about indigenous peoples to arrive at her conclusions about the nature of Indian spirituality and attitudes toward gender.

49. The term "divine within" comes from Warren Felt Evans (1817–89), one of the earliest and most influential New Thought teachers; the in-dwelling God's place in Unity theology is most clearly articulated in the chapter "The Secret Place of the Most High" in Emile Cady's *Lessons in Truth*, as discussed in Nathaniel Braden, *Spirits in Rebellion*, 233–63. On Hopkins's Christian Science, see chapter 2, note 51, above. Details about Unity's theology are explored in Dell deChant, "Myrtle Fillmore," and John Simmons, "Forgotten Contributions of Annie Rix Militz."

50. Braden, *Spirits in Rebellion*, 261.

51. DeChant, "Myrtle Fillmore," 107. Unity was not alone in conceptualizing God as Father-Mother. Mary Baker Eddy's Church of Christ, Scientist proffered a similar image, as did Emma Curtis Hopkins's Christian Science Association, within which Charles and Myrtle Fillmore studied in the 1880s.

52. "Hazelden: More Than Just Treatment," 18.

53. McElrath, *Further Reflections*, 33.

54. Interview, Mark Crea.

55. McElrath, *Further Reflections*, 52.

56. Karen Casey, email to the author, 22 May 2003.

57. Interview, Mark Crea.

58. Karen Casey, email to the author, 22 May 2003.

59. McElrath, *Further*, 31.

60. Interview, Jim Erickson.

61. Interviews, Rebecca Post, Alan Borne, and Bill Hammond.

62. Jerry Spicer, email to the author, 23 May 2003.

63. On "merger mania" in 1980s trade publishing, see Compaine and Gomery, *Who Owns the Media?*, 66–67.

64. Interview, Tom Grady.

65. Feldman, "On the Road to Recovery," 52; McElrath, *Further Reflections*, 31.

66. Swift and Williams, "Recovery for the Whole Family," 8.

67. McElrath, *Further Reflections*, 34.

68. "HCI Books Celebrates"; Braus, "Selling Self-Help," 50; Claudia Black, email to the author, 14 March 2009.

69. The "Progression of 'Loving Too Much' and Recovery" chart in Norwood's book copies M. M. Glatt's "Alcohol Addiction and Recovery," which appeared in the *British Journal of Addiction* in 1958.

70. Norwood, *Women Who Love Too Much*, 5.

71. Shapiro, "Advice Givers Strike Gold," 64. For a more complete account of the *Women Who Love Too Much* phenomenon, including discussion of the fact that what appear in the book as "case studies" are in fact episodes from Norwood's own life as a codependent, see Faludi, *Backlash*, 347–56.

72. Feldman, "On the Road to Recovery," 52.

73. Beattie, *Codependent No More*, 36. Further citations are noted parenthetically in the text.

74. Feldman, "On the Road to Recovery," 52.

75. Elizabeth Taylor, "Taking Care of Herself," 106; *New York Times Book Review*, 12 November 1989, 62.

76. Interviews, Tom Grady, Jerry Spicer, and Harry Swift.

77. Interviews, Rebecca Post and Jerry Spicer.

78. Interview, Jerry Spicer.

79. McElrath, *Further Reflections*, 35.

80. Ibid., 17.

81. The survey found that 70 percent overall used non-CAL materials in addition to CAL, but that figure included such materials as a local newsletter, a list of meetings, or a membership directory. Besides *24 Hours* and *The Little Red Book*, 11 percent of groups used midcentury pamphlets, including "Who—Me?" a thirty-five-question quiz intended to determine whether the reader was an alcoholic, developed in the early 1940s by Dr. Robert Seliger of Johns Hopkins Hospital and reprinted in a variety of locations. Also popular was "A Guide to the 12 Steps," which may have been a reprinting of the Akron pamphlet of that name (see chapter 2, note 53, above) or of the oft-reprinted "Detroit Pamphlet" described in chapter 3, note 60, above (Conference Report 1966, 22). Further citations to annual conference reports in this section appear parenthetically in the text, with year and page number indicated, unless otherwise noted.

82. The following citations are to General Service Conference reports. On making *Twenty-four Hours* a CAL text: 1972, 31; 1976, 26. Requests for meditation book: 1968, 27; 1978, 46. Requests for Big Book–related publications appear in various ways. For facsimile edition of the first edition: 1973, 31; 1980, 30; for concordance: 1977, 26; for pocket edition: 1970, 31; 1977, 26. On general problems with literature, see "Literature Is No Substitute for Handshakes and Sponsorship" and "Literature Array Responds to Needs and Fills a Big Budget Gap," 1975, 20–21; also Trustee's Litera-

ture Committee Report of that year, 33; also "Presentation on Literature: Too Much? Too Specialized?," 1979, 13.

83. The desire to distinguish CAL from non-CAL publications dates back to the designation's inception (see chapter 3). On designating via the statement "Conference Approved," see 1956, 14; on designating with circle and triangle logo, see 1955, 13; 1959, 21. The conference reiterated the importance of designating non-CAL as such when it was offered for sale by groups in 1972, 31. On need to segregate CAL from non-CAL publications in displays, see 1973, 15; 1975, 40.

84. Quoted in Dick B., "AA Conference Approved Myths," <http://www.dickb.com/conference-approved.shtml>.

85. This was a repeated occurrence: see 1968, 27; 1975, 40–41; 1978, 46.

86. For young alcoholics, "What Happened to Joe?" (comic format) and "Young People in AA" appeared in 1967, followed by "Too Young?" in 1977. "Time to Start Living," for older alcoholics, appeared in 1979 and was replaced by "AA for Older Alcoholics" in 2001. The first literature aimed at clergy and prison inmates appeared in 1961: "Members of the Clergy Ask About Alcoholics Anonymous" and "Memo to an Inmate Who Might be An Alcoholic." These were replaced in the 1970s by "A Clergyman Looks at AA" (1970) (retitled "The Clergy Asks" in 1987) and "It Sure Beats Sitting in a Cell" (1978). "AA and the Armed Services" appeared in 1974. "AA and the Gay/Lesbian Alcoholic" and "AA for the Native North American" were published in 1989; "Can AA Help Me Too? Black/African Americans Share Their Stories" appeared in 2001. All dates and titles from "AA Pamphlets," <http://www.silkworth.net/aa/aa_pamphlets.html.>.

87. The Literature Committee acknowledged its own slow pace. A presentation on "How a Trustee Committee Handles Literature" in 1981 recounted that the suggestion to develop a pamphlet addressed to the older alcoholic had been submitted to the Literature Committee in 1956 and approved in 1957. But because few stories and ideas from members were submitted when they were solicited, the idea was tabled—and revived in 1977 to be completed in 1979. "The process could have been faster if, in 1956, some chief or boss had given the order, and if AA had an authoritarian structure," the speaker explained. "But would the result have been more beneficial to all of us, both present members and those yet to come?" (1981, 13).

88. AA as an institution has never kept track of its membership or the duration or quality of the sobriety of its members. The only data that they have attempted to capture is length of involvement with the AA group; a summary of the data from the 1977 through 1989 Triennial Surveys of the membership notes simply that 56 percent of those who stay in the group for three months are still active at the end of twelve months (Shehan et al., "Alcoholics Anonymous (AA) Recovery Outcome Rates"). The foreword to the second edition of the Big Book, however, makes a bolder claim: "Of alcoholics who came to AA and really tried, 50% got sober at once and remained that way; 25% sobered up after some relapses, and among the remainder, those who stayed with AA showed improvement" (BB, xx). This success rate has been touted by traditionalists as evidence of the efficacy of AA in the good old days, and current low rates of success—some "Back to Basics" groups claims they are as low as

5 percent, but do not disclose the data from which that figure is derived—are concomitantly used to indicate the weakness of contemporary AA. Bracketing the glaring problem of data collection, Glenn Chesnut has pointed out that such comparisons are meaningless, since midcentury midwestern AA groups typically "either (a) prescreen[ed prospects] and/or (b) exclude[d] people from [their] sample who only came to a relatively few meetings and then dropped out because of lack of real internal motivation." He argues that groups that resort to such filtering practices today also achieve similarly high rates of success.

89. Tom P. Jr., "Gresham's Law and Alcoholics Anonymous," 5. Original emphasis. Tom P. Jr. was a cofounder of All Addicts Anonymous, a traditionalist group in upstate New York connected to the East Ridge community and recovery center (founded 1964). *24 Magazine*, originally titled *Way Out*, began publishing in 1970. It became the *Ridge Review* in the mid-1980s, and it continues today as *24 Newsletter*. My thanks to Matt Dingle of East Ridge for providing me with this history.

90. Ibid., 13, 11.

91. "Mose Yoder's AA Lead, 1976," 40–41; Walter S., "This Is the Bright Star Press."

92. AA Commonplaces are discussed in detail in Travis, " 'Handles to Hang on to Our Sobriety.' "

93. Information on CTM edition from Charles Bishop and Bill Pittman, *To Be Continued*, entry 976. The General Service Conference report of 1986 explained the CTM situation thus: "The copyright on the first edition of the Big Book lapsed in 1967, and the copyright on the new material in the second edition lapsed in 1983—both because of a failure to renew them in a timely fashion. There was a mistaken belief that registering the copyright on the second edition in 1956 served to revive the copyright on the first edition; the misconception continued, with respect to the second edition, when the third edition was copyrighted in 1976" (8). On legal exchanges, see Conference Report 1986, 28–29.

94. On disputes over copyright and trademark in Mexico, see Conference Reports 1994, 24, and 1995, 55. On Quebecois and European translations, see 1998, 22. A sympathetic account of anti-GSO publishing is Charles Bishop's "Spirituality versus Legalism in Alcoholics Anonymous," <http://dickb.com/fear.shtml>.

95. Joe McQ. of Little Rock and Charlie P. of Maysville, Arkansas, who began to travel and promote their "Joe and Charlie Curriculum" in the mid-1980s, are perhaps the best known of the traditionalist sobriety guide-authors. Other examples of the genre include *Searcy's Book* by Searcy W. (Dallas, 1990); *Back to Basics*, by Wally P. (Tucson, 1997); *The Primary Purpose Big Book Study*, by Clifford B. and Myers R. (Dallas, 2000), and *Unofficial Guide to the Twelve Steps*, compiled by AA Members in Texas and edited by Paul O. (Laguna Nigel, Calif., 1990).

96. Jim H., "Editorial Statement," <http://aabbsg.de/oppf/OPPF0101.htm>.

97. Mitchell K., *How It Worked*, 226–27.

98. Ibid., 226–29. Original emphasis.

99. In one odd moment during the Conference question and answer session in 1970, this belief was spelled out directly. A delegate asked, "What procedure is used to select the staff at the GSO and why are men being discriminated against?" The

unequivocal answer: "Men are not discriminated against. Any man who feels he is qualified for the position has every right to apply; any interested A.A. member is encouraged to apply, as staff openings do occur from time to time. Some general qualifications are: (1) At least four years of continuous sobriety in A.A., (2) A good background in a business or service organization (in or out of A.A.), (3) Experience in speaking at A.A. meetings and (4) Knowledge of a foreign language (particularly Spanish and French) can prove useful, but this is not essential" (Conference Report 1970, 31).

100. For discussions of this phenomenon from a variety of perspectives, see, for example, Douglas, *Feminization of American Culture*; Huyssen, *After the Great Divide*, 44–64; Macdonald, "Masscult and Midcult"; and Radway, "On the Gender of the Middlebrow Consumer."

101. Huyssen, *After the Great Divide*, 47.

102. Conference Report 1982, 21.

103. On the relationship between low-tech, nonprofessional print forms and the creation of identity, see, for example, Berlet, "Write Stuff"; Danky, "Oppositional Press"; and Garvey, "Out of the Mainstream and into the Streets."

Chapter 5

1. *Feminist Bookstore News* 11, no. 6 (September 1983): 16.

2. Paul, "Gay and Alcoholic," 154. On the community-forming nature of feminist bookstores, see also Junko Onosaka, *Feminist Revolution in Literacy*, and Ann Enke, *Finding the Movement*, especially 62–103.

3. Herman, "Twelve-Step Program"; Faludi, *Backlash*, 350; Rapping, *Culture of Recovery*, 107, 164. For similar criticisms of recovery as a depoliticizing agent, see, for example, Echols, *Daring to Be Bad*, 243–87; and Kaminer, "Feminism's Identity Crisis" and *I'm Dysfunctional*.

4. I use quotation marks around "postfeminism" to signal the hotly contested nature of this term within feminist circles. The word first appeared in Susan Bolotin's 1982 *New York Times Magazine* article, "Voices from the Post-Feminist Generation," denominating young women whose values resonated with those of Second Wave feminists but who rejected the term "feminist" to describe themselves. It has since taken on two contradictory meanings, neatly parsed by Ann Braithwaite in "The Personal, the Political, Third Wave, and Postfeminisms." In the first, its meaning is a "largely negative, sometimes even hostile reaction against an earlier feminism [in which] the prefix 'post' . . . becomes equivalent to 'anti.'" The second meaning uses "post" in the same fashion as "postmodern" or "postcolonial," to achieve a sense of critical friction with a precursor term and "signif[y] some continuing relationship to feminism [despite] the changes in feminist thinking over the last forty years rather than a rupture with it" (337–41). Braithwaite points out that the latter definition has proven popular with Australian and British feminists, while scholars in the United States tend to default to the former definition and therefore be hostile to its deployment. For an example of the former stance, see Brooks, *Postfeminisms*; for the latter, see Hawkesworth, "Semiotics of Premature Burial," and Hall and Rodriguez, "Myth of Postfeminism."

5. Hanisch, "Personal Is Political."

6. On consciousness raising, see chapter 4, note 46.

7. This chapter's interest in "varieties" of feminist experience poses a set of thorny terminological challenges, as the varied feminists in question use different terms to describe themselves. In general, I use "women's" and "feminist" interchangeably to indicate attitudes, institutions, and discourses centered in women's experiences and seeking to improve their positions in the world. Within that broad category, I distinguish "liberal" from "radical" feminism based on their political modalities, assuming the first to be oriented primarily to institutional reform and civic equity, the second to societal revolution and personal liberty. Within "radical" feminism, Alice Echols ("Cultural Feminism" and *Daring to be Bad*) has identified two clashing groups: "politicos" coming out of the New Left who favored a materialist critique of society and advocated for a movement toward androgyny, and "cultural feminists" who emerged from and retained significant commitments to the idea of lesbian separatism, believed in the reality of gender difference, and advocated for a world remade along the lines of "the female principle." It is this latter group that I mean when I use the term "radical feminist" in this chapter. Verta Taylor and Nancy Whitier have argued that the term "lesbian feminism" should be used to describe this formation ("Collective Identity"), but I use "lesbian" here fairly narrowly, to indicate a commitment to same-sex female coupledom and the culture that supported it. I use "black feminist" or "woman of color feminist" to denominate women of color, lesbian and straight, within the radical feminist camp; I use "womanist" to describe the perspective of women of color who reject the term "feminist" because of its association with white privilege. The history and the tensions of these varying strains of feminism are discussed in Tong, *Feminist Thought*.

8. Sandmaier, *Invisible Alcoholics*, 74.

9. Tong, *Feminist Thought*, 32.

10. On the imprecision in contemporary epidemiological accounts of female drinking, see Edith Lisansky Gomberg, "Gender Issues." Laura Schmidt and Constance Weisner discuss the ambiguous statistics in more detail in "The Emergence of Problem-Drinking Women," which draws on the work of, among others, Kaye Middleton Fillmore, "'When Angels Fall,'" and Elizabeth Morrissey, "Contradictions Inhering."

11. Sandmaier, *Invisible Alcoholics*, xv; Morrissey, "Contradictions Inhering," 65.

12. Schmidt and Weisner, "Emergence of Problem-Drinking Women," 313.

13. Sandmaier, *Invisible Alcoholics*, 75; Beckman and Amaro, "Patterns of Women's Use," 319.

14. Anthony is a fascinating figure. A journalist and peace activist during the Second World War, she refused to testify before the House Un-American Activities Committee during the Red Scare of the 1950s, and for some time lived as an exile in the Caribbean, having renounced U.S. citizenship. She was cleared of wrongdoing and reinstated as a citizen in the late 1960s. In 1965 she earned a Ph.D. in theology from St. Mary's College at the University of Notre Dame. Anthony lectured on behalf of the National Council on Alcoholism from 1976 until 1991; during those years she also worked as a substance abuse coordinator at South County Mental Health Center

and founded Wayside House, a treatment center for chemically dependent women, both in Delray Beach, Florida.

15. Wilsnack and Beckman, *Alcohol Problems in Women*, ix.

16. Leland, "Alcohol Use and Abuse."

17. Sandmaier, *Invisible Alcoholics*, 6.

18. Braiker, "Therapeutic Issues," 357. See also Morrissey, "Contradictions Inhering," 77–80.

19. For an overview of this crucial development in women's and gender history, see Satter, "Sexual Abuse Paradigm."

20. Wilsnack, "Drinking, Sexuality, and Sexual Dysfunction," 215–16.

21. Braiker, "Therapeutic Issues," 352.

22. Kirkpatrick, *Goodbye Hangovers*, xv.

23. Kirkpatrick, *Turnabout*, 108. Biographical information on Kirkpatrick is drawn from her memoirs, which are imprecise and, in some places, inconsistent.

24. Kirkpatrick, *Turnabout*, 160, 108. Ellipsis in original.

25. Ibid., 164.

26. Kirkpatrick, *Goodbye Hangovers*, 28–37.

27. Kaskutas, "Women for Sobriety," 180. Original emphasis.

28. Kirkpatrick, *Turnabout*, 161.

29. Kirkpatrick, *Goodbye Hangovers*, 34. Original emphasis.

30. Kaskutas, "Women for Sobriety," 182.

31. Kirkpatrick, *Goodbye Hangovers*, 58.

32. Ibid., 43–68.

33. Kirkpatrick, *Turnabout*, 173.

34. Ibid., 149, and Kirkpatrick, *Goodbye Hangovers*, 165–70.

35. Kirkpatrick, *Goodbye Hangovers*, 144. The sixth of the keys is Step 8, "the fundamental object of life is emotional and spiritual growth."

36. Ibid., 157, 167.

37. Ibid., 139.

38. Kaskutas, "Women for Sobriety," 178, and Kaskutas, "Pathways to Self-Help," 260.

39. "Mary," WFS Outreach Coordinator, email to the author, 21 October 2008.

40. Kaskutas, "Women for Sobriety," 185. Kaskutas reports that the "fixed contribution" was mandatory, but Mary, the current Outreach Coordinator for WFS, describes it as voluntary. The two stances may reflect a change over time.

41. On the development of such feminist institutions, see Myra Marx Ferree and Patricia Yancey Martin, *Feminist Organizations*.

42. Schmidt and Weisner, "Emergence of Problem-Drinking Women," 314–15; Morrissey, "Contradictions Inhering."

43. On gay male bars, see Berube, *Coming Out under Fire*, and Chauncey, *Gay New York*. While less central to lesbian life, bars were still extremely important in the creation of lesbian space. See, for example, Enke, *Finding the Movement*, 25–61; Elizabeth Kennedy, *Boots of Leather*; and Nestle, "Femme's Feminist History."

44. For an overview of this phenomenon, see Paul, "Gay and Alcoholic."

45. Nardi, "Alcoholism and Homosexuality," 11. Fifield discusses the report and resistance to her findings in Borden, *History of Gay People*, 197–204.

46. Swallow, *Out from Under*, vii. Further citations noted parenthetically in the text.

47. The concept of interior colonization originated with Afro-Caribbean psychologist and anti-colonial activist Frantz Fanon, but its best-known articulation within the predominately white U.S. women's liberation movement appeared in Kate Millett's best-selling *Sexual Politics* (1968).

48. Swallow, "The Politics of Hope," talk given at the Coming Out Whole Conference, Ann Arbor, Michigan, 5 April 1986, typescript with additions in hand, 21. Jean Swallow Papers (GLC 50), James C. Hormel Gay and Lesbian Center, San Francisco Public Library (hereafter JS Papers), Box 5.

49. In addition to the September 1983 promotional section, *Feminist Bookstore News* ran a feature on "Women and Alcoholism" in September 1984, and then devoted an entire issue to recovery in 1989.

50. Swallow to Loretta A. Barrett, 10 August 1984, JS Papers, Box 3.

51. Swallow, "CV," JS Papers, Box 5.

52. See, for example, " 'Language of Angels' Plot/Character/Step Outline," notes in hand, 11 November 1991. In these notes, Swallow maps out an unpublished novel, placing plot points on a calendar and correlating them with the 12 Steps whose insights they are supposed to illustrate. JS Papers, Box 2.

53. hooks, *Sisters of the Yam*, 7 and passim.

54. hooks, *Talking Back*, 30. Among the foundational nonfiction texts exploring both the difficulty and the necessity of black self-recovery are Fanon, *Black Skin, White Masks* (1952; U.S. edition 1967); James Baldwin, *Nobody Knows My Name* (1961); and Audre Lorde, *Sister Outsider* (1984).

55. Allan, *Womanist and Feminist Aesthetics*, 75, 72.

56. Christian, *Black Feminist Criticism*, 94.

57. Alice Walker, "Womanist," xii. Original emphasis.

58. On Walker's depression, sense of drift, and turn to mysticism in the late 1970s, see Evelyn C. White's *Alice Walker*, 261–300. On the "religion of love," see Alice Walker, *Same River Twice*, 33. Walker is quoted on violence in "Alice Walker Makes the Big Time."

59. See, for example, Selzer, "Race and Domesticity," and, to a lesser extent, Henry Louis Gates's treatment of the novel in his *The Signifying Monkey*.

60. Allen's alcoholism and recovery is discussed in Evelyn White, *Alice Walker*, 300–306.

61. Alice Walker, *Color Purple*, 1–2. Further citations are noted parenthetically in the text.

62. Berlant, "Race, Gender, and Nation."

63. Walker names Shug's faith as "paganism" and discusses her own embrace of that religious tradition in, among other places, *Anything We Love* (4–26) and *Same River Twice* (20–35).

64. Alice Walker, "Womanist," xi. Original emphasis.

65. Cannon in Sanders et al., "Roundtable Discussion," 136.

66. Rapping, *Culture of Recovery*, 128.

67. Further research is needed into this dynamic and the similar one that may

have been produced by the appearance in 1970 of the gay mutual-help organization Alcoholics Together. Audrey Borden's chapter on Alcoholics Together in *A History of Gay People in Alcoholics Anonymous* is particularly suggestive in this regard.

68. Ferree and Martin, *Feminist Organizations*.

69. Morrissey, "Contradictions Inhering." Rapping also makes this argument over the course of her book.

70. "Mary," WFS Outreach Coordinator, email to the author, 21 October 2008.

71. These ideas form the substance of Verta Taylor and Leila Rupp's arguments in "Women's Culture" and of Nancy Whittier's *Feminist Generations*.

72. Quoted in Staggenborg, "Beyond Culture versus Politics," 520.

73. Swallow, *Out from Under*, 101.

74. Cheryl Miller, "Out from Under," 18.

75. Swallow, "Our Big Dreams," 7, undated typescript (ca. 1992), JS Papers, Box 4.

76. "Politics of Hope," 11, JS Papers, Box 4.

77. Ibid., 18–21.

78. See correspondence and meeting notes, JS Papers, Box 5.

79. Swallow, "Our Big Dreams," 5, JS Papers, Box 4.

80. See workbooks and conference notes, JS Papers, Box 4.

81. Unless otherwise noted, information on the industry's prepublication perception of *The Color Purple*, and on the packaging and marketing of the novel, is from interviews with Susan Ginsburg, John Glusman, and Irene Skolnick.

82. Mitgang, "Alice Walker Recalls."

83. Kleinfeld, "Problems and a Few Solutions."

84. Kleinfeld, "Shifting Paperback Market." On the marketing and design issues that made quality paperbacks "hot" in the early 1980s, see Stephanie Girard, "Standing at the Corner."

85. Watkins, "Some Letters Went to God."

86. McDowell, "Paperbacks" and "Trade Paperbacks Reshaping."

87. O'Brien, "Alice Walker: An Interview"; Rosenfeld, "Profiles in Purple and Black," E1. In "The Changing Same," Deborah McDowell argues that the way the novel uses epistolary form and the canon of black women's writing make Walker's intention to speak first and foremost to a black female audience clear.

88. Some black feminist critics found white women's comfort with the novel troubling. See, for example, bell hooks, "Writing the Subject," and Harris, "On *The Color Purple*." Sales figures from Evelyn White, *Alice Walker*, 362.

89. Bobo, *Black Women as Cultural Readers*, 75–77.

90. McCullough, "New Spin."

91. On rise of recovery specialty stores, see Margaret Jones, "Getting Away," and Rivkin, "Recovery Stores."

92. In 1992, *American Demographics* reported that women purchased more than 70 percent of self-help books, and a Gallup survey showed that those who bought books dealing with self-improvement and motivation (the two categories that correlate most closely to recovery) tended to be college educated and over thirty-five, with higher than average earning power. Braus, "Selling Self Help," 51; Wood, "Gallup Survey," 33.

93. hooks, *Sisters of the Yam*, 14.

94. It would be useful, for example, to know how and to what extent being in recovery, either as a personal quest or as part of an organized group, has affected women's individual or collective participation in structured agitation for social change over the long term. Such a study might allow us to arrive at a somewhat more conclusive argument about the politics of women's recovery, one derived from empirical evidence rather than from predetermined positions vis-à-vis "the political." Neither the critics nor the supporters of women's recovery, however, have sought to decamp from their theoretical strongholds long enough to undertake such a wide-ranging and data-driven inquiry, which is unfortunately beyond the scope of this archive-based historical project.

95. See chapter 1, note 81, above.

Chapter 6

1. Rapping, *Culture of Recovery*, 17.

2. Lowney, *Baring Our Souls*, 140.

3. Program air dates: 29 October, 2 December, 11 December 1986; 6 January, 12 February, 16 April, 9 June, 11 June, 12 June, 29 July 1987. At one time Burrelle's Information and Transcript Services offered a complete list of *Oprah Winfrey Show* air dates, program topics, and guests to researchers, but they no longer provide that service. I am deeply grateful to Janice Peck for sharing her personal copies of this resource with me.

4. Buchman, *Remaking the World*, 5.

5. Winfrey quoted in LaTonya Taylor, "Church of O," <http://www.christianitytoday.com/ct/2002/april1/1.38.html>.

6. Illouz, *Glamour of Misery*, 5.

7. Winfrey curtailed the book club in the spring of 2002, then revived it the following year with a focus on "classic" literature. That phase lasted through the fall of 2005, when she returned to intermittently showcasing contemporary works (fiction and nonfiction), a practice that continues as of this writing. The post-2002 incarnations of the book club differ significantly in their intention, substance, production values, and degrees of author and reader involvement with on-air and on-line content; therefore claims made about the original club should not be extended to these later incarnations.

8. Preeminent examples of this reading of talk show discourse can be found in Masciarotte, " 'C'mon Girl' "; Shattuc, *Talking Cure*; and Gamson, *Freaks Talk Back*.

9. Greene and Winfrey, *Make the Connection*, 2. Further citations are noted parenthetically in the text.

10. "Diets Don't Work," <http://www.rebeccashouse.org/Rebecca_about.asp>. The program is the creation of Rebecca Cooper, a licensed clinical psychologist and eating disorder survivor.

11. No definitive—or even particularly useful—biography of Winfrey has yet been written; the many titles on the market cobble their accounts together from press clippings. Thus while there are no doubt elements of truth in this "official" account, it is extremely difficult to know to what extent it is the product of Winfrey's public

relations apparatus. Since Winfrey's control over access to information about her life is remarkably strong, it is unclear whether this fundamental informational question will ever be resolved.

12. Mair, *Real Story*, 204.

13. For an excellent short overview of Winfrey's religious upbringing, see LaTonya Taylor, "Church of O."

14. Quoted in Love, *Oprah Winfrey Speaks*, 120.

15. Mair, *Real Story*, 344. For a discussion of how Winfrey's spirituality reflects the traditions of African humanism and spirituality, see Denise Martin, "Oprah Winfrey and Spirituality."

16. Harrison, "Importance of Being Oprah," 54.

17. The term "the Black church" is typically used to indicate those Protestant denominations—especially Methodist, Baptist, and Pentecostal—into which enslaved African Americans in the South were assimilated. As blacks moved north during the Great Migration, congregants from these traditional faiths occasionally encountered New Thought doctrine, with fascinating and complicated results. The best known of these hybrid faith communities was Father Divine's (George Baker's) Peace Mission movement, centered around New York City in the 1920s and 1930s and discussed in Satter, "Marcus Garvey, Father Divine" and in Griffith, *Born Again Bodies*, 141–59. A more recent example is Oakland, California's East Bay Church of Religious Science, the subject of Darnise Martin's *Beyond Christianity*. Perhaps the largest such enterprise (and the one most directly connected to Oprah Winfrey) can be found in the ministry of Divine Science minister Iyanla Vanzant, whose Inner Visions Worldwide Institute awaits scholarly analysis.

18. Quoted in Lowe, *Oprah Winfrey Speaks*, 122.

19. Quoted in LaTonya Taylor, "Church of O." This criticism is echoed, although from a slightly different theological perspective, in Kate Maver, "Making the New Age Normal," <http://www.equip.org/site/apps/nlnet/content3.aspx?c=muI1LaMNJrE&b=4136305 &content_id={1F1840BF-9455}-42E8-8B77-18B1B35EFFC0}&notoc=1.>

20. Delaney: 22 April 1987; Siegel: 11 November 1987 and 17 October 1988; Fulghum: 20 December 1988. Hay claims to have been invited on the show, but a gap in the transcript record during the period in which she would have appeared makes it impossible to confirm this (see Mark Oppenheimer, "Queen of the New Age," 62).

21. Harrison, "Importance of Being Oprah," 30, 28, 48. The term "New Age," frequently used by critics seeking to disparage Winfrey's beliefs, is misleading. While in its early years *The Oprah Winfrey Show* did examine topics such as witches (24 June 1987) and astrology (25 May 1988) and feature guests like Shirley MacLaine talking about past life regression (20 November 1986), the paranormal, the occult, and other phenomena associated with the "New Age" have historically played only minor roles in Winfrey's decidedly New Thought spirituality.

22. This generalization is based on the episode titles and guests listed in the Burrelle's Transcripts lists mentioned above. These are usually clear about what an episode will be about, and usually list celebrity guests (including authors) by name, but there are exceptions. Unfortunately, it is no longer possible to clarify ambiguities (or do any other research into the content of the programs themselves) because in

2007 Harpo Inc. discontinued its contract with Burrelle's Transcript Service in order to sell *Oprah Winfrey Show* transcripts via the Oprah.com web site. However, only transcripts from programs airing since the spring of 2005 have thus far been made available.

23. Williamson, *Return to Love*, 9. Further citations are noted parenthetically in the text.

24. *A Course in Miracles* is a volume of teachings "scribed" by Helen Schucman, with assistance from William Thetford. During the late 1960s, Schucman received extensive communications from a voice she claimed was that of Jesus Christ, and her transcriptions form the base of the course. Despite the popularity of the course (sources suggest over 1.5 million copies have been sold), to date no serious scholarship to speak of has delved into its principles or its followers, although intriguing discussions of the book's complicated copyright history can be found in the journalistic "How Jesus Got His Copyright Back," by Michael Braunstein (<http://www.jcim.net/How%20Jesus.pdf>), and in the legalistic "Gutenberg's Legacy," by Thomas F. Cotter.

25. "Marianne Williamson," 8.

26. Quoted in Peck, *Age of Oprah*, 107; Peck, *Age of Oprah*, 105.

27. "Conversations with Oprah: Deepak Chopra," 1. The fourth and fifth "Conversations" featured Holocaust survivor Elie Wiesel and attorney and novelist Andrew Vachss, who, along with Winfrey, had lobbied throughout 1992 for passage of the National Child Protection Act, which created a nationwide database of child sex offenders. Neither the Vachss nor the Wiesel transcripts are currently available for study. (M. Scott Peck, it should be noted, is no relation to the critic Janice Peck.)

28. "Deepak Chopra," 12, 9.

29. "Deepak Chopra," 16; "Conversations with Oprah: M. Scott Peck," 6.

30. "Conversations with Oprah: Maya Angelou," 7, 8, 11, 6, and passim, 15.

31. "Deepak Chopra," 23; "M. Scott Peck," 11, 12.

32. "M. Scott Peck," 11; "Deepak Chopra," 20.

33. "Deepak Chopra," 16–17; "M. Scott Peck," 20.

34. "Deepak Chopra," 20.

35. "Syndie Shows," 10.

36. "Good News," 5 November 1993; "Kindness," 15 February 1994; "Angels," 6 July 1994; Williamson, 11 January 1994; Dossey, 6 April 1994.

37. "Aliens," 18 April 1994; "Rapist," 18 May 1994; "Hussies," 20 August 1993.

38. Competitors' toxic titles cited in Abt and Seesholtz, "Shameless World," 181, and Shattuc, *Talking Cure*, 145, 146.

39. Mair, *Real Story*, 340.

40. "M. Scott Peck," 18.

41. On talk show wars see Abt and Seesholtz, "Shameless World," and Timberg, *Television Talk*.

42. Quoted in Lowe, *Oprah Speaks*, 128.

43. Dana Kennedy, "Oprah Act Two," <http://www.ew.com/ew/article/0,,303583,00.html>.

44. Quoted in Adler, *Uncommon Wisdom*, 76.

45. Johnson and Fineman, "Oprah Winfrey: A Life in Books," 60; quoted in Lowe, *Oprah Speaks*, 150, 126.

46. Mair, *Real Story*, 340.

47. Shattuc, *Talking Cure*, 154–55.

48. "Smelled Bad," 8 December 1994; "What Now?," 8 February 1995.

49. "Marianne Williamson," 11, 3; Redfield and Moore, 28 October 1994; Covey, 23 March 1995.

50. "Thank You," 19 September 1994; "Forgive," 1 December 1994; "Dreams," 16 January 1995; "Miracle," 14 April 1995; "Compassion," 21 June 1995.

51. "Season Premiere," 6.

52. Quoted in LaTonya Taylor, "Church of O." Original emphasis.

53. Quoted in Parkins, "Oprah Winfrey's Change Your Life TV," 145.

54. " 'Change Your Life'—Log On with Oprah," <http://www.findarticles.com/p/articles/mi_moEIN/is_1998_Oct_19/ai_53093122>. Vanzant is the founder of Inner Visions Institute for Spiritual Development, "a network of spiritual and holistic practitioners . . . [who] believe that empowerment is a function of knowing who you are, why you are on the planet and the role you play in the divine order of life." She calls Joel Goldsmith, former Christian Science practitioner and founder of the metaphysical offshoot The Infinite Way, her "Master" and was ordained a "minister of New Thought Christianity" after studying with Dr. Barbara King at the Hillside Truth Chapel in Atlanta. *In the Meantime*, 6; "Almasi" of Inner Visions Worldwide, email to the author, 19 August 2008.

55. Quoted in Parkins, "Change Your Life TV," 149.

56. Harrison, "Importance of Being Oprah," 28–30.

57. "Oprah Begins," 65.

58. "Deepak Chopra," 16.

59. This theme has become significantly more pronounced since 2002, thanks in part to growing participation by Suze Orman. It reached a crescendo in February 2007 when Winfrey showcased Rhonda Byrne's "think and grow rich" film *The Secret* over the course of two programs, sparking noticeable critical backlash. See, for example, Birkenhead, "Oprah's Ugly Secret," <http://www.salon.com/mwt/feature/2007/03/05/the_secret/>, and Ehrenreich, "Power of Negative Thinking," <http://www.nytimes.com/2008/09/24/opinion/24ehrenreich.html?_r=1&scp=1&sq=%22The%20Power%20of%20Negative%20Thinking.%22%20&st=cse&oref=slogin>.

60. Wang, "Everything's Coming Up Rosie"; Maio, "Next Wave," 11.

61. Sellers, "Business of Being Oprah," *Fortune*, 1 April 2002, <http://www.mutualofamerica.com/articles/Fortune/2002_04_08/Oprah1.asp>.

62. " 'Change Your Life'—Log On with Oprah."

63. "Spirit and Self," <http://www.oprah.com/spiritself/ss_landing.jhtml>. The site text has changed since the original access date, and no longer includes the statements about mission and purpose.

64. Quoted in Lowney, *Baring Our Souls*, 91.

65. Quoted in ibid., 140–41.

66. The club selected two memoirs: Maya Angelou's 1981 *The Heart of a Woman* (18 June 1997) and Malika Oufkir's 1999 *Stolen Lives: Twenty Years in a Desert Jail* (20

June 2001). Three short children's books by Bill Cosby, *The Meanest Thing to Say*, *The Treasure Hunt*, and *The Best Way to Play* (all 1997) were featured on 8 December 1997. The definition of "recent" was flexible, as one spokesperson noted: "The only real criteria we have is that the author has to be alive, so that he or she can appear on the program" (quoted in Rooney, *Reading with Oprah*, 109).

67. Max, "Oprah Effect"; Lehmann, "Book Fatigue."

68. For criticism in this vein, see, for example, Farr, *Reading Oprah*; McHenry, *Forgotten Readers*, 307–15; and Rooney, *Reading with Oprah*.

69. 18 October 1996, 17.

70. 23 June 2000, 11.

71. 15 June 1999, 16; 28 March 2000, 11; 5 April 2002, 12.

72. 18 November 1996, 13.

73. Janice Peck notes that Barbara Kingsolver (23 August 2000) also attempted to assert the conscious labor and practice that led to *The Poisonwood Bible*, only to have Winfrey "corral" the discussion. Peck, "Oprah Effect," 169.

74. 6 March 1998, 11, 4. For additional discussion of the *Paradise* episode, especially as evidence of Morrisonian exceptionalism, see Aubry, "Beware the Furrow."

75. Johnson and Fineman, "Oprah Winfrey: A Life in Books," 48.

76. Clemetson, "Oprah on Oprah," <http://www.newsweek.com.id/80655>.

77. Identification queries: 9 April 2000, 12; 9 May 1997, 15.

78. Postings to the web site's book club bulletin boards reveal a variety of reading modes and lively disagreement over meaning, as Kimberly Chabot Davis reveals in her reading of comments on *The Bluest Eye* in "Politics of Cross-Racial Empathy." See also Peck, "Oprah Effect."

79. Booth, *Company We Keep*, 138. Original emphasis.

80. Braden, *Spirits in Rebellion*, 108. Substantive images and talk of openness occur, for instance, in episodes devoted to Christina Schwartz's *Drowning Ruth*, Isabel Allende's *Daughter of Fortune*, Malika Oufkir's *Stolen Lives: Twenty Years in a Desert Jail*, Janet Fitch's *White Oleander*, and Ann-Marie McDonald's *Fall on Your Knees*.

81. 8 April 1997, 9. Additional citations are noted parenthetically in the text.

82. 18 June 1997, 4. Additional citations are noted parenthetically in the text.

83. 26 May 2000, 2, 8. Additional citations are noted parenthetically in the text.

84. Other love- and spirit-cultivating practices are discussed in Lofton, "Practicing Oprah," and Parkins, "Change Your Life TV."

85. 24 January 2001, 18; 23 August 2000, 2.

86. Curry, "Oprah Comes Full Circle," <http://www.msnbc.msn.com/id/12821 015/>.

87. Johnson and Fineman, "Oprah Winfrey: A Life in Books," 53.

88. Curry, "Oprah Comes Full Circle."

89. Quoted in LaTonya Taylor, "Church of O," 1.

90. Huber, *American Idea of Success*, 172.

91. hooks, *Talking Back*, 8.

92. Quoted in Stanley, "Specter of Oprah," 46.

93. Ibid., 47.

94. Winfrey quoted in Peck, *Age of Oprah*, 159.

95. Reinarman, "Twelve-Step Movements," 95, 97–98.

96. It is important to note that Winfrey has discussed and, to some extent, supported these and other progressive concerns on her program, though rarely with the consistency and to the extent that progressives would like.

97. On this point see, for example, Wallis, *God's Politics*.

98. Tompkins, *Sensational Designs*, 127, 133.

99. On this topic, see also Agnew, *Worlds Apart*; Elizabeth Clark, " 'Sacred Rights of the Weak' "; and Kete, *Sentimental Collaborations*.

100. On empowerment through literacy, see, for example, Hall, " 'Oprahfication' of Literacy," and Aubry, "Beware the Furrow"; on dismantling cultural hierarchy, see Farr, *Reading Oprah*, and Rooney, *Reading with Oprah*. On the latent progressivism of recovery, see Room, " 'Healing Ourselves.' "

Afterword

1. *A Million Little Pieces* was published as a memoir to much fanfare in 2003; it was the first pick of Oprah's Book Club when the club turned from "classics" back to contemporary titles in fall 2005. In the book Frey claimed, among other things, to have a lengthy arrest record for drug possession and distribution as well as felony assault and disorderly conduct, and to have served three months in prison. In January 2006, the muckraking web site The Smoking Gun revealed that he was in fact once arrested on a drunk-driving charge and spent a few hours at the police station while friends arranged bail. The site also suggested Frey's book exaggerated his role in the accidental death of a high school classmate, changed details of the purported suicide of the girlfriend he met in rehab, and lied about receiving a root canal without benefit of anesthesia ("A Million Little Lies"). Despite the charges, Frey insisted he had told what he called "the emotional truth" of his experiences, and that the details were relatively unimportant. Winfrey originally stood by him, and then withdrew her support, castigating him on her program for lying. For a nuanced reading of how the Winfrey-Frey affair played out, see Adam Miller, "Man Who Kept Oprah Awake at Night."

2. The clinic's name is never mentioned in the book, but Frey has named it in interviews since.

3. Frey, *Million Little Pieces*, 9. Further references cited parenthetically in the text.

4. Frey made his debt to modernism explicit in articles surrounding the publication of *A Million Little Pieces*, invoking as his role models authors like William Burroughs, Ferdinand Céline, and Ernest Hemingway. See Joe Hagan, "New Staggering Genius," and Karen Valby, "James Frey Does Not Care."

5. Gilbert and Gubar, *No Man's Land*.

6. Douglas, *Terrible Honesty*. Citations noted parenthetically in the text. Douglas actually touches on the founding of Alcoholics Anonymous in her text, treating it briefly (138–39), along with the development of New Thought religions, as a revolt against ecclesiastical and medical authority.

7. Kimberly Chabot Davis, *Postmodern Texts*, 2.

8. Even among those who would recuperate Victorian women's culture, there has

been dissent. On the tension within the academy and the feminist movement about whether to abandon this project (ironically, often called "recovery") in order to publish more explicitly oppositional women authors, see Murray, *Mixed Media*, especially chapters 2 and 4.

9. One substratum of academic inquiry where the investigation of recovery culture might find a home is within the slowly but steadily growing domain of scholarship on middlebrow culture. This woman-centered realm of earnest realism has always distanced itself from modernism's (and postmodernism's) most ambitious formal experiments, and has been the source of male critical disdain as a result. Scholars treating the middlebrow have been attentive to the importance of spirituality to their readers (see, for example, Long, *Book Clubs*, and Smith, "What Would Jesus Read?") and taken seriously the ways that identification and other forms of affective engagement motivate their reading practices (see, for example, Ehrhardt, *Writers of Conviction*, Harker, *America the Middlebrow*, and Radway, *Feeling for Books*). But they have also identified as a central feature of middlebrow culture its instrumental value: its promise to middle- and upper-middle-class readers that by reading it, they will allay their anxieties about their cultural incompetencies and better negotiate the competitive knowledge economy of late capitalism (see, for example, Rubin, *Making of Middlebrow Culture*, and Turner, *Marketing Modernism*). While recovery culture may be instrumental, its instrumentalities are decidedly not directed at keeping up with the Joneses. As a result, while there are some clear affinities, recovery sits somewhat uneasily within the terrain of the middlebrow.

10. In addition to the left-leaning critics previously cited in the text, see also the somewhat more libertarian and/or communitarian arguments against recovery or "therapeutic" culture made by Bellah et al. in *Habits of the Heart*; Berlant in "Subject of True Feeling," "Poor Eliza," and *Queen of America*; Imber, *Therapeutic Culture*; Lasch, *Culture of Narcissism*; Lasch-Quinn, *Race Experts*; and Rieff, *Triumph of the Therapeutic*.

11. Aubry, "Afghanistan Meets the *Amazon*"; Davis, *Postmodern Texts* and "Politics of Cross-Racial Empathy."

12. Grossberg, *We've Gotta Get Out*, 86–87. The classic interpretation of American populism as a precondition or sign of illiberalism is Hofstadter, *Age of Reform*. For more balanced accounts, see McMath, *American Populism*, and Kazin, *Populist Persuasion* and *Godly Hero*. The capture of late twentieth-century populist energies by the Republican Party is documented in Perlstein, *Before the Storm*.

BIBLIOGRAPHY

Archival Sources
Dallas, Tex.
Searcy W.'s Library, The White House Group [of Alcoholics Anonymous]
New York, N.Y.
Alcoholics Anonymous Archives
Providence, R.I.
John Hay Library, Brown University
Chester H. Kirk Collection on Alcoholism and Alcoholics Anonymous
Dr. Bob Archives—The Robert Holbrook Smith Collection of Books,
Manuscripts, and Memorabilia
San Francisco, Calif.
James C. Hormel Gay and Lesbian Center, San Francisco Public Library
Jean Swallow Papers

Twelve-Step Publications
"AA Pamphlets." <http://www.silkworth.net/aa/aa_pamphlets.html>. 13 May 2007.
AAWS [Alcoholics Anonymous World Services, Inc.]. "The AA Archives." <http://www
.aa.org/lang/en/en_pdfs/f-47_theaaarchives.pdf>. 20 March 2009.
——. "AA Preamble." <http://www.aa.org/lang/en/en_pdfs/smf-92_en.pdf>. 20
March 2009.
——. *The AA Service Manual Combined with Twelve Concepts for World Service by Bill
W.* New York, 2001.
——. *Alcoholics Anonymous: Seventy Years of Growth.* New York, 2005.
——. *Alcoholics Anonymous: The Story of How Many Thousands of Men and Women
Have Recovered from Alcoholism.* 4th ed. New York, 2001.
——. *Alcoholics Anonymous Comes of Age.* New York, 1957, 1985.
——. "Archives Guidelines." <http://www.aa.org/lang/en/en_pdfs/mg-17_archives
.pdf>. 20 March 2009.
——. "Archives Workbook." <http://www.aa.org/lang/en/pdf/products/m-44i_
archivesworkbook.pdf>. 20 March 2009.
——. Conference Reports, 1951–2006.
——. "Do You Think You're Different?" New York, 1976.
——. *Dr. Bob and the Good Oldtimers.* New York, 1980.
——. "Estimates of AA Groups and Members." <http://www.aa.org/lang/en/subpage
.cfm?page=74>. 14 November 2008.
——. "Let's Be Friendly with Our Friends." New York, 1958.
——. "Oral History Kit." <http://www.aa.org/lang/en/en_pdfs/en_oralhistorieskit
.pdf>. 20 March 2009.

——. *Pass It On: The Story of Bill Wilson and How the AA Message Reached the World.* New York, 1984.

——. "Three Talks to Medical Societies by Bill W., Co-Founder of AA." New York, 1950.

——. "The Twelve Steps of Alcoholics Anonymous." <http://www.aa.org/en_pdfs/smf-121_en.pdf>. 1 March 2009.

——. *Twelve Steps and Twelve Traditions.* New York, 1952.

——. "The Twelve Traditions of Alcoholics Anonymous." <http://www.aa.org/pdf/products/p-28_thetweltradofaa.pdf>. 8 March 2009.

Adult Children of Alcoholics Anonymous. "Early History." <http://www.adultchildren.org/lit/EarlyHistory.s> 13 February 2007.

Al-Anon Family Groups. *The Al-Anon Family Groups.* Virginia Beach, n.d.

——. *From Survival to Recovery: Growing Up in an Alcoholic Home.* New York, 1994.

——. "Introduction." <http://www.al-anon.alateen.org/pdf/mediakit/mkintro.pdf>. 20 March 2009.

Alcoholics Anonymous of Akron, Ohio. "A Guide to the Twelve Steps of Alcoholics Anonymous." Akron: Akron Area Intergroup Office, ca. mid-1940s. Rev. ed., 1999.

——. "A Manual for Alcoholics Anonymous." Akron: Akron Area Intergroup Office, ca. mid-1940s. 6th rev. ed., 1999.

——. "Second Reader for Alcoholics Anonymous." Akron: Akron Area Intergroup Office, ca. mid-1940s. Rev. ed., 1999.

——. "Spiritual Milestones in Alcoholics Anonymous." Akron: Akron Area Intergroup Office, ca. mid-1940s. Rev. ed., 1999.

Augustine Fellowship. "What Is Sex and Love Addicts Anonymous?" <http://www.slaafws.org/>. 7 March 2009.

"Authors of Stories from the Book *Alcoholics Anonymous.*" <http://silkworth.net/aabiography/storyauthors.html>. 5 October 2008.

B., Clifford, and Myers R. *The Primary Purpose Group Big Book Study Guide.* Dallas: Primary Purpose Group, 2000.

B., Dick. "Conference Approved Myths." <http://www.dickb.com/conference-approved.shtml>. 14 August 2006.

——. *Dr. Bob and His Library: A Major AA Spiritual Source.* Kihei, Maui, Hawaii: Paradise Research Publications, 1992.

——. *The Good Book and the Big Book: AA's Roots in the Bible.* Rev. ed. Kihei, Maui, Hawaii: Paradise Research Publications, 1995.

——. *Good Morning! Quiet Time, Morning Watch, Meditation, and Early AA.* Kihei, Maui, Hawaii: Paradise Research Publications, 1996.

——. *The James Club and the Original AA Program's Absolute Essentials.* 4th ed. Kihei, Maui, Hawaii: Paradise Research Publications, 2008.

B., Jim. "Memoirs of Jimmy: The Evolution of Alcoholics Anonymous." <http://www.aabibliography.com/jim_burwell_aahistory.html>. 10 March 2009.

B., Mel. *New Wine: The Spiritual Roots of the Twelve Step Miracle.* Center City, Minn.: Hazelden, 1991.

"Big Book Changes." <http://www.barefootsworld.net/aabigbookchanges.html>. 1 March 2009.

"Bill D–. AA Member #3." <http://www.scratchinpost.net/barefootbob/aabilld-aa3.html>. 9 March 2009.

"Biography: 'The Lone Endeavor.'" <http://silkworth.net/aabiography/patcooper.html>. 10 March 2009.

Bishop, Charles, Jr. "Spirituality Versus Legalism in Alcoholics Anonymous." 1999. <http://dickb.com/fear.shtml>. 17 May 2007.

Bishop, Charles, and Bill Pittman. *To Be Continued . . . The Alcoholics Anonymous World Bibliography 1935–1994*. Wheeling: Bishop of Books, 1994.

Chicago Area Alcoholics Anonymous. "AA: God's Instrument." Chicago, n.d.

——. "AA Is a Tender Trap." Chicago, n.d.

——. "Alcoholics Anonymous: The Long Haul." Chicago, n.d.

——. "Alcoholics Anonymous 'Willingness.'" Chicago, n.d.

——. "The Devil and AA." Chicago, n.d.

——. "Impressions of AA." Chicago, n.d.

——. "It's All in the Mind." Chicago, n.d.

——. "Out of the Fog." Chicago, n.d.

Chesnut, Glenn. "The Ancestor of the Little Red Book." <http://hindsfoot.org/mnclass1.html>. 29 April 2008.

——. "Classic Protestant Liberalism and AA." <http://hindsfoot.org/ProtLib.html>. 26 April 2007.

——. "The Earliest Printings of Richmond Walker's *24 Hours a Day*." <http://hindsfoot.org/rwcvphot.html>. 14 July 2006.

——. "Early Black AA Along the Chicago-Gary-South Bend Axis." <http://hindsfoot.org/Nblack1.html>. 4 October 2008.

——. "The First Edition of the Little Red Book." <http://hindsfoot.org/ed02.html>. 29 April 2008.

——. *The Lives and Teachings of AA Old Timers*. 2 vols. South Bend, Ind.: iUniverse, 2005.

——. "Note." Preface to "An Interpretation of the 12 Steps (The Detroit Pamphlet)." <http://hindsfoot.org/Detro.html>. 9 October 2008.

——. "Richmond Walker and New York, 1953–1954." 2004. <http://health.groups.yahoo.com/group/AAHistoryLovers/message/1999>. 14 July 2006.

——. "Richmond Walker and the Twenty-Four Hour Book." 2003. <http://hindsfoot.org/RWfla1.html>. 14 July 2006.

Clutterers Anonymous. "What Is Clutterers Anonymous?" <http://www.clutterersanonymous.net>. 14 February 2007.

Co-Dependents Anonymous. "The Welcome of Co-Dependents Anonymous." <http://www.codependents.org/foundation-docs-welcome.php >. 5 October 2007.

Debtors Anonymous. "History of Debtors Anonymous." <http://www.debtorsanonymous.org/about/history.htm>. 7 March 2009.

Emotions Anonymous. "Emotions Anonymous." <http://www.emotionsanonymous.org>. 14 February 2007.

Gamblers Anonymous. "History." <http://www.gamblersanonymous.org/history.html>. 15 March 2007.

GSOWatch. "Documents Concerning AA History." <http://gsowatch.aamo.info/aaws/index.htm>. 9 October 2008.

H., Jim. "Editorial Statement." *Our Primary Purpose Forum* 1, no. 1 (1994). <http://aabbsg.de/oppf/OPPF0101.htm>. 15 May 2007.

Hepatitis C Anonymous, Inc. "HCV Hepatitis C Anonymous." <http://www.hcvanonymous.com/default.htm>. 14 February 2007.

K., Mitchell. *How It Worked: The Story of Clarence H. Snyder and the Early Days of Alcoholics Anonymous in Cleveland, Ohio*. Washingtonville, N.Y.: AA Big Book Study Group, 1991.

The Language of the Heart: Bill W.'s Grapevine Writings. New York: AA *Grapevine*, 1988.

Narcotics Anonymous. "Basic Information." <http://www.na.org/basic.htm>. 20 July 2008.

———. *It Works, How and Why: The 12 Steps and 12 Traditions of Narcotics Anonymous*. Van Nuys, Calif., 1993.

———. *Miracles Happen: The Birth of Narcotics Anonymous in Words and Pictures*. Chatsworth, Calif., 1998

———. *Narcotics Anonymous*. Van Nuys, Calif., 1987.

Nicotine Anonymous. "A Brief History." <http://www.nicotine-anonymous.org/admin/prod_images/Brief%20History%20of%20Nicotine%20Anonymousrevised.pdf>. 7 March 2009.

P., Tom Jr. "Gresham's Law and Alcoholics Anonymous." *24 Magazine* (July 1976): 4–22.

P., Wally. *Back to Basics: The Alcoholics Anonymous Beginner's Meetings*. Tucson: Faith with Works Publishing, 1997.

———. *But, for the Grace of God: How Intergroups & Central Offices Carried the Message of Alcoholics Anonymous in the 1940s*. Wheeling: Bishop of Books, 1995.

S., Buddy. "How AA Got Started in Arkansas." 1983. Typescript in the author's possession.

S., Clarence. *AA Sponsorship . . . Its Opportunities and Its Responsibilities*. Cleveland: Cleveland Central Committee, 1944. Reprinted in Mitchell K., *How It Worked: The Story of Clarence H. Snyder and the Early Days of Alcoholics Anonymous in Cleveland, Ohio*. Washingtonville, N.Y.: AA Big Book Study Group, 1991.

S., Walter. *Handles for Sobriety*. East Moline, Ind.: Bright Star Press, n.d.

———. *Stinkin' Thinkin': (Thoughts for)*. East Moline, Ind.: Bright Star Press, n.d.

———. "This Is the Bright Star Press." East Moline, Ind.: Bright Star Press, n.d.

Shehan, Arthur. "*Alcoholics Anonymous* First Editions." Typescript in author's possession.

S[hehan], Arthur, Tom E., and Glenn C[hesnut]. "Alcoholics Anonymous (AA) Recovery Outcome Rates." Updated edition, 11 October 2008. <http://hindsfoot.org/recout01.pdf>. 18 March 2009.

O., Paul. ed. *Unofficial Guide to the Twelve Steps*. Laguna Nigel, Calif., 1990.

W., Ed, and Barry C. *The Little Red Book*. 50th anniversary ed. Center City, Minn.: Hazelden, 1996.

W., Searcy. *Searcy's Book: Two Different Proven Methods on How to Experience the 12 Steps of AA*. Dallas, 1990.

White Bison, Inc. *The Red Road to Wellbriety: In the Native American Way*. Center City, Minn.: Hazelden, 2006.

Wilson, Bill. "AA History and How The Big Book Was Put Together." Talk given in Fort Worth, 1954. <http://www.barefootsworld.net/aabook1954.html>. 25 October 2008.

Wilson, Lois. *Lois Remembers: Memoirs of the Co-founder of Al-Anon and the Wife of the Co-founder of Alcoholics Anonymous*. Virginia Beach: Al-Anon Family Group Headquarters, 1979.

Workaholics Anonymous. "The History of Workaholics Anonymous." <http://www.workaholics-anonymous.org/page.php?page=history>. 7 March 2009.

Yoder, Mose. *Grateful Thoughts*. Ca. mid-1960s. Rev. ed., ca. mid-1990s.

——. "Mose Yoder's AA Lead, 1976." In *The Journey of Mose and Mary Yoder*, complied and transcribed by Katie Yoder-Hochstetler, edited by Lisa Mae Menold-Hochstetler, 25–42. Mogadore, Oh.: privately printed, 2005.

Interviews and Correspondence with the Author

"Almasi." Inner Visions Worldwide. August 2008.

Black, Claudia. March 2009.

Borne, Allan. April 2005.

C., Pam. March 2009.

Casey-Elliott, Karen. June 2003; December 2005.

Crea, Mark. April 2003.

Erickson, Jim. July 2003.

Filiatreau, Amy. August 2007.

G., Karen. August 2008.

Ginsburg, Susan. May 2005.

Glusman, John. March 2005.

Grady, Tom. June 2003.

Hammond, Bill. April 2005.

Kauffman, Louis. May 2003.

L., Elisabeth. November 2005.

M., Vinnie. September 2001.

"Mary." Women for Sobriety. October 2008.

Post, Rebecca. May 2003.

Rott, Ruby. December 2005.

Santon, Judit. September 2001.

Skolnick, Irene. April 2005.

Spicer, Jerry. May 2003.

Spohn, David. June 2003.

Swift, Harry. July 2003.

The Oprah Winfrey Show *Transcripts*

"Book Club Finale" [Maya Angelou, *The Heart of a Woman*]. 18 June 1997.

"Book Club—Toni Morrison" [*Paradise*]. 6 March 1998.

"Conversations with Oprah: Maya Angelou." 13 July 1993.

"Conversations with Oprah: Deepak Chopra." 12 July 1993.

"Conversations with Oprah: Dr. M. Scott Peck." 14 July 1993.

"How'd They Do That?" [Jacquelyn Mitchard, *The Deep End of the Ocean*]. 18 November 1996.

"The Man Who Kept Oprah Awake at Night" [James Frey, *A Million Little Pieces*]. 26 October 2005.

"Marianne Williamson." 14 December 1994.

"Newborn Quintuplets Come Home." 18 October 1996.

"Oprah's Book Club" [Melinda Haynes, *Mother of Pearl*]. 9 September 1999.

"Oprah's Book Club" [Alice Hoffman, *Here on Earth*]. 9 April 1998.

"Oprah's Book Club" [Barbara Kingsolver, *The Poisonwood Bible*]. 23 August 2000.

"Oprah's Book Club" [Sue Miller, *While I Was Gone*]. 23 June 2000.

"Oprah's Book Club" [Toni Morrison, *The Bluest Eye*]. 26 May 2000.

"Oprah's Book Club—*Daughter of Fortune* [Isabel Allende]." 28 March 2000.

"Oprah's Book Club—*Fall on Your Knees* [Ann-Marie MacDonald]." 5 April 2002.

"Oprah's Book Club—*House of Sand and Fog* [Andre Dubus]." 24 January 2001.

"Salute to Mothers" [Shari Reynolds, *The Rapture of Canaan*]. 9 May 1997.

"Season Premiere." 8 September 1998.

"Selena's Family" [Ursula Hegi, *Stones from the River*]. 8 April 1997.

Books, Articles, Dissertations, and Papers

Abrams, Harry N. "Interview." By Paul Cummings. 14 March 1972. Archives of American Art, Smithsonian Institution. <http://www.aaa.si.edu/collections/oralhistories/transcripts/abrams72.htm>.

Abt, Vicki, and Mel Seesholtz. "The Shameless World of Phil, Sally, and Oprah: TV Talk Shows and the Deconstructing of Society." *Journal of Popular Culture* 28 (Summer 1994): 171–91.

Adler, Bill, ed. *The Uncommon Wisdom of Oprah Winfrey: A Portrait in Her Own Words*. New York: Carol Publishing, 2000.

Agent Orange [pseud.]. "The Orange Papers: One Man's Analysis of Alcoholics Anonymous." *The Orange Papers*. <http://www.orange-papers.org>. 17 May 2007.

Agnew, Jean-Christophe. *Worlds Apart: The Market and the Theater in Anglo-American Thought, 1550–1750*. Cambridge: Cambridge University Press, 1986.

Ahlstrom, Sydney E. *A Religious History of the American People*. New Haven, Conn.: Yale University Press, 1972.

Alexander, Jack. "Alcoholics Anonymous: Freed Slaves of Drink, Now They Free Others." *Saturday Evening Post*, 1 March 1941. 9–11, 90–92.

"Alice Walker Makes the Big Time." *California Living*, 15 August 1992. In *Alice Malsenior Walker: An Annotated Bibliography, 1968–1986*, edited by Louis H. Pratt and Darnell D. Pratt. Westport, Conn.: Meckler Corp., 1988.

Allan, Tuzyline Jita. *Womanist and Feminist Aesthetics: A Comparative Review*. Athens: Ohio University Press, 1995.

Allen, Chaney. *I'm Black & I'm Sober: A Minister's Daughter Tells Her Story about Fighting the Disease of Alcoholism—and Winning*. Minneapolis: Compcare, 1978.

Antze, Paul. "Symbolic Action in Alcoholics Anonymous." In *Constructive Drinking: Perspectives on Drink from Anthropology*, edited by Mary Douglas, 149–81. Cambridge: Cambridge University Press, 1987.

Apple [pseud]. "Deprogramming from Alcoholics Anonymous." *AADeprogramming*. <http://www.aadeprogramming.org>. 18 March 2007.

Asbury, Herbert. *The Great Illusion: An Informal History of Prohibition*. New York: Greenwood Press, 1979.

Aubry, Timothy. "Afghanistan Meets the *Amazon*: Reading *The Kite Runner* in America." *PMLA* 124, no. 1 (2009): 25–43.

———. "Beware the Furrow of the Middlebrow: Searching for Paradise on *The Oprah Winfrey Show*." *Modern Fiction Studies* 52, no. 2 (2006): 350–73.

Augustine. *City of God*. <http://www.clerus.org/bibliaclerusonline/en/bsq.htm>. 12 March 2009.

Bateson, Gregory. "The Cybernetics of 'Self': A Theory of Alcoholism." In *Steps to an Ecology of the Mind: Collected Essays in Anthropology, Psychiatry, Evolution, and Epistemology*, 309–37. San Francisco: Chandler Publishing, 1972.

Baylor, Courtney. *Remaking a Man*. New York: Moffat, Yard, and Company, 1919.

Beattie, Melody. *Codependent No More: How to Stop Controlling Others and Start Caring for Yourself*. New York: Harper/Hazelden, 1987.

Beckman, Linda J., and Hortensia Amaro. "Patterns of Women's Use of Alcohol Treatment Agencies." In *Alcohol Problems in Women: Antecedents, Consequences, and Intervention*, edited by Sharon C. Wilsnack and Linda J. Beckman, 319–48. New York: Guilford Press, 1984.

Beckwith, Sarah. *Christ's Body: Identity, Culture, and Society in Late Medieval Writings*. New York: Routledge, 1993.

Bederman, Gail. *Manliness and Civilization: A Cultural History of Gender and Race in the United States, 1880–1917*. Chicago: University of Chicago Press, 1995.

———. " 'The Women Have Had Charge of the Church Long Enough': The Men and Religion Forward Movement of 1911–1912 and the Masculinization of Middle-Class Protestantism." *American Quarterly* 41 (September 1989): 432–65.

Bellah, Robert, et al. *Habits of the Heart: Individualism and Commitment in American Life*. Berkeley: University of California Press, 1985.

Bepko, Claudia, ed. *Feminism and Addiction*. New York: Haworth Press, 1991.

Berlant, Lauren. "Poor Eliza." *American Literature* 70 (September 1998): 635–668.

———. *The Queen of America Goes to Washington City: Essays on Sex and Citizenship*. Durham, N.C.: Duke University Press, 1997.

———. "Race, Gender, and Nation in *The Color Purple*." *Critical Inquiry* 14, no. 4 (1988): 831–59.

———. "The Subject of True Feeling: Pain, Privacy, and Politics." In *Transformations: Thinking through Feminism*, edited by Sara Ahmed, Jane Kilby, Celia Lury, Maureen McNiel, and Beverly Skaggs, 33–47. London: Routledge, 2000.

Berlet, Chip. "The Write Stuff: U.S. Serial Print Culture from Conservatives out to Neo-Nazis." *Library Trends* 56, no. 3 (2008): 570–600.

Berube, Allan. *Coming Out under Fire: The History of Gay Men and Women in World War Two*. New York: Free Press, 1990.

"Between the Sheets: The History of Overeaters Anonymous and Its Food Plans."
Shutitdown.net. <http://www.shutitdown.net/text/oa.html#15>. 15 March 2007.

Birkenhead, Peter. "Oprah's Ugly Secret." 5 March 2007. <http://
www.salon.com/mwt/feature/2007/03/05/the_secret/>. 8 May 2007.

Black, Claudia. *It Will Never Happen to Me.* Bainbridge Island, Wash.: MAC
Publishing, 1982.

Blum, Eva Maria, and Richard H. Blum. *Alcoholism: Modern Psychological Approaches
to Treatment.* San Francisco: Jossey-Bass, 1967.

Bobo, Jacqueline. *Black Women as Cultural Readers.* New York: Columbia University
Press, 1995.

Bolotin, Susan. "Voices from the Post-Feminist Generation." *New York Times
Magazine.* 17 October 1982, 28+.

Booth, Wayne C. *The Company We Keep: An Ethics of Fiction.* Berkeley: University of
California Press, 1988.

Borden, Audrey. *The History of Gay People in Alcoholics Anonymous, from the
Beginning.* New York: Haworth Press, 2007.

Bordo, Susan. *The Male Body.* New York: Farrar, Strauss, and Giroux, 1999.

Braden, Charles Samuel. *Spirits in Rebellion: The Rise and Development of New
Thought.* Dallas: Southern Methodist University Press, 1963.

Brady, Maggie. "Culture in Treatment, Culture as Treatment: A Critical Appraisal of
Developments in Addictions Programs for Indigenous North Americans and
Australians." *Social Science and Medicine* 41, no. 11 (1995): 1487–98.

Braiker, Harriet. "Therapeutic Issues in the Treatment of Alcoholic Women." In
Alcohol Problems in Women: Antecedents, Consequences, and Intervention, edited
by Sharon C. Wilsnack and Linda J. Beckman, 349–68. New York: Guilford Press,
1984.

Braithwaite, Ann. "The Personal, the Political, Third-Wave, and Postfeminisms."
Feminist Theory 3, no. 3 (2002): 335–44.

Brandes, Stanley. *Staying Sober in Mexico City.* Austin: University of Texas Press,
2002.

Braunstein, Michael. "How Jesus Got His Copyright Back." *Heartland Healing*,
November–December 2004. <http://www.jcim.net/How%20Jesus.pdf>). 10
November 2008.

Braus, Patricia. "Selling Self-Help." *American Demographics* (March 1992): 48–52.

Brereton, Virginia Lieson. *From Sin to Salvation: Stories of Women's Conversions,
1800 to the Present.* Bloomington: Indiana University Press, 1991.

Brisbort, Alan. "Dry Drunk: Is Bush Making a Cry for Help?" *American Politics
Journal*, 24 September 2002. <http://www.americanpolitics.com/
20020924Bisbort.html>. 18 July 2008.

Brodhead, Richard H. *Cultures of Letters: Scenes of Reading and Writing in Nineteenth-
Century America.* Chicago: University of Chicago Press, 1993.

Brooks, Ann. *Postfeminisms: Feminism, Cultural Theory, and Cultural Forms.* New
York: Routledge, 1997.

Brown, Sally, and David Brown. *A Biography of Mrs. Marty Mann: The First Lady of
Alcoholics Anonymous.* Center City, Minn.: Hazelden, 2001.

Buchman, Frank. *Remaking the World: The Speeches of Frank Buchman*. London: Blandford Press, 1947.

Bufe, Charles. *Alcoholics Anonymous: Cult or Cure?* Tucson, Ariz.: See Sharp Press, 1998.

Bush, George W., and Mickey Herskowitz. *A Charge to Keep: My Journey to the White House*. New York: Harper Paperbacks, 2001.

Cain, Arthur. "Alcoholics Anonymous: Cult or Cure?" *Harper's Magazine*, February 1963, 48–52.

Cain, Carole. "Personal Stories: Identity Acquisition and Self-Understanding in Alcoholics Anonymous." *Ethos* 19, no. 2 (1991): 210–53.

Camfield, Gregg. "The Moral Aesthetics of Sentimentality: A Missing Key to *Uncle Tom's Cabin*." *19th-Century Literature* 43, no. 3 (1988): 319–45.

Campbell, Ted. *The Religion of the Heart: A Study of European Religious Life in the Seventeenth and Eighteenth Centuries*. Columbia: University of South Carolina Press, 1991.

Cantril, Hadley. *The Psychology of Social Movements*. New York: John Wiley, 1941.

Carnegie, Dale. *How to Win Friends and Influence People*. New York: Simon and Schuster, 1936.

Carwardine, Richard. *Transatlantic Revivalism: Popular Evangelicalism in Britain and America, 1790–1865*. Westport, Conn.: Greenwood Press, 1978.

Casey, Karen. *Each Day a New Beginning: Daily Meditations for Women*. Center City, Minn.: Hazelden, 1982.

——. *The Love Book*. Center City, Minn.: Hazelden, 1985.

——. "The Portrayal of American Indian Women in a Select Group of American Novels." Ph.D. diss., University of Minnesota, 1979.

Casey, Karen, and Martha Vanceburg. *The Promise of a New Day*. Center City, Minn.: Hazelden, 1983.

Cermak, Timmen. *Diagnosing and Treating Co-Dependence*. Minneapolis: Johnson Institute Books, 1986.

" 'Change Your Life'—Log On with Oprah." *Business Wire*. 19 October 1998. <http://www.findarticles.com/p/articles/mi_m0EIN/is_1998_Oct_19/ai_53093122>. 11 November 2006.

Chauncey, George. *Gay New York: Gender, Urban Culture, and the Makings of the Gay Male World, 1890–1940*. New York: Basic Books, 1994.

"Chavez Extends Anti-Bush Tirade on Visit to Harlem." *Breitbart.com*. <http://www.breitbart.com/article.php?id=060921201049.4stienz0&show_article=1>. 18 July 2008.

Chavigny, Katherine. "Reforming Drunkards in Nineteenth-Century America: Religion, Medicine, Therapy." In *Altering American Consciousness: Historical Perspectives on Drug and Alcohol Use, 1800–1997*, edited by Sarah W. Tracy and Caroline J. Acker, 108–23. Amherst: University of Massachusetts Press, 2004.

Cheever, Susan. *My Name is Bill: Bill Wilson: His Life and the Creation of Alcoholics Anonymous*. New York: Simon and Schuster, 2004.

Christian, Barbara. *Black Feminist Criticism: Perspectives on Black Women Writers*. New York: Pergamon Press, 1985.

Clark, Elizabeth B. " 'The Sacred Rights of the Weak': Pain, Sympathy, and the Culture of Individual Rights in Antebellum America." *Journal of American History* 82, no. 2 (1995): 463–93.

Clark, Walter Houston. *The Oxford Group, Its History and Significance*. New York: Bookman Associates, 1951.

Clemetson, Lynette. "Oprah on Oprah." *Newsweek*, 8 January 2001, 38–44. <http://www.newsweek.com/ID/80655>. 22 March 2009.

Clinton, Bill. *My Life*. New York: Knopf, 2004.

Compaine, Benjamin, and Douglas Gomery, eds. *Who Owns the Media? Competition and Concentration in the Mass Media Industry*. Mahwah, N.J.: Lawrence Erlbaum Associates, 2000.

Connor, Tracy. "Newser's Book: Ford Saw Clinton as a Sex 'Addict.' " *New York Newsday*. 28 October 2007. <http://www.nydailynews.com/news/us_world/2007/10/28/2007-10-28_newsers_book_ford_saw_clinton_as_a_sex_a.html>. 18 July 2008.

Conrad, Peter, and Joseph W. Schneider. *Deviance and Medicalization: From Badness to Sickness*. Philadelphia: Temple University Press, 1992.

Cotter, Thomas F. "Gutenberg's Legacy: Copyright, Censorship, and Religious Pluralism." *California Law Review* 91 (March 2003): 323–92.

Covington, Stephanie. *Helping Women Recover: A Program for Treating Addiction*. San Francisco: Jossey-Bass, 1999.

Coyhis, Don, and William L. White. "Alcohol Problems in Native America: Changing Paradigms and Clinical Practices." *Alcoholism Treatment Quarterly* 20, no. 3/4 (2002): 157–65.

Crane, R. S. "Suggestions toward a Genealogy of the 'Man of Feeling.' " *ELH* 1, no. 3 (1934): 205–30.

Crowley, John W., and William L. White. *Drunkard's Refuge: The Lessons of the New York Inebriate Asylum*. Amherst: University of Massachusetts Press, 2004.

Culler, Jonathan. *On Deconstruction: Theory and Criticism after Structuralism*. Ithaca, N.Y.: Cornell University Press, 1982.

Cunningham, Raymond J. "The Emmanuel Movement: A Variety of American Religious Experience." *American Quarterly* 14 (Spring 1962): 48–63.

Curry, Ann. "Oprah Comes Full Circle." *NBC News Dateline*. 21 May 2006. <http://www.msnbc.msn.com/id/12821015/>. 6 July 2008.

Danky, James. "The Oppositional Press." In *A History of the Book in America*, vol. 5, edited by David Nord, Joan Shelley Rubin, and Michael Schudson. Chapel Hill: University of North Carolina Press, forthcoming.

Dannenbaum, Jed. *Drink and Disorder: Temperance Reform in Cincinnati from the Washingtonian Revival to the WCTU*. Champaign: University of Illinois Press, 1984.

Darnton, Robert. "What Is the History of Books?" In *Reading in America: Literature and Social History*, edited by Cathy Davidson, 27–52. Baltimore: Johns Hopkins University Press, 1989.

Darrah, Mary C. *Sister Ignatia: Angel of Alcoholics Anonymous*. Chicago: Loyola University Press, 1992.

Davis, David Brion. *The Problem of Slavery in Western Culture*. Ithaca, N.Y.: Cornell University Press, 1966.

Davis, Kimberly Chabot. "Oprah's Book Club and the Politics of Cross-Racial Sympathy." *International Journal of Cultural Studies* 7, no. 4 (2004): 399–419.

——. *Postmodern Texts and Emotional Audiences: Identity and the Politics of Feeling*. West Lafayette: Purdue University Press, 2007.

deChant, Dell. "Myrtle Fillmore and Her Daughters: An Observation and Analysis of the Role of Women in Unity." In *Women's Leadership in Marginal Religions: Explorations Outside the Mainstream*, edited by Catherine Wessinger, 102–24. Urbana: University of Illinois Press, 1993.

Decker, Jeffrey Louis. *Made in America: Self-Styled Success from Horatio Alger to Oprah*. Minneapolis: University of Minnesota Press, 1998.

Denzin, Norman K. *The Alcoholic Self (Sociological Observations)*. Thousand Oaks, Calif.: Sage Publications, 1987.

——. *The Recovering Alcoholic (Sociological Observations)*. Thousand Oaks, Calif.: Sage Publications, 1987.

Derrida, Jacques. *Of Grammatology*. Trans. Gayatri Chakravorty Spivak. Baltimore: Johns Hopkins University Press, 1976.

"Diets Don't Work." *Rebecca's House Eating Disorder Treatment Programs*. <http://www.rebeccashouse.org/Rebecca_about.asp>. 22 March 2009.

Dobson, Joanne. "Reclaiming Sentimental Literature." *American Literature* 69, no. 2 (1997): 263–88.

Douglas, Ann. *The Feminization of American Culture*. New York: Knopf, 1977.

——. *Terrible Honesty: Mongrel Manhattan in the 1920s*. New York: Farrar, Straus, and Giroux, 1995.

Driberg, Tom. *The Mystery of Moral Re-Armament: A Study of Frank Buchman and His Movement*. New York: Knopf, 1965.

Dubiel, Richard M. *The Road to Fellowship: The Role of the Emmanuel Movement and the Jacoby Club in the Development of Alcoholics Anonymous*. Lincoln, Neb.: iUniverse, 2004.

Echols, Alice. *Daring to Be Bad: Radical Feminism in America, 1967–1975*. Minneapolis: University of Minnesota Press, 1989.

Ehrenreich, Barbara. *The Hearts of Men: American Dreams and the Flight from Commitment*. New York: Anchor Books, 1983.

——. "The Power of Negative Thinking." New York *Times*, 23 September 2008. <http://www.nytimes.com/2008/09/24/opinion/24ehrenreich.html?_r=1&scp=1&sq=ehrenreich.%20power%20of%20negative%20thinking&st=cse>. 22 March 2009.

Ehrhardt, Julia. *Writers of Conviction: Zona Gale, Dorothy Canfield Fisher, Rose Wilder Lane, and Josephine Herbst*. Columbia: University of Missouri Press, 2004.

Enke, Anne. *Finding the Movement: Sexuality, Contested Space, and Feminist Activism*. Durham, N.C.: Duke University Press, 2007.

Fahey, David. *Temperance and Racism: John Bull, Johnny Reb, and the Good Templars*. Lexington: University Press of Kentucky, 1996.

Faludi, Susan. *Backlash: The Undeclared War against American Women*. New York: Crown, 1991.

Fager, Wes. "The $traights Dot Com." <http://www.thestraights.com/>. 7 May 2008.

Farr, Cecilia Konchar. *Reading Oprah: How Oprah's Book Club Changed the Way America Reads*. Albany: State University of New York Press, 2004.

Feldman, Gayle. "On the Road to Recovery with Prentice Hall, Ballantine, Et Al." *Publishers Weekly*, November 3, 1989, 52–53.

Feminist Bookstore News 11, no. 6 (September 1983).

Ferree, Myra Marx, and Patricia Yancey Martin, eds. *Feminist Organizations: Harvest of the New Women's Movement*. Philadelphia: Temple University Press, 1995.

Fillmore, Kaye Middleton. " 'When Angels Fall': Women's Drinking as Cultural Preoccupation and as Reality." In *Alcohol Problems in Women: Antecedents, Consequences, and Intervention*, edited by Sharon C. Wilsnack and Linda J. Beckman, 7–36. New York: Guilford Press, 1984.

Fingarette, Herbert. *Heavy Drinking: The Myth of Alcoholism as a Disease*. Berkeley: University of California Press, 1988.

Fisher, Philip. *Hard Facts: Setting and Form in the American Novel*. New York: Oxford University Press, 1985.

Foucault, Michel. *Discipline and Punish: The Birth of the Prison*. New York: Pantheon Books, 1977.

Fox, Emmet. *The Sermon on the Mount*. New York: Harper and Brothers, 1938.

Franklin, Benjamin. *The Autobiography and Other Writings*. Selected and edited by L. Jesse Lemisch. New York: Signet Classics, 1961.

Frey, James. *A Million Little Pieces*. New York: Nan Talese/Doubleday, 2003.

Galanter, Marc. *Cults: Faith, Healing, and Coercion*. New York: Oxford University Press, 1999.

Gamson, Joshua. *Freaks Talk Back: Tabloid Talk Shows and Sexual Non-Conformity*. Chicago: University of Chicago Press, 1998.

Garrett, Michael Tlanusta, and Jane J. Goodman. "Mending the Broken Circle: Treatment of Substance Dependence among Native Americans." *Journal of Counseling & Development* 78, no. 4 (2000): 379–88.

Garvey, Ellen Gruber. "Out of the Mainstream and into the Streets: Small Press Magazines, the Underground Press, and Artists' Books." In *Perspectives on American Book History*, edited by Scott Casper, Joanne Chaison, and Jeffrey Groves, 367–402. Amherst: University of Massachusetts Press, 2002.

Gates, Henry Louis. *The Signifying Monkey: A Theory of African-American Literary Criticism*. New York: Oxford University Press, 1988.

Giddens, Anthony. *Modernity and Self-Identity: Self and Society in the Late Modern Age*. Stanford, Calif.: Stanford University Press, 1991.

Gilbert, James. *Men in the Middle: Searching for Masculinity in the 1950s*. Chicago: University of Chicago Press, 2005.

Gilbert, Sandra M., and Susan Gubar. *No Man's Land: The Place of the Woman Writer in the Twentieth Century*. 3 vols. New Haven, Conn.: Yale University Press, 1988.

Girard, Stephanie. " 'Standing at the Corner of Walk and Don't Walk': Vintage Contemporaries, *Bright Lights, Big City*, and the Problem of Betweenness." *American Literature* 68, no. 1 (1996): 161–85.

Gomberg, Edith Lisansky. "Gender Issues." In *Recent Developments in Alcoholism*, vol. 11: *Ten Years of Progress*, edited by Marc Galanter, 95–107. New York: Plenum Press, 1993.

——. "Special Populations." In *Alcohol, Science, and Society Revisited*, edited by Edith Lisansky Gomberg, Helen Raskin White, and John A. Carpenter, 337–54. Ann Arbor: University of Michigan Press and the Rutgers Center for Alcohol Studies, 1982.

Gomery, Douglas. "The Book Publishing Industry." In *Who Owns the Media: Competition and Concentration in the Mass Media Industry*, edited by Benjamin Compaine and Douglas Gomery. Mahwah, N.J.: Lawrence Erlbaum and Associates, 2000.

Goodman, Paul. *Of One Blood: Abolition and the Origins of Racial Equality*. Berkeley: University of California Press, 1998.

Graham, Allan W., and Terry Schulz, eds. *Principles of Addiction Medicine*. Chevy Chase, Md.: American Society of Addiction Medicine, 1998.

Grateful Members. *The Twelve Steps for Everyone . . . Who Really Wants Them*. Minneapolis: Compcare, 1977.

Greene, Bob, and Oprah Winfrey. *Make the Connection: Ten Steps to a Better Body— and a Better Life*. New York: Hyperion, 1996.

Greene, John Gardner. "The Emmanuel Movement, 1906–1929." *New England Quarterly* 7 (September 1934): 494–532.

Griffith, R. Marie. *Born Again Bodies: Flesh and Spirit in American Christianity*. Berkeley: University of California Press, 2004.

Griffiths, Paul J. *Religious Reading: The Place of Reading in the Practice of Religion*. New York: Oxford University Press, 1999.

Grossberg, Lawrence. *We Gotta Get Out of This Place: Popular Conservatism and Postmodern Culture*. New York: Routledge, 1992.

Gusfield, Joseph. *Symbolic Crusade: Status Politics and the American Temperance Movement*. Urbana: University of Illinois Press, 1963.

Gutjahr, Paul C. *An American Bible: A History of the Good Book in the United States, 1777–1880*. Stanford, Calif.: Stanford University Press, 1999.

Haaken, Janice. "From Al-Anon to ACOA: Codependence and the Reconstruction of Caregiving." *Signs* 18, no. 2 (1993): 321–45.

Hagan, Joe. "Meet the New Staggering Genius." *New York Observer*, 23 February 2003.

Haggard, Howard. "Critique of the Concept of the Allergic Nature of Alcohol Addiction." *Quarterly Journal of Studies on Alcohol* 5, no. 2 (1944): 233–41.

Hall, Elaine, and Marnie Salupo Rodriguez. "The Myth of Postfeminism." *Gender and Society* 17, no. 6 (2003): 878–902.

Hall, R. Mark. "The 'Oprahfication' of Literacy: Reading 'Oprah's Book Club.' " *College English* 65, no. 6 (2003): 646–67.

Hanisch, Carol. "The Personal Is Political." *The "Second Wave" and Beyond*. Alexandria, Va.: Alexander Street Press, 2006. <http://scholar.alexanderstreet.com/pages/viewpage.action?pageId=2259>. 4 July 2008.

Harbaugh, Lyn. "Sister Francis and the Ministry of High Watch: From New Thought to Alcoholics Anonymous." BA honors thesis, Smith College, 1995.

Harker, Jamie. *America the Middlebrow: Women's Novels, Progressivism, and Middlebrow Authorship between the Wars*. Amherst: University of Massachusetts Press, 2007.

Harris, Jennifer, and Elwood Watson, eds. *The Oprah Phenomenon*. Lexington: University Press of Kentucky, 2007.

Harris, Trudier. "On *The Color Purple*, Stereotypes, and Silence." *Black American Literary Forum* 18, no. 4 (1984): 155–61.

Harrison, Barbara Grizutti. "The Importance of Being Oprah." *New York Times Magazine*, 11 June 1989, 28–30, 46, 48, 54, 130, 134–35.

Hartigan, Francis. *Bill W.: A Biography of Alcoholics Anonymous Cofounder Bill Wilson*. New York: Macmillan, 2001.

Hatch, Nathan. *The Democratization of American Christianity*. New Haven, Conn.: Yale University Press, 1989.

Hawkesworth, Mary. "The Semiotics of Premature Burial: Feminism in a Post-feminist Age." *Signs* 29, no. 4 (2004): 961–85.

Hazelden Catalogue, 1969. Collection of the author.

"HCI Books (Health Communications, Inc.) Celebrates 25 Years in Publishing." N.d. Press release in author's possession.

Hebdige, Dick. *Subculture: The Meaning of Style*. London: Methuen, 1979.

Hendler, Glenn. *Public Sentiments: Structures of Feeling in Nineteenth-Century American Literature*. Chapel Hill: University of North Carolina Press, 2001.

Henley, William Ernest. "Invictus." 1875. <http://www.bartleby.com/103/7.html>. 25 March 2005.

Herman, Ellen. "The Twelve-Step Program: Cure or Cover?" *Utne Reader* (November-December 1988): 52–63. Reprint of "Getting to Serenity: Do Addiction Programs Sap Our Political Vitality?" *Out/Look* (Summer 1988): 16–21.

Hersey, Brook. "The Controlled Drinking Debates: A Review of Four Decades of Acrimony." April 2001. <http://www.doctordeluca.com/Library/AbstinenceHR/FourDecadesAcrimony.htm>. 18 July 2008.

Hill, Napoleon. *Think and Grow Rich!* 1937. Greenwich, Conn.: Fawcett Books, 1960.

Hofstadter, Richard. *The Age of Reform: From Bryan to F.D.R.* New York: Knopf, 1955.

Hoganson, Kristin. *Fighting for American Manhood: How Gender Politics Provoked the Spanish-American and Philippine-American Wars*. New Haven: Yale University Press, 2000.

Holder, Harold, Richard Lennox, and James Blose. "The Economic Benefits of Alcoholism Treatment: A Summary of Twenty Years of Research." *Journal of Employee Assistance Research* 1, no. 1 (1992): 63–82.

hooks, bell [Gloria Watkins]. *Sisters of the Yam: Black Women and Self-Recovery*. Boston: South End Press, 1993.

——. *Talking Back: Thinking Feminist, Thinking Black*. Boston: South End Press, 1989.

——. "Writing the Subject: Reading *The Color Purple*." In *Alice Walker*, edited by Harold Bloom, 251–28. New York: Chelsea House, 1989.

"How It All Started." *Association of Camps Farthest Out*. <http://www.acfona.org/index.asp?pageId=34>. 7 May 2008.

Huber, Richard M. *The American Idea of Success*. New York: McGraw-Hill, 1971.

Huyssen, Andreas. *After the Great Divide: Modernism, Mass Culture, Postmodernism, Theories of Representation and Difference*. Bloomington: Indiana University Press, 1986.

Hyde, Lewis. *The Gift: Imagination and the Erotic Life of Property*. New York: Vintage Books, 1983.

Imber, Jonathan, ed. *Therapeutic Culture: Triumph and Defeat*. New Brunswick, N.J.: Transaction, 2004.

Irvine, Leslie. *Codependent Forevermore: The Invention of Self in a Twelve Step Group*. Chicago: University of Chicago Press, 1999.

Jackson, Mary S. "Afrocentric Treatment of African American Women and Their Children in a Residential Chemical Dependency Program." *Journal of Black Studies* 26, no. 1 (1995): 17–30.

Jackson, Mary S., Richard C. Stephens, and Robert L. Smith. "Afrocentric Treatment in Residential Substance Abuse Care: The Iwo San." *Journal of Substance Abuse Treatment* 14, no. 1 (1997): 87–92.

James, William. *The Varieties of Religious Experience*. 1902. Reprint, with an introduction and notes by Wayne Proudfoot, New York: Barnes and Noble Classics, 2004.

Janzen, Ron. *The Rise and Fall of Synanon: A California Utopia*. Baltimore: Johns Hopkins University Press, 2001.

Jellinek, E. M. *The Disease Concept of Alcoholism*. New Haven, Conn.: Hillhouse Press, 1960.

——. "The First (1943) Summer Session of the School of Alcohol Studies." *Quarterly Journal of Studies on Alcohol* 4, no. 2 (1943): 187–94.

——. "Notes on the First Half Year's Experience at the Yale Plan Clinics." *Quarterly Journal of Studies on Alcohol* 5, no. 2 (1944): 279–302.

——. "Outline of Basic Policies." *Quarterly Journal of Studies on Alcohol* 3, no. 1 (1942): 103–24.

——. "Phases of Alcohol Addiction." *Quarterly Journal of Studies on Alcohol* 13, no. 4 (1952): 673–84.

——. "Phases in the Drinking History of Alcoholics." *Quarterly Journal of Studies on Alcohol* 7, no. 1 (1946): 1–88.

Jensen, George H. *Storytelling in Alcoholics Anonymous: A Rhetorical Analysis*. Carbondale: Southern Illinois University Press, 2000.

Johnson, Bruce Holley. "The Alcoholism Movement in America: A Study in Cultural Innovation." Ph.D. diss., University of Illinois, 1973.

Johnson, Marilyn, and Dana Fineman. "Oprah Winfrey: A Life in Books." *Life*, September 1997, 46–48, 53, 54, 56, 60.

Jones, Margaret. "The Rage for Recovery." *Publishers Weekly*, 25 November 1990, 16–24.

Jones, Robert Kenneth. "The Development of Medical Sects." *Journal of Religion and Health* 22, no. 4 (1983): 307–21.

Jordan, Judith, et al. *Women's Growth in Connection: Writings from the Stone Center*. Boston: Guilford Press, 1991.

Kaminer, Wendy. "Feminism's Identity Crisis." *Atlantic Monthly*, October 1993, 51–68.

——. *I'm Dysfunctional, You're Dysfunctional: The Recovery Movement and Other Self-Help Fashions.* Boston: Addison-Wesley, 1992.

——. "Is Clinton a Sex Addict?" *Slate.* 22 March 1998. <http://www.slate.com/id/2495/>. 31 August 2008.

Kaskutas, Lee. "Pathways to Self-Help among Women for Sobriety." *American Journal of Drug and Alcohol Abuse* 22, no. 2 (1996): 259–81.

——. "Women for Sobriety: A Qualitative Analysis." *Contemporary Drug Problems* 16 (Summer 1989): 177–200.

Kasl, Charlotte Davis. *Many Roads, One Journey: Moving Beyond the Twelve Steps.* New York: HarperCollins, 1992.

Katz, Alfred H. *Self-Help in America: A Social Movement Perspective.* New York: Twayne, 1993.

Kazin, Michael. *A Godly Hero: The Life of William Jennings Bryan.* New York: Anchor Books, 2007.

——. *The Populist Persuasion: An American History.* Ithaca, N.Y.: Cornell University Press, 1998.

Keller, Mark. "On Defining Alcoholism." *Alcohol and Health Research World* 15, no. 4 (1991), <http://findarticles.com/p/articles/mi_m0847/is_/ai_12754549>. 26 July 2006.

Kennedy, Dana. "Oprah Act Two." *Entertainment Weekly*, 9 September 1994. <http://www.ew.com/ew/article/0,,303583,00.html>.

Kennedy, Elizabeth. *Boots of Leather, Slippers of Gold: The History of a Lesbian Community.* New York: Routledge, 1993.

Kerr, K. Austin. *Organized for Prohibition: A New History of the Anti-Saloon League.* New Haven: Yale University Press, 1985.

Kete, Mary Louise. *Sentimental Collaborations: Mourning and Middle-Class Identity in Nineteenth-Century America.* Durham, N.C.: Duke University Press, 2000.

Kimmel, Michael. *Manhood in America: A Cultural History.* New York: Free Press, 1996.

Kirkpatrick, Jean. *Goodbye Hangovers, Hello Life.* New York: Atheneum, 1986.

——. *Turnabout: Help for a New Life.* New York: Doubleday, 1978.

Kitchen, Victor Constant. *I Was a Pagan.* New York: Harper and Brothers, 1934.

Klein, Joe. "Bill Clinton: Who Is This Guy?" *New York Magazine*, 20 January 1992. <http://nymag.com/ncws/features/40563>.

Kleinfeld, N. R. "Problems and a Few Solutions." *New York Times*, 28 December 1980, sec. 7, p. 3.

——. "The Shifting Paperback Market." *New York Times*, 10 October 1980, sec. D, p. 1.

Kurtz, Ernest. "Alcoholics Anonymous and the Disease Concept." *Alcoholism Treatment Quarterly* 20, no. 3/4 (2002): 5–40.

——. *Not-God: A History of Alcoholics Anonymous.* Center City, Minn.: Hazelden Educational Services, 1979.

L., Elisabeth. *Food For Thought: Daily Meditations for Overeaters.* Center City, Minn.: Hazelden, 1980.

Lasch, Christopher. *The Culture of Narcissism: American Life in an Age of Diminishing Expectations.* New York: Norton, 1978.

Lasch-Quinn, Elizabeth. *Race Experts: How Racial Etiquette, Sensitivity Training, and New Age Therapy Hijacked the Civil Rights Revolution*. New York: Norton, 2001.

The Layman with a Notebook. *What Is the Oxford Group?* New York: Oxford University Press, 1933.

Lean, Garth. *On the Tail of a Comet: The Life of Frank Buchman*. Colorado Springs: Helmers and Howard, 1988.

Lears, T. J. Jackson. "From Salvation to Self-Realization: Advertising and the Therapeutic Roots of the Consumer Culture, 1880–1930." In *The Culture of Consumption: Critical Essays in American History, 1880–1980*, edited by Richard Fox and T. J. Jackson Lears, 3–38. New York: Pantheon Books, 1983.

———. *No Place of Grace: Antimodernism and the Transformation of American Culture, 1880–1920*. New York: Pantheon Books, 1981.

Lehman, Chris. "Oprah's Book Club Fatigue." *Slate*. 10 April 2002. <http://www.slate.com/id/2064224/>. 30 October 2008.

Leland, Joy. "Alcohol Use and Abuse in Ethnic Minority Women." In *Alcohol Problems in Women: Antecedents, Consequences, and Intervention*, edited by Sharon Wilsnack and Linda J. Beckman, 66–96. New York: Guilford Press, 1984.

Lender, Mark Edward, and James Kirby Martin. *Drinking in America: A History*. New York: Free Press, 1982.

Lerner, Harriet Goldhor. "Problems for Profit." *Women's Review of Books* 7, no. 7 (1990): 15–16.

Levin, Jerome D. *The Clinton Syndrome: The President and the Self-Destructive Nature of Sexual Addiction*. Rocklin, Calif.: Prima Publishing, 1998.

Levine, Harry G. "The Discovery of Addiction: Changing Conceptions of Habitual Drunkenness in America." *Journal of Studies on Alcohol* 15 (1978): 493–506.

Lewis, Jay. "The Federal Role in Alcoholism Research, Treatment, and Prevention." In *Alcohol, Science, and Society Revisited*, edited by Edith Lisansky Gomberg, Helen Raskin White, and John A. Carpenter, 385–99. Ann Arbor: University of Michigan Press and the Rutgers Center for Alcohol Studies, 1982.

Lippy, Charles. *Do Real Men Pray? Images of the Christian Man and Male Spirituality in White Protestant America*. Knoxville: University of Tennessee Press, 2005.

"Live Your Best Life." <http://www.oprah.com/spiritself/ss_landing.jhtml>. 3 May 2001.

Lobdell, Jared. *This Strange Illness: Alcoholism and Bill W.* New York: Aldine de Gruyter, 2004.

Lofton, Kathryn. "Practicing Oprah; or, the Prescriptive Compulsion of Spiritual Capitalism." *Journal of Popular Culture* 39, no. 4 (2006): 599–621.

Long, Elizabeth. *Book Clubs: Women and the Uses of Reading in Everyday Life*. Chicago: University of Chicago Press, 2003.

Longshore, Douglas, Cheryl Grills, Kiku Annon, and Rhumel Grady. "Promoting Recovery from Drug Abuse: An Africentric Intervention." *Journal of Black Studies* 28, no. 3 (1998): 319–33.

Lowe, Janet, ed. *Oprah Winfrey Speaks*. New York: John Wiley and Sons, 1998.

Lowney, Kathleen S. *Baring Our Souls: TV Talk Shows and the Religion of Recovery, Social Problems and Social Issues*. New York: Aldine de Gruyter, 1999.

Macdonald, Dwight. "Masscult and Mid-Cult." In *Against the American Grain*, 3–75. New York: Random House, 1962.

Maio, Elsie. "The Next Wave: Soul Branding." *Design Management Journal* 10, no. 1 (1999): 10–16.

Mair, George. *Oprah Winfrey: The Real Story*. New York: Birch Lane, 2002.

Mann, Marty. "Formation of a National Committee for Education on Alcoholism." *Quarterly Journal of Studies on Alcohol* 5, no. 2 (1944): 354–58.

Maraniss, David. *First in His Class: A Biography of Bill Clinton*. New York: Simon and Schuster, 1996.

Marsden, George M. *Fundamentalism and American Culture: The Shaping of Twentieth Century Evangelicalism, 1870–1925*. New York: Oxford University Press, 1980.

Martin, Darnise. *Beyond Christianity: African Americans in a New Thought Church*. New York: New York University Press, 2005.

Martin, Denise. "Oprah Winfrey and Spirituality." In *The Oprah Phenomenon*, edited by Jennifer Harris and Elwood Watson, 147–64. Lexington: University Press of Kentucky, 2007.

Masciarotte, Gloria-Jean. "C'mon Girl: Oprah Winfrey and the Discourse of Feminine Talk." *Genders* 11 (1991): 81–110.

Maver, Kate. "Oprah Winfrey and Her Self-Help Saviors: Making the New Age Normal." *Christian Research Institute*. Statement DN403, 23, no. 4 (2001) <http://www.equip.org/site/apps/nlnet/content3.aspx?c=muI1LaMNJrE&b=4136305&content_id={1F1840BF-9455-42E8-8B77-18B1B35EF}FC0}&notoc=1>. 27 March 2006.

Max, D. T. "The Oprah Effect." *New York Times Magazine*, 26 December 1999, 36–41.

Maxwell, Milton. "The Washingtonian Movement." *Quarterly Journal of Studies on Alcohol* 11 (September 1950): 410–52.

McClellan, Michelle. " 'Lady Tipplers': Gendering the Modern Alcoholism Paradigm." In *Altering American Consciousness: The History of Alcohol and Drug Use in the United States, 1800–2000*, edited by Sarah W. Tracy and Caroline Jean Acker, 267–97. Amherst: University of Massachusetts Press, 2004.

McDowell, Deborah. " 'The Changing Same': Generational Connections and Black Women Novelists." *New Literary History* 18, no. 2 (1987): 281–302.

McDowell, Edwin. "Paperbacks: Turmoil in the Racks: The Second Paperback Revolution." *New York Times*, 29 September 1985, sec. 7, p. 35.

——. "Trade Paperbacks Reshaping Book Publishing." 22 April 1985, *New York Times*, sec. C, p. 13.

McElrath, Damien. *Further Reflections on Hazelden's Spiritual Odyssey*. Center City, Minn.: Hazelden, 1999.

——. *Hazelden: A Spiritual Odyssey*. Center City, Minn.: Hazelden, 1987.

——. *The Quiet Crusaders: The Untold Story Behind the Minnesota Model*. Center City, Minn.: Hazelden, 2001.

McGee, Micki. *Self-Help, Inc.: Makeover Culture in American Life*. New York: Oxford University Press, 2005

McHenry, Elizabeth. *Forgotten Readers: Recovering the Lost History of African-American Literary Societies*. Durham, N.C.: Duke University Press, 2002.

McKenney, Ruth. *Industrial Valley*. New York: Harcourt Brace, 1939.

McLoughlin, William G. *Revivals, Awakenings, and Reform*. Chicago: University of Chicago Press, 1978.

McMath, Robert C. Jr. *American Populism: A Social History, 1877–1898*. New York: Hill and Wang, 1990.

Meacham, Andrew. "AMA Declares All Drug Dependencies Diseases." *U.S. Journal of Drug and Alcohol Dependence* 11, no. 7 (1987): 1–20.

——. *Selling Serenity: Life among the Recovery Stars*. Boca Raton, Fla.: SIRS-Mandarin, 1999.

Menninger, Karl A. *Man against Himself*. New York: Harcourt, 1938.

Mercadante, Linda. *Victims and Sinners: Spiritual Roots of Addiction and Recovery*. Louisville: Westminster John Knox Press, 1996.

Meyer, Donald. *The Instructed Conscience: The Shaping of the American National Ethic*. Philadelphia: University of Pennsylvania Press, 1972.

Michael, John. *Sober, Clean, and Gay!* Minneapolis: Compcare, 1977.

Milgram, Gail Gleason. "The Summer School of Alcohol Studies: An Historical and Interpretive Review." In *Alcohol Interventions: Historical and Sociocultural Approaches*, edited by David Strug, S. Priyandarsini, and Merton Hyman, 59–74. New York: Haworth Press, 1986.

Miller, Adam. "The Man Who Kept Oprah Awake at Night: How and Why We Read the Lies of James Frey's *A Million Little Pieces*." BA honors thesis, College of William and Mary, 2008.

Miller, Cheryl. "Out from Under: A Talk with Writer/Editor Jean Swallow." *Feminist Writers Guild National Newsletter* (Summer 1986): 18–19.

Miller, Laura. "Is Clinton a Sex Addict?" *Salon*, January 1998. <http:// www.salon.com/feature/1998/01/cov_26feature.html>. 31 August 2008.

"A Million Little Lies: Exposing James Frey's Fiction Addiction." <http:// www.thesmokinggun.com/archive/0104061jamesfrey1.html>. 10 January 2006.

Mitgang, Herbert. "Alice Walker Recalls the Civil Rights Battle." *New York Times*, 16 April 1983, sec. 1, p. 13.

Morrissey, Elizabeth. "Contradictions Inhering in Liberal Feminist Ideology: Promotion and Control of Women's Drinking." *Contemporary Drug Problems* 13, no. 1 (1986): 65–88.

Moskowitz, Eva S. *In Therapy We Trust: America's Obsession with Self-Fulfillment*. Baltimore: Johns Hopkins University Press, 2001.

Murray, Simone. *Mixed Media: Feminist Presses and Publishing Politics*. London: Pluto Press, 2004.

Musto, David. *The American Disease: Origins of Narcotic Control*. 3rd ed. New Haven, Conn.: Yale University Press, 1999.

Nardi, Peter. "Alcoholism and Homosexuality: A Theoretical Perspective." In *Alcoholism and Homosexuality: Directions for Counseling and Therapy*, edited by Thomas O. Ziebold and John Mongeon, 9–25. New York: Haworth Press, 1981.

Nathan, Peter. "Human Behavioral Research on Alcoholism, with Special Emphasis on the Decade after the 1970s." In *Alcohol, Science, and Society Revisited*, edited by Edith Lisansky Gomberg, John A. Carpenter, and Helen Raskin White, 279–94. Ann Arbor: University of Michigan Press, 1983.

Nelson, Barbara. *Making an Issue of Child Abuse: Political Agenda Setting for Social Problems*. Chicago: University of Chicago Press, 1984.

Nelson, Dana. *National Manhood: Capitalist Citizenship and the Imagined Fraternity of White Men*. Durham, N.C.: Duke University Press, 1998.

Nestle, Joan. "Femme's Feminist History." In *The Feminist Memoir Project: Voices from Women's Liberation*, edited by Ann Snitow and Rachel DuPlessis, 338–49. New York: Three Rivers Press, 1998.

Noll, *The Rise of Evangelicalism: The Age of Edwards, Whitefield, and the Wesleys*. Downer's Grove, Ill.: InterVarsity Press, 2003.

Norwood, Robin. *Women Who Love Too Much*. New York: Putnam, 1985.

O'Brien, John. "Alice Walker: An Interview." In *Alice Walker: Critical Perspectives, Past and Present*, edited by Henry Louis Gates, 326–46. New York: Amistad, 2000.

Ohmann, Richard. *Selling Culture: Magazines, Markets, and Class at the Turn of the Century*. New York: Verso, 1996.

O'McCarthy, Michael. "Is Bush a 'Dry Drunk'? This Is a Serious, Not Just a Provocative, Question." *Buzzflash Reader Commentary*, 10 March 2003. <http://www.buzzflash.com/contributors/03/03/10_drunk.html>. 17 July 2008.

Onosaka, Junko. *Feminist Revolution in Literacy: Women's Bookstores in the United States*. New York: Routledge, 2006.

Oppenheimer, Mark. "Queen of the New Age." *New York Times Magazine*, 4 May 2008, 60–65.

"Oprah Begins Thirteenth Season with 'Renewed Mission.' " *Jet*, 9 September 1998, 65.

O'Reilly, Edmund B. *Sobering Tales: Narratives of Alcoholism and Recovery*. Amherst: University of Massachusetts Press, 1997.

Page, Penny Booth. "E. M. Jellinek and the Evolution of Alcohol Studies: A Critical Essay." *Addiction* 92, no. 12 (1997): 1619–37.

Parkins, Winfrey. "Oprah Winfrey's Change Your Life TV and the Spiritual Everyday." *Continuum: Journal of Media and Cultural Studies* 15, no. 2 (2001): 145–57.

Parsons, Elaine Frantz. *Manhood Lost: Fallen Drunkards and Redeeming Women in the Nineteenth-Century United States*. Baltimore: Johns Hopkins University Press, 2003.

Paul, Jay P. "Gay and Alcoholic: Epidemiological and Clinical Issues." *Alcohol Health and Research World* 15, no. 2 (1991): 151–60.

Peabody, Richard Rogers. *The Common Sense of Drinking*. Boston: Little, Brown, and Company, 1931.

———. "Psychotherapeutic Procedure in the Treatment of Chronic Alcoholism." *Mental Hygiene* 14 (January 1930): 109–28.

Peck, Janice. *The Age of Oprah: The Making of a Cultural Icon for the Neoliberal Era*. Boulder, Colo.: Paradigm Publishers, 2008.

———. "The Oprah Effect: Texts, Readers, and the Dialectic of Signification." *Communications Review* 5, no. 1 (2002): 143–78.

Peele, Stanton. *Diseasing of America: Addiction Treatment out of Control*. Lexington, Mass.: Lexington Books, 1989.

——. *The Truth about Addiction and Recovery*. New York: Simon and Schuster, 1991.

Peele, Stanton, Charles Bufe, and Archie Brodsky. *Resisting 12-Step Coercion: How to Fight Forced Participation in AA, NA, or 12-Step Treatment*. Tucson, Ariz.: See Sharp Press, 2000.

Perlstein, Rick. *Before the Storm: Barry Goldwater and the Unmaking of the American Consensus*. New York: Hill and Wang, 2001.

Pfeil, Fred. *White Guys: Studies in Postmodern Domination and Difference*. New York: Verso, 1995.

Pfister, Joel, and Nancy Schnog. *Inventing the Psychological: Toward a Cultural History of Emotional Life in America*. New Haven, Conn.: Yale University Press, 1997.

Pittman, Bill. *AA: The Way It Began*. Seattle: Glen Abbey Books, 1988.

——. Foreword to the fiftieth anniversary edition of *The Little Red Book*. Center City, Minn.: Hazelden, 1996.

Pratt, Louis H., and Darnell D. Pratt. *Alice Malsenior Walker: An Annotated Bibliography, 1968–1986*. Westport, Conn.: Meckler Corp., 1988.

Radway, Janice. *A Feeling for Books: The Book of the Month Club, Literary Taste, and Middle-Class Desire*. Chapel Hill: University of North Carolina Press, 1997.

——. "On the Gender of the Middlebrow Consumer and the Threat of the Culturally Fraudulent Female." *SAQ: South Atlantic Quarterly* 93, no. 4 (1994): 871–93.

Raphael, Matthew J. *Bill W. and Mr. Wilson: The Legend and Life of AA's Cofounder*. Amherst: University of Massachusetts Press, 2000.

Rapping, Elayne. *The Culture of Recovery: Making Sense of the Self-Help Movement in Women's Lives*. Boston: Beacon Press, 1996.

Reinarman, Craig. "Twelve-Step Movements and Advanced Capitalist Culture: On the Politics of Self-Control in Postmodernity." In *Cultural Politics and Social Movements*, edited by Barbara Leslie Epstein, Marcy Darnovsky, and Richard Flacks, 90–109. Philadelphia: Temple University Press, 1995.

Reynolds, David. "The Feminization Controversy: Sexual Stereotypes and the Paradoxes of Piety in 19th-Century America." *New England Quarterly* 53, no. 1 (1980): 96–106.

Rice, John Steadman. *A Disease of One's Own: Psychotherapy, Addiction, and the Emergence of Co-Dependency*. New Brunswick, N.J.: Transaction Publishers, 1995.

Rieff, Philip. *The Triumph of the Therapeutic: Uses of Faith after Freud*. London: Chatto and Windus, 1966.

Riehle, Wolfgang. *The Middle English Mystics*. Translated by Bernard Standring. London: Routledge and Kegan Paul, 1977.

Rivkin, Jacqueline. "Recovery Stores: A Sense of Mission." *Publishers Weekly*, 23 November 1990, 26–28.

Robertson, Nan. *Getting Better: Inside Alcoholics Anonymous*. New York: Morrow, 1988.

Robinson, Sally. *Marked Men: White Masculinity in Crisis*. New York: Columbia University Press, 2000.

Roebuck, M. Christopher, Michael T. French, and A. Thomas McClellan. "DATStats: Results from 85 Studies Using the Drug Abuse Treatment Cost Analysis Program (DATCAP)." *Journal of Substance Abuse Treatment* 25, no. 1 (2003): 51–57.

Roizen, Ron. "The American Discovery of Alcoholism, 1933–1939." Ph.D. diss., University of California Berkeley, 1991.

———. "The Great Controlled-Drinking Controversy." In *Recent Developments in Alcoholism*, vol. 5, edited by Mark Galanter, 245–79. New York: Plenum Press, 1987.

———. "Paradigm Sidetracked: Explaining Early Resistance to the Alcoholism Paradigm at Yale's Applied Physiology Laboratory, 1940–1944." <http://www.roizen.com/ron/sidetracked.htm>. 15 July 2008.

Romano, Lois, and George Lardner Jr. "1986: A Life-Changing Year; Epiphany Fueled Candidate's Climb." *Washington Post*, 25 July 1999. <http://www.washingtonpost.com/wp-srv/politics/campaigns/wh2000/stories/bush072599.htm>. 30 July 2008.

Room, Robin. "Addiction Concepts and International Control." *Global Drug Policy: Building a New Framework*. Paris: Senlis Council, 2003. 15–23.

———. "Alcoholism and Alcoholics Anonymous in U.S. Films, 1945–1962: The Party Ends for the 'Wet Generations.' " *Journal of Studies on Alcohol* 50, no. 4 (1989): 368–83.

———. "Alcoholics Anonymous as a Social Movement." In *Research on Alcoholics Anonymous: Opportunities and Alternatives*, edited by Barbara S. McCrady and William R. Miller, 167–87. New Brunswick, N.J.: Rutgers Center of Alcohol Studies, 1993.

———. " 'Healing Ourselves and Our Planet': The Emergence and Nature of a Generalized 12-Step Consciousness." *Contemporary Drug Problems* 19, no. 4 (1992): 717–40.

———. "Sociological Aspects of the Disease Concept of Alcoholism." In *Research Advances in Alcohol*, vol. 7, edited by R. G. Smarts et al., 47–91. New York: Plenum Press, 1983.

Rooney, Kathleen. *Reading with Oprah: The Book Club That Changed America*. Fayetteville: University of Arkansas Press, 2005.

Rose, Howard. *The Quiet Time*. New York: The Oxford Group, 1937. <http://www.aabibliography.com/pdffiles/quiettimerose.pdf>.

Rosenfeld, "Profiles in Purple and Black: 'Womanist' Alice Walker and the Love of Life." *Washington Post*, 15 October 1982, E1.

Rotskoff, Lori. *Love on the Rocks: Men, Women, and Alcohol in Post-World War II America*. Chapel Hill: University of North Carolina Press, 2002.

Rubin, Joan Shelley. *The Making of Middlebrow Culture*. Chapel Hill: University of North Carolina Press, 1992.

Rudy, David. *Becoming Alcoholic: Alcoholics Anonymous and the Reality of Alcoholism*. Carbondale: University of Southern Illinois Press, 1986.

Rudy, David, and Arthur Greil. "Is Alcoholics Anonymous a Religious Organization? Meditations on Marginality." *Sociological Analysis* 50, no. 1 (1988): 41–51.

Rumbarger, John J. "The 'Story' of Bill W.: Ideology, Culture, and the Discovery of the Modern American Alcoholic." *Contemporary Drug Problems* 20, no. 4 (1993): 759–82.

Russell, A. J. *For Sinners Only*. London: Hodder and Stoughton, Ltd., 1932.

Sandage, Scott. *Born Losers: A History of Failure in America*. Cambridge, Mass.: Harvard University Press, 2005.

Sanders, Cheryl J., Katie G. Cannon, Emilie M. Townes, M. Shawn Copeland, bell hooks, and Cheryl Townsend Gillespie. "Roundtable Discussion: Christian Ethics and Theology in Womanist Perspective." In *The Womanist Reader*, edited by Layli Phillips, 126–57. New York: Routledge, 2006.

Sanders, Mark. "The Response of African American Communities to Alcohol and Other Drug Problems: An Opportunity for Treatment Providers." *Alcoholism Treatment Quarterly* 20, no. 3/4 (2002): 167–74.

Sandmaier, Marian. *The Invisible Alcoholics: Women and Alcohol Abuse in America*. New York: McGraw-Hill, 1980.

Satter, Beryl. *Each Mind a Kingdom: American Women, Sexual Purity, and the New Thought Movement, 1875–1920*. Berkeley: University of California Press, 1999.

———. "Marcus Garvey, Father Divine, and the Gender Politics of Race Difference and Race Neutrality." *American Quarterly* 48, no. 1 (1996): 43–76.

———. "The Sexual Abuse Paradigm in Historical Perspective: Passivity and Emotion in Mid-20th Century America." *Journal of the History of Sexuality* 12, no. 3 (2003): 424–64.

Schaef, Anne Wilson. *Co-Dependence: Misunderstood, Mistreated*. New York: Harper Perennial, 1986.

Schmidt, Laura, and Constance Weisner. "Developments in Alcoholism Treatment." In *Recent Developments in Alcoholism,* vol. 11: *Ten Years of Progress*, edited by Marc Galanter, 369–96. New York: Plenum Press, 1993.

———. "The Emergence of Problem Drinking Women as a Special Population in Need of Treatment." In *Recent Developments in Alcoholism*, vol. 12: *Women and Alcoholism*, edited by Marc Galanter, 309–32. New York: Plenum Press, 1995.

Schmidt, Leigh Eric. *Restless Souls: The Making of American Spirituality*. San Francisco: Harper San Francisco, 2005.

Sellers, Patricia. "The Business of Being Oprah." *Fortune*, 1 April 2002, 50–58.

Selzer, Linda. "Race and Domesticity in *The Color Purple*." *African American Review* 29, no. 1 (1995): 67–82.

Shapiro, Laura. "Advice Givers Strike Gold." *Newsweek*, 1 June 1987, 64–65.

Shattuc, Jane. *The Talking Cure: TV Talk Shows and Women*. New York: Routledge, 1997.

Sheldon, Charles M. *In His Steps: "What Would Jesus Do?"* Chicago: Smith-Andrews, 1897.

Shlaes, Amity. *The Forgotten Man: A New History of the Great Depression*. New York: HarperCollins, 2007.

Silkworth, William Duncan. "Alcoholism as a Manifestation of Allergy." *Medical Record* 145 (1937): 249–51. <http://silkworth.net/silkworth/allergy.htm>. 15 February 2006.

Simmons, John K. "The Forgotten Contributions of Annie Rix Militz to the Unity School of Christianity." *Nova Religio* 2, no. 1 (1998): 76–92.

Simonds, Wendy. *Women and Self-Help Culture: Reading Between the Lines*. New Brunswick, N.J.: Rutgers University Press, 1992.

Smith, David E., Millicent E. Buxton, Rafiq Bilal, and Richard B. Seymour. "Cultural Points of Resistance to the 12-Step Recovery Process." *Journal of Psychoactive Drugs* 25, no. 1 (1993): 97–108.

Smith, Erin. "What Would Jesus Read?: Scenes of Religious Reading and Writing in Twentieth-Century America," forthcoming.

Sontag, Susan. *Illness as Metaphor*. New York: Farrar, Straus and Giroux, 1978.

Spicer, Jerry. *The Minnesota Model: The Evolution of the Multidisciplinary Approach to Addiction Recovery*. Center City, Minn.: Hazelden, 1993.

"Spirit and Self." *Oprah*. <http://www.oprah.com/spiritself/ss_landing.jhtml>. 3 May 2001.

Staggenborg, Suzanne. "Beyond Culture Versus Politics: A Case Study of a Local Women's Movement." *Gender and Society* 15, no. 4 (2001): 507–30.

Stallybrass, Peter, and Allon White. *The Politics and Poetics of Transgression*. Ithaca, N.Y.: Cornell University Press, 1986.

Stanley, Tarshia. "The Specter of Oprah Winfrey: Critical Black Female Spectatorship." In *The Oprah Phenomenon*, edited by Jennifer Harris and Elwood Watson, 35–50. Lexington: University Press of Kentucky, 2007.

Starker, Stephen. *Oracle at the Supermarket: The American Preoccupation with Self-Help Books*. New Brunswick, N.J.: Transaction Publishers, 1989.

Susman, Warren. " 'Personality' and the Making of 20th-Century Culture." In *Culture as History: The Transformation of American Society in the 20th Century*. New York: Pantheon, 1984.

Swallow, Jean. *Leave a Light on for Me*. San Francisco: Spinsters/Aunt Lute, 1986.

———. *The Next Step: Lesbians in Long-Term Recovery*. Boston: Alyson Publications, 1994.

———. *Out from Under: Sober Dykes and Our Friends*. San Francisco: Spinsters, Ink Press, 1983.

Swift, Harold. *Program Management: AA and Bibliotherapy*. Center City, Minn.: Hazelden, 1984.

Swift, Harold, and Terrence Williams. *Recovery for the Whole Family*. Center City, Minn.: Hazelden, 1975.

Sykes, Charles. *A Nation of Victims: The Decay of the American Character*. New York: St. Martin's Press, 1992.

"Syndie Shows Mostly on the Rebound." *Daily Variety*, 29 July 1993, 10.

Szalavitz, Maia. *Help at Any Cost: How the Troubled-Teen Industry Cons Parents and Hurts Kids*. New York: Riverhead, 2006.

Tabor, Michael "Cetewayo." "Capitalism Plus Dope Equals Genocide." New York [?]: Black Panther Party, 1970. <http://marxists.anu.edu.au/history/usa/workers/black-panthers/1970/dope.htm>. 7 March 2009.

Taylor, Elizabeth. "Taking Care of Herself." *Time*, 10 December 1990: 106+.

Taylor, LaTonya. "The Church of O." *Christianity Today*, 1 April 2002. <http://www.christianitytoday.com/ct/2002/april1/1.38.html>. 10 July 2007.

Taylor, Verta. "Social Movement Continuity: The Women's Movement in Abeyance." *American Sociological Review* 54, no. 4 (1989): 761–75.

Taylor, Verta, and Leila J. Rupp. "Women's Culture and Lesbian Feminist Activism: A Reconsideration of Cultural Feminism." *Signs* 19, no. 1 (1993): 32–61.

Taylor, Verta, and Marieke Van Willigen. "Women's Self-Help and the Reconstruction of Gender: The Postpartum Support and Breast Cancer Movements." *Mobilization: An International Journal* 1, no. 2 (1996): 123–42.

Thomsen, Robert. *Bill W.* New York: Harper and Row, 1985.

Thornton, Sarah. "General Introduction." In *The Subcultures Reader*, edited by Ken Gelder and Sarah Thornton, 1–10. New York: Routledge, 1997.

Timberg, Bernard. *Television Talk: A History of the TV Talk Show.* Austin: University of Texas Press, 2002.

Tompkins, Jane P. *Sensational Designs: The Cultural Work of American Fiction, 1790–1860.* New York: Oxford University Press, 1985.

Tong, Rosemary. *Feminist Thought: A More Comprehensive Introduction.* Boulder, Colo.: Westview Press, 2008.

Tonigan, J. Scott. "Introduction: Effectiveness and Outcome Research." In *Recent Developments in Alcoholism*, vol. 18, *Research on Alcoholics Anonymous and Spirituality in Addiction Recovery*, edited by Marc Galanter and Lee Ann Kaskutas, 349–55. New York: Springer, 2008.

Tracy, Sarah. *Alcoholism in America: From Reconstruction to Prohibition.* Baltimore: Johns Hopkins University Press, 2005.

Travis, Trysh. " 'Handles to Hang on to Our Sobriety': Commonplace Books and Surrendered Masculinity in Alcoholics Anonymous." *Men and Masculinities* 2008. DOI: 10.1177/1097184X08318182. 26 May 2008.

———. "Print Culture in the AA Fellowship." *Social History of Drugs and Alcohol: An Interdisciplinary Journal* 19 (2004): 28–62.

Trevino, Javier. "Alcoholics Anonymous as Durkheimian Religion." *Research in the Social Scientific Study of Religion* 4 (1992): 182–208.

Trice, Harrison, and William Sonnenstuhl. "Contributions of AA to Employee Assistance Programs." *Employee Assistance Quarterly* 1, no. 1 (1985): 7–31.

Trimpey, Jack. "Alcoholics Anonymous: Of Course It's a Cult." *Journal of Rational Recovery* 9, no. 5 (1997). <http://www.positiveatheism.org/rw/ofcourse.htm>. 23 April 2007.

———. "Recovery Group Disorders Are Real." 2004. <http://www.rational.org/html_member_area/reasons_cancel.html>. 8 March 2009.

———. *The Small Book: A Revolutionary Alternative for Overcoming Alcohol and Drug Dependence.* New York: Delacorte Press, 1992.

Turner, Catherine. *Marketing Modernism between the Two World Wars.* Amherst: University of Massachusetts Press, 2003.

Unger, Craig. *The Fall of the House of Bush: The Untold Story of How a Band of True Believers Seized the Executive Branch, Started the Iraq War, and Still Imperils America's Future.* New York: Scribner, 2007.

Upshaw, William D. *Bombshells for Wets and Reds, the Twin Devils of America.* Cincinnati: God's Bible School, 1936.

U.S. Census Bureau. *Statistical Abstract of the United States, 2007.* 126th ed. Washington, D.C., 2006.

Uzzell, Thomas H. "The Love Pulps." *Scribner's*, April 1938, 36–41.

———. *Narrative Technique: A Practical Course in Literary Psychology.* New York: Harcourt Brace, 1923.

Valby, Karen. "James Frey Does Not Care What You Think about Him (Please Love Him)." *Entertainment Weekly*, 4 April 2003, 63.

Valverde, Mariana. *Diseases of the Will: Alcohol and the Dilemmas of Freedom.* Cambridge: Cambridge University Press, 1998.

Vanzant, Iyanla. *In the Meantime: Finding Yourself and the Love You Want.* New York: Fireside, 1999.

Walker, Alice. *Anything We Love Can Be Saved: A Writer's Activism.* New York: Random House, 1998.

——. *The Color Purple: A Novel.* New York: Pocket Books, 1985.

——. *The Same River Twice: Honoring the Difficult: A Meditation on Life, Spirit, Art, and the Making of the Film, "The Color Purple," Ten Years Later.* New York: Scribner, 1996.

——. "Womanist." In *In Search of Our Mothers' Gardens: Womanist Prose*, xi–xii. New York: Harcourt Brace Jovanovich, 1983.

Walker, Richmond. *Twenty-four Hours a Day.* 1954; rev. ed., Center City, Minn.: Hazelden, 1975.

Wallis, Jim. *God's Politics: Why the Right Gets It Wrong and the Left Doesn't Get It.* New York: HarperOne, 2006.

Wang, Jennifer Hyland. " 'Everything's Coming Up Rosie': Empower America, Rosie O'Donnell, and the Construction of Daytime Reality." *Velvet Light Trap* no. 45 (March 2000): 20–35.

Warhol, Robyn R., and Helena Michie. "Twelve-Step Teleology: Narratives of Recovery/Recovery as Narrative." In *Getting a Life: Everyday Uses of Autobiography*, edited by Sidonie Smith and Julia Watson, 327–50. Minneapolis: University of Minnesota Press, 1996.

Warner, Nicholas. "Temperance, Morality, and Medicine in the Fiction of Harriett Beecher Stowe." In *The Serpent in the Cup: Temperance in American Literature*, edited by David S. Reynolds and Deborah J. Rosenthal, 136–52. Amherst: University of Massachusetts Press, 1997.

Washington, Peter. *Madame Blavatsky's Baboon: A History of the Mystics, Mediums, and Misfits Who Brought Spiritualism to America.* New York: Schocken Books, 1993.

Watkins, Mel. "Some Letters Went to God." *New York Times*, 25 July 1982, sec. 7, p. 7.

Weber, Max. *From Max Weber: Essays in Sociology.* Translated and edited by H. H. Gerth and C. Wright Mills. New York: Oxford University Press, 1946.

Weber, Timothy P. "The Two-Edged Sword: The Fundamentalist Use of the Bible." In *The Bible in America: Essays in Cultural History*, edited by Nathan Hatch and Mark Noll, 101–20. New York: Oxford University Press, 1982.

Weijl, Simon. "Theoretical and Practical Aspects of Psychoanalytic Therapy of Problem Drinkers." *Quarterly Journal of Studies on Alcohol* 5, no. 2 (1944): 200–211.

Weisner, Constance, and Robin Room. "Financing and Ideology in Alcohol Treatment." *Social Problems* 32, no. 2 (1984): 167–84.

White, Evelyn C. *Alice Walker: A Life.* New York: Norton, 2004.

White, William L. *Slaying the Dragon: The History of Addiction Treatment and*

Recovery in America. Bloomington, Ill.: Chestnut Health Systems/Lighthouse Institute, 1998.

Whittier, Nancy. *Feminist Generations: The Persistence of the Radical Women's Movement*. Philadelphia: Temple University Press, 1995.

Wiener, Carolyn L. *The Politics of Alcoholism: Building an Arena around a Social Problem*. New Brunswick, N.J.: Transaction Books, 1981.

Williamson, Marianne. *A Return to Love: Reflections on the Principles of a Course in Miracles*. New York: HarperCollins, 1992.

Wilsnack, Sharon C. "Drinking, Sexuality, and Sexual Dysfunction in Women." In *Alcohol Problems in Women: Antecedents, Consequences, and Intervention*, edited by Sharon C. Wilsnack and Linda J. Beckman, 189–228. New York: Guilford Press, 1984.

Wilsnack, Sharon C., and Linda J. Beckman, eds. *Alcohol Problems in Women: Antecedents, Consequences, and Intervention*. New York: Guilford Press, 1984.

Winchell, Donna Haisty. *Alice Walker*. New York: Twayne, 1992.

Wing, Nell. *Grateful to Have Been There: My 42 Years with Bill and Lois, and the Evolution of Alcoholics Anonymous*. Park Ridge, Ill.: Parkside Publishing Corporation, 1992.

Woititz, Janet. *Adult Children of Alcoholics*. Deerfield Beach, Fla.: Health Communications, Inc., 1983.

Wood, Leonard. "The Gallup Survey." *Publishers Weekly*, 14 October 1988, 33.

Woods, Randall B. *LBJ: Architect of American Ambition*. New York: Free Press, 2006.

Wuthnow, Robert. *Sharing the Journey: Support Groups and the Quest for a New Community*. New York: Free Press, 1996.

INDEX

AA (Alcoholics Anonymous): General Service Office, 1, 15, 52, 138, 140–41, 143, 145, 148, 151–52, 173–74, 178–80, 300 (n. 68), 306–7 (n. 99); membership of, 3–4, 36, 93, 96, 144, 273, 274; organizational structure of, 5, 51, 52, 93, 97; vs. therapy, 7, 49, 119; efficacy of, 8–9, 17, 176, 280–81 (n. 20), 305–6 (n. 88); evolution of, 9–10, 12–13, 49, 83, 93, 119–20, 141–42, 172–73; founding of, 29–33; vs. professional treatment, 49, 52, 54, 56; gender relations within, 53–54, 79–80, 181–82, 195–97, 306–7 (n. 99); characterized as cult, 61–63, 103, 130; critique of possessive individualism within, 62–63, 92, 101–2; financial contribution limits, 63, 289 (n. 9); history of, 64–69, 75, 116, 297 (n. 19); attitudes toward women within, 79–80, 144, 163–64, 171; AA Way of Life, 82–83, 85, 98–100, 103, 109, 136–37, 149, 173, 176, 181, 289 (n. 10); and "man on the bed," 89–91, 100, 125; gift economy of, 92–100; as subculture, 103; General Service Conference, 136, 138–40, 142–43, 148, 172–74, 306 (n. 93); ecumenism of, 137, 148, 179; conspiracy theories, 138, 205; Trustees' Literature Committee, 140–41, 148, 175, 305 (n. 87); commercialization of, 181–82; feminization of, 181–83, 267; and marriage, 293 (n. 66), 298 (n. 33); and race, 295 (n. 90), 300 (n. 73). *See also* Big Book; Midwestern AA; Traditionalist AA; 12 Steps; 12 Traditions; Women in AA

AA literature: and AA historians, 9–10, 78, 281 (n. 25), 291 (n. 38); amateur authorship, 9–10, 15, 16, 80, 161, 179–80, 182–83, 281 (n. 25); and self-made man, 65–66, 92; and surrender, 79, 104; midwestern, 80–85, 99, 102–3, 135–37, 139, 142, 145, 147, 173, 179, 259, 292–93 (n. 53), 299 (n. 60), 304 (n. 81); reading of, 82, 107–9, 150–51; and gender, 83–85, 127, 155, 293 (n. 66); and service work, 88, 129, 136–37, 142; and alcoholic equalitarianism, 90–91, 104; publication and distribution of, 97, 110, 120–21, 133, 143, 151–52; and 12-Step calls, 115; Bill Wilson's desire for control of, 120–21, 138–42, 143, 300 (n. 72); standardization of, 137, 140–43, 173–74; sales of, 138–39; and AA philosophy, 139–40, 300 (n. 73); Conference Approved Literature, 140–43, 148–49, 152, 158, 161, 173–78, 218, 304 (n. 81), 305 (nn. 83, 86); and Hazelden, 151–52, 165; controversies over, 173–81, 182, 305 (n. 88); and traditionalist AA, 176–80; Frey's rejection of, 266–67, 270. *See also* Big Book; *Little Red Book*

Abstinence: and disease concept, 22, 34–35, 47; and temperance movement, 24–25, 94; and psychoanalysis, 28; as deviant behavior, 61–62; AA sobriety distinguished from, 85, 99; and Women for Sobriety, 196; and feminist recovery, 206; vs. controlled-drinking proponents, 287 (n. 82)

Acceptance, 158, 169, 235, 242, 244

Addiction: defined, 2–3; to processes, 4, 6, 52–57, 187; as spiritual sickness, 15, 16; and feminism, 144, 201, 218; multiple addictions, 150, 173; to food, 155, 230, 232–33, 241, 256; etiology of, 158–59, 217; and women, 158–59, 163, 193–94, 200, 203–7, 226; to emotions, 168; political economy of, 205, 221; racialized experiences of, 228; and *The Oprah Winfrey Show*, 229–30, 232; alcohol distinguished from drug, 283 (n. 7); alcohol merged with drug, 287 (n. 82). *See also* Disease concept; 12-Step approaches to addiction

Adult Children of Alcoholics, 54–56, 168, 217, 229, 282 (n. 29)

African Americans, 46–47, 175, 209–17, 228, 236–37, 286 (n. 81), 295–96 (n. 90), 313 (n. 17)

AIDS epidemic, 203

Al-Anon, 4, 6, 52–55, 167, 169, 204, 282 (n. 27), 298 (n. 32)

Alateen, 52, 55

Alcoholic equalitarianism: worldview of, 63; and Christian traditions, 86–87, 91, 289 (n. 10); and identification, 87, 91, 124; and 12th-Step call, 88–91; and gift economy, 92, 180; and 12 Traditions, 96, 100; principles of, 101–2, 119; critics of, 103; and reading, 109; and 12-Step narrative form, 129–30; and CAL, 141–42; and gender inclusiveness, 144, 156; and women, 163–64; and diversity, 172–73, 175, 182; and traditionalist AA, 183; and Winfrey, 252, 257; and race, 300 (n. 73)

Alcoholic Foundation, 93, 121, 138, 140, 148

Alcoholics Anonymous. See AA (Alcoholics Anonymous)

Alcoholism: and dry drunk, 2, 15, 63, 279 (n. 9); and temperance, 24; psychoanalytic view of, 26–29, 35, 36; as allergy, 33–36, 67–69, 116, 122; as man's disease, 53, 83, 144, 288 (n. 101); surrender as antidote, 65, 69, 149, 164; and soul sickness, 83, 101; co-alcoholism, 220. See also Alcoholism Movement; Disease concept; Women's alcoholism movement

Alcoholism Movement: and disease concept, 36–37, 40, 44, 47, 49, 56; diversity within, 36–37, 189; relationship with AA, 50, 97–98; literature of, 137–38; growth of, 152

American Indians, 46–47, 161, 175, 228, 286 (n. 81), 296 (n. 90), 303 (n. 48)

American Medical Association, 43, 190, 287 (n. 82)

Amos, Frank, 115, 120, 121, 134

Anderson, Dan, 150–51, 153

Angelou, Maya, 239–40, 250, 253–55

Anonymity, 8, 11, 42, 49, 98, 102, 116, 297 (n. 19)

Anonymous Publishing, 179

Anthony, Susan B., 191–92, 308–9 (n. 14)

Anticolonialism, 205, 209, 214–16, 224

Anti-intellectualism: of Oxford Group, 72;

of midwestern AA, 81–83, 249; of AA, 102, 197; of Big Book, 122; of recovery movement generally, 157; in Oprah's Book Club, 249–50. See also Pragmatic focus of AA

Asceticism, 70–72, 74, 79–81, 83, 101, 113, 157

Barry C., 81, 145, 152

Beattie, Melody, 169–71, 218, 225

Bible: reading of, 82, 107–8, 110–12, 114–15; and Oxford Group, 112–13, 135, 146; and Big Book, 141–42; and Richmond Walker, 147, 149; and sobriety guides, 179; in *The Color Purple*, 215; and Winfrey, 236

Bibliotherapy, 154, 166, 171

Big Book: reading, 12, 107–9, 136; and disease concept, 34–35, 122–23; on self-will, 62, 67–69, 164; "Bill's Story" in, 64, 73, 74, 120–21, 123, 126; on amends, 88; and 12th-Step call, 89, 294 (n. 78); on 12 Steps, 103, 124–25, 297–98 (n. 29); Q. Method of annotating, 107–8, 296 (n. 2); planning of, 118–21; and commercialism, 120–21, 131–36; publication of, 120–21, 126, 129, 134, 298 (n. 37); and pragmatic focus of AA, 122–25; and identification, 124, 126, 129–30; and spirituality, 125–26, 139, 291 (n. 34); and 12-Step narrative form, 126–31, 175, 298 (nn. 32, 33); editing of, 131–34, 284–85 (n. 44), 299 (n. 53); sales of, 134, 137–39, 143, 300 (n. 68); and intensive vs. extensive reading, 135; talismanic properties of, 136, 141–42; and consumerism, 147; and Hazelden, 150–51, 153–54, 166; editions of, 173–74, 178–79, 275, 306 (n. 93); Frey on, 266–67; distribution of, 276–77; on sex, 290 (n. 29)

Bill W. See Wilson, William ("Bill")

Black, Claudia, 168, 222, 230

Buchman, Frank, 30–32, 34, 70–72, 75, 112, 116–17, 147, 230–31, 290 (nn. 29, 32)

Bush, George W., 1, 279 (n. 9)

Butler, Pat, 149, 150, 152

CAL (Conference Approved Literature), 140–43, 148–49, 152, 158, 161, 173–78, 218, 304 (n. 81), 305 (nn. 83, 86)

Capitalism: and addiction, 47, 205; and self-made man, 65; behavioral norms of, 92, 96; and sentimental culture, 102, 262; and consumerist reading, 113; and feminist recovery, 209; in *The Color Purple*, 214, 224; and Winfrey, 257–58; and social categories, 260. *See also* Commercialism; Consumerism; Market economy

Carnegie, Dale, 85, 294 (n. 75)

Carry the Message, Inc. (CTM), 178–79, 306 (n. 93)

Casey, Karen: and Hazelden, 154–56, 160; and New Thought, 154, 161–62, 231; and Unity, 154, 161–63, 198; and self-will, 157, 164; and traditionalist AA, 158, 160–62, 164; influence of American Indian spirituality on, 161, 303 (n. 48); and publishing trends, 225. See also *Each Day a New Beginning* (Casey)

Catholics, 75, 161, 291 (n. 39)

Chemical dependency, 47, 55–57, 150

Chesnut, Glenn, 9, 75, 146, 148, 149, 281 (n. 25), 291 (n. 38), 306 (n. 88)

Childhood sexual abuse: and women's addiction, 193–94; of Swallow, 203, 208, 220, 222; in *The Color Purple*, 209, 211–13; of Winfrey, 230, 250, 253, 256; of Angelou, 239, 250, 253

Chopra, Deepak, 239, 240–41, 245

Christian Science, 76, 79, 161, 292 (n. 51), 303 (n. 51)

Clarence S., 135, 180

Clinton, Bill, 1, 2, 3, 258

Codependence: and therapy, 55–57; and treatment industry, 167–68; and Hazelden, 168–69; and antifeminism, 188; and Swallow, 203–4, 207–8, 220–22; and publishing, 225; and *The Oprah Winfrey Show*, 229, 232

Co-Dependents Anonymous, 4, 6, 9, 54–56, 217, 282 (n. 29), 288 (n. 107)

Collins, Patricia Hill, 257, 259

The Color Purple (Alice Walker): and childhood sexual abuse, 209, 211–13; as feminist recovery text, 209, 211, 213, 216–17, 224–25; epistolary form of, 211, 214, 311 (n. 87); and 12-Step narrative form, 211, 216, 224; patriarchy in, 212–14; and spirituality, 214–16; marketing of, 222–24, 311 (n. 81); Winfrey's relationship to, 256–57

Commercialism: of recovery, 13, 16, 225–26, 228, 257; and Big Book, 120–21, 131–36; and direct marketing, 138, 300 (n. 66); of Hazelden, 172; and traditionalist AA, 173; of AA, 181–82; of Winfrey, 245–46, 257. *See also* Consumerism

Commodity exchange, 92, 96, 98

Communications circuits, 14–15, 58–59, 142, 145, 172, 183

Community: progressive notions of, 7; recovery culture as form of, 9; and religious rejection of world, 62–63, 83; as challenge to socioeconomic order, 65; and interdependency, 84; and self-in-relation, 85, 101–3, 260, 294 (n. 72); women's, 160, 190, 219; and self, 217–25; and Winfrey, 250; and Oprah's Book Club, 260–61; and identification, 271

Consciousness-raising, 154, 159–60, 189, 198, 203, 207, 235

Conservative politics, 23, 54, 67, 189, 261, 290 (n. 20)

Consumerism: and temperance movement, 26; and abstinence, 62; and gendered behavioral norms, 63; and self-will, 67–68, 69; and secularism, 71; Oxford Group's rejection of, 72, 114; as threat to sobriety, 80, 82, 99, 147; and 12-Step narrative form, 130; AA critique of, 147; and recovery, 189; and quality paperbacks, 223–24. *See also* Capitalism; Commercialism; Market economy

Consumerist reading, 113–14, 120, 165

Controlled drinking, 67–68, 128, 287 (n. 82)

Conversion, 34, 73, 78, 120, 125, 131, 291 (n. 34)

Criminal justice system, 6, 24, 36, 41, 44, 48–49, 51, 172

Cults, 5, 61–63, 103, 130, 288–89 (n. 2)

Debtors Anonymous, 6, 52

Decolonization, 216, 245, 256

Devotional practice, 77–78, 161–62

Devotional reading: in AA meetings, 107; and Oxford Group, 112, 135; importance of, 115–16; and Dr. Bob Smith, 115, 117; and Bill Wilson, 115, 175; and midwestern AA, 135–36; and Big Book, 136, 142; and *Twenty-four Hours a Day*, 145–46; and CAL, 174–75

Direct marketing, 138, 300 (n. 66)

Disease concept: critics of, 22–23, 44, 47, 52, 183, 225, 287 (n. 82); and political economy, 23, 58–59; metaphorical dimensions of, 24, 57–58, 65; origins of, 24, 33–36; and Big Book, 34–35, 122–23; "handiness" of, 35–37, 42, 50, 56, 78; and Alcoholism Movement, 36–37, 40, 44, 47, 49, 56; language of, 36, 58, 78; and National Council on Alcoholism, 37, 38, 44–45; and Yale Center of Alcohol Studies, 37–43; and National Committee for Education on Alcoholism, 41–44; and federal government, 45–46; and role of AA, 49–52, 56, 59; and process addictions, 52–57; and women, 144, 158, 193; and Hazelden, 149; and Adult Children of Alcoholics, 168; imprecision of, 194; and Women for Sobriety, 196; feminist critique of, 217

Diversity: within recovery, 7; of AA, 103, 144–45, 172–75, 180–83; in addict population, 150; and alcoholic equalitarianism, 172–73, 175, 182; and CAL, 174–75, 305 (n. 86)

Divine within, 146, 161–64, 198, 214, 231, 237, 240, 303 (n. 49)

Dr. Bob. *See* Smith, Robert ("Dr. Bob")

Donahue, Phil, 230, 232, 233, 241

Dorothy S.M., 115, 131

Douglas, Ann, 268, 317 (n. 6)

Each Day a New Beginning (Casey): and surrendered life, 157–58; and self-esteem, 158–59, 163–64, 170; and gender differences, 159–60, 163, 170; and Higher Power, 160–64; sales of, 164, 225; distribution of, 167

Ebby T., 74, 78, 116

Eddy, Mary Baker, 76, 292 (n. 51), 303 (n. 51)

Ed W., 81, 145, 152, 157

Emmanuel Movement, 27, 146

Empowerment, 195, 197, 211, 213, 258

Ethnic identity–based treatment, 7, 46–47, 205, 228, 286 (n. 81)

Evangelicalism, 7, 30, 86–88, 102, 284 (n. 31), 294 (n. 76). *See also* Oxford Group

Exman, Eugene, 120–21

Faludi, Susan, 188, 218, 219

Family systems therapy, 55, 218

Family treatment, 57, 153, 168, 193

"Felt truth," 35, 194

Feminism: and post-12-Step recovery, 7, 16; relationship with AA, 8, 54, 164, 187; in women's treatment programs, 46; and addiction, 144, 201, 218; consciousness-raising as tool of, 154, 159, 189, 207, 235; Second Wave, 157, 159, 188–89, 219, 226, 228, 303 (n. 46); equity as goal for, 160; skepticism of recovery, 187, 189, 201, 217; Reagan-era backlash against, 188–89, 220; liberal, 189–92, 194–95, 200–201, 204–5, 218–19, 226, 308 (n. 7); and "personal is political," 189, 220, 226–27; "postfeminism," 189, 307 (n. 4); radical, 189–90, 199–201, 205–7, 219, 226–27, 308 (n. 7); women of color, 190, 219, 226–27, 308 (n. 7); womanism, 210–11, 214–16, 222, 227, 231, 245, 252, 254, 256–57, 308 (n. 7); defined, 303 (n. 46), 308 (n. 7)

Feminist recovery: as depoliticizing, 188–90, 219–20, 225; political nature of work, 189–90, 207, 218, 226–27; and child sexual abuse, 194; relationship with AA, 196–97, 204; and women's alcoholism movement, 199–200; and self-esteem, 203–6, 235; and sobriety, 206–7, 217, 227; and African Americans, 209–17; and *The Color Purple*, 209, 211, 213, 216–17, 224–25; and post-12-Step recovery, 217, 228; cultural work of, 280 (n. 18)

Feminization: of piety, 79–85; of AA, 181–83, 267

Fifield, Lillen, 202, 203

Fillmore, Charles, 154, 161, 162, 303 (n. 51)

Fingarette, Herbert, 22, 44

Food addiction, 155, 230, 232–34, 241, 256

Food for Thought, 155, 164, 167

Ford, Betty, 1, 190

Foucault, Michel, 9, 13

Four Absolutes, 31, 72, 116, 147

Fox, Emmet, 115, 121

Freud, Sigmund, 27, 28–29

Frey, James, 265–68, 270, 317 (n. 1)

Gays. *See* Lesbians and gays

Gender differences, 144, 159–60, 163, 170, 192, 197, 308 (n. 7)

Gender equity, 191–92, 195, 200, 201, 205, 217

Gender relations: within AA, 53–54, 79–80, 181–82, 195–97, 306–7 (n. 99); within treatment community, 195, 196; Alice Walker on, 210, 212, 214; and feminist recovery, 218, 228

Gender roles: and addiction, 54; behavioral norms, 63; and founding of AA, 64, 65–66; alcoholism enmeshed in, 68; and surrender, 80; and AA literature, 83–85, 127, 155, 293 (n. 66); ideal of femininity, 159, 198; and Beattie, 170; and women's alcoholism movement, 190–91, 201, 204; Victorian ideologies of, 191; and Women for Sobriety, 198; and sentimental power, 262. *See also* Masculinity

Gift economy, 92–100, 132, 136–42, 145, 180, 183, 300 (n. 73)

The Grapevine, 39–40, 94–95, 99, 138–39, 174, 285 (n. 56)

Great Depression, 64–65, 127, 290 (n. 20)

Greene, Bob, 233–34, 236, 238–40

Hank P., 131, 132, 133

Harper and Brothers, 120–21, 297 (n. 25)

Harper San Francisco, 167, 171

Harpo, Inc., 231, 245–46, 257, 261

Hazelden: literature sales, 13, 167, 170–71; relationship with AA, 145, 149, 150–55, 169, 171–72; treatment protocol of, 149–51, 154; and *Twenty-four Hours a Day*, 149–52, 155–56, 166, 302 (n. 41); and Big Book, 150–51, 153–54, 166; Counselor Training Program, 150, 152, 154, 166; multidisciplinary approach of, 150–53; Educational Materials Division, 152, 154–55, 164–68, 171–72; professionalism in, 152–53, 171–72; Family Program, 153, 167; Literary Advisory Committee, 153–56, 164; and bibliotherapy, 154, 166, 171; and Casey, 154–56, 160; and codependence, 168–69; and Frey, 265–66

Health Communications Incorporated (HCI), 13, 168

Hegi, Ursula, 251–53

Hill, Napoleon, 85–86, 294 (n. 75)

hooks, bell, 209, 227, 257

Hopkins, Emma Curtis, 79, 161, 292 (n. 51), 303 (n. 51)

Hughes, Harold, 45, 46, 50

Humanist psychology, 8, 55, 152, 158–60, 169

Idealism, 76–77, 237–41, 242, 245, 248–49, 257, 260–62

Identification: and alcoholic equalitarianism, 87, 91, 124; in AA Way of Life, 98; and common language, 118; and Big Book, 124, 126, 129–30; and 12-Step narrative form, 126–31; and reading, 131–32, 318 (n. 9); and Winfrey, 250–52, 254–55; and community, 271

Identity: ethnic identity–based treatment, 7, 46–47, 205, 228, 286 (n. 81); of alcoholic, 62; of white, middle-class male, 67; and surrendered self, 74, 80; reestablishment of, 83; and community, 84; of women, 159–60; sexual identity, 201, 213

Identity politics, 101, 145, 175, 269

Inebriety physicians, 25, 33, 36

Inner child, 221, 222

Insurance industry, 47–48, 57

Interior colonization, 47, 205, 222, 224, 227, 228, 310 (n. 47)

Jack V., 153, 156, 163, 164

Jacoby Club, 146, 301 (n. 5)

James, William, 76–78, 265, 292 (n. 44)

Jellinek, E. M., 38–44, 47, 50, 56, 192, 285 (n. 56), 288 (n. 101)

Johnson, Lyndon B., 45

Kaminer, Wendy, 22–23, 130, 218–19, 282 (n. 29)

Keswick Convention, 30, 284 (n. 31)

Kirkpatrick, Jean, 195–200, 204, 219, 231

Kurtz, Ernest, 9, 34, 35, 69, 281 (n. 25), 291 (n. 38), 295 (n. 84)

"Language of the heart," 15–16, 103, 180

Lears, T. J. Jackson, 100–101

Left/Progressive thought, 23, 257–62

Lesbians and gays, 175, 187–88, 201–9, 213, 218, 220–21, 261, 308 (n. 7), 309 (n. 43), 311 (n. 67)

Liquor industry, 26, 38, 39, 205

Literary marketplace, 13–16, 121, 132, 171

Little Red Book: history of, 81, 293 (n. 61); and surrender, 81–82, 145, 147; and AA Way of Life, 82–83, 85, 136–37, 176, 289 (n. 10); religiosity of, 139, 300 (n. 72); and anti-intellectualism, 157; use of, 173, 304 (n. 81); web sites promoting, 179

Love: and Oxford Group, 31, 72; and surrendered self, 63; and mysticism, 77; and AA sobriety, 83; and womanism, 210; and Alice Walker, 211, 217, 222, 225; and Swallow, 221, 225; and wounded self, 222; and Winfrey, 236, 238, 240, 242, 244–45, 248, 251, 254–56, 261–62; celebrated by Oprah's Book Club, 254–56, 260, 262; and social difference, 259

Mann, Marty, 41–45, 50, 56, 98, 138, 144, 192, 231, 285 (n. 63)

Market economy: of trade publishing, 13–16, 121, 132, 171, 222–24; and self-will, 62; uncritical belief in, 67; AA's relationship to, 92, 96, 98–99, 103, 172, 181–82; and AA literature, 110, 138–40; and 12-Step narrative form, 133; and anti-materialism, 147. See also Capitalism; Commercialism; Consumerism

Masculinity: and alcoholism, 53, 83, 144, 288 (n. 101); and possessive individualism, 63; hegemony of, 65–66, 69, 79–80, 85, 100–103, 182, 290 (n. 16), 294 (n. 72); as mandated in American culture, 67–69, 85; and self-will, 68, 79–80, 85, 182; and surrender, 74, 80, 84–85, 139, 147, 181–82, 261; redefined within AA, 80, 84–85, 101; and sobriety, 80–81, 83–84, 102–3; and rational thinking, 84, 291 (n. 35); in AA literature, 127, 155; and modernism and postmodernism, 269. See also Gender roles

McElrath, Damian, 151, 152–53, 172

Mel B., 9, 77, 292 (n. 43)

Melodrama, 132, 133, 134, 247

Menninger, Karl, 27, 28, 29

Mexican Americans, 175, 296 (n. 90)

Middlebrow culture, 132, 318 (n. 9)

Midwestern AA: literature of, 80–85, 99, 102–3, 135–37, 139, 142, 145, 147, 173, 179, 259, 292–93 (n. 53), 299 (n. 60), 304 (n. 81); anti-intellectualism of, 81–83,

249; and leaderless structure, 93; philosophical framework of, 117; and Big Book, 125, 134–35; and intensive vs. extensive reading, 135–36. See also Traditionalist AA

Minorities. See Diversity; and specific minorities

Mitchard, Jacquelyn, 248–49

Mitchell K., 135, 180

Modernism, 267, 268–69, 317 (n. 4), 318 (n. 9)

Modernity, 21, 62, 72, 110, 132–33, 141

Morrison, Toni, 223, 247, 249, 254–55

Multiculturalism, 175, 248

Mutual aid: and 12 Traditions, 6, 52, 99; and recovery, 7, 118; and Washingtonian Temperance Society, 94; and 12-Step calls, 128–29; and Hazelden, 150; and Women for Sobriety, 196, 218

Mysticism: of Oxford Group, 70, 112, 113; and spirituality, 75–77, 83; and surrender, 77, 79; and New Thought, 78, 146; Lears on, 100–101; and religious reading, 114, 141; and Higher Power, 163; and Women for Sobriety, 199; and Alice Walker, 211; and Winfrey, 231, 243, 248, 249, 250

Narcotics Anonymous, 4, 52, 282 (n. 27)

National Coalition for Women's Alcoholism Programs, 191

National Committee for Education on Alcoholism, 37, 38, 41–44, 50, 98, 138, 192

National Committee for the Homeless and Institutional Alcoholic, 44–45

National Council on Alcoholism (NCA), 44–45, 47, 191

National Council on Alcoholism and Drug Dependence, 287 (n. 82)

National Institute of Mental Health (NIMH), 45, 46

National Institute on Alcohol Abuse and Alcoholism (NIAAA), 46–48, 143–44, 286 (n. 79)

National Organization for Women, 191, 200

Negativity, 238–39, 240

New Thought: relationship with AA, 7, 78–79; and Mann, 43; and AA cofounders, 62, 76, 161, 292 (nn. 42, 44); idealism of,

70, 76–77, 237–41, 242, 245, 248–49, 257, 260; development of, 75; divine within, 146, 161, 164, 198, 231, 237, 240, 303 (n. 49); and Casey, 154, 161–62, 231; and Beattie, 169; and Kirkpatrick, 198–99; and Winfrey, 231, 237–38, 242–43, 245, 247, 251–52, 255, 257, 261, 313 (n. 21), 313–14 (n. 22), 315 (n. 59); vs. "New Age," 237, 313 (n. 21); and African Americans, 313 (n. 17). *See also* Emmanuel Movement; Unity

Norwood, Robin, 168–69, 218, 304 (n. 71)

Oppression, 160, 204–7, 210, 211, 214, 216–17, 219, 221–24, 227, 255

Oprah's Book Club: history of, 231, 312 (n. 7); cultural work of, 246–47, 280 (n. 18); featured books of, 247–48, 315–16 (n. 66), 316 (n. 80); and New Thought, 247–50; reading in, 248–52, 254–56, 316 (n. 78); and recovery, 256–57; and social difference, 259; and community, 260–61; and Frey, 265–68, 270, 317 (n. 1)

The Oprah Winfrey Show: addiction topics, 229–30, 232; as ministry, 241–47; and Oprah's Book Club, 247, 251–53, 257. *See also* Winfrey, Oprah

Orality: of AA meetings, 11, 107, 108, 118–19; and expansion to print forms, 109–10, 120–21, 131, 145; and metaphysics of presence, 119, 136, 141, 297 (n. 22); and style of Big Book, 123; and "drunk-ologues," 130; as antimodern communi-cative mode, 141

"Outside issues," 16, 49, 98, 160, 217–18, 260

Overeaters Anonymous, 4, 52, 155, 188, 233

Oxford Group: history of, 30–31; and alco-holic squad, 32, 114–18, 231; and ecumenism, 33, 74–75; AA influenced by, 62, 116–17, 122, 141, 296 (n. 7); asceticism of, 70–72, 80–81, 83, 113; meditative practice of, 70, 112–14, 146, 162, 297 (n. 10); mysticism of, 70, 112–13; reading practices of, 70, 109, 112–16, 296 (n. 7); and Bill Wilson, 116, 146, 231; tensions with AA, 134–35; and Richmond Walker, 146–47; and sexual impurity, 290 (n. 29)

Patriarchy, 159–60, 163, 187, 201, 203, 205, 212–14

Peck, Janice, 239, 258, 316 (n. 73)

Peck, M. Scott, 239, 240, 241, 255

Peele, Stanton, 22, 23, 44

Personal responsibility, 23, 56, 219, 257–58, 259

Pittman, Bill, 9, 291 (n. 39)

Political economy: and disease concept, 23, 58–59; of addiction, 205, 221; and Winfrey, 257, 260

Politics: conservative, 23, 54, 67, 189, 261, 290 (n. 20); Left/Progressive, 23, 226–28, 257–62; politicized recovery, 47, 189–90, 207, 211, 217–18, 226–27, 312 (n. 94); race politics, 47, 210, 214, 222–24, 252, 254–58, 260, 281 (n. 81), 295 (n. 90), 300 (n. 73); identity politics, 101, 145, 175, 269; as "outside issues," 160, 217–18. *See also* Feminism; Feminist recovery

Popular culture: recovery-infused, 4–6; and publicizing disease concept, 23, 57, 61; and psychoanalytic explanations of alcoholism, 29, 35; academic accounts of, 265, 267, 269–70

Possessive individualism, 62, 63, 92, 101–2, 259, 260

Postmodernism, 9, 268–69, 307 (n. 4), 318 (n. 9)

Post-12-Step recovery: agents of, 6–7; forms of, 16; theorizing of, 187; and fem-inist recovery, 217, 228; market for, 225–26; evolution of, 227–28; texts of, 265

Power of mind, 77–78, 198–99, 244–45

Power relations, 65, 67, 80, 85, 99, 102, 159–60, 189, 217–18, 228

Pragmatic focus of AA: and spirituality, 33, 54, 78–79, 291 (n. 39); and disease con-cept, 35–37, 42, 50, 56, 78; and Big Book, 122–25. *See also* Anti-intellectualism

Print culture: of recovery, 11–15, 265–66, 270, 282 (n. 27); and women, 12, 282 (n. 28); and treatment industry, 13, 15–16, 199; and communications circuit, 14–15, 142; and disease concept, 59; vs. orality, 109–10, 120–21, 131, 145; and midwestern AA, 136–37; and women in AA, 155–57; underground, 180, 182–83, 208. *See also* AA literature; Hazelden

Process addictions, 4, 6, 52–57, 187
Prohibition, 25–26, 61, 64, 94, 127
Protestantism: and Prohibition, 25; and Oxford Group, 70, 71, 76, 83; and surrender, 73–74; and AA spirituality, 75, 161, 163; and Christian equalitarianism, 86–87, 102, 289 (n. 10), 294 (n. 76); and Bible reading, 110–11; and devotional reading, 146. *See also* Evangelicalism
Psychoanalysis, 8, 26–29, 35, 36, 122

Quality paperbacks, 223–24

Race politics: in treatment, 47, 281 (n. 81); and Alice Walker, 210, 214, 222–24; and Winfrey, 252, 254–58, 260; in AA, 295 (n. 90), 300 (n. 73)
Raphael, Matthew J., 10, 67, 78, 122, 281 (n. 26), 285 (n. 44), 296 (n. 7), 298 (nn. 29, 35)
Raphael, Sally Jessy, 230, 241
Rapping, Elayne, 188, 218, 219, 229, 230, 282 (nn. 26, 29)
Rational thinking, 70, 84, 102, 197–98, 291 (n. 35)
Reading: in AA, 11–12, 107–9, 115, 296 (n. 2); in Oxford Group, 70, 109, 112–16, 296 (n. 7); of AA literature, 82, 107–9, 150–51; of Bible, 82, 107–8, 110–12, 114–15; religious vs. consumerist, 113–18, 120, 141, 142, 154, 165; intensive vs. extensive, 114, 135–36, 140, 142–43, 154; and identification, 131–32, 318 (n. 9); and Hazelden, 151, 153–54; as bibliotherapy, 154, 166, 171; Winfrey's promotion of, 246–47; in Oprah's Book Club, 248–52, 254–56, 316 (n. 78). *See also* Devotional reading
Reagan, Ronald, 49, 219–20, 258
Recovery: meaning of, 3–7, 9, 11, 15, 24; as subculture, 4–5, 14; scholarly neglect of, 8, 265–68, 270–71; print culture of, 11–15, 265–66, 270, 282 (n. 27); scholarly criticism of, 12, 22–23, 258–60, 282 (n. 29), 318 (n. 10); commercialization of, 13, 225–26, 228, 257; "politicized," 47, 189–90, 207, 211, 217–18, 226–27, 312 (n. 94); professionalization of, 52; and gender, 54; feminist critics of, 159, 217–20, 225–26, 230, 258; as depoliticizing, 188–90, 218–20, 222, 227, 258–60;

and Winfrey, 229–31, 256, 262; aesthetics of, 270, 271; as populist culture, 270–71; as social movement, 280 (n. 18); and middlebrow culture, 318 (n. 9). *See also* Feminist recovery; Post-12-Step recovery; 12 Steps
Religiosity: Big Book's avoidance of, 122–25; of midwestern literature, 137, 139, 142, 300 (n. 72); of *Twenty-four Hours a Day*, 148–49, 174; and AA Way of Life, 149, 173; of Casey, 160–63. *See also* Spirituality
Research Council on Problems of Alcohol (RCPA), 38, 39
Rockefeller, John D., 93, 119, 121
Roizen, Ron, 10, 281 (n. 26)
Room, Robin, 10, 36, 39–40, 48, 53, 58, 64, 280 (n. 18), 281 (n. 26), 287 (n. 82), 289 (n. 11)
Rotskoff, Lori, 10, 54, 64, 65, 83, 281 (n. 26)
Rush, Benjamin, 24, 68

Sandmaier, Marian, 190, 192–93
Secularism, 64, 71, 125, 148, 198–99, 263
Self: and codependence, 55–56, 170; AA's spiritually grounded ideal of, 62–63; surrendered, 63, 74, 80, 98, 103, 133, 158, 177; universal alcoholic selfhood, 90–92, 175; female, 158–60, 190, 227–28; and community, 217–25; and identification, 250–52; and sponsorship, 259–60
Self-disclosure, 119, 132, 133
Self-esteem: in Big Book, 86; and Casey, 158–59, 163–64, 170; and women's alcoholism movement, 194–95; and Women for Sobriety, 196, 199; and feminist recovery, 203–6, 235; Winfrey's belief in importance of, 235, 250
Self-improvement, 85–86
Self-in-relation: and AA fellowship, 85, 101–3, 260, 294 (n. 72); and 12-Step call, 89; and 12 Traditions, 92, 96, 98–100; self-made man contrasted with, 100, 294 (n. 72); social difference inimical to, 259
Self-made man, 65–66, 79, 92, 100, 101, 103, 294 (n. 72)
Self-will: Big Book on, 62, 67–69, 164; in market economy, 62; and sobriety, 67,

80–81; and masculinity, 68, 79–80, 85, 182; and anti-intellectualism, 82, 157; and 4th-Step inventory, 86, 87; and making amends, 88; and 12 Traditions, 93, 100; and spirituality, 103; and reading, 112–14; and Richmond Walker, 147–48; and Winfrey, 234

Sentimental culture, 102, 130, 261–62, 270, 317–18 (n. 8)

Sexuality: sex addiction, 1, 15, 188; AA attitudes toward, 144; Oxford Group concerns with, 290 (n. 29). *See also* Childhood sexual abuse; Lesbians and gays

Silkworth, William Duncan, 33–35, 67, 116, 122

Smith, Anne, 53, 114

Smith, Robert ("Dr. Bob"): and founding of AA, 29–30; and disease concept, 34, 35, 117, 238; and Victorian success ideology, 70; and spirituality, 75, 76, 79, 231; influence on midwestern AA, 81, 93, 293 (n. 53); and reading, 114–15, 117; philosophy of, 118–19, 139, 170; and writing of Big Book, 119–20, 125, 131, 139; relationship with Bill Wilson, 125, 142; death of, 136, 138; and suspicion of women, 144

Smithers, R. Brinkley, 43–44, 45, 50

Sobriety: as deviant, 61; and self-will, 67, 80–81; and powerlessness, 69; and surrender, 79–82, 147; "AA sobriety" vs. "sobriety, period," 80–85, 88, 99–100, 206; consumerism as threat to, 80, 82, 99, 147; and masculinity, 80–81, 83–84, 102–3; service as key to maintaining, 88–92; social difference inimical to, 101–2, 259; and Big Book, 125, 126; and women in AA, 144; modeling of, 173; and efficacy of AA, 176, 305–6 (n. 88); guides to, 179; and traditionalist AA, 179; feminist skepticism of, 201; and feminist recovery, 206–7, 217, 227; emotional sobriety, 220–21

Social difference, 231–32, 251–57, 259, 262

Sontag, Susan, 21–22, 23, 24, 57–58

Soul sickness, 71, 83, 101

Special populations, 46, 144–45, 163, 167, 202

Spirituality: in AA, 6, 8, 52, 62, 65, 67, 74–79, 116, 123, 125, 128, 136–37, 174–75,

179, 217; and post-12-Step recovery, 7; vs. religion, 11, 32, 62, 70, 75, 291 (n. 38); vs. professionalization, 52, 149–53, 172, 175, 180, 182; and Al-Anon, 53–54; and religious rejections of world, 62, 63, 70, 74; and mysticism, 75–77, 83; and sobriety, 79, 80–82, 147; Lears on, 100; and Big Book, 125–26, 139, 291 (n. 34); and 12-Step narrative form, 128–29; of Richmond Walker, 146–47, 231; of Casey, 160–64; American Indian, 161, 286 (n. 81), 303 (n. 48); of Women for Sobriety, 198–99; and *The Color Purple*, 214–16; of Winfrey, 230–31, 235–40, 242–46, 255, 257–58, 260–61; AA historians on, 291 (n. 38); and middlebrow culture, 318 (n. 9)

Sponsorship, 88, 117, 139, 173, 259–60

Subcultures, 4–5, 14, 103, 173

Substance abuse, 47, 52, 57, 143, 283 (n. 7), 287 (n. 82)

Surrender: surrendered self, 63, 74, 80, 98, 103, 133, 158, 177; as antidote to alcoholism, 65, 69, 149, 164; and 12 Steps, 69, 124; Bill Wilson's experience of, 72–74; and masculinity, 74, 80, 84–85, 139, 147, 181–82, 261; and mysticism, 77, 79; and AA sobriety, 79–82, 147; and feminization of piety, 79–85; and *Little Red Book*, 81–82, 145, 147; Dr. Bob Smith's attitude toward, 117; and midwestern pamphlet literature, 136, 142; surrendered life, 145, 147, 157–58, 176, 179, 301 (n. 6); and Casey, 157–58; and codependence, 169; and Women for Sobriety, 196–97

Swallow, Jean, 159, 203–9, 220–22, 225, 310 (n. 52)

Swift, Harry, 153–57, 164–68, 171

Temperance movement: gospel temperance, 1, 36, 74, 119, 125; and abstinence, 24–25, 94; Washingtonian Temperance Society, 94–95, 97, 99; AA's distance from, 96. *See also* Prohibition

"Terrible honesty," 268–69, 271

Therapy: therapeutic recovery culture, 6, 143–44; relationship to AA, 7, 49, 119; and disease concept, 49, 56; and codependence, 55–57; family systems, 55, 218; incorporation into Hazelden treatment, 150–52, 154, 166, 169; bibliotherapy, 154, 166, 171; as dilution of AA spirituality, 172–73, 175, 180, 182; and feminists, 190

Three-part disease, 81, 145, 151, 164, 175, 194, 204

Tileston, Mary Wilder, 152, 155

Tom P. Jr., 176, 182, 306 (n. 89)

Traditionalist AA: and midwestern AA literature, 83, 136–37, 142, 173; religiosity of, 117, 149, 173; and Hazelden, 153, 171–72; and surrendered self, 157; and Casey, 158, 160–62, 164; print culture of, 176–80, 182–83; and women in AA, 181–83, 225, 306–7 (n. 99); feminist recovery compared to, 206; and efficacy, 305–6 (n. 88)

Treatment industry: growth of, 4, 27, 45–49, 57, 143–44, 171, 191; relationship with AA, 7, 49, 50–52, 98, 172–73, 182; and print culture, 13, 15–16, 199; and disease concept, 22, 23, 57; and National Council on Alcoholism, 44; and insurance, 47–48; and managed care, 57, 171; and bibliotherapy, 154, 166, 171; special populations within, 167, 202; and women within, 191–93, 200–201, 218–19, 222, 226; masculinism of, 192, 226

Trimpey, Jack, 22, 61, 62

12-Step approaches to addiction: varieties of, 3–6, 52–53, 280 (n. 19); efficacy of, 8–9, 71, 176, 280–81 (n. 20); commodification of, 147, 164; and Hazelden, 149–53; and codependence, 168–70; and Women for Sobriety, 196

12-Step calls, 88–91, 92, 115, 128–29

12-Step narrative form: and identity formation, 9; and identification, 126–31; aesthetics of, 130–34, 298 (n. 39); and The Color Purple, 211, 216, 224; and Winfrey, 233–34

12 Steps: culture of, 6; and Bill Wilson, 32, 124; and process addiction, 52–57; and surrender process, 69, 124; self-improvement compared to, 85–86; 4th-Step inventory, 86, 87, 234; and making amends, 88; in Big Book, 103, 124–25, 297–98 (n. 29); as suggested program, 103; benefits of working, 123, 147; and midwestern AA, 139; Tom P. Jr. on, 176;

and feminists, 190; and Winfrey, 233, 245; organizations using, 280 (n. 19). *See also* AA (Alcoholics Anonymous)

12 Traditions: and "outside issues," 16, 49–50, 98, 260; and process addictions, 52; nonprofessionalism, 56; function of, 91–93, 96; and Bill Wilson, 92, 95–100, 140, 295 (n. 83); and local customs, 97, 295–96 (n. 90); and Hazelden, 153; organizations using, 280 (n. 19)

Twenty-four Hours a Day (Richmond Walker): publishing of, 145–49; and surrendered self, 145, 147, 301 (n. 6); sales of, 147–49, 152, 164; religiosity of, 148–49, 174; and Hazelden, 149–52, 155–56, 166, 302 (n. 41); revised to address women, 155–56, 301 (n. 4), 302 (n. 41); and active fellowship, 170; use of, 173, 304 (n. 81)

Underground print culture, 180, 182–83, 208

Unity, 76, 154, 161–64, 198, 238, 292 (n. 44), 303 (n. 51)

Uzzell, Thomas, 131–34, 299 (n. 53)

Vanzant, Iyanla, 244, 313 (n. 17), 315 (n. 54)

Victorian culture, 64, 191, 268, 269

Victorian success ideology, 65–66, 70, 73, 91, 100–101

Walker, Alice, 209–11, 214–16, 222–24, 236, 310 (n. 63). See also *The Color Purple* (Alice Walker)

Walker, Richmond, 145–47, 157, 231, 301 (n. 5). See also *Twenty-four Hours a Day* (Richmond Walker)

Walter S., 176, 177

Washingtonian Temperance Society, 94–95, 97, 99

Weber, Max, 62–63, 70, 77, 83–84, 101, 103

White, William L., 10, 35, 36, 45, 47, 51, 144, 150, 181, 281 (n. 26)

Williamson, Marianne, 238–41, 243–44

Wilson, Lois, 52, 53, 67, 75, 76

Wilson, William ("Bill"): and founding of AA, 29–33, 78; and Oxford Group, 30–31, 116, 231; and 12 Steps, 32, 124; and disease concept, 33–35, 56, 238; and

Alcoholism Movement, 42, 45, 50; "Bill's Story," 64, 73–74, 120–21, 123, 126; and Victorian success ideology, 66–67; and surrender, 72–74; and spirituality, 75–76, 79, 231, 236, 291 (n. 39); and 12 Traditions, 92, 95–100, 140, 295 (n. 83); and Rockefeller, 93; and reading, 114–15, 175; and anonymity, 116, 297 (n. 19); philosophy of, 117–19, 170; and writing of Big Book, 119–27, 131, 285 (n. 44), 297–98 (n. 29); and need to control AA literature, 120–21, 138–42, 143, 300 (n. 72); and sales of Big Book, 134, 137–38; on women in AA, 144; on sex, 290 (n. 29); on race in AA, 295 (n. 90), 300 (n. 73)

Winfrey, Oprah: as recovery icon, 229–31, 256, 262; and food addiction, 230, 232–34; and New Thought, 231, 237–38, 242–43, 245, 247, 251–52, 255, 257, 261, 313 (n. 21), 313–14 (n. 22), 315 (n. 59); and transcendence of social difference, 231, 251–57, 259; "Oprah's Story," 232–36, 241–42; and social issues, 232, 261, 317 (n. 96); biography of, 234, 312–13 (n. 11); and African American religious tradition, 236–37; critics of, 246–48, 257–59, 261–63; and Frey, 317 (n. 1)

Wing, Nell, 78, 292 (n. 44)

Woititz, Janet, 168, 230

Womanism, 210–11, 214–16, 222, 227, 231, 245, 252, 254, 256–57, 308 (n. 7)

Women: and print culture, 12, 282 (n. 28); and alcoholism as man's disease, 53, 83, 144, 288 (n. 101); and feminization of piety, 79–85; and disease concept, 144, 158, 193; and Hazelden, 150, 156; and addiction, 158–59, 163, 193–94, 200, 203–7, 226; and community, 160, 190, 219; and alcoholic equalitarianism, 163–64; as symbol of cultural degradation, 181–82; women of color, 190, 219, 226–27, 308 (n. 7); and liquor advertising, 205; book-buying habits of, 223–24, 226, 311 (n. 92). *See also* Feminism; Feminist recovery

Women for Sobriety (WFS), 195, 196–200, 201, 204, 218, 219, 226

Women in AA: inclusion of, 69, 127, 144–45, 218; and print culture, 155–57; and traditionalist AA, 181–83, 225, 306–7 (n. 99)

Women's alcoholism movement: and gender roles, 190–91, 201, 204; and invisibility, 190–91, 193, 194; and stigma, 190–93, 195; and liberal feminism, 191–92, 194, 226; and gender equity, 192, 195, 201; and self-esteem, 194–95; and empowerment, 195, 197; and feminist recovery, 199–200

Women's bookstores, 187, 204, 207

Word-of-mouth program, 31–32, 93, 118–19, 122, 124, 133

Works Publishing, Inc., 121, 138

World War I, 64, 66–67, 73, 127

Yale Center of Alcohol Studies, 37–43

Yale Plan Clinics, 40, 46, 50

Yale Summer School of Alcohol Studies, 40–41, 50, 137–38

Yoder, Mose, 176–77